Banished

Migrations in History

―――

Edited by
Catherine Brice, Maddalena Marinari,
Anna Mazurkiewicz und Machteld Venken

Volume 1

Banished

Traveling the roads of exile in nineteenth-century Europe

Edited by
Delphine Diaz and Sylvie Aprile

Translated by Adrian Morfee

DE GRUYTER
OLDENBOURG

The translation of the book was supported by the Agence nationale de la recherche, Institut universitaire de France, Institut Convergences Migrations, Institut des sciences sociales du politique and the Centre de recherches en histoire européenne comparée.

ISBN 978-3-11-135685-3
e-ISBN (PDF) 978-3-11-073227-6
e-ISBN (EPUB) 978-3-11-073234-4
ISSN 2701-1437

Library of Congress Control Number: 2021941932

Bibliographic information published by the Deutsche Nationalbibliothek
The Deutsche Nationalbibliothek lists this publication in the Deutsche Nationalbibliografie; detailed bibliographic data are available on the Internet at http://dnb.dnb.de.

© 2023 Walter de Gruyter GmbH, Berlin/Boston
This volume is text- and page-identical with the hardback published in 2022.
Published in French as *Les Réprouvés. Sur les routes de l'exil dans l'Europe du XIXe siècle*
© 2021 Editions de la Sorbonne, Paris
Cover illustration: Honoré Daumier: *The Fugitives*, The Ethel Morrison Van Derlip Fund, Minneapolis Institute of Arts, Gallery G354.
Printing and binding: CPI books GmbH, Leck

www.degruyter.com

Acknowledgements

The publication of this book was supported by the French National Research Agency (ANR), as part of a "young researchers" program running from 2016 to 2020, called AsileuropeXIX (Défi Flash Asile), "A European history of political exile and asylum in nineteenth-century Europe". This program was coordinated by Delphine Diaz and hosted by the "Centre d'études et de recherche en histoire culturelle" (Cultural History Studies and Research Center) at the University of Reims Champagne-Ardenne.

The collective writing of this book, whose purpose is to synthesize the contributions to the AsileuropeXIX program, was launched in February 2019 at a workshop hosted by the Villa Finaly in Florence. We extend our warm thanks to the Chancellery of the Universities of Paris for having provided so exceptional a setting for our team to pursue work on the European history of exile.

The book was first published in French by the Éditions de la Sorbonne under the title *Les Réprouvés. Sur les routes de l'exil dans l'Europe du XIXe siècle*. This English version has only been made possible thanks to the support of the "Institut universitaire de France", the "Institut Convergences Migrations", the "Institut des sciences sociales du politique" (Institute of Social Science of Politics) and the "Centre de recherches en histoire européenne comparée" (Comparative European History Research Center), for which we express our gratitude. Our thanks also go to Adrian Morfee who translated and helped improve the present work.

Table of Contents

Sylvie Aprile and Delphine Diaz
Introduction —— 1

Sylvie Aprile, Delphine Diaz and Antonin Durand
Chapter 1 Times of exile —— 11

Delphine Diaz, Laurent Dornel and Hugo Vermeren
Chapter 2 Taking in and casting out —— 39

Sylvie Aprile, Alexandre Dupont and Hugo Vermeren
Chapter 3 Travel and transit —— 75

Sylvie Aprile and Delphine Diaz
Chapter 4 Living far away —— 107

Constance Bantman, Catherine Brice and Alexandre Dupont
Chapter 5 Politics in exile —— 141

Sylvie Aprile, Delphine Diaz, Alexandre Dupont and Antonin Durand
Chapter 6 Gender and exile —— 175

Romy Sánchez and Fabrice Bensimon
Chapter 7 European homelands, global vistas —— 205

Sylvie Aprile and Laure Godineau
Chapter 8 Returns and memories —— 241

Sylvie Aprile and Delphine Diaz
Conclusion —— 279

Printed sources —— 283

Bibliography —— 285

List of figures and tables —— 303

List of contributors —— 305

Index —— 307

Sylvie Aprile and Delphine Diaz
Introduction

While "every history worthy of the name is contemporary",[1] that of the refugees going into exile in the nineteenth century, and circulating throughout Europe and beyond, resonates strongly with the topical phenomenon of migration. Since summer 2015, the idea of a "migrant crisis" has moved center stage in political debate and the media, with repeated references to the "uncommon or historic" nature of the arrival of exiles and asylum seekers on the European continent.[2] At the same time, the UN High Commissioner for Refugees recorded the unprecedented figure of 65 million refugees, asylum seekers, and displaced people worldwide.[3]

This renewed political and media interest in migration and exile and in the legal category of "refugee" has led many working in the social sciences to place these phenomena in a longer perspective, so as to detach them from the immediacy of the present day and its inevitably shortsighted viewpoint. By re-examining the history of Europeans on the move, or more precisely, Europeans *obliged* to move, this book investigates exile on a continent where, in the nineteenth century, banished individuals circulated frequently and in large numbers. From the outset, they modified social equilibriums, sparked political changes in the lands of departure, transit, and refuge, and triggered reactions of attachment, distrust, or rejection even in the places where they found asylum. Still, it is not this book's purpose to compare two very distant and distinct European situations, that constituting the starting date for this study, the year 1815, immediately after the Congress of Vienna, and that of Europe 200 years later, marked by the arrival of exiles in the wake of wars and major upheavals in the Middle East, the Horn of Africa, and the Sahel. Just as it is not possible to compare the political situation at these two dates, the definitions attached to the words "exile" and "refugee" in 1815 were not the same as two hundred years later. In the early nineteenth century, the noun "exile" no doubt carried a dual meaning, referring both to an individual banished from court on sovereign order – hence an internal exile – and

---

[1] Benedetto Croce, *Contributo alla critica di me stesso*. English translation of the essay by RG Collingwood, published under the title *Benedict Croce: an autobiography* (Oxford: Clarendon Press, 1927).
[2] Emmanuel Blanchard and Claire Rodier, "Crise migratoire': ce que cachent les mots," *GISTI / Plein droit*, 111/4 (2016): 3.
[3] According to the annual statistical report by the UN High Commissioner for Refugees (HCR): accessed April 8, 2021, https://www.unhcr.org/576408cd7.

those expelled beyond their homeland's national borders. As for the term "refugee", it was a way of designating individuals constrained to leave their country for political reasons and who, having broken all ties with their state of origin, relied on the assistance of their host country to subsist.[4] Indeed, the question of financial assistance became central to the definition of "refugee", which in French emerged as an administrative category in its own right under the July monarchy. European terminology for forced migration in the nineteenth century drew on a variety of terms and approaches,[5] from *refugee*, firmly part of English vocabulary since the Huguenots,[6] to *emigrado* in Spain, commonly used to refer to political exile.[7] At the time there was no unified definition of a refugee, and it had nothing in common with the legal concept which emerged in Europe after the Geneva Convention was adopted in 1951. The latter introduced the criterion of individual persecution as its touchstone. Conversely, in the early nineteenth century, politicians, administrators, and diplomats were already keenly interested in exiles and refugees, and ways of perceiving them were already largely shaped by law.[8]

Without seeking to compare the past and the present term by term, this book endeavors to shed light on other "asylum crises" associated with exiles and refugees affecting Europe experienced after the Napoleonic wars.[9] Studying them suggests we should relativize the supposedly unparalleled nature of the contemporary situation. Furthermore, this book strives to show that this history of exile

---

4 Maurice Block (ed.), *Dictionnaire de l'administration française* (Paris: Berger-Levrault et fils, 1856), 1412.
5 On European terminology for forced migration, see Delphine Diaz & Alexandre Dupont (eds.), "Les mots de l'exil dans l'Europe du XIXᵉ siècle," *Hommes & Migrations* 1321 (April-May 2018).
6 *Cf.* Thomas C. Jones, "Refugee", lexicographical resources on the website of the AsileuropeXIX program, accessed April 8, 2021, https://asileurope.huma-num.fr/le-vocabulaire-de-lexil/refugee.
7 *Cf.* Alexandre Dupont, "Emigrado, emigración", lexicographical resources on the website of the AsileuropeXIX program, accessed April 8, 2021, https://asileurope.huma-num.fr/le-vocabulaire-de-lexil/emigracion-emigrado: "from the outset, emigrado thus designated an individual who had to leave his country for political reasons, with the important nuance that the emigrado was fleeing from repression, unlike the *desterrado* who had been sentenced to deportation".
8 See for example the corpus of administrative circulars on foreign refugees that the AsileuropeXIX team has gathered for France for the period 1830–1870, accessed April 8, 2021, https://asileurope.huma-num.fr/circulaires-sur-les-refugies.
9 Rather than speaking of a "migrant crisis", we can use the expression "asylum crisis" to describe the upheavals caused by the arrival of many exiles and asylum seekers in Europe as of summer 2015. See Karen Akoka, "Crise des réfugiés, ou des politiques d'asile?," *La Vie des idées*, May 31, 2016. ISSN: 2105–3030, accessed April 8, 2021, http://www.laviedesidees.fr/Crise-des-refugies-ou-des-politiques-d-asile.html

and asylum in nineteenth-century Europe was never a purely and exclusively European phenomenon. Not only did the exiles circulating on the continent and taking refuge there come from far more distant horizons – the Americas, particularly, and the Ottoman Empire – but European exiles themselves were continually pushing back the frontier of where they sought refuge.[10] They did not hesitate to settle in Anatolia in the Ottoman Empire, in North African colonies and protectorates, or even on the other side of the Atlantic, or in Oceana, as was the case for many British Chartists deported to Australia who remained in exile after serving their sentence. Like any other migration, exile in Europe is now "studied as a whole and placed in a global context".[11]

While the geographical area studied here is primarily European, our endeavor presupposes placing Europe within the global dynamics identified and analyzed by recent historiography.[12] The focus undoubtedly falls on some countries more than others, due to the way in which this book has been written, as part of a transnational research program by authors wishing to compare and analyze several given spaces the better to apprehend the departure and taking in of nineteenth-century refugees.[13] For our purpose of studying the reception and protection of refugees, and comparing them to the other foreign migrants, four nation-states drew our attention, which had existed and been firmly established within Europe for differing lengths of time: namely, Great Britain, the most liberal in terms of receiving foreigners during this century, France, which acted as a

---

10 On transatlantic exiles, see Delphine Diaz, Jeanne Moisand, Romy Sánchez and Juan Luis Simal, *Exils entre les deux mondes. Migrations et espaces politiques atlantiques au XIXe siècle* (Bécherel: Les Perséides, 2015).
11 Dick Hoerder, Jan Lucassen, and Leo Lucassen "Terminologies and concepts of migration research," in *The Encyclopedia of Migration and Minorities in Europe from the 17th Century to the Present*, ed. Klaus J. Bade, Pieter C. Emmer, Leo Lucassen, and Jochen Oltmer (Cambridge: Cambridge University Press, 2013), xxv.
12 *Cf.* Christopher Alan Bayly, *The Birth of the Modern World, 1780–1914* (Oxford: Blackwell Publishing, 2004); Jürgen Osterhammel, *The Transformation of the World. A Global History of the 19th Century*, translated from the German (Princeton: NJ, Princeton University Press, 2014), and Pierre Singaravélou and Sylvain Venayre, *Histoire du monde au XIXe siècle*, (Paris: Fayard, 2017).
13 This book stems from collective work by the team of researchers on the "jeunes chercheuses jeunes chercheurs" AsileuropeXIX program, coordinated by Delphine Diaz, funded by the Agence nationale de la recherche for the period 2016–2020, and hosted by the Centre d'études et de recherche en histoire culturelle (EA 2616) at the Université de Reims Champagne-Ardenne. For discussion of the initial postulates and scientific objectives of this program, see *id.*, "Pour une histoire européenne de l'exil et de l'asile politiques au XIXe siècle: le programme de recherches AsileuropeXIX", *Diasporas, Circulations, Migrations, Histoire* 28/2 (2016): 163–176.

nodal point due to its central role as a receiving and a sending state,[14] as well as Switzerland, and Belgium.

Our purpose of shedding light on how refugees passed through or settled in these four countries also stems from the wealth of new historiography, which has generated material for debate. Bernard Porter's first book about refugees in Great Britain, published in 1979, focuses on the very liberal legal framework governing asylum. He demonstrates that as a result of the abrogation of the 1826 Aliens Act, exiled Europeans were totally free to settle there up until 1905, despite a more repressive Aliens Act being adopted, though in fact never enforced, for a two-year period as of 1848. Additionally, his book examines the situation of refugees in London. Porter describes their assorted geographical provenances and ideological leanings, though this variety did not prevent their having many points of contact.

Following the publication of this seminal work, a 1987 book by Marc Vuilleumier, a historian of the labor movement, examined the conditions in which exiles were received in the nineteenth century in another land of European exile. He reassesses Switzerland's role in immigration in the late modern period, draws up a typology of exiles who took refuge in the Confederation, and sketches out a map of the cantons most concerned.[15] In France, interest in political exiles developed in parallel with studies of foreign immigration, which took off in the 1980s. The first to address this question was Gérard Noiriel in his book *La Tyrannie du national. Le droit d'asile en Europe (1793–1993)*,[16] republished seven years later under the title *Réfugiés et sans papiers. La République face au droit d'asile, XIXe-XXe siècle*.[17] It sets out to show how France was riven by debate between recognizing human rights – chief among them the right of asylum – and protecting its national interests within a broader European context. Noiriel also examines the relations the state and administration built up with foreigners come to seek refuge in France for political reasons.

This approach struck a chord. In 2000, Frank Caestecker studied the emergence of a policy to receive foreigners in Belgium after the country gained inde-

---

[14] The fact that France is center stage in this book also reflects the fact that most of its contributors are French.
[15] Marc Vuilleumier, *Immigrés et réfugiés en Suisse: aperçu historique* (Zurich: Pro Helvetia, 1987), translated into Italian as *Immigrati e profughi in Svizzera. Profilo storico*, 1990.
[16] Gérard Noiriel, *La Tyrannie du national. Le droit d'asile en Europe (1793–1993)* (Paris: Calmann-Lévy, 1991).
[17] Gérard Noiriel, *Réfugiés et sans papiers. La République face au droit d'asile, XIXe-XXe siècle* (Paris: Hachette, 1998, first edition, republished in 2006).

pendence.[18] His book shows that the new Belgian state, still struggling throughout the 1830s to win recognition for its independence, had rapidly grasped the scale of the risk posed by taking in foreign exiles, perceived as "archetypal political actors capable of imperiling the precarious diplomatic equilibrium" to which the new monarchy owed its existence.[19]

Still, western Europe was not the only part of the world to take in political exiles in the nineteenth century. The kingdom of Piedmont-Sardinia took in Italians from the rest of the peninsula after the failed 1848–1849 revolutions, together with many Hungarians and French driven out by the events of the Second Republic, as Ester De Fort has demonstrated.[20] As for Spain, its role in taking in migrants has not as yet been reassessed, despite its granting asylum to hundreds of Italian exiles during the *Trienio Liberal* (1820–1823), and then to French outcasts in the 1850s and again during the *Sexenio democrático* (1868–1874).[21] On the other hand, the latest Spanish historiography, rather than focusing on the relatively small number of foreigners taking refuge in Spain, has sought to describe and explain a far larger phenomenon, that of the enforced collective departures of Spaniards throughout the nineteenth century.[22] While the six countries mentioned above are at the heart of this book,[23] the history of exile and refugees far exceeded the perimeter thus drawn. Looking east, other lands that historically banished or received exiles included the German states, the Austrian Empire,[24] Russia, and Poland, while, looking west and south, the cases of Greece

---

18 Frank Caestecker, *Alien Policy in Belgium, 1840–1940: the Creation of Guest Workers, Refugees and Illegal Immigrants* (New York: Berghahn Books, 2000).
19 Caestecker, *Alien Policy*, 5.
20 Ester De Fort, "Esuli in Piemonte nel Risorgimento. Riflessioni su di una fonte," *Rivista storica italiana* 115/2 (2003): 648–88.
21 Apart from the article published by Manuel Morán Orti, "La cuestión de los refugiados extranjeros. Política española en el Trienio liberal," *Hispania* 173 (1989): 985–1016.
22 Among this vast body of scholarship, we confine ourselves to citing the following titles: Rafael Sánchez Mantero, *Liberales en el exilio. La emigración política en Francia en la crisis del Antiguo Régimen* (Madrid: Rialp, 1975); Juan Bautista Vilar, *La España del exilio. Las Emigraciones políticas españolas en los siglos XIX y XX* (Madrid: Síntesis, 2006); Jordi Canal (ed.), *Exilios. Los Éxodos políticos en la historia de España, siglos XV-XX* (Madrid: Sílex, 2007); Juan-Luis Simal, *Emigrados. España y el exilio internacional, 1814–1834* (Madrid: Centro de Estudios Políticos y Constitucionales – Asociación de Historia Contemporánea, 2012).
23 These six countries – France, Belgium, Great Britain, Switzerland, Italy, and Spain – form the geographical area studied by the AsileuropeXIX program from which this book issues.
24 Among the extensive literature, see Heléna Tóth, *An Exiled Generation: German and Hungarian Refugees of Revolution, 1848–1871* (New York: Cambridge University Press, 2014).

and Portugal would need to be included to appreciate the full complexity of the itineraries taken by migrants and the conditions in which they were received.[25]

This book thus sets out to study the departure, travels, and reception of these exiles in nineteenth-century Europe, from the Congress of Vienna through to the period 1870–1880. Our work draws on the many approaches to the history of migration, relying on certain fruitful concepts and frameworks of analysis relating to circular migrations, migration chains, and the border controls set up to sift and limit flows.[26] Nevertheless, it intends to focus on one particular form of migration, that experienced by those forced to leave their country because of their political beliefs.

Though the European and Atlantic revolutions of the late eighteenth century no doubt led many outcasts to go into exile – first among whom the counterrevolutionary émigrés, who were exceptionally numerous for the period, and to whom we shall refer in the following chapters – it was only after the end of the Napoleonic wars that exile became a veritable "political institution",[27] almost a rite of passage for opponents, revolutionaries, and patriots yearning for a nation-state. The "century of exiles" remained a coherent phenomenon up until the 1870s–1880s,[28] when banishment started to recede as a tool of repression in Europe. Furthermore, the development of great migrations for economic reasons together with the development of new schemes to control mobility were major turning points ushering in a new era for refugees.[29]

So how may we introduce what is both an appraisal of several decades' research and ongoing investigation of varied spaces and themes, shedding light on trajectories which crisscrossed, ran alongside, or remained distant from each

---

25 On Portugal, see Grégoire Bron, "Révolution et nation entre le Portugal et l'Italie: les relations politiques luso-italiennes des Lumières à l'Internationale libérale de 1830" (PhD diss., Paris/Lisbon, EPHE-Instituto superior de ciências do trabalho e da empresa, 2013).
26 On the new approaches in migration history on a global scale, see Dirk Hoerder, Immanuel Ness and Sari Safitri (eds.), *The Encyclopedia of Global Human Migration* (New York: Wiley Publishers, 2012).
27 To use Carlo Cattaneo's still famous expression about the migration of Ugo Foscolo, who turned exile into a veritable institution in the Italian peninsula. Carlo Cattaneo, *Ugo Foscolo e l'Italia* (Milan: Politecnico, 1861), 34.
28 Sylvie Aprile, *Le Siècle des exilés. Bannis et proscrits, de 1789 à la Commune* (Paris: CNRS Éditions, 2010).
29 History scholarship on exile is closely linked and indebted to the many works by historians who have conceptualized and developed the history of migration. See Dirk Hoerder, and others, "Terminologies and Concepts of Migration Research," in *The Encyclopedia of Migration and Minorities in Europe from the 17th Century to the Present*, ed. Klaus J. Bade, Pieter C. Emmer, Leo Lucassen and Jochen Oltmer (Cambridge: Cambridge University Press, 2013), Dirk Hoerder et al., eds., *The Encyclopedia of Global Human Migration* (New York: Wiley Publishers, 2012).

other? To answer these questions, which call for countless nuances, we have decided to adopt several viewpoints and have selected paths of exile illustrating the full diversity of the phenomenon, following both a quantitative and a qualitative methodology. What did these men and women moving around nineteenth-century Europe have in common? No doubt their experience of rupture and precarity, be it real or imagined, and their removal from their homeland, be it near or far, brief or lasting. The experience of heading into exile, primarily the preserve of intellectual and political elites at first, gradually affected larger and more sociologically diverse groups after the turning point of 1848.

The traces these nineteenth-century outcasts left in the archives of the police and justice system involved in tracking and monitoring them, and on occasions employing them, are more voluminous than those from any other period. They were also – before, during, and after their exile – men and women of letters, journalists, thinkers, and writers, who, in the press and in literature (broadly defined), voiced their aspirations, fears, and observations of the landscapes and societies before their eyes. Nowadays, they seem especially present through the vast correspondences they left behind. They wrote many letters to those they had left behind – their entourage, family members, and friends – sometimes evading censorship to do so, but also wrote copiously to each other, as illustrated by the correspondence of Giuseppe Mazzini (1805–1872), Karl Marx (1818–1883), and Alexander Herzen (1812–1870) – to mention but a few famous names still spontaneously associated with the idea of "exile politics".

We draw on the concept of *exopolitie* (exile polity, or exopolitics) – formulated by Stéphane Dufoix in reference to the space in which exiles position themselves and act in relation to one another, outside the country in reference to which they act – to cast light on the political thought, divisions, and reconfigurations generated by exile in the nineteenth century.[30] Action by exiles took place in highly varied political situations, which are analyzed here, ranging from the slightest and most moderate to bloody assassination attempts. They were conducted by exiles whose ideological choices reflected the complex spectrum of political cultures of the period, from counterrevolutionaries and royalists to liberals, republicans, socialists, federalists, anarchists, and so on.

Their alternative way of doing politics from exile leads us to study different forms of commitment which can cast light on present-day disaffection with political institutions such as parliaments, the executive, and trade unions. The figure of the nineteenth-century exile who, by definition, left traditional places of

---

30 Stéphane Dufoix, *Politiques d'exil. Hongrois, Polonais et Tchécoslovaques en France après 1945* (Paris: Presses universitaires de France, 2002), 29.

debate, such as the parliamentary chamber, or places of authority, such as a prison, thus chime with the present-day weakness of those currently excluded and the range of political possibilities available to them. Yet we in no way wish to present a vision of nineteenth-century exile as conducive to moderation and conciliation, for it had many negative, shameful, and destructive aspects – as illustrated by the role of rumor, plotting, and violence by anonymous and desperate protagonists or self-proclaimed heroes.

The many dimensions of exile are also linked to the specific attendant porosity between the public and the private sphere. The expatriation of nineteenth-century exiles took a particular form, modifying the place of men and women, and by extension the role of the couple and family, and associated visions of femininity and masculinity. How else may we understand the tribunal of exiles Alexander Herzen wished to set up to condemn his wife Natalia's lover, the German exile Georg Herwegh?[31] Although the words of these banished men and women may at times seem amusing, at others annoying, we should avoid the temptation to downplay the role they played, for they are one of the keys to our European past.

To apprehend these exiles and grasp the diversity of their situations and stances, we have opted for a methodology and way of writing that enables us to track these protagonists as closely as possible, thanks to the use of primary sources and secondary literature. The history of the state and reception provisions in place are inseparable from that of civil society in Europe. Social and economic change form the backdrop shaping the movement of the exiles we are seeking to follow. In tracing their itineraries throughout their migration, we have compared administrative and diplomatic archives of the lands of departure, transit, and refuge, as well as examining sources left by the exiles themselves. This work gives pride of place to analyzing these itineraries, and allows the banished to speak in their own words, reproducing the texts they wrote, the speeches they gave about their migration, and including the literary, pictorial, or photographic works in which they deplored or celebrated their time in exile. Nevertheless, giving voice to outcasts themselves implies focusing on those who left correspondence, diaries, or memoirs, leaving in the shadows all those from less privileged social classes who could not write or who did not leave a written record of their experience.

---

31 Simone Rist, "L'affaire Herwegh," *Revue des études slaves*, LXXVIII/2–3 (2007): 229–42. "The Herwegh affair was a family affair, a private affair which, at the auspices of its protagonists, became a public affair. When viewed externally and with hindsight, the affair looks like a second-rate tragicomedy, yet it was not a fiction, and involved people experiencing and suffering from the passions of an intimate drama".

Casting light on the key moments in their heading into exile entails going over the specific chronology of their movements, while bringing out the complexity of the reasons pushing Europeans to leave their homeland. Admittedly, the tempo of the uprisings and revolutions which rocked the European continent over the course of the century heavily influenced that of their departures. Nevertheless, there was a nearly continuous flow of exiles between the 1830s and the 1848 revolutions, and then from 1849 to the 1870s, involving not only former insurgents but also legitimists and counterrevolutionaries (chapter 1). In order to better understand the conditions in which these refugees from across the political spectrum were received and treated, we need to examine the national provisions for receiving them introduced by the European states coming to their assistance, bearing in mind that these same states also selected and expelled refugees. In addition to the perspective of host states and societies (chapter 2), the viewpoints of those involved in these migrations are central to this work. It thus addresses the theme of departure into exile via the material experience of crossing borders in the nineteenth century (chapter 3), and that of continuing with professional and family life, both of which were comprehensively interrupted by forced expatriation (chapter 4). Yet expatriation did not simply mean rupture and despondency, for it could also generate new ways of reinventing one's life and pursuing political commitments from abroad (chapter 5). Those involved in these travels are envisaged in all their diversity, with much room devoted to women and children, many of whom were also forced to move, though they have long been eclipsed in the gender-specific historiography of these migrations (chapter 6). While this book seeks primarily to examine the exiles of Europeans in Europe, the phenomenon also needs interpreting on a global scale, as illustrated by the many exiles departing for the colonies and the Americas (chapter 7). Finally, it closes on the topic of exiles' (impossible or difficult) return to their home countries, together with an examination of how the memory of exile was subsequently constructed, and on occasions viewed as a foundational experience (chapter 8).

Sylvie Aprile, Delphine Diaz and Antonin Durand
Chapter 1 Times of exile

In addition to providing an overview of the tides of exile around Europe, this chapter focuses on the role played by countries of origin, going over the political events and wars causing people to head into exile. It enters the world of nineteenth-century outcasts through the complex timeframes of their migrations.

In 1815, upheavals across Europe drove a flurry of military and civilian displacements. Some people headed home, others departed. But their journeys and circulations were characterized by uncertainty, and their paths crossed. One obvious example is the return of Louis XVIII, followed by his precipitate departure during the Hundred Days, when Napoléon landed in France only to be exiled shortly after on St Helena. The about-turns of these great figures reverberated around Europe, and their effects were felt in the colonies even. After 1816 and the adoption of the misleadingly named "amnesty law" in France,[1] many members of the regicidal National Convention headed for Belgium, while certain remnants of the imperial army took refuge in America, at the Champ d'Asile.[2] On occasions, it was a matter of prudently slipping across the nearest border. During the Hundred Days, a young aristocrat who had rejoined King Louis XVIII's military household went into refuge in Switzerland, then in Savoy, before returning to the French shore of Lake Leman in late June 1815, aboard a boatman's rowboat, who rented him a little house, once used by douaniers, some quarter of an hour from the village. This fleeting far from glorious exile was the young Alphonse de Lamartine.[3]

The purpose of the Congress of Vienna was to establish new borders, but it in fact fueled the tensions and hopes of various monarchic branches, of military leaders who did not disarm, and of peoples subjected to victorious emperors. The history of migrations, which has largely accompanied the revived interest in the

---

[1] The "amnesty law" of January 12, 1816 was granted by Louis XVIII to all those who had taken part in the "rebellion and usurpation by Napoléon Bonaparte", except the members of the Bonaparte family and the members of the regicidal National Convention who were instructed to leave France within one month.

[2] Particularly Rafe Blaubarf, *Bonapartists in the Borderlands: French Exiles and Refugees on the Gulf Coast 1815–1835* (Tuscaloosa: University of Alabama Press, 2005) and Éric Saugera, *Reborns in America: French Exiles and Refugees in the United States and the Vine and Olive Adventure 1815–1865* (Tuscaloosa: University Alabama Press, 2011).

[3] Two hundred years later, the boatman's house is visible on the shore of the lake, and the municipality has had verses from Lamartine's *Lac* engraved on the port jetty – even though they were penned about another lake.

history of exile, has as a matter of convenience long proceeded by constructing successive logical sequences, suggesting a series of regular and continuous waves. But the changes and spatial frameworks are in fact more complex, for both migrations and exiles. Flows waxed and waned but never wholly dried up, while the early nineteenth century saw a "trickle" rather than great waves, to extend the aquatic metaphor. The destinations were also highly varied, illustrating the many reasons for departure – fleeing repression by a regime against which one had risen up, following once powerful leaders now cast down, or hatching plots and scheming revolutions from afar. The timeframes were complex too: the ten years Napoleon spent on St Helena are in no way comparable to Lamartine's few days of exile lying low on the other shore of Lake Leman, more as a deserter than a refugee.

Is it possible to quantify European political exile during this period? Many researchers have addressed this question, often in monographs on a particular national group or place of refuge. Very reliable estimations are thus available for the number of foreigners in Paris under the July Monarchy,[4] or in London in the aftermath of 1848.[5] But broadening the focus to gauge the extent of the phenomenon throughout Europe poses methodological problems. First, not all places of refuge and all national groups have been studied equally, and much work remains to be done, for example, on central Europe, despite pioneering research by Heléna Tóth.[6] Second, the heterogeneity of the available sources means that it can be hazardous to add new groups, for their contours change depending on whether they are apprehended via archives about assistance to refugees, or those about monitoring them, or whether they include or exclude women. Matters become even more fraught once we try to separate political exiles from economic migrations, for an infinite continuum of nuances exist between these two ideal types. Moments of political crisis together with the revolutionary episodes of 1820–1821, 1830, and 1848 obviously caused political exiles to depart in substantial though varying numbers. But these events often coincided with periods of recession and unemployment, making any separation between political and economic motives largely artificial.

The purpose of this chapter is thus to periodize, spatialize, and quantify political exiles in nineteenth-century Europe. In terms of chronology, it is a matter of showing that while major political changes caused fluctuations in pace and

---

[4] Delphine Diaz, *Un asile pour tous les peuples. Exilés et réfugiés étrangers en France au cours du premier XIXe siècle* (Paris: Armand Colin, 2014).
[5] Sabine Freitag (ed.), *Exiles from European Revolutions. Refugees in Mid-Victorian England*, (Oxford-New York: Berghahn Books, 2003).
[6] Tóth, *An Exiled Generation*.

scale, these should not hide the complexity of individual itineraries or the diversity of national cases. Looking at the geography of exile flows should help untangle this complexity, with particular attention to the paths taken by exiles, often not a straightforward transfer from country of departure to country of arrival. In terms of quantities, rather than gathering numbers which are far too disparate to yield any overall estimate of the number of exiles, the objective is to make the flows commensurable, and to map individual and collective trajectories within the European circulations of exiles.

1 The Congress of Vienna: restoring powers and controlling the vanquished

The representatives of the victorious powers did not specifically debate the question of exile and asylum, but they were committed to stabilizing populations and confining or else expelling those who had collaborated with the now defeated Napoleonic order. The Final Act of the Congress of Vienna simplified the map of Europe. The German mosaic of 350 states was pared down to just 39, united in a Germanic Confederation. The Italian peninsula was hence divided into seven states. Russia now encompassed most of the former Duchy of Warsaw, transformed into a Kingdom of Poland in personal union with the Tsar. Prussia received Swedish Pomerania, northern Saxony, Westphalia, and most of Rhineland. Austria gained control of Lombardy, Venetia, the Adriatic coast (Illyria and Dalmatia), the Tyrol, and Salzburg. Spain and Portugal were reunited with their sovereigns, though their colonial empires were gradually broken up. These territorial annexations did not take aspirations to unity into account, and the return of monarchs quite clearly caused abrupt or negotiated departures. Aspirations to unification (in Italy, and partly in German states) went ignored, as did those to a constitutional regime, as called for by progressive bourgeois swathes. Many of the young Germans who had been called to arms in 1813 by sovereigns promising them a free and united Germany, to the battle cry of *"Vivat Teutonia!"* ("Long live Germany!"), were bitterly disappointed. Secret societies, particularly the carbonari in the Italian peninsula, started to develop and nourish new ideas.

Thus most of the circulations of exiles in the early nineteenth century, echoing those of earlier political circulations, arose from dissent with the order of Vienna. The exiles of the beginning of the century were necessarily marked by the displacements of émigrés during the French Revolution and by the exodus of planters from Saint-Domingue. All these experiences, to which should be added the passage of armies through Europe and the Atlantic, carved out deeply bedded routes, shaped representations, and profoundly marked the policies introduced. The French Revolution had occasioned the first mass exile of the late modern period, that of the "counterrevolutionaries", which was not comprised solely of migrating aristocrats, no doubt numbering around 150,000 people in all. There was nothing comparable in the rest of the nineteenth century, but this initial emigration influenced exiles and authorities in lands of departure and arrival.

Other even older memories were also reactivated, such as that of the 200,000 Huguenots who had fled the kingdom of France after the revocation of the Edict of Nantes in 1685 for Germany, Britain, and the Netherlands, or the less studied departure of 45,000 English and Irish military and civilian Jacobites who left Britain after James II fled in 1689.[7] But the phenomenon did not solely draw inspiration from the past; exiles innovated at times, as did the government's taking them in and casting them out. Exiles borrowed from the paths taken by international volunteers journeying throughout Europe, while governments wondered how best to control and monitor the newcomers, or else relegate them to a distance. Was exile a civilized sentence? This topic was debated by the powers at the Congress of Vienna who, without forsaking execution for political convicts, preferred to keep them at a distance. As Caroline Shaw has shown, this humanitarianism went hand-in-hand with the abolition of the slave trade and slavery.[8] The geography of European exile was thus not solely continental, and played a role in establishing a British empire in the Mediterranean with the taking of Malta in 1800, the Ionian Isles in 1809, and the occupation of Corfu from 1815 to 1864.[9] It is also important to have an overall vision, and consideration of the paths taken by exiles encourages us to take the broad picture into account: Garibaldi, for instance, was a revolutionary circulating between the two worlds of Europe and the Americas as a combatant and an exile;[10] equally, the French conquest of Algeria was largely conducted by the bat-

---

[7] On this neglected exile and the reasons why it has been neglected, see Guy Chaussinand-Nogaret, "Une élite insulaire au service de l'Europe: les Jacobites au xviie siècle," *Annales. Économies, sociétés, civilisations* 28th year, 5 (1973): 1097–1122.
[8] Caroline E. Shaw, *Britannia's Embrace. Modern Humanitarianism and the Imperial Origins of Refugee Relief* (Oxford: Oxford University Press, 2015).
[9] Robert Holland, *Blue-Water Empire, The British in the Mediterranean since 1800* (London: Allen Lane, 2013).
[10] Lucy Riall, "Travel, Migration, Exile: Garibaldi's global Fame," *Italy* 19/1 (2014): 41–52.

talions of the French Foreign Legion, made up of exiled Italians, Spaniards, and Poles.[11]

2 Asylum for peoples and refuge for kings (1815 – 1848)

Delphine Diaz has sketched an overview of the political refugees who came to settle in France in the years 1820 – 1830. There is no pan-European synthesis of similar scale, and what follows is only schematic. The difficulty in apprehending these forced displacements stems from their instability and tendency to be knocked off course. Sojourns outside the homeland were never thought of as definitive by exiles, who lived in fear of new measures being unleashed against them. Still, by following the broad lines of the political changes toppling or reinstating thrones, we may sketch out a chronology and map the movements of exiles in the early nineteenth century.

The 1820s: the Mediterranean exile of those who had fought for freedom

Conveniently but also because their situations were closely linked, one point clearly transpires for the first decade after the Congress of Vienna: it was southern Europe which was on the move, rocked by revolts, revolutions, and *pronunciamientos*. The main exile currents thus flowed out of Spain and Italy. Most arrived in two European countries which took them in, but with seemingly very different policies, namely France and Britain. Nevertheless, we need to consider the Mediterranean as a whole to understand these displacements and circulations. For a long time, the Mediterranean's key role in political migrations was not explicit. But in the first decades of the nineteenth century, it acquired a central place. Throughout the century the Mediterranean – which has emerged as a category of historical analysis as evidenced by the authors working under the recent editorship of Maurizio Isabella and Konstantina Zanou – was a central space for voluntary and forced connections and circulations.[12]

---

11 Delphine Diaz, "Indésirables en métropole, utiles en Algérie? Les réfugiés politiques étrangers et la colonisation (1830 – 1852)," *Revue d'histoire du XIXe siècle*, 51 (2015/2): 190 *et seq.*
12 Maurizio Isabella & Konstantina Zanou (eds.), *Mediterranean Diasporas, Politics and Ideas in the long 19th Century* (New York: Bloomsbury, 2016).

The *afrancesados* were the first great migration spawned by the defeat of Napoléon. These Spaniards who had collaborated with the French occupier went abroad, especially to neighboring France after the battle of Vitoria in June 1813. This was mass immigration, with the scholarship agreeing on a figure of nearly 12,000 Spaniards going into exile. The historian Juan Lopéz Tabar, who has gone over the figures, reached the same number, though was able to obtain reliable information for only 4,172 of them.[13] Estimates by the French government were revised downwards in 1815, when they were said to number 5,000 to 6,000, a figure it is hard to check in the absence of statistical tools about *afrancesados* returning to Spain, or else continuing on their travels, heading especially for Britain. The amnesty granted by Ferdinand VII on February 15, 1818 and the establishment of a liberal regime in January 1820 further reduced this figure. In addition to being a mass exile, it was also a family and aristocratic phenomenon, mainly comprised of Joseph Bonaparte's senior administrators, accompanied by their wives and children. Initially, the wives were forbidden from returning to the Iberian Peninsula, as were Joseph's supporters. During the Liberals' brief spell in power during the *Trienio liberal* (1820–1823), pro-absolutists crossed the border into France, but liberal exiles resumed with the "expedition of the Hundred Thousand Sons of Saint Louis" in 1823, which reinstated Ferdinand VII on the throne. On withdrawing from Spain, the French army took nearly 12,500 prisoners with it,[14] not including volunteer exiles. In 1824 these prisoners obtained the right to return home with an indemnity and an assigned itinerary. They were also allowed to remain in France as refugees and enjoy the same status as their compatriots who had come of their own accord. A small proportion of prisoners took this option, but it led to confusion between the various situations.

In addition to choosing France, Spanish liberals also headed for the land of liberalism, namely Britain, and once in London earnestly debated liberal principles. Others opted for Latin America and took part in the revolutionary conflicts on the American subcontinent. Here, the Mediterranean was part of a vaster space, that of an empire which, though dismembered, still looked towards another maritime space, namely the Atlantic. Juan Luis Simal has shown that Spanish exiles were actively involved in two-way politicization on either side of the ocean, maintaining political relationships and promoting intellectual processes

---

13 Juan López Tabar, *Los famosos traidores: los afrancesados durante la crisis del Antiguo Régimen (1808–1833)* (Madrid: Biblioteca nueva, 2001), 107.
14 Archives nationales de France, F7 11 991, note from the ministry of the interior, weekly report on prisoners of the Spanish war, December 23, 1823, quoted in Diaz, *Un asile pour tous les peuples*, 46.

and ideological transfers via exchanges between Spain, Latin America, and the United States.[15] Fifty or so liberals from the Iberian Peninsula and from Cuba settled in the United States. In December 1823, three Cuban parliamentarians arrived from the *Cortes* in Madrid: Félix Varela, Leonardo Santos Suárez, and Tomás Gener. Along with the parliamentarian from Porto Rico, they were the only American representatives to have remained in the *Cortes* after most of their peers departed, in February 1822, in a definitive break with the process of constitutional reform to the Spanish Empire initiated a decade earlier. In 1823 they were unable to return home, for the Creole authorities and elite had accepted the restoration of Ferdinand VII.

The Iberian peninsula was not the only source of exiles on the American continent. The wars of independence in the Americas, followed by internal conflict between the new nations, led many thousands of Spaniards who had remained in the Latin American republics to go into exile for political reasons, without having to re-cross the Atlantic from West to East. Hispanophobia peaked in Mexico with the expulsion laws of the late 1820s. The 7,148 Spaniards who left Mexico between 1807 and 1829 traveled to the United States, England, or France. Conversely, exiled Spaniards clearly cooperated with Hispano-Americans in preparing insurrections in Spain.

Contact was not only personal but also intellectual. The Hispano-Spaniards, particularly in Britain, responded to the surging demand for publications from the new authorities and elites in the Hispano-American republics wishing to provide the middle classes with works of general interest on education and economics. Rudolf Ackermann, a German settled in London, built up a circle of unemployed Spaniards, including the engineer José María de Lanz y Valdívar (1764–1839),[16] who in 1820 wrote the *Essai sur la Composition des Machines*. Ackermann's most ambitious publishing project was the *Catechisms*, a series of books teaching the basics about the arts and sciences. These were a great success in Latin America, with thousands of copies being printed.[17]

The French authorities often confused these exiles from Spain with other liberals from Naples and Piedmontese due to their shared political influences. It was after the adoption of the 1812 Cadiz constitution, and under the influence of the 1820 Spanish *pronunciamiento*, that the members of the secret societies of the Kingdom of Two Sicilies and of Piedmont sought to take power. On the heels of their defeat, they headed for the country which inspired them, Spain.

---

15 Juan Luis Simal, "Exils et circulations des idées politiques entre Amérique hispanique et Espagne après les indépendances (1820–1836)," *Revue d'histoire du XIXe siècle* 51 (2015): 35–51.
16 See chapter 5 for further details about this figure.
17 Simal, "Exils et circulations," 47.

The ideological and socio-economic contours of the leading partisans were once again fairly alike, being mainly military officers, students, and members of the liberal professions. The French expedition also caused them to leave Spain and scatter across Europe and the Americas. They did not select their destinations for proximity to their country of origin, but rather for political proximity. Above all, the exiles in question – at most 1,000 individuals – sought to organize themselves alongside such great figures of exile as Ugo Foscolo, Giuseppe Pecchio, and Santorre di Santarosa.[18]

Liberalism also drove the political movements that marked 1820s Portugal, causing its partisans to go into exile. These upheavals were felt throughout the Empire, for Dom Pedro, the son of the king of Portugal, John VI, became emperor of Brazil in 1822. The king's accession in 1826 resulted in a serious crisis between, on the one hand, supporters of Dom Pedro, who had remained in Brazil with his daughter, who was still a minor, and, on the other, John VI's second son Dom Miguel, who was ultra-intransigent and opposed to any constitution. His regency sparked a civil war, causing Portuguese liberals to go into refuge once again in 1828, heading via the Azores for England and France. One of them, Almeida Garrett, was closely involved in building a network of what historians of Portuguese liberalism have defined as the "system of Southern liberty".[19]

Another Mediterranean source of exile to be affected by major political upheavals in the 1820s was Greece. The origin of the uprisings here was different, and may be traced back to spring 1821, with the outbreak of the war of independence against the Ottoman Empire. Greek independence, proclaimed on January 1, 1822, was the point of departure for a war which consumed all Europe, with volunteers hurrying to the Greeks' assistance. The circulation of exiles was thus caught up with that of combatants going to fight alongside the Greeks. Ten years later, Greece was victorious, but over the course of this decade, many insurgents left the country and placed their family in safety abroad. Records also show that, unusually, there were as many women as men among the small number of Greek exiles in France in 1826.[20] Another specificity was that though some of the Greek community settled in Paris, far more did so in the south of France, especially in the ports of Marseille and Toulon where they dis-

---

18 On this Italian exile during the 1820s, see Maurizio Isabella, *Risorgimento in Exile. Italian Émigrés and the Liberal International in the Post-Napoleonic Era*, (Oxford: Oxford Press, 2009), and Agostino Bistarelli, *Gli esuli del Risorgimento* (Turin: Il Mulino, 2011).
19 Gabriel Paquette, "An Itinerant Liberal: Almeida Garrett's Exile Itineraries and Political Ideas in the Age of Southern European Revolutions (1820–1834)," in *Mediterranean Diasporas*, ed. Maurizio Isabella and Konstantina Zanou, 46.
20 Diaz, *Un asile pour tous les peuples*, 51.

embarked, and in Corsica. In 1830 there were 400 Greek exiles in Marseille, but the sources do not allow us to differentiate combatants and patriots from the merchants and sailors who traditionally moved around the Mediterranean but had now retrenched their activities to the great French port.[21]

Proscribed dynasties

The many exiles whose itineraries we have followed stemmed largely from having fomented failed insurrections. But members of European royal families and their courts also underwent forced migrations, either heading into exile or returning from it to retrieve their throne. In the conclusion of a book edited by Bruno Dumons, *Rois et reines en exil*, Jean-Clément Martin rightly highlights the singular nature of these atypical exiles who, though not needing to prove the legitimacy of their cause, had to maintain their rank and remain worthy of their bloodline.[22] In 1814–1815 Louis XVIII arrived in France, left it, then re-returned from exile. However, most of the émigrés had preceded him to France, returning under the Empire. In 1830 Charles X, for his part, had to head back down the same road he had taken when leaving France in 1789. His family and circle stayed first in England, then in Scotland, before moving to outside Prague. The royal family subsequently took up residence in Frohsdorf, in 1839, when the Duke of Blacas Charles X's trusted confidant, acquired the castle and estate of Frohsdorf, 25 miles outside Vienna, for the sum of 175,000 florins from his own exchequer.[23]

To these French examples we may add the journeying of the Spanish and Portuguese kings. However, during these years exile acquired a particular meaning, for it was not solely a withdrawal but also a complex form of expiation, endowed with a legendary dimension. The figure of Napoléon condemned to reside on Elba and especially then on St Helena left a deep and lasting impact on ways of viewing and imagining exile.[24] In *La Légende des siècles* (1827), Victor Hugo identified the exiled Emperor with Prometheus:

---

21 Diaz, *Un asile pour tous les peuples*, 52.
22 Jean-Clément Martin, "Exils princiers? L'occasion de comprendre une rupture historique," in *Rois et princes en exil, une histoire transnationale du politique dans l'Europe du XIXe siècle*, ed. Bruno Dumons (Paris: Éditions Riveneuve, 2015), 151–160.
23 See chapter 8 in this book about memory of the royal family's exile at Frohsdorf.
24 Max Andréoli, "Napoléon Bonaparte: trois îles, trois exils," *Studia romanica* 4 (2002): 97–114.

St Helena! Lesson! Fall! Example! Agony!
England exhausting its genius with hatred
Set about devouring this great man in full daylight,
And the universe witnessed once again this Homeric spectacle;
The chain, the rock scorched by the African sky,
And the Titan – and the Vulture![25]

The 1820s – often overlooked due to a focus on the return to order – were profoundly marked by ceaseless political movements, with a far more complex map and chronology than suggested by accounts built around "restoration". The men and women circulating during this decade did so in the name of ideals which, though taken largely from the past, could also be characterized by modern national sentiment, which emerged as one of the main drivers of political movements and their corollary, exile politics.

The 1830s: extending the domain of exile

The combats of the previous decade continued into the 1830s, but the lands of departure and exile and the map of exile became more diverse and complex. Circulations intensified in Europe, the Americas, and North Africa. The reasons for departure also became more varied. In addition to being caused by conflicts between liberalism and authoritarian monarchism, or a response to foreign occupations, exiles were now driven by national aspirations, a phenomenon which was already present in Italy and was gathering momentum in Germany. But the main country embodying exile during this decade was the martyred nation of Poland which, unlike Greece, did not benefit from an inrush of European military volunteers, and instead came to symbolize European political exile through its many personalities and anonymous soldiers cast out onto the roads.

Though the revolutions of the 1830s did not affect all European countries, they altered the political map of Europe.[26]

Louis-Philippe's France came to embody liberal asylum, like Britain. The governments of Louis XVIII and of Charles X had not conducted a policy of rejecting exiles, but the new monarch wished to embrace an even broader policy

---

[25] Victor Hugo, "Le retour de l'Empereur", *La Légende des siècles* (Paris: Gallimard, collection de la Pléiade, 1950), 594. This image of the "hideous" rock where the emperor is pinned down appears again in "L'expiation", the fifth book of *Châtiments*. Cf. Max Andréoli, 113, translated by Adrian Morfee.

[26] Sylvie Aprile, Jean-Claude Caron, & Emmanuel Fureix (eds.), *La Liberté guidant les peuples. Les révolutions de 1830 en Europe* (Seyssel: Champ Vallon, 2013).

Fig 1, translation: Previous revolts: Pink: Independence; Light pink: Autonomy; Rose: Constitution granted; Yellow: Failed liberal uprisings; **1830 revolutions:** Yellow (star): July Revolution; Light orange: Constitution granted; light green: Conservative block (Holy Alliance); dark green: Failure and repression; purple Line: Limit of the German confederation.
1. Hanover, 2. Brunswick, 3. Hesse-Cassel, 4. Parma, 5. Modena, 6. Church states.

of more ostensible welcome, overseen by regulations to count and control the flow of political refugees. The latter, principally from Spain, Portugal, the Italian peninsula, and above all Poland, were viewed as posing a risk of unrest. As a French deputy, Dupin, declared to parliament on February 21, 1832: "tranquility could be disturbed by the presence of Spanish, Italian, or Polish refugees in certain places, for we now have refugees from all nations".[27]

This new concern occasioned closer counting of the number of exiles, and triggered new debates. The figure of the exile as a category was no longer identified solely with a handful of nations and a few political positions. The Spaniards numbered not only liberals, but also their enemies, Carlists, legitimists who had fled Spain during the First Carlist War of 1833–1840. Larger numbers of Italians came to France. They also came from more diverse origins. Together with liberal exiles taking refuge primarily in Spain, and, like Spanish liberals,

---

[27] Diaz, *Un asile pour tous les peuples*, 53.

entertaining hopes of popular uprisings, there were now candidates for exile fleeing Austrian domination in Venetia. The newly arrived Poles were more numerous and received greater assistance. The members of the "great emigration" started arriving in sizeable numbers in winter 1831. In the Russian part of Poland, a liberal uprising was triggered in November 1830 in the wake of revolutions in France and Belgium (in July and August respectively). The victorious military uprising in Warsaw resulted in the Polish army taking power and the flight of Grand Duke Konstantin. A provisional government was set up on December 3, 1830, but soon found itself facing a counteroffensive by the Russian army. In September 1831, Russian troops were at the gates of Warsaw. When the city surrendered on the 7th of the month, thousands of Poles had to leave the country, and most chose to head for France. The newly formed kingdom of Belgium also took in Poles from the great emigration, as did Britain and America. Out of the 8,000 or so former insurgents who fled Warsaw in late 1831, probably 6,000 went to France, with no hope of return in the short term. There was a certain degree of social homogeneity among Polish exiles, as most were army officers from the minor nobility. Indeed, non-commissioned officers and soldiers had more difficulty obtaining passports from the French consulate or diplomatic authorities. Although the mass arrival of 1831–1832 was spectacular, Polish émigrés continue to arrive throughout the 1830s. Another wave headed to France after the February 1846 Kraków uprising against Austrian domination ended in defeat.

The reception Poles received in France also played a major role in how their cause was covered in the press. Just as a few years earlier writers and intellectuals – Musset, Hugo, Montalembert, Vigny, and Béranger – had mobilized in favor of Greece, they now came out in favor of the Polish cause, which was also a Catholic and liberal one. When General Sébastiani declared to the chamber that "order reign[ed] in Warsaw", Lafayette answered that "all France [was] Polish".[28] The banished were received triumphantly, and Casimir Delavigne's song *La Varsovienne* was on everyone's lips. In 1833, Adam Mickiewicz – a friend of Jules Michelet and Edgar Quinet, and a professor at the Collège de France – brought out a book called *Livre de la nation polonaise et des pèlerins polonais*, giving temporary embodiment to the hopes of crushed Poland. In England, a group of exiles based in Portsmouth and at St Helier on Jersey founded the Communes of the Polish people. Among the Poles who went into exile in Western Europe, some headed for the newly independent Belgium, which was home to about 100 Polish

---

28 Speech by General Lafayette, September 11, 1831, *Mémoires, correspondances et manuscrits du Général Lafayette, publiés par sa famille* (Brussels: Société belge de librairie, 1839), vol. 2, 531.

refugees after 1833, admittedly fewer than in France or Britain at that time. This lesser-known part of the great emigration has been researched by Idesbald Goddeeris.[29] The Poles in Belgium included a famous and more radical figure than the head of the emigration in France – Prince Adam Jerzy Czartoryski, who had taken up residence in Paris – namely Joachim Lelewel, whose brief stay in France was cut short by an expulsion order in 1833, on which he departed for Brussels where he resided for nearly thirty years. A pro-Polish current developed in Belgium supported by Belgian liberals, resulting in the formation of short-lived committees and the organization of subscriptions and lotteries. The Polish diaspora no doubt traveled the furthest due to the long duration of their exile, the sheer numbers involved, and Poland's position on the edge of continental empires. Katarzyna Papiez has recently discovered the existence of a colony founded in 1842 by a group of Polish exiles at Adampol, forty kilometers from Istanbul. They had decided to settle there because Prince Czartoryski, a former foreign affairs minister under Tsar Alexander I, wished to pursue a diplomatic policy via a network of clandestine agencies he had set up, whose main branch was in Istanbul.[30]

German political emigration was on a more modest scale, and it is hard to differentiate the circulation of intellectuals from that of the very large numbers of migrant workers.[31] In the 1840s there were 70,000 Germans in the French capital, forming what was no doubt the largest group of émigrés. The vast majority of this "German colony" was composed of craftsmen, day laborers, street sweepers, and unqualified workers. These temporary migrants had come to Paris for economic reasons, being unable to meet their basic needs in their home country. Some of the many German craftsmen who came to settle in Paris for a few years were politicized, but their political formation often occurred in France. It is thus difficult to identify the "exiles" among this migrant group. The term was used solely for the few journalists and writers who had settled in Paris and Brussels after having been harried and expelled from Germany. German political exiles sought to escape the vast surveillance and censorship system put in place by Metternich. Paris, viewed as the seat of revolution in Europe, had become the

---

29 Idesbald Goddeeris, *La Grande Émigration polonaise en Belgique (1831–1870). Élites et masses en exil à l'époque romantique à l'époque romantique* (Bern: Peter Lang, 2013).
30 Katarzyna Papiez, "Adampol/Polonezköy, refuge et colonie agricole: un laboratoire de la polonité en exil dans l'empire ottoman au xixe siècle," in Delphine Diaz & Alexandre Dupont (eds.), *Les mots de l'exil dans l'Europe du xixe siècle, Hommes & Migrations* 1321 (April-June 2018): 65–75.
31 Jacques Grandjonc, "Les émigrés allemands sous la monarchie de Juillet: documents de surveillance policière 1833-février 1848," *Cahiers d'études germaniques* 1 (1972): 115–249.

preferred meeting place for German political "activists". Having escaped censorship, they could publish freely and follow events back in their home country, even though they were under permanent surveillance by the French police and Prussian and German informers. It was in these circumstances that Karl Marx arrived in Paris in 1843 and was expelled in 1845. The encounter between German political exiles, craftsmen, and workers helped spawn the modern labor movement in the 1830s and 1840s. The social critique these German exiles and émigrés formulated in their newspapers and pamphlets or voiced within their associations established a close link between political exile and economic immigration. But they brought with them to the capitals of Europe new and at times clashing ideas. They were not driven by secret military liberal or legitimist actions but by social and national aspirations. Although the various utopian, communist, and socialist currents often clashed and did not join up their operations, they built new and more radical networks which were no doubt a greater source of concern to the authorities than earlier liberal movements had been. The United States was an ideal land for people whose government wanted to be rid of them. The economist Friedrich List (1789–1846), who had been imprisoned in Asperg fortress for having severely criticized the Wurtemberg administration, was released in 1825 on pain of leaving the country for the United States. He settled in Pennsylvania where he discovered a coal seam which he mined with local landowners, set up a railway network, wrote one of the major works of political economy, and conducted an argument with Adam Smith. In 1832 List returned to Leipzig in Saxony, where he set about the task of improving the transport system.

In the wake of the Paris revolution of July 1830, Italian migration to the French capital increased, since events in the peninsula were now in phase with the revolutionary wave initiated in France. The Orléans regime gave Italian patriots its encouragement, and the Duchy of Ferrara reciprocated in August by acclaiming the July Revolution in France. But it was in January 1831 that the first uprisings occurred in the Papal States and in the Duchy of Modena; by the following month, all central Italy was in the grip of insurrection. This revolutionary outbreak caused neighboring Austria to step in, sending its troops against Modena in March 1831. By mid-July 1831 France was pressuring Austria to rapidly withdraw its troops from central Italy. Further uprisings took place in the autumn, leading to a second Austrian intervention. This time France too was drawn into weighing on future events in central Italy, sending an expeditionary force to Ancona in April 1832, thus ending Austria's monopoly over Italian affairs.

César Vidal estimates that France granted a total of 1,500 passports to subjects of the Pope after the 1831 troubles.[32] In addition to diplomatic sources, ministry of the interior statistics on foreign refugees in receipt of subsidies allows us to place a more exact figure on the number of Italian exiles under the July Monarchy, even though these lists only include individuals receiving assistance. In September 1831, for the French territory as a whole, 1,524 Italian refugees were recorded as receiving government subsidies.

The conditions under which people banished from central Italy could reside in France were strictly controlled. Indeed, this was the case for all foreign refugees, even prior to the first law on the residency of refugees being adopted in April 1832. While most settled in the south-east and east of the country, particularly the Italian depot in Mâcon, some were authorized to live in the capital. Of the 1,524 Italian exiles assisted by the French government, 257 had settled in the department of Seine. Thus only 16.8% of subsidized refugees had the right to reside in Paris, and these privileged exiles were mainly from the social and intellectual elites of their country of origin. The records of the ministry of the interior include 216 magistrates, officers, landowners, attorneys, doctors, or students, but only 9 non-commissioned officers, soldiers, workers, or servants, with the 32 women and children being counted separately. Elites comprised the vast majority of subsidized refugees, with only 4% of Italian exiles residing in Paris in 1831 being from the lower classes. This was not specific to Italian exiles, since the French ministry of the interior, together with the Paris police authorities, did their utmost to refuse access to the capital to all refugees with insufficient resources.

Among the notables from Italy residing in Paris were Princess Cristina di Belgiojoso of Lombardy, who arrived in May 1831, Count Terenzio Mamiani della Rovere, who arrived a few months later, and the professors Vincenzo Gioberti (from 1831 to 1834) and Giuseppe Ferrari (1837 to 1841), together with famous men of letters, such as Niccolò Tommaseo (1802–1874), a writer of Dalmatian origin, forced by the censors to leave Florence in 1834. This group of liberal exiles residing in Paris, mainly from the Papal States, but also from Lombardy and Tuscany, frequently met as of 1835 in the salon held by Princess Belgiojoso in her residence on Rue d'Anjou. This acted as the rallying point for the great figures of Italian exile; Niccolò Tommaseo mentions it twenty-seven times in his diary entries between January 1835 and March 1837.[33] It was also attended by French pol-

---

[32] César Vidal, *Louis-Philippe, Mazzini et la Jeune Italie (1832–1834)* (Paris: Les Presses modernes, 1934), 46.
[33] Delphine Diaz, "Un asile pour tous les peuples? Proscrits, exilés et réfugiés étrangers en France 1813–1852" (PhD diss., Université Paris 1 Panthéon-Sorbonne, 2012), 520–21.

iticians and men of letters, such as the historian François-Auguste Mignet, the philosopher Victor Cousin, and the poet Alfred de Musset.

It was during the 1830s that the group of Italian liberals exiled in Paris was most united. As of the following decade, the return home of Italian political immigrants started to be felt both in the capital and across France as a whole. Whereas in 1832 the French government provided assistance to 964 Italians in all, about 11.4% of the total number of registered refugees, the figure dropped slowly over the course of the second half of the decade, declining from 708 in 1835 to only 543 refugees by 1839.

In the 1830s, political exile reflected the harsh censorship and repression muzzling internal public opinion, hindering reforms and curbing socio-political unrest. Although it might initially seem paradoxical, exile tended to strengthen the place of those who were outside where politics was conducted and voiced, turning them into heroes and constructing nostalgic visions previously the preserve of exiled kings. It was in exile that innovations and utopias were forged. Initially, the émigré could cast around for material solutions, and seek a return to arms in a post-revolutionary period marked by the Napoleonic wars. But secret agitation and attempted power grabs tended to gradually unravel and lose their appeal. To avoid being excluded or cut off from political contest, exiles were able to draw on a time of reflection which could bring their project to fruition, or on occasions radicalize it. It was in Paris between 1843 and 1845 that Karl Marx met German workers, an encounter which led him from liberalism to socialism. Paris was also where he forged his steadfast friendship with Engels, which lasted throughout his exile and hence his life. Was exile a factor here? It is hard to say; nevertheless, this early phase gave rise to many fraternal relations, as well as to numerous political divisions.

3 1848 and its aftermath

Exiles amidst revolutionary upheaval

The 1848 revolutions engendered an important shift in European exile. Many European states were affected by revolutionary movements of various natures, so 1848 stands out for the unprecedented number of people heading into exile, giving rise to what Heléna Tóth calls an "exiled generation".[34] As exile became a mass phenomenon, those involved became socially more diverse, with workers

---

34 Tóth, *An Exiled Generation*.

and vagabonds now rubbing shoulders with lettered elites.[35] But exile was not solely a consequence of revolutionary unrest, it also contributed to its spread. While events were concentrated around the year 1848, the chronology of troubles enabled exiled agitators to take part in new plots or protests in their country of refuge.

Unrest first broke out in Messina in the Kingdom of the Two Sicilies in 1847, where riots against the order established by the Congress of Vienna took up the watchword "Pius IX, Italy, Constitution". The movement soon spread across Sicily with major demonstrations in Palermo in January 1848, leading King Ferdinand II to grant the first 1848 constitution, on January 29. The Grand Duke of Tuscany soon followed suit, in turn, constrained to submit to a fundamental law promulgated on February 17, 1848.

Even though the events in Paris in February 1848 reverberated more strongly around Europe, they only occurred a few days later, starting on February 22, after a republican banquet planned in Paris was banned. As is well known, the revolutionary dynamic then spread throughout Europe, particularly the German states and the Austrian Empire, sparing only Britain. Initially, monarchs were caught off guard and made concessions. Nearly all the places concerned introduced a constitution, though often briefly, accompanied by a first experimentation with universal male suffrage. Exiles played a far from negligible role in this phase of revolutionary expansion. Several of the most emblematic figures, such as Giuseppe Mazzini and Giuseppe Garibaldi in Italy, and Karl Marx in Germany, returned from their place of relegation to combat the conservative monarchies in their country of origin. Others poured their revolutionary energies into serving new causes, such as István Türr (1825–1908), a Hungarian patriot in refuge in Piedmont, who took part in the first war of independence against the Austrians (March-August 1848). Exiles needed to transpose their "nationality-based" ideals to a different context. Such an endeavor was in no way certain: while Italian and Hungarian patriots certainly had a common enemy in Austria, once it became a matter of dividing up territories, or establishing a hierarchy between nations and political regimes, then transferring patriotism from one country to another became problematic.

---

35 The reader is referred to chapter 4 for a collective portrait of exiles and their social origins.

From repression to flight

Exiles thus started out as protagonists in the 1848 revolutions, before falling victim to the phases of repression washing over the continent after the opening months of the year and through to the aftermath of Louis Napoléon Bonaparte's coup in 1851. The repression of revolutions in Lombardy-Venetia by Austria's General Joseph Radetsky in summer 1848, the suppression of the Prussian parliament by Frederick William IV in November 1848, the dissolution of the Frankfurt parliament in April 1849, the recapturing of Rome by pontifical forces with the support of the French army, and the defeat of Hungarian patriots against the joint advances by Austrian and Russian troops in autumn 1849 all triggered mass forced displacements of people seeking to escape repression. Admittedly, the liberal revolutions had on occasions resulted in certain individuals being subjected to banishment: for instance, the French law of May 26, 1848, forbade King Louis-Philippe and his family from entering French territory for perpetuity, while Pope Pius IX went into voluntary exile on November 15, 1848, after the assassination of Pellegrino Rossi,[36] before the proclamation of the Roman Republic blocked access to the city and those who had remained faithful to him.[37] But it was with the return of conservative forces that it became a mass phenomenon. Hence after the failed insurrection in Baden and recapture of Freiburg-im-Breisgau by the Grand Duchy's loyalist forces, no fewer than 9,000 men converged on Switzerland. Equally, in Saxony, repression of protests sparked by Frederick Augustus II's dissolution of parliament led several thousand insurgents to take flight. Among them was the composer Richard Wagner, who settled in Zürich for twelve years.[38] It is estimated that about 30,000 of those involved in the 1848 revolutions in Italy fled repression by the Kingdom of the Two Sicilies, Venetia, Lombardy (the latter two in Austrian hands), and central duchies, initially taking refuge in Piedmont before fanning out across Europe and the Americas.[39]

---

36 Born in Carrare in 1787, Pellegrino Rossi became a professor of law in Bologna in 1815, before settling initially in Geneva then in Paris. He arrived in France in 1833, was naturalized on August 13, 1834, and named ambassador to Rome in 1845. He was removed from this post due to the February 1848 revolution, and called to head the pontifical constitutional government. He was assassinated in Rome by a republican on November 15, 1848.
37 On the use of the figure of Pius IX in Italian political debate, see Ignazio Veca, *Il mito di Pio IX. Storia di un papa liberale e nazionale* (Roma: Viella, 2018).
38 On Wagner's exile in Switzerland, see the documentary by Andy Sommer, "Wagner. Un génie en exil," with Antoine Wagner, length: 54 minutes. Documentary released on June 18, 2013, distributed by Outhere Distribution France.
39 Gian Biagio Furiozzi, *L'emigrazione politica in Piemonte nel decennio preunitario* (Firenze: L. S. Olschki, 1979).

The number of Italians in London also rose, reaching 1,600 refugees in 1851.[40] These increased numbers made the migratory paths more complex since traditional places of asylum were themselves in the throes of revolutionary unrest or else hard pushed to take in a rapidly expanding population, thus becoming lands of departure in turn.

The chronology of exile followed a different pattern in France, where the regime issuing from the 1848 revolution was one of the most durable in Europe. Thanks to the longevity of the republican regime, France initially seemed the last remaining refuge for liberals persecuted in their country of origin. In a letter to Jules Michelet dated March 10, 1850, the Romanian refugee Démètre Brătianu noted that France was "in a way, the general headquarters for revolutionary forces from the whole of Europe".[41] The republic's policy of taking in political refugees often extended further than partisans and sympathizers. Hence the law of exile against the Bonaparte family was abrogated on October 14, 1848, despite the risk this posed to the regime itself.

The coup by Louis Napoléon Bonaparte meant that France went from being a land of asylum to one where liberals and republicans were persecuted. The sentence of exile was, for that matter, reintroduced by a decree of January 1852. Thus according to the expression of Victor Hugo, who had personally taken refuge in Belgium, then Jersey, and finally Guernsey, "we witness the somber matter of France being chased out of France".[42] Among the 10,000 or so republicans who left the country, mainly clandestinely, many headed for neighboring countries, especially England, which took in 4,500, but also Switzerland and Belgium.[43] Like Amédée Saint-Ferréol who left Paris for Brussels in the wake of the coup, they came to seek "liberty, open-air, movement, constitutional government, and a people in peaceful enjoyment of liberal institutions".[44]

It was not only French republicans who were targeted once the Second Empire was established; additionally, many liberals who had been taken in and as-

---

40 Maurizio Isabella, "Italian Exiles and British Politics before and after 1848," in *Exiles from European Revolutions*, 59–87.

41 Ion Breazu, *Michelet și românii. Studiu de literatură comparată* (Michelet and the Romanians. A study in comparative literature) (cluj: Carta Româneasca, 1935), 130.

42 Victor Hugo, *Histoire d'un crime*, IV, 12, "Les expatriés", electronic edition with a preface and notes by Jean-Marc Hovasse & Guy Rosa, undated, [1877], available online, accessed April 11, 2021: http://www.groupugo.univ-paris-diderot.fr/Hcr_critique/Cadres_Hcr_critique.htm?Submit3=Edition+critique.

43 Fabrice Bensimon, "The French Exiles and the British," in *Exiles from European Revolutions*, 88–102.

44 Amédée Saint-Ferréol, *Les Proscrits français en Belgique: ou la Belgique contemporaine vue à travers l'exil* (Paris: Godet jeune, 1875), vol. 1, 71.

sisted by the July Monarchy and the republic were now deemed undesirable after the coup, leading the Polish refugee Franciszek Ordynski to observe in 1851 that "the government of this country is hounding foreigners".[45] Exiles in Paris were obliged to flee en masse towards neighboring countries, in uncoordinated manner, disrupting the assistance networks and international attempts to organize the exile movement. Alexander Herzen, a Russian refugee in Paris who had been obliged to return hastily to Italy after the repression of the labor movement, was worried at this dispersal: "where are those with whom I argued? They are all dispersed, all persecuted; some are in prison, others have long since crossed the Ocean, one is in Cairo, the other in hiding in Switzerland, and one wandering in London ... who was right?".[46]

Political migrations in the wake of the 1848 revolutions resulted in a larger number of countries becoming lands of exile. The United States emerged as a major destination, chosen by some but thrust upon others. Several thousand liberals and democrats from the German states took refuge there, often after having vainly sought asylum in Switzerland or England.[47] For example, Julius Fröbel (1805–1893), a mineralogist by training and democrat member of the Frankfurt parliament, after taking part in the 1849 uprising in Vienna and escaping a death sentence, settled in New York as a journalist.[48] Eight thousand Hungarians took refuge in the United States between 1848 and 1862, peaking when the former head of the provisional government, Lajos Kossuth, sailed there in 1851.[49] Certain utopian socialists also viewed the New World as the place to realize their ideas, such as Étienne Cabet's disciples, of whom between 1,000 and 1,500 followed him to the United States between 1848 and 1860.[50] South

---

45 Letter from Franciszek Ordynski to J. F. Zieliski, November 28, 1851, municipal library of Torun, quoted in Slawomir Kalembka, "Les émigrés polonais victimes de répression politique (1848–1870)," in *Répression et prison politiques en France et en Europe au XIXe siècle. Actes du colloque de 1986 organisé par la Société d'histoire de la révolution de 1848 et des révolutions du XIXe siècle*, ed. Alain Faure (Paris: Créaphis, 1990), 306.
46 Alexandre Herzen, *Lettres de France et d'Italie (1847–1852)*, translated into French from the Russian by Natalie Herzen, presentation by Marc Vuilleumier (Paris-Geneva: Slatkine, 1979) [1871], letter XII, 272.
47 Marianne Walle, "'Le pain amer de l'exil'. L'émigration des Allemands révolutionnaires (1848–1850) vers les États-Unis," in *Themenportal Europäische Geschichte*, 2007, available online, accessed April 9, 2021, <www.europa.clio-online.de/essay/id/artikel-3327>.
48 Carl Wittke, *Refugees of Revolution: The German Forty-Eighters in America* (Philadelphia: University of Pennsylvania Press, 1952), 325–326.
49 István Kornél Vida, *Hungarian Émigrés in the American Civil War: A History and Biographical Dictionary* (Jefferson: McFarland, 2012).
50 Michel Cordillot, *Utopistes et exilés du Nouveau Monde. Des Français aux États-Unis, de 1848 à la Commune* (Paris: Éditions Vendémiaire, 2013).

America also attracted many outcasts. In 1853 Argentina became a federal republic, offering asylum and an appearance of political stability that was hard to come across in Europe. It was often after complex itineraries marked by repeated expulsions and refusals of asylum that liberal and republican exiles found lasting refuge in the Americas. Thus Friedrich Sorge (1828–1906), who had taken up arms at the age of nineteen during the Forty-Eighter movement in Saxony, fled Germany under threat of a death sentence. He first took refuge in Switzerland, whence he was expelled to Belgium, where he was equally unwelcome, and had to head for England before leaving Europe for the United States in June 1852.

The Ottoman Empire, where some pioneering exiles had settled in the 1840s, also became a major destination in the wake of the 1848 revolutions. Over 5,000 Hungarians flocked there after their revolution was put down. Although nearly all of them were initially confined to camps near the border, hoping for a rapid turn, some settled there lastingly, or else went to Istanbul where the population in the European neighborhoods grew considerably.[51] The Ottoman Empire also looked like a solution for those rejected by traditional places of refuge. Thus Adriano Lemmi (1822–1906), a former secretary to Kossuth and a friend of Mazzini who was expelled from Piedmont in 1853, ended up taking refuge in Constantinople after having failed to obtain asylum in Switzerland.[52]

Colonial lands also seemed to combine political refuge with the possibility of settling, even though the window of opportunity opened by the July Monarchy exhorting refugees to settle in Algeria was pulled shut under the Second Republic.[53] But refugees from southern Europe now turned to other lands, with the Balearics becoming the part of Spain to take in the most exiles in the 1840s and 1850s.[54] As of the French law of March 1852, and especially that of May 30, 1854, on the transportation of common criminals sentenced to hard labor, the principle of deportation took precedence over that of refuge. Between 1852 and 1867, over 18,000 people were handed down a – sometimes light – prison sentence plus transportation to Guyana for perpetuity.[55]

---

51 Tóth, *An Exiled Generation*, chap. 1, 20–3. See too György Csorba, "Hungarian Emigrants of 1848–49 in the Ottoman Empire," in *The Turks*, ed. Hasan Celâl Güzel et al. (Ankara: Yeni Türkiye Publications, 2002), vol. 4, 224.
52 Emilio Costa, "L'espulsione di Adriano Lemmi dal Regno di Sardegna nel marzo del 1853," in *Mazzini e i repubblicani italiani. Studi in onore di Terenzio Grandi nel suo 92° compleanno*, (Turin: Palazzo Carignano, 1976), 239–259.
53 Diaz, "Indésirables en métropole", 187–204.
54 Juan B. Vilar, *La emigración española al Norte de Africa (1830–1999)* (Paris: Hachette, 1996).
55 Marc Renneville, "Les bagnes coloniaux: de l'utopie au risque du non-lieu," *Criminocorpus* [online], The penal colonies, presentation of the issue, accessed April 9, 2021, http://journals.openedition.org/criminocorpus/173.

While the years immediately following the 1848 revolutions saw a peak in forced mobility, the 1850s and 1860s saw these flows partially subside, with people returning from exile in waves of varying degrees of coordination. In Second Empire France, several operations were conducted between 1852 in 1859 to pardon individuals or grant collective amnesties, enabling most French exiles to return, though some turned down a pardon which, rather than restoring their rights, made them dependent on the emperor's goodwill.[56] Conversely, the Czech economist František Ladislav Rieger (1818–1903), a member of the 1848 constituent assembly who, on being forced to flee repression in Bohemia, had taken refuge in France and then in England, returned to Prague in 1851, where his past as an exile meant he was turned down for a post at Charles University.

Despite the reduced flow of exiles characterizing the two decades after 1848, Europe was still shaken by after-shocks of varying intensity, triggering new peaks in forced mobility. Thus the Warsaw uprising in January 1863 occasioned further exiles, mainly of people from the urban classes and the bourgeoisie. Once again it was France that took in most of the Polish insurgents, with 3,400 of them registered there in 1866,[57] reaching 6,000 during the last five years of the Second Empire, most of whom lived in Paris. As for the others, they headed for Switzerland, home to about 2,000 of them in 1865, Italy, Saxony, Bavaria, England, or, lastly Belgium, where 180 of them found refuge.

The end of the century did not mark the end of exile. The founding of the states so fervently hoped for by the national movements of the early nineteenth century, together with the establishment of the republic in France, did not in fact put an end to these forced displacements. On the contrary, wars together with social and religious conflicts exacerbated and radicalized certain political currents, which also became increasingly international.

---

56 Aprile, *Le Siècle des exilés*, 229–255.

57 Jerzy Wojciech Borejsza, *Emigracja polska po powstaniu styczniowym* (Warsaw: Państwowe wydawnictwo naukowe, 1966). These and the following figures have been taken up and completed by Goddeeris, *La Grande Émigration*, 159–173.

4 An exiles' international? Communards, cantonalists, and anarchists

The crisis of the 1870s

The age of revolutionary internationals, which opened with the creation of the International Workingmen's Association in London in 1864, provided political exiles with an opportunity to structure their actions.[58] It also saw new forms of unrest develop, casting thousands of men and women onto the roads of exile, including French communards, Spanish cantonalists, German socialists, and Italian anarchists. In the early 1870s, a new generation of exiles was formed.

The return of war to Spain was a first important factor causing forced displacements. The redrawing of borders also sparked mass population movements, such as when Alsace and Moselle were annexed to Germany under the treaty signed at the Galerie des Glaces in Versailles, causing the displacement of 128,000 French citizens who refused to become German subjects. The German troops advancing on Paris also gave rise to exiles, at times short-lived, both within France and abroad. Equally, growing instability in the Balkans, flaring up in revolts in Bosnia-Herzegovina in 1875 and especially in Bulgaria in 1876, triggered military intervention by Russia and caused many Muslims, referred to as *muhacir* (literally "migrants"), to flee to Anatolia: there were 17,600 recorded departures of Muslims from Bosnia-Herzegovina towards continental Turkey between 1893 and 1899.[59]

Due to their number, and the way their misfortune echoed throughout Europe, French communards played a key role in this new exile movement, even though the case of Paris has attracted more scholarly attention than communes in the south of France or their colonial emulators. Alongside deportees, some of whom were also sentenced to hard labor, no fewer than 4,000 people who had participated to varying degrees in the functioning of the Commune were forced to flee France to escape repression. Many settled in London where they rubbed shoulders with Parisians who had left that city to flee the Franco-Prussian war, or the Commune itself. There were thus several concurrent strata of exiles, some from opposed political camps, all forced in their flight to converge on the same

---

[58] Fabrice Bensimon, Quentin Deluermoz, and Jeanne Moisand, "*Arise Ye Wretched of the Earth": The First International in a Global Perspective* (Leiden: Brill, 2018).
[59] Philippe Gelez, "La spécificité musulmane dans l'évolution démographique de la Bosnie-Herzégovine durant la seconde moitié du XIXe siècle (1850–1914)," *European Journal of Turkish Studies* 12 (2011), accessed April 9, 2021, https://journals.openedition.org/ejts/4382#tocto3n3.

place. Thus in addition to taking in Napoléon III, who went into refuge after his defeat at Sedan, the United Kingdom was simultaneously home to people from eastern France who had fled the Prussian advance, Parisians wishing to escape the Commune, and communards seeking to escape repression. London thus became a privileged destination for French artists, such as the sculptor Jean-Baptiste Carpeaux, who struggled to sell his works in France and so left for economic reasons, Claude Monet, who crossed the Channel to flee war, and Jules Dalou, a figure from the Paris communard movement who settled there for genuinely political reasons.[60] While certain exiles settled lastingly in England, most of those who had fled the war soon returned to France. As for the former communards, most of them remained in England awaiting an amnesty law which was only passed in 1880, and some stayed beyond this date. Constance Bantman has calculated that there were still about one hundred left in 1890.[61]

In addition to London, which remained the privileged destination for communards, exiles in the early 1870s continued to head for the traditional refuges of the Forty-Eighters. Switzerland was thus a favored destination of those who had been banished. It served as a rallying point for actors in several provincial communalist movements, to the extent that the influx of refugees was felt there prior even to the bloody events in Paris marking the end of the Commune.[62] Thus Jules Guesde, who supported the communard movement from Montpellier, escaped a five-year prison sentence by settling in Switzerland, later going to Italy for a few years, before returning to France in 1876, slightly before most communards. Gustave Courbet also went into refuge in Switzerland after having served a first prison sentence.

Equally, Belgium took in 1,252 French outcasts between 1871 and 1880, mainly workers and craftsmen.[63] Many found work in the manufactories in Brussels or else for construction companies transforming the urban landscape of the Belgian

---

60 Caroline Corbeau-Parsons (ed.), *Les Impressionnistes à Londres. Artistes français en exil (1870–1904)*, catalogue of an exhibition at the Petit Palais, June 21 to October 14, 2018 (Paris: Paris Musées, 2018).
61 Constance Bantman, *The French Anarchists in London, 1880–1914. Exile and Transnationalism in the First Globalisation*, Studies in Labour History no.1 (Liverpool: Liverpool University Press, 2013).
62 Marc Vuilleumier, "La Suisse", in *1871: Jalons pour une histoire de la Commune de Paris*, special issue of the *International Review of Social History*, ed. Jacques Rougerie, 17–1 (1972): 272–302.
63 Francis Sartorius and Jean-Luc Depaepe, eds., *Les Communards en exil. Etat de la proscription communaliste à Bruxelles et dans les faubourgs 1871–1880*, Cahiers Bruxellois, t. XV-XVI, fasc. 1–2 (1970–1971).: See too Quentin Dupuis, "Génétique de l'exil des communards à Bruxelles (1871–1880)," in "La Commune et les étrangers", *Migrance*, 35 (2010): 113–122.

capital. Others changed jobs several times to make ends meet, such as Charles Aconin, a law student and captain with the 248th Battalion during the Commune, who started by teaching Roman law in Brussels before becoming an inspector with a life insurance company, Le Monde.[64] Though harder to count in the absence of a formal asylum policy, several dozen communards, mainly not from Paris, took refuge in Spain, such as a leather worker and laborer from Nîmes, Émile Henry, who took refuge in Saragossa and then Barcelona after having taken part in the Paris commune, or Karl Marx's son-in-law, Paul Lafargue.[65] Lastly, the United States took in 200 to 300 communards fleeing repression, who mostly settled in New Jersey and New York, the nerve center of US socialism.[66]

Finally, the colonies, being distant, were a particularly secure destination for deporting people. The most striking example is New Caledonia, where Louise Michel was deported from 1873 to 1880. These distant colonies were also a place of temporary exile for those seeking to escape repression. Thus nearly 2,000 Spanish cantonalists, fleeing the collapse of the short-lived autonomous Republic of Cartagena, landed in Algeria in 1874, where they endeavored to reactivate the reception networks in Oran to overcome the French authorities' hostility.[67]

Towards transnational networks

The repression of the communards and their emulators, whether they fled abroad or were deported – when not simply executed – is a long-standing topic of historiography. Yet the counterrevolutionary exile of the 1860s and 1870s has long been overshadowed by memories of the Commune. Though it no doubt involved smaller numbers, it nevertheless encapsulates how reception policies differed depending on the political inclination of the refugees. The case of the Spanish

---

64 Daisy Devreese, "La proscription en Belgique (1871–1880)," in *1871: Jalons*, 253–271. See "Charles Aconin", *Dictionnaire biographique du mouvement ouvrier*, accessed April 9, 2021, http://maitron-en-ligne.univ-paris1.fr/spip.php?article50997.
65 Jeanne Moisand, "Les exilés de la 'République universelle'. Français et Espagnols en révolution," in *Exils entre deux mondes. Migrations et espaces politiques atlantiques au XIXe siècle*, ed. Delphine Diaz et al. (Paris: Les Perséides, 2015), 169.
66 Michel Cordillot, "La proscription communaliste aux États-Unis," in *Aux origines du socialisme moderne. La Première Internationale, la Commune de Paris, l'exil* (Paris: Éditions de l'Atelier, 2010), 177.
67 Jeanne Moisand, "Que faire d'exilés indésirables? Les cantonalistes espagnols en Algérie française (1874)," *Diasporas. Circulations, migrations, histoire* 33/1 (2019): 159–171.

Carlists studied by Alexandre Dupont illustrates the scale of the phenomenon.[68] In the wake of the "glorious" revolution of 1868 and Isabella II's departure into exile, the Carlist movement enjoyed a second lease of life with the abdication of the pretender, Don Juan, in favor of his son, Don Carlos. In the years of political confusion that followed, particularly during the second Carlist war (1872–1876), many Carlists sought refuge in France in the light of the fluctuating fortunes of war: it is estimated that 15,000 headed there in late February 1876. French policy toward them was ambiguous. The republican regime displayed great firmness, implementing virtually systematic internment and holding the Carlists at a distance from the border, but the exiles also enjoyed significant support among local populations along the border.[69]

The exiles of the 1870–1871 crisis, like those after the 1848 revolutions, lasted for varying lengths of time.[70] Those who had fled war were the first to return once new forms of stability were established, with the exception of the populations of Alsace and Lorraine, the vast majority of whom remained in France. German and Italian national unification enabled exiled patriots to return home, where many reaped the rewards for their commitment to the cause by being elected to parliament or municipal councils, or else appointed to university posts. The return of the banished communards and cantonalists occurred over longer and more uncertain timeframes. Only the amnesty laws – first the partial law of 1879, then the general one of 1880 – gave rise to a mass return of former communards to France. Laure Godineau has calculated that within a six-week period between September and October 1880, no fewer than 2,000 communards returned to Paris.[71]

The 1860s to the 1890s were marked by the setting up of the International Workingmen's Association in 1864, followed by the Workers' International in 1889, and were lastly the years when labor and socialist organizations developed networks, having found that exile not only offered a way of escaping per-

---

[68] Alexandre Dupont, *Une Internationale blanche. Histoire d'une mobilisation royaliste transnationale entre France et Espagne dans les années 1870* (Paris: Éditions de la Sorbonne, 2020).
[69] Alexandre Dupont, "L'exil carliste espagnol dans le sud de la France des années 1870. Entre catégorisations du réfugié et protestations populaires," *Hommes & Migrations* 1321 (2018), 93–100.
[70] For a comparative approach to post-1848 exiles in London, see Thomas C. Jones & Robert Tombs, "The French Left in Exile: quarante-huitards and communards in London, 1848–1880," in *A History of the French in London: Liberty, Equality, Opportunity*, ed. Martyn Cornyk and Debra Kelly (London: Institute of Historical Research, 2013), 165–191.
[71] Laure Godineau, "Le retour d'exil, un nouvel exil? Le cas des communards," *Matériaux pour l'histoire de notre temps*, 67/1 (2002): 11–16. On return from exile, the reader is referred to chapter 8 of this book.

secution, but also furthered the circulation of ideas. Bismarck's antisocialist laws engendered major flows of German socialists to England and Switzerland.[72] Once again, London served as the epicenter for a movement bringing together former French communards who had turned down the amnesty, Italian anarchists, and German socialists who all sought to organize themselves during the International Workers Congress of summer 1881.[73] While anarchists – the bogeyman of sources of repression – failed to establish any veritable European network, they were present throughout Europe, often having fled the Italian peninsula, and were highly visible due to their practice of propaganda through action.[74]

From the Congress of Vienna through to the 1870s and 1880s, exile was a major cause of migration, and its timeframes need to be viewed in parallel with those of the uprisings, revolutions, and civil wars punctuating the century, causing the banished to leave their homeland. But departures into exile continued during the periods between these upheavals. As for the places concerned by these forced migrations, they ranged across Europe, though the most favored host countries, which we shall discuss shortly, tended to lie in the north and west of the continent.

Exile did not disappear in the 1870s and 1880s, far from it. But forced expatriation gradually became a less prominent feature of European repression, at a time when the reality of the nation-state was emerging: "many national revolutionaries fought for the idea of the nation-state and became political refugees as a result".[75] These decades also saw more people departing, primarily to improve their economic situation rather than escape political repression, though some left for both reasons. The "European mass exodus" thus helped eclipse the visibility of political exiles,[76] who nevertheless continued to circulate in Europe, as illustrated by anarchist groups at the end of the century, who increasingly encountered rigid border controls.

---

[72] Marc Vuilleumier, "La question des réfugiés dans les luttes politiques de Genève entre 1848 et 1857," *Revue des Archives fédérales suisses*, special issue about refuge in Switzerland after the 1848 revolutions, 25 (1999): 147–196.
[73] Constance Bantman, "'Anarchistes de la bombe, anarchistes de l'idée': les anarchistes français à Londres, 1880–1895," *Le Mouvement Social* 246/1 (2014): 47–61.
[74] Davide Turcato, "Italian Anarchism as a Transnational Movement, 1885–1915," *International Review of Social History* 52 (2007): 407–444.
[75] Klaus Bade, *Migration in European History* (Oxford: Blackwell Publishing, 2003), 148.
[76] Bade, *Migration*, 188.

Delphine Diaz, Laurent Dornel and Hugo Vermeren
Chapter 2 Taking in and casting out

The example of the Polish politician and historian Joachim Lelewel (1786–1861) may serve to illustrate how European states' policies to receive and expel émigrés could influence the paths of nineteenth-century exiles. After teaching history at Vilnius University, then serving as a minister in the Polish national government headed by Prince Adam Czartoryski, Lelewel responded to the Russian victory over the Warsaw uprising by heading west into exile in 1831. According to the account by his compatriot Léonard Chodźko, "he walked to the Prussian border which he crossed at [...] Strasbourg, bearing a passport under a different name. He arrived in Paris on October 29, 1831, after having encountered difficulties in Germany".[1]

Once established in France, Lelewel became the chair of the Polish national committee, a republican organization, in which capacity he addressed the French chamber of deputies on behalf of refugees in November 1832.[2] A few months after, Lelewel was removed from Paris and assigned residence in Tours, before being expelled from France to Belgium. This forced journeying from Tours led him through Rouen and Abbeville on his way to Brussels, to avoid passing via Paris, a precaution which did not prevent outbursts of support in places where he stopped over. Along the way, he received funds collected by champions of the Polish cause, but preferred to give them to other "outcasts more unfortunate than himself".[3] Though Lelewel spent most of his exile in Brussels, he returned to Paris for medical treatment, dying there in 1861. The funeral procession to the cemetery where he was buried in Montmartre acted as a reminder of the importance of his brief period of exile in Paris.

This example suggests just how essential it is to examine reception and expulsion policies in tandem when considering the asylum granted to nineteenth-century exiles. This chapter sets out to show the impact of reception policies – or

---

[1] Léonard Chodźko, "Notice biographique sur Joachim Lelewel," in *Les Polonais et les Polonaises de la révolution du 20 novembre 1830. Portraits des personnes qui ont figuré dans la dernière guerre de l'indépendance polonaise, lithographiés par les artistes les plus distingués et accompagnés d'une biographie pour chaque portrait*, ed. Joseph Straszewicz (Paris: Pinard, 1834), 13.
[2] Léonard Chodźko and Joachim Lelewel, *Adresse des Polonais réfugiés en France à la Chambre des députés* (Paris: Fournier, November 24, 1832), 5.
[3] *Le Journal de Rouen*, quoted in *Le Constitutionnel*, 230, August 18, 1833, 3: see Delphine Diaz, "Les expulsions de réfugiés étrangers, Pratiques administratives et mobilisations de l'opinion publique. France, 1832–1852," *Diasporas. Circulations, migrations, histoire* 33/1 (2019): 29.

restrictions on reception – decreed by the European states where exiles took refuge. At a finer scale, it examines local policies and reactions by civil society which did much to influence how exiles and refugees were received at this period. How did local political decisions anticipate, supplement, or modify state provisions for selecting exiles and taking them in? What role did civil society play in mechanisms to admit or expel refugees? How were these selection and expulsion policies implemented, and how were refugees targeted? These are the questions this chapter sets out to answer.

1 How states went about taking in refugees

In taking in European exiles, whose migrations were occasioned by the revolutions, repressions, civil wars, and wars of independence punctuating the nineteenth century, states were led to adopt both a legislative and an administrative response to managing these atypical foreign populations. This chapter examines how political authorities sought to distinguish "refugees" from other foreigners on their territory, emphasizing the *enforced* and *political* nature of their migration. This desire to single out refugees from other foreigners resulted in fluctuations in the standard terminology, as well as giving rise to legislation and regulations endeavoring to provide a legal definition of this group.

Laws and norms to differentiate foreigners from refugees

In France, foreigners had been subject to laws since the Revolution, which all sought to differentiate them from citizens "with the attribute of being French".[4] Under the Convention, the law of August 1, 1793, stipulated that foreigners not domiciled in France prior to July 14, 1789, were to be reported and arrested. Under the Directory, the law "about passports" adopted on October 19, 1797 (28 vendémiaire, Year VI) established a lasting framework for conducting identity checks and selecting foreigners authorized to remain in France:

> All foreigners traveling inside the Republic or residing there without a mission recognized by the French government from neutral and friendly powers, or without the title of citizen, are placed under the special surveillance of the executive Directory, which may withdraw their passports and enjoin them to leave French territory should it deem their presence likely to disturb public order.

---

4 The term "nationality" did not yet exist in French statute law.

But it was especially under the July Monarchy that lawmakers turned their attention to refugees, with the laws on "foreign refugees" of April 21, 1832, May 1, 1834, and 24 July, 1839. These were the first to delineate a category of foreigners who were in fact already treated separately by the administration. Though intended as a temporary measure, to be prolonged if needed, and while making no attempt to define the legal contours of this group,[5] these laws were nevertheless the only ones of the period to single out refugees as a specific category of foreigners. To better understand how these laws were applied, we need to study the associated regulations, though this task is complicated by gaps in the central police archives. The ministry of the interior had a refugees bureau: between March 1831 and February 1836, the main bureau in its administration was officially called the "Sûreté de l'État, réfugiés" (state security, refugees), and it produced voluminous correspondence and statistics about refugees.[6] Research conducted jointly in the French national and many local (*départementale*) archives has brought to light 142 circulars issued by the ministry of the interior during the July Monarchy.[7] These texts call on prefects to better distinguish genuine political refugees from "deserters", "vagrants", and "migrants" usurping the title of refugee. As for the latter, they were subdivided into several groups, since the ministry requested that prefects distinguish them by nationality,[8] as well as in the light of their political persuasions.

Hence the laws on refugees inherited from the July Monarchy were crucial in making a pragmatic if at times hesitant distinction between refugees, who, on being granted this administrative title, received subsidies, were issued with a certificate, and had to comply with regular summons, and other foreigners who escaped such recognition and oversight. The laws on refugees which were adopted, renewed, and modified in the 1830s established a framework whose influence,

---

5 See the speech by Gaillard de Kerbertin on March 4, 1834 requesting that the law of April 21, 1830 be extended: "passed for one year, and extended only for another year, by the law of April 16, 1833, and expiring at the end of the current session, unless you deem it appropriate to renew it once again", quoted in *Archives parlementaires*, 2nd series, vol. 87, 104.
6 Delphine Diaz, "Les réfugiés en France au prisme des circulaires du ministère de l'Intérieur (1830–1870): pour une étude conjointe des discours et pratiques de l'administration," *Hommes & Migrations* 321 (2018): 34.
7 This research was conducted by two members of the AsileuropeXIX ANR program team (Delphine Diaz and Hugo Vermeren), and the assembled corpus of administrative circulars about refugees is available on its website, accessed April 11, 2021, https://asileurope.huma-num.fr/circulaires-sur-les-refugies.
8 *Recueil des circulaires et instructions émanées du ministère de l'Intérieur de 1831 à 1837 inclusivement* (Paris: Dupont, 1848), vol. 2, circular no. 13 from the ministry of the interior, April 23, 1833.

though fluctuating, continued to make itself felt. This legislation, though temporarily suspended under the Second Republic by the provisional government in March 1848,[9] was re-established a few months later, on December 13, 1848.[10] The Second Empire then decided to stop applying the July Monarchy's laws on refugees, as stated in a circular of April 1853 issued by the ministry of general police, asserting that "the special laws concerning refugees have ceased to exist; the government, in no longer calling for their prolongation, feels that common law suffices".[11] Nevertheless, the same circular simultaneously lays down principles "from which the administration shall never depart". These, in fact, were heavily inspired by the laws of the July Monarchy and attendant regulations, with an emphasis on keeping refugees away from cities and borders.[12]

France was not, however, the only country to pass legislation about its foreign population while progressively seeking to circumscribe the group of refugees in its midst. During the decisive decade of the 1830s, the newly formed kingdom of Belgium also passed legislation on foreigners. The law of September 22, 1835, which started by listing the cases in which foreigners could be sentenced to internment or expulsion, stipulates that the administrative measure of expulsion could not be applied to foreigners authorized to establish domicile in the kingdom, nor to those married to a Belgian woman with whom they had children born in Belgium, nor to those decorated with the Iron Cross.[13] In 1841, the Belgian Parliament tightened the law by removing the exceptions for this second category of foreigners; as Maïté Van Vyve observes, the expulsion law was "one of the pillars of a liberal and minimalist immigration policy".[14] Every three years the government had to ask the chamber of representatives to extend this law, which never failed to spark lively debate about taking in foreigners.

The term "refugee" does not figure once in this Belgian legislative text, but that in no way precluded its extensive use in the correspondence and administrative circulars emanating from the ministry of justice, more specifically its gen-

---

9 Archives départementales des Bouches-du-Rhône, 4 M 956, circular from the ministry of the interior, March 18, 1848.
10 Diaz, *Un asile pour tous les peuples*, 107.
11 Archives départementales de la Somme, 4 M 1228, circular no. 10 from the ministry of general police, April 9, 1853.
12 The first article of the circular of April 9, 1853 forbade on principle refugees from residing in or passing through Paris, Lyon, and Marseille, while the second article prohibited Spanish refugees from staying near the Pyrenees border.
13 Archives générales du Royaume de Belgique, Police des étrangers, 866, Annales parlementaires, Chambre des représentants, March 3, 1898, text of the law of September 22, 1835.
14 Maïté Van Vyve, "Les perceptions de l'étranger, du réfugié et de l'expulsé dans les débats parlementaires en Belgique (1835–1875)," *Hommes & Migrations* 1321 (2018): 54.

eral security administration in charge of policing foreigners. Thus a letter sent out in July 1849 by the ministry of justice alerted the head of Belgian diplomacy to the arrival on its borders of *"political refugees* that the French authorities appear predisposed to send to Belgium",[15] while a letter from the ministry of foreign affairs to the security administration provided a "table of *political refugees* [...] successively authorized to reside provisionally in Belgium".[16]

Under the Belgian law of September 1835 as applied by the general security bureau, refugees taken in by the kingdom could receive very different administrative treatment depending on whether they obtained a residency permit or not. In April 1850, a letter from the ministry of foreign affairs to the Belgian ambassadors in Paris, Vienna, and Berlin reminded them that foreign refugees settled in Belgium were divided into two categories:

> The first includes refugees who have obtained provisional and revocable residency permits, the prolonging of which is subordinate to how they conduct themselves there; consequently, these refugees may be sent back at any moment by administrative measures. The second category includes refugees who have acquired a residence in the country, and who may only be expelled under a royal expulsion order and in the circumstances stipulated by the law of September 22, 1835.[17]

Like all other foreigners, the situation of refugees established in the kingdom varied in vulnerability depending on their marital and legal status.

But certain other countries chose not to establish any such hierarchy among foreigners. Britain stood out for not controlling immigration within its borders between 1826, when the Aliens Act of 1793 was declared obsolete, and 1905, when a new Aliens Act was passed.[18] During this period, foreigners entered their national territory freely and could not be expelled; at the same time, there was no legal distinction between refugees and other foreigners. This liberal tradition of taking foreigners in was not called into question – not even during the 1890s, when Britain was the only European country to take in foreign anar-

---

15 Archives générales du Royaume de Belgique, Police des étrangers, 246, letter from the ministry of justice to the ministry of foreign affairs, July 5, 1849.
16 Archives générales du Royaume de Belgique, Police des étrangers, 250, letter from the ministry of foreign affairs to the ministry of justice, March 14, 1850.
17 Archives du ministère des Affaires étrangères belge, Correspondance politique, 1841–1851, letter from the ministry for foreign affairs to the Belgian ambassadors in Paris, Vienna, Berlin, April 8, 1850.
18 Bernard Porter, *The Refugee Question in mid-Victorian Politics* (Cambridge: Cambridge University Press, 1979), 3. While an Aliens Act was briefly in force during this period, from 1848 to 1850, it was not applied in practice.

chists, despite pressure from British public opinion, which tended to question the principle of accepting them.[19]

It was only in 1905, when a new Aliens Act was passed, that those arriving in the country due to political or religious persecution were singled out for specific treatment. For them, and solely for them, access to British territory could not be refused on the grounds that they lacked the financial resources or that they might one day become a "financial burden" on the nation.[20] Nevertheless, the word "refugee" does not appear once in this law, which only refers indirectly to foreign refugees as immigrants with a somewhat specific status.

Assistance policies

State policies devised during the nineteenth century to take in refugees and grant them special treatment also need to be understood through parliamentary debates, laws, and other more general legal texts about them. The financial lens may also provide indications about the wish to make special provisions for refugees, who were able to benefit from state-run assistance schemes. For many political exiles, going into exile, sometimes preceded by the confiscation or sequestration of assets,[21] implied a loss of revenue, together with difficulty in accessing any assets they might still have. In these circumstances, many refugees underwent social relegation and a brutal drop in their standard of living, sometimes to the point of poverty or absolute penury.[22] In French parliamentary debates under the July Monarchy, these forms of relegation or destitution were suggested by the frequent use of the expression "wretched refugees",[23] referring both to the

---

19 Shaw, *Britannia's Embrace*, 206 et seq.
20 *Aliens Act*, August 11, 1905: "in the case of an immigrant who proves that he is seeking admission to this country solely to avoid prosecution or punishment on religious or political grounds or for an offence of a political character, or persecution, involving danger of imprisonment or danger to life or limb, on account of religious belief, leave to land shall not be refused on the ground merely of want of means, or the probability of his becoming a charge on the rates".
21 Catherine Brice, "Politique et propriété: confiscation et séquestre des biens des exilés politiques au XIXe siècle. Les bases d'un projet," *Mélanges de l'École française de Rome – Italie et Méditerranée modernes et contemporaines* 129–2 (2017), accessed April 3, 2018, doi: 10.4000/mefrim.3095. See chapter 3 in this book.
22 The reader is referred to chapter 4 about social life in exile.
23 See for example the speech by Dupin the elder to the chamber of deputies on February 21, 1832, quoted in *Archives parlementaires*, 2nd series, vol. 75, 460: "the land of France cannot but congratulate itself on what it has done for the wretched of all nations".

nostalgia of a class cut off from their homeland and to the material difficulties besetting them in their country of asylum.

Enquiring into the material circumstances in which refugees were taken in thus entails considering any state financial provision for exiled settlers, either in response to a straightforward emergency or to provide more regular, perhaps even lasting assistance for political émigrés. Several reasons were used to explain why exiles should be granted financial assistance. The first was to present them as brothers in religion, or else as brothers from another denomination to whom assistance was due in the name of the dominant religion, as arose when (Protestant) Britain assisted French (Catholic) émigrés during the French Revolution. In her book about refuge in Britain, Caroline Shaw contends that there could no longer be any religious ground justifying this government assistance to foreign Catholics. Still, she emphasizes that the government launched a campaign in spring 1793 to which British parishioners responded by donating £38,000 to assist French émigrés, proving that religious, philanthropic, and political reasons were often inextricably linked.[24]

Arguments of a religious nature were often supplemented by a stance insisting on the compassion due to foreigners who had lost everything, justifying the assistance provided by the nation in these terms. In France under the First Restoration, Charles-Louis Clément (1768–1857), parliamentarian for Doubs and a member of the former legislative body under the Empire, explained in October 1814 that it was the duty of Louis XVIII's monarchy to provide assistance to Spanish refugees even though they had supported the Napoleonic authorities retreating from Spain. As Clément remarked in a speech to the chamber of deputies, three-quarters of these *afrancesados* had no resources.[25] He argued that it was not up to the chamber to "judge the behavior" of this "aggregation of exiles", made up of officers, landowners, merchants, employees, elderly, women, and children, to whom assistance was owed in their wretchedness. The justification that assistance was due to foreigners who had lost everything on grounds of charity explains why Louis-Philippe's France assisted Spanish *afrancesado* refugees up until 1820. In addition to appeals to charity, there was also a humanist – even proto-humanitarian – justification for succoring refugees. Caroline Shaw shows this for Britain, where aid to refugees was increasingly viewed from the early nineteenth century as an entitlement due to foreigners whose dignity

---

24 Shaw, *Britannia's Embrace*, 32–33.
25 Speech given by Charles-Louis Clément to the chamber of deputies on October 8, 1814, quoted in Jérôme Mavidal & Émile Laurent (eds.), *Archives parlementaires parlementaires de 1787 à 1799. Recueil complet des débats législatifs et politiques des chambres françaises* (Paris: Dupont, 1868), 2nd series, vol. 13, 210.

was to be preserved, rather than as a self-interested recompense for any military, material, or moral support these refugees might provide to the country.[26] As of the 1830s, liberals also put forward other possible interpretations of aid to refugees. Rejecting the principle of charity, they argued for the eminently political dimension to the aid foreigners received, considered as brothers in politics. In a speech to the chamber of deputies on October 26, 1831, Lafayette responded to a stern speech about refugees by the president of the council, Casimir Perier, retorting that France should adopt an assistance policy worthy of the name on the grounds of political fraternity,[27] particularly towards Poles of the "great emigration", these "brothers of the North":

> Had it been a matter of individuals cast onto our land by chance, I would have supported charity; but here I call for fraternity.
> The exiles in question are our brothers in freedom; I say it with pride, the disciples of '89; they are the disciples of the doctrine proclaimed in France on the sacred right and duty of resisting oppression.[28]

In justifying assistance on grounds other than simple charity, Lafayette proposed an eminently *political* interpretation for helping refugees. This was not without problems under the July Monarchy, confronted with taking in liberal refugees as well as legitimists such as Spanish Carlists during and after the first Carlist war (1833–1840),[29] who received assistance as of 1835 despite their opposition to liberalism. After 1848, the kingdom of Piedmont-Sardinia adopted the political argument to justify its provision for refugees, most of whom came from other states on the Italian peninsula.[30] As Ester De Fort notes, the way refuge was organized was "not motivated by purely humanitarian reasons, but by the desire – on the part of the more lucid representatives of liberalism south of the Alps – to turn Piedmont into 'a sort of Italian asylum'",[31] as Massimo D'Azeglio put it in 1849.

---

26 Shaw, *Britannia's Embrace*, 39.
27 On the links between fraternity and exile, see Gilles Bertrand, Catherine Brice, and Gilles Montègre, *Fraternité, pour l'histoire du concept. Cahiers du CRHIPA*, Grenoble, 2012, and Catherine Brice and Sylvie Aprile (eds.), *Exil et fraternité en Europe au XIXe siècle*, (Pompignac: Éditions Bière, 2013).
28 *Journal des Débats politiques et littéraires*, October 27, 1831, 4.
29 For discussion of Carlist refugees in France, see Emmanuel Tronco, *Les Carlistes espagnols dans l'Ouest de la France, 1833–1883* (Rennes: Presses universitaires de Rennes, 2010).
30 Gian Biago Furiozzi, *L'emigrazione politica*.
31 Ester De Fort, "Une fraternité difficile. Exil et associationnisme dans le royaume de Sardaigne après 1848," in *Exil et fraternité*, ed. Catherine Brice and Sylvie Aprile, 145.

Whether justified on religious or political grounds, assistance of varying degrees of generosity depending on the country and political regime was granted to foreigners considered to be "refugees". In late eighteenth-century Britain, the level of financial assistance was substantial, be it for loyalists from the thirteen colonies in the wake of the American war of independence or émigrés from the French Revolution. The amount allocated to French émigrés was determined by a scale based on social class, a symbolic and financial hierarchy which, according to the Duchess of Gontaut's memoirs, was keenly resented by beneficiaries:

> M. de Saint-Blancard [...] depicted the state of mind of our compatriots who were hurt on receiving assistance offered by the government even. They were upset by the differences in rank, with the sub-lieutenant envying the general's pension.[32]

Over the course of the nineteenth century, the level of assistance Britain granted to refugees followed a downwards trend, even though certain liberals – especially Spaniards and Italians – received financial support as voted by parliament. Large numbers of Spanish veterans of the war of independence against France, many of whom were inspired by liberalism and had left Ferdinand VII's Spain after the *Trienio liberal* of 1820–1823, found asylum in Britain where they received assistance. Thomas C. Jones emphasizes that:

> Spanish exiles were sorted into "classes" depending on their prior position, and received monthly pensions of different amounts. The most important, the "first class", received £5 per month, "second class" exiles £4, the "third class" £3 10 shillings, the 'fourth class" £3, and the "fifth class £2 8 shillings.[33]

In France at the same period, refugee assistance was likewise calculated depending on military rank or prior civilian position in the country of origin. From the end of the Empire to the Bourbon Restoration, Spanish *afrancesado* refugees were subject to a complex scale with twelve different classes. But the general assistance scales adopted under the July Monarchy tended to simplify this hierarchy somewhat, whittling it down to five classes which remained proportionally unchanged in each revision to the scales in 1833, 1837, 1839, and 1843. At the same time, the rate for each class was progressively reduced, seeking to lessen what detractors denounced as a financial burden on the monarchy. Whereas the assistance scales under the July Monarchy varied depending on the refugee's

---

[32] Marie Joséphine Louise de Gontaut-Biron, *Mémoires de la duchesse de Gontaut, gouvernante des enfants de France pendant la Restauration, 1773–1836* (Paris: Plon, 1891), 29.
[33] Thomas C. Jones, "Définir l'asile politique en Grande-Bretagne (1815–1870)," *Hommes & Migrations* 1321 (2018): 17.

nationality, with Poles receiving significantly more than Italians and Spaniards, the Second Republic decided to abolish such differences based on national origin, while maintaining those based on social rank.

Gradation of assistance based on social or geographic origin was not, however, an absolute norm in European countries implementing refugee assistance policies in the nineteenth century. In Switzerland, where over 10,000 German refugees arrived in the years 1848–1849, the Berne federal council decided to grant these former revolutionaries assistance in the form of daily sums of money without any distinction based on status. The Confederation allocated the sum of 50 centimes per day to the most needy, a policy which cost a total of 1.5 million Swiss francs for the years 1849 1850.[34] As of winter 1849, a few months after emergency relief was granted to refugees, the federal council sought to curb the cost incurred:

> In order to increasingly restrict subsidies for maintaining refugees to the limits established by the federal assembly decree of August 1849, to prevent them reaching individuals who do not really need them or do not deserve them, and to reduce the considerable expenses resulting from this subsidy, the federal council has decided [...] that as of February 1, 1850, subsidies from the federal treasury will only be granted to refugees for whom they are indispensable.[35]

The federal treasury placed conditions on payment of subsidies to refugees, who had to prove "sufficiently their status as a political refugee", to be unable to meet their own needs, to be too compromised to return to their country of origin, and be of good behavior.[36]

These restrictions introduced to Swiss policy to assist German refugees as of winter 1849 thus lead us to examine the conditionality of such policies. Helping refugees was a matter of enabling them to get through the ordeal of exile. But it also provided a way of monitoring their movements, their loyalty, and their morality. Gérard Noiriel has demonstrated this for refugees in France in the nineteenth century: "if the question of subsidies was of such importance for the authorities, it is because it made it easier to conduct the major form of police

---

34 Cédric Humair, *1848. Naissance de la Suisse moderne* (Lausanne: Éditions Antipodes, 2009), 124.
35 Archives du Canton de Vaud, Lausanne, K VII e 10-A, circular from the Swiss federal council to all confederate states, Berne, December 26, 1849.
36 Archives du Canton de Vaud, Lausanne, K VII e 10-A, circular from the Swiss federal council to all confederate states, Berne, December 26, 1849.

activity of the period, namely controlling people's movements".[37] Administering help to refugees, obliging them to reside in "depots", and keeping up-to-date records on them, served the additional purpose of limiting refugees' mobility, who were under constant watch by the administration.[38]

Other countries drew inspiration from this system, which though financially generous restricted the freedoms accorded to refugees. Thus in 1833, a few months after the first French law on exiles of April 1832, introducing the principle of assigning place of residence, Belgium created depots where the first Polish refugees were placed. Nevertheless, as of June 1834, this strict system was loosened, and Poles were able to receive Belgian assistance provided they settled in one of the obligatory places of residence.[39]

Financial aid for refugees was subject to certain conditions: choice of place of residence, complying with summons, and a morality requirement. In France, a seriously indebted or miscreant refugee could be struck off the assistance register by the prefect of the department where they resided. In addition to being conditional, assistance was generally devised as a temporary measure, and after initially granting it to certain groups, some countries then suspended the policy. For example, as of the 1830s, the British government decided to stop organizing assistance or issuing calls to civil society to assist refugees. On the contrary, it was society itself which, deeming the state response to be unsatisfactory, assumed the lead role in assisting them.

While it is useful to place the treatment of refugees in Europe in the context of state policies devised for this category of foreigners, a top-down approach is nevertheless insufficient. First, because in certain cases civil society set up assistance schemes before the state then stepped in. This was notably the case in Barcelona where, after the arrival of Italian liberals fleeing repression in 1821, the garrison and municipality organized assistance for refugees before the Spanish authorities provided more systematic assistance during the *Trienio Liberal*.[40] But if the state approach was insufficient, it is also because in many host countries – Britain first and foremost – civil society stepped in to make up for a state deemed to be falling short.

---

[37] Gérard Noiriel, *Réfugiés et sans-papiers. La République face au droit d'asile, XIXe-XXe siècle* (Paris: Hachette, 2006), 51.
[38] The July Monarchy thus devised an "individual refugee certificate".
[39] Goddeeris, *La Grande Émigration*, 33.
[40] Morán Orti, "La cuestión de los refugiados," 989.

2 Civil societies and refugees

Other (non-state) actors played a key role in host countries throughout the period. The level of mobilization varied widely from one country or region to another, and from one period to another, depending on the social and geographic origin and ideological leanings of the refugees. The liberal and mainly wealthy exiles of the 1820s and 1830s were followed by more massive waves of activists from less prosperous classes after 1848. Of course, the way these refugees were received could also depend on their number, their personal fortune, and their social status, as well as the political choices of the receiving populations. The first institutional contact often took place locally, at the level of municipalities, before any subsequent state assistance. Thus in France, it was mayors who organized public charity, placing refugees in hospitals and hospices where they were accommodated free of charge or at a reduced rate.[41] In western France in the 1830s, the municipal and departmental authorities were omnipresent, as emphasized by the sub-prefect of Mortagne in the department of Orne:

> The Mortagne municipal authorities were actively involved in procuring for Polish refugees residing there the help they so needed. The municipal council, in a deliberation I authorized it to conduct, decreed that a register is to be opened at the town hall to record charitable gifts from citizens.[42]

In November 1845, faced with the arrival of forty or so refugees from Romagna "in the most absolute unemployment", the mayor in Saumur admitted he was "unable to find liberal or industrial employ for each". When in May 1848 nearly 500 Germans arrived in Besançon, the mayor and commissioner distributed bread, cooking pots, plates, and firewood.

Elsewhere in Europe, the local authorities were in the front line. In Brussels, the burgomaster, Nicolas Rouppe, chaired a committee for political refugees as of 1833.[43] In Turin, the *Comitato centrale per i soccorsi all'emigrazione italiana* was presided by the municipal director of finances, succeeded by Abbot Cameroni.[44]

---

[41] Gérard Noiriel, *La Tyrannie du national. Le droit d'asile en Europe 1793–1993* (Paris: Calmann-Lévy, 1991), 64.
[42] Quoted in Valentin Guillaume, "L'autre exil. Trajectoires migratoires et stratégies d'insertion de la Grande Émigration polonaise de 1831 dans l'Ouest de la France" (PhD diss., Paris, EHESS, 2016), 140.
[43] Godderis, *La Grande Émigration*, 214.
[44] Ester De Fort, "La Mecca d'Italia," in *1860–1861. Torino Italia Europa* (Turin: Archivio Storico della Città di Torino, 2010), 46.

In the 1850s in Piedmont, the French authorities played a crucial role in identifying émigrés and in their treatment.[45]

What kind of solidarity for which exiles?

In all host countries, the arrival of exiles gave rise to extremely varied kinds of support from civil society. First, the very powerful family bonds within European aristocracies provided long-standing forms of solidarity predating exile. In 1828 a certain number of Portuguese liberals decided to settle in Paris because they had ties there. The mother of the Marquis de Santa Iria was a certain Montboissier Beaufort de Canillac, related to Lafayette, while the Marquis de Fronteira was a distant cousin of the de Choiseul family.[46] The progressive nobles forming this circle of liberal exiles could draw on significant resources enabling them to lead a sparkling social life in the salons of Faubourg Saint-Germain.[47] In 1829, members of the French titled nobility including the Duc de Chartres, Duc de Guiche, Duc de Mouchy, and Madame de Noailles flocked to the ball held in support of Portuguese exiles.

Nevertheless, such ties were not solely family ones, and a veritable "liberal international" – initially aristocratic but increasingly bourgeois – set about taking exiles in.[48] Whig aristocrats and liberal nobles from Lombardy, Piedmont, and Naples were part of the same liberal, wealthy, cosmopolitan circle, and had already met prior to 1821 in Milan, Florence, or Genoa.[49] The Marquis de Palmela established the political center for Portuguese liberalism in London, where he was ambassador and led a very active social life. He was friends with the progressive Whigs (Lord Holland, Lord Grey, Lord Brougham, Sir James Mackintosh,

---

45 Antonin Durand, "Éloigner les Barabbas: sur une campagne d'expulsion d'étrangers en Piémont en 1853," *Diasporas. Circulations, migrations, histoire* 33/1 (2019): 119 –136, 122.

46 Grégoire Bron, "La diplomatie du libéralisme portugais et la solidarité aristocratique internationale (1828 –1832)," *Ler Historia* 68 (2015): 9 – 31.

47 Grégoire Bron, "L'exil libéral portugais du début du XIXe siècle (1808 –1834)," *Mélanges de la Casa de Velázquez. Nouvelle série* 48/1 (2018): 315 – 321.

48 Maurizio Isabella has shown that diasporas of Italian, Greek, and Spanish patriots were built up by waves of exiles, ultimately creating a liberal international. Isabella, *Risorgimento in Exile*. See too Agostino Bistarelli on the contacts between Italian exiles and the *Casas del Pueblo* and the *Sociedades Patrióticas* in Catalonia during the Liberal Triennium (1820 –1823): Bistarelli, *Gli esuli*, 96.

49 Maurizio Isabella, "Italian Exiles and British Politics before and after 1848," in *Exiles from European Revolutions*, 63– 66.

and Lord Russell) whose political ideas he adopted, and he attended Princess Lieven's salon, balls at the Austrian embassy, and meetings at the Traveller's Club. In Paris, the Comte de Cavour attended the salons of Madame de Circourt, Duchesse de Rohan, and Madame de Boigne during his third stay there in 1842–1843, as well as the houses of Madame la Cisterna and Princess di Belgiojoso. Parisian salons opened their doors to political exiles. Baron Gérard's salon was attended by liberally-minded Spaniards, including the Spanish poet and statesman Francisco Martínez de la Rosa. Lafayette's salon, the "home of European liberals", was renowned for its Tuesdays, and was frequented by Germans, Italians, and Poles.[50] In Turin, salons such as Olimpia Savio's, where the intelligentsia met, welcomed émigrés and were attended by such figures as Mancini, Guerrazzi, and Mamiani.

This "liberal archipelago", as Walter Bruyère Ostells calls it,[51] functioned broadly as a network driven by a certain number of high-profile individuals. In Belgium, Félix de Mérode – a patriot and liberal Catholic who knew Lafayette – received many Polish refugees, some of whom were recruited by the Belgian army.[52] When Lelewel was expelled from France, Alexandre Gendebien provided him with accommodation in his château at Mielmont, near Namur. On inheriting Gaasbeck castle, Count Giuseppe Arconati-Visconti and his wife Costanza took in many exiles during the 1820s. One of the centers for the Italian refugee movement was the house of Louis de Potter (1786–1859), a rich young Belgian aristocrat and radical liberal who had lived in Italy, and companion of the painter Matilde Malenchini.[53] In London, the poet Thomas Campbell – the author of "Stanzas to the Memory of the Spanish Patriots", editor of the *New Monthly Magazine* since 1821, and a friend of Manuel Eduardo de Gorostiza – held gatherings at home. The Duke of Wellington provided accommodation for General Álava.[54] The Whig aristocracy and Bentham's circle were at the center of an international network of progressive politicians and thinkers dotted across continental Europe. After 1821, exiles from Lombardy and Piedmont were taken in by this

---

50 Diaz, *Un asile pour tous les peuples*, 201–203. Lafayette provided Lelewel with accommodation at his La Grange estate for a while.
51 Walter Bruyère-Ostells, *La Grande armée de la liberté* (Paris: Tallandier, 2009).
52 Goddeeris, *La Grande Émigration*, 233–240.
53 Anton van de Sande and Hans de Valk, "Italian refugees in the Netherlands during the Restoration 1815–1830. Report on a Current Investigation," in *L'Émigration politique en Europe aux XIXe et XXe siècles. Actes du colloque de Rome (3–5 mars 1988)* (Roma: École Française de Rome, 1991), 191–204.
54 Vicente Llorens, *Liberales y románticos. Una emigración española en Inglaterra 1823–1834* (Madrid: Editorial Castalia, 1968), second edition, 44–45.

Whig aristocracy, typically at Holland House (the most cosmopolitan aristocratic circle in England) where they became acquainted with the members of the *Edinburgh Review* such as Sydney Smith and William Empson, and historians such as Thomas Macaulay, as well as rubbing shoulders with Spanish exiles. Lord Holland, the main benefactor of Spanish liberal exiles, had adopted the Whig reformist tradition, initiated by Charles James Fox and identified with defending English freedoms against despotism, as well as with humanitarian causes such as the campaign against the slave trade.[55] Equally, other figures played a major role, such as John Bowring, and Lord Dudley Coutts Stuart who held the annual "Polish balls" to assist the Poles.[56] In Paris, – and in addition to Lafayette – Benjamin Constant, Jean-Baptiste Say, and Armand Carrel were also actively involved in supporting exiles, particularly Italians.

Part of this liberal international had links with organizations of differing transnational extent and varying degrees of secrecy which were involved in taking in banished individuals, such as the Carbonari and the freemasons. Large numbers of Neapolitans and Piedmontese joined the French Carbonari, particularly in south-eastern France, after the failed uprising of 1820–1821, as did Spaniards after 1823–1824. Thus the Di Aceto brothers from Sicily, known as being two of the "most zealous Carbonari in the Kingdom of the Two Sicilies" made contact with other banished Carbonari on arriving in Marseille in 1823.[57] After 1821 many refugees flocked to Brussels, which became one of the hubs of the Carbonari movement outside Italy: Giovanni Berchet, Federico Confalonieri, Giovita Sclavini, and Vincenzo Gioberti all stayed at Gaasbeck Castle.[58] But the death of Filippo Buonarroti in 1837 caused the Carbonari to withdraw from Belgium, where other associations such as the *Trou* stepped in and replaced them to varying degrees. Félix Delhasse, a friend of Buonarroti, and a leading figure in the Belgian democrat movement, played an important role for exiles.[59] Between 1821 and 1823 Guglielmo Pepe and Giuseppe Pecchio were involved in exporting the Carbonari movement to Spain, expanding their network of conspiracy to in-

---

55 Isabella, *Risorgimento in Exile*, 29, and Juan Francisco Fuentes, "Afrancesados y libérales," in *Exilios. Los éxodos políticos en la historia de España. Siglos XV-XX*, ed. Jordi Canal (Madrid: Sílex, 2007), 137–166.
56 Bernard Porter, "The Asylum of Nations: Britain and the Refugees of 1848," in *Exiles from European Revolutions*, 50.
57 Diaz, *Un asile pour tous les peuples*, 246–247.
58 Anton van de Sande and Hans de Valk, "Italian Refugees," 199.
59 Francis Sartorius, "Des débuts de la monarchie de Juillet à la fin du Second Empire: intellectuels et hommes politiques français en exil en Belgique," *Revue d'histoire du XIXe siècle* 11/1 (1995): 35–49.

clude Spanish and Portuguese liberals.⁶⁰ Freemasonry also played a part in taking in certain outcasts, particularly from Spain and Portugal.⁶¹ In the early 1830s Auguste Lanclou, a republican military officer from Lyon exiled in Belgium, was admitted to a Belgian lodge.⁶² In France, at least fifteen Portuguese and many *afrancesados* were members of French lodges or else lodges under French influence.⁶³

Support networks linking up the politically like-minded were also at work, particularly the "white" pro-Carlist international. In western France, some of the Carlist support committees were run by legitimists, as Emmanuel Tronco has shown. In the Poitou region – including Vendée – "exiles for the cause became the faithful auxiliaries of noble households, mainly estate owners who continued to reside permanently on their lands".⁶⁴ In Maine-et-Loire, the thirty or so refugees in the department lived in a house provided free of charge by the Comte de Quatrebarbes, a legitimist through and through. Vendée was even more attractive, particularly Luçon and Fontenay-le-Comte, as were Ille-et-Vilaine, Mayenne, and Sarthe, where Carlists received strong support from the aristocrats and such as the Comtesse Anatole de Montesquiou.

Legitimist networks were activated once again in the 1860s and 1870s during the final Carlist upheaval. A transnational solidarity network was built up among legitimists and Carlists, with the French playing a leading part. Legitimists opened their châteaux to the Carlists: Henry de Larralde accommodated Don Carlos at the Château d'Urtubie in Urrugne, while Marguerite, her children, and the Marquis de la Romana resided at Tartifume, a property of the Vicomte de Curzay, a relative of the Marquis de Carayon-Latour. In May 1875, the Duchesse de Chevreuse – La Rochefoucauld's daughter – held a ball to collect donations for the "wounded *from both camps*". It was attended by nearly 2,000 people and raised Fr.42,000.⁶⁵ The salons of Faubourg Saint-Germain also acted as places of counterrevolutionary sociability.

Religious networks also played a longstanding and important role in this loose-knit legitimist cluster. They had been crucial in the 1830s when a part of the French clergy, with its legitimist leanings, had felt it their duty to support

---

60 Isabella, *Risorgimento in Exile*, 22.
61 Anne Leblay, "Proscrits ibériques à Paris au temps des monarchies constitutionnelles (1814–1848)" (PhD diss., Paris, EHESS, 2013), 548.
62 Sartorius, "Des débuts de la monarchie de Juillet," 37.
63 Leblay, "Proscrits ibériques," 550–552.
64 Tronco, *Les Carlistes espagnols*, 293–294.
65 Dupont, *Une internationale blanche*, 375.

the combat of Carlist ecclesiastics.⁶⁶ A few decades later, priests who had long been exiled in Bordeaux provided financial backing for "the Cause", as did Carmelites in the town, promoting it within the secrecy of the confessional. Monastic buildings also became a safe refuge, since they could not be searched; when the Jesuits were expelled from France many took exile in Spanish monasteries.⁶⁷ Still, the church did not always play a partisan role. As soon as the first waves of Carlist exiles arrived in France, for example, charitable works came to their assistance, such as the Société de Saint-Vincent-de-Paul.

An emotional welcome

Support for exiles could provide an opportunity for special occasions. In France, Belgium, and Britain, funeral processions were "moments of fraternal union", as were liberal banquets.⁶⁸ In Brussels in 1838 and in 1848, annual celebrations of the Polish insurrection of November 29 provided a way of expressing mass support for Polish exiles. Special religious services were held, such as that of April 18, 1861 in Brussels attended by 2,000 Belgians after the Warsaw riots in February.⁶⁹ On May 10, 1874, legitimists in Marseille celebrated a mass at Notre-Dame-de-la-Garde to implore divine protection for Don Carlos's army.⁷⁰

As of the 1840s, especially after 1848, there was a change in the social and political complexion of exiles, and another type of internationalism emerged, particularly a socialist international. Exiles came increasingly from the middle and working class,⁷¹ bringing other support networks into play. In Belgium, socialists had consistently presented themselves as championing refugees as of the early days of the kingdom.⁷² It was also in Belgium that the International Democrat Association was born, the fruit of concerted action by German, French, and Belgian democrats. This association, founded in late September 1847 by Adalbert von Bornstedt, the editor of the *Deutsche Brüsseler Zeitung*, presented itself as an

---

66 Leblay, "Proscrits ibériques," 541–547.
67 Jean-Marc Delaunay, "Des réfugiés en Espagne: les religieux français et les décrets du 29 mars 1880," *Mélanges de la Casa de Velázquez* 17 (1981): 291–319.
68 Sylvie Aprile, "Exils français et fraternités européennes," in *Exil et fraternité*, 28.
69 Goddeeris, *La Grande Émigration*, 240.
70 Dupont, *Une internationale blanche*, 380.
71 On the Poles, see Krzysztof Marchlewicz, "Continuities and Innovations: Polish Emigration after 1849," in *Exiles from European Revolutions*, 107.
72 Nicolas Coupain, "L'expulsion des étrangers en Belgique (1830–1914)," *Revue belge d'histoire contemporaine* 33/1–2 (2003): 5–48.

international association, and was chaired by the Belgian Lucien Jottrand, seconded by Karl Marx. It managed to attract many exiles,[73] focusing its efforts on Poles, with Polish commemorations acting as landmark events in its development.[74] The German socialists who started arriving in London as of 1849 (about 1,500 in all) were able to count on an assistance network in the form of the *Communistischer Arbeiter Bildungsverein (CABV),* also known as the Communist League, chaired by August Willich and Karl Schapper. The CABV had three branches, including a Social and Democratic Committee for Refugees run Marx and Engels, who were refugees themselves. The Communist League was dissolved in 1852 at Marx's suggestion, and many former activists joined the first IWA in 1864,[75] which later took in many communards, often via the intermediary of Chartist activists.

Though Chartism went into decline as 1842, it had taken an interest in the fate of refugees from a very early date.[76] As of 1836 William Lovett, Henry Hetherington, and other artisan radicals founded the London Workingmen's Association (LWA) whose internationalism was based on personal ties: Lovett knew Mazzini, who was the friend of Stanislas Worcell, a major figure in Polish émigré circles between 1834 and 1857. The LWA and Polish refugees were henceforth closely linked. But refugees from other nationalities were not overlooked. In 1839 French refugees had founded the Société Démocratique Française, run by Berrier-Fontaine and Chilman, veterans of the Société des Droits de l'Homme Républicaine, then by Auguste Juin (known as Jean Michelot); in 1844, it organized assistance for recently arrived Spanish refugees. From that stage on, French and Spanish radicals attended Chartist meetings.[77] Within the Chartist movement, Julian Harney, who ran the Fraternal Democrats, was the main architect of closer ties with refugees thanks to his personal ties with Berrier-Fontaine, Chilman, and Michelot, as well as with Karl Schapper, Wilhelm Weitling, Friedrich Engels, and Joseph Moll. The first meeting of the Fraternal Democrats was held to protest against oppression in Poland. Its objective was to attract democrats from all nations, and, backed up by its newspaper, the *Northern Star*, it became the largest of the multinational organizations during the Chartist period. The Fraternal Democrats were joined by the French and German democrat societies, meeting on

---

73 Sartorius, "Des débuts de la monarchie de Juillet," 41.
74 Goddeeris, *La Grande Émigration*, 310.
75 Christine Lattek, "German Socialism in London after 1849: the Communist League of August Willich and Karl Schapper," in *Exiles from European Revolutions*, 187–208.
76 Iowerth Prothero, "Chartists and Political Refugees," in *Exiles from European Revolutions*, 209–229.
77 Prothero, "Chartists and Political Refugees," 216.

Sundays, but, according to Iowerth Prothero, remained a coterie without any monopoly over relations with refugees. In 1846 a People's International League was set up, largely at the instigation of artisan radical William Linton, who had met Mazzini in 1844. This attracted primarily Italians and Poles, while the French and Germans tended to prefer the Fraternal Democrats.[78]

English radicals and chartists in London and a dozen or so cities including Birmingham, Manchester, Liverpool, and Sheffield organized subscriptions for refugees, as well as demonstrations and petitions voicing their support for the February 1848 revolution in France, or for Kossuth and the cause of Hungarian sovereignty.[79] Chartism also asserted its support for the Paris Commune, and in Nottingham, in a borough previously held by Feargus O'Connor, working-class republicans collected funds for refugee communards.[80]

In addition to these various traditional forms of solidarity and reception, not destined specifically for refugees, dozens of committees and associations were set up across Europe with the sole purpose of supporting exiles. These originated in the great wave of philhellenism which, in the 1820s, had swept the German states, Switzerland, then Paris and various other French towns, as well as London.[81] Some of these committees were set up by exiles themselves, others by well-known figures in host countries. As yet, no comparative history of these committees has been conducted. We here sketch what seems to be one of the very first humanitarian nexuses.[82]

These various committees tended to be organized within national networks, via local committees or bureaus, as well as international ones. Thus the Central Polish Committee in Paris was part of a transnational network in that it was in contact with committees in Switzerland, United Kingdom, and the United States.[83] With a few exceptions, the committees had meagre means and were of limited duration. The charitable actions they undertook, largely copying those of the earlier philhellenic committees, changed little over the course of the period: subscriptions advertised mainly in the press; social gatherings,

---

[78] Shaw, *Britannia's Embrace*, 62.
[79] Margot Finn, *After Chartism. Class and nation in English radical politics, 1848–1874* (Cambridge: Cambridge University Press, 1993), 63–99.
[80] Finn, *After Chartism*, 287–289.
[81] Diaz, *Un asile pour tous les peuples*, 229.
[82] The situation in Piedmont was slightly different. The exiles leaving Turin and towns in the Kingdom of Sardinia were not really foreigners: coming primarily from territories under Austrian domination, they fought to create an Italian nation. In a sense, people from Piedmont, Lombardy, Tuscany, and Naples were all Italians in the making.
[83] Diaz, *Un asile pour tous les peuples*, 232.

balls, concerts, and theatre performances; exhibitions of works produced by exiles; and charity collections and bazaars. These charitable actions were often run by women. In Brussels, a Lady's Committee chaired by Zoé de Gamond (1806–1854) organized a grand exhibition in February 1834 of over 700 paintings, which were sold or used as lottery prizes.[84] At roughly the same time in Paris, wealthy businessmen's wives, such as Madame Cheuvreux, wives of politicians seeking recognition, such as Duchesse Decazes, and members of families ennobled by Napoléon I, such as the Baronne Friant, chose, in the tradition of patronage, to organize "patriotic donations". They thus sold at their homes tickets for events organized by the Polish Committee in support of Poland at war.[85] In Besançon, a Ladies Relief Committee displayed its support for German refugees in May 1848.[86] In Piedmont, many committees included women, generally the wives and daughters of local notables, members of "this provincial bourgeoisie which had become the ruling class and which, on inheriting the social duties once upheld by the aristocracy, had reinterpreted them in their own manner".[87] These committees enabled women to exert considerable political and social influence and to attract a clientele of protégés.

While support for exiles could extend as far as purchasing and delivering arms, these committees also provided emergency assistance (food, clothing, and lodging), distributed money raised by subscriptions, and sought to find work for exiles, though not as often as the latter wished. In Piedmont, the two main committees, the one run by Cameroni and the *Società dell'Emigrazione italiana* (SEI), helped very many exiles find a job, particularly in public employment and the army.[88] A certain number of Lombard aristocrats even founded the *Stabilimento industriale* in 1851, a fairly unique enterprise, in order to benefit especially "honest working émigrés who prefer work to charity". The *Stabilimento* was a sort of joint-stock company, which also received state support through the *Comitato centrale*. By June 1851 it had already employed over eighty refugees in various types of administrative work (as copyists, accountants, translators, and so on). It received backing from the *Gazzetta del Popolo*, which defined the enterprise in the following terms: "the best way to do good for those experiencing difficult circumstances does not consist in charity in the simple form

---

84 Goddeeris, *La Grande Émigration*, 220.
85 Guillaume, *L'autre exil*, 120.
86 Fernand Rude, *Les Réfugiés allemands à Besançon sous la Deuxième République*, (Besançon: Millot, 1939), 12.
87 Ester De Fort, "Une fraternité difficile," 147.
88 Ester De Fort, "La Mecca d'Italia," 49.

of alms, but rather in procuring the means by which they can overcome their painful situation".[89]

While exchanges between these relief and refugee committees could be on a good and lasting footing – in London, for example, the Chartists were on good terms with the French socialists,[90] with the French Democrat Society readily taking part in Chartist meetings – at times relations could be ambivalent and marred by political tensions. The Central Committee for Poles, for example, included virtually no Poles in its ranks, and it had complicated relations with the National Polish committee run by Joachim Lelewel, despite the latter being on friendly terms with Lafayette. At times the European Central Democrat committee run by Mazzini clashed with the Italian committees in London and Paris, as did the Franco-Spanish-Italian Democrat Committee of his rival Giuseppe Montanelli. As is well known, there were tensions between, on the one hand, the Polish National Committee and the Young Poland section of the Polish Democrat Society, and, on the other, the various pro-Polish committees around Europe. Thus when the London Literary Association of the Friends of Poland sought to encourage Poles to emigrate to the United States, no longer having the funds to support them, the Polish Democrat Society protested energetically – despite being chaired by Prince Adam Jerzy Czartoryski's friend Lord Dudley Coutts Stuart – for any Pole emigrating across the Atlantic would be one less combatant for the cause.[91] In France in 1833, the notables of Argentan founded a Polish committee to take in exiles in this town. But relations between the committee and the refugees became tense when the former made their financial support virtually conditional on the latter renouncing all political activity. The Argentan refugees quite simply returned the money they had received.[92] Most of the time, exiles came together within national organizations, in a form of ethnic clustering, and did not join the committees assisting them, especially as the latter were very short-lived.

Lastly, relations between populations and exiles were ambivalent and varied according to the region and period, preferable. In all host countries and at all times, the arrival of exiles could trigger waves of enthusiasm. In Brussels, Paris, and London, Poles were often welcomed as heroes. The same was true

---

[89] Gian Battista Furiozzi, *L'emigrazione politica*, 38. This is the book to consult for the history of the *Comitato centrale* and the SEI.
[90] Fabrice Bensimon, "The French Exiles and the British," in *Exiles from European Revolutions*, 97.
[91] Krzysztof Marchlewicz, "Continuities and Innovations: Polish Emigration after 1849," in *Exiles from European Revolutions*, 112.
[92] Diaz, *Un asile pour tous les peuples*, 235.

in smaller towns. Thus in Bergerac in March 1833, the *garde nationale* accompanied by several hundred men and women, went out to meet the exiles and escort them along the final miles.[93] A few weeks later, in August, the *garde nationale* at Château-du-Loir (Sarthe), with the mayor's authorization, went to meet the fourteen Poles sent to their village by the prefect of the department. On hearing the sound of drums, the inhabitants joined the procession and each exile had soon found somewhere to lodge.[94] It was once again to help Poles that in January 1834 the people of Marseille rallied to prevent their expulsion to Algiers.[95] Overall, in the early 1830s, Poles were fairly well received, and it was not rare for them to settle, find work, and marry local women, as was the case in Clermont-Ferrand.[96] In Belgium, Poles were also enthusiastically received on several occasions. In England, certain exiles were warmly welcomed, such as Kossuth in Southampton in 1851, or Garibaldi in 1864, though they were feted more as heroes than as refugees.[97] Lastly, in Turin, in the wake of their defeat at Novare (March 1849), the republican soldiers *of* the *Colonna mantovana* were taken aback by the warmth of the welcome they received from a population known for its political moderation.[98]

From fraternity to mistrust

Any such enthusiasm, in addition to often being directed more towards Poles than Spaniards or Italians, was, however, short-lived, giving way to indifference or mistrust. In the kingdom of Sardinia, the increasingly suspicious and intolerant attitudes there may be attributed to changes in the social composition of exiles as of 1848: there were fewer aristocrats, intellectuals, and people of private means, and more men from mixed social backgrounds, often accompanied by their family and less inclined to establish ties with native elites, who viewed them with mistrust and deemed them a supplementary burden on the state, or

---

[93] Pierre Pageot, *Le Périgord terre d'asile. Réfugiés, évacués rapatriés en Dordogne au cours des XIXe et XXe siècles* (Paris: L'Harmattan, 2005), 17.
[94] Valentin Guillaume, "*L'autre exil*" 111.
[95] Archives nationales de France, BB^{18} 1353, file 101 A8, "Désordres à Marseille à l'occasion de l'embarquement pour Alger de 29 officiers polonais déportés".
[96] Pierre Gerbet, "La vie des réfugiés politiques à Clermont-Ferrand de 1815 à 1870," *Bulletin historique et scientifique de l'Auvergne*, 63 (1943): 17–21.
[97] Bernard Porter, *The Refugee Question*, 109–110.
[98] De Fort, "La Mecca d'Italia," 46.

a threat to public order even.[99] Admittedly Britain took in refugees throughout the century, and expelled none, but that does not mean that they were appreciated. Most refugees in England were ignored or despised, and very few Britons were openly friends with the French, especially after the affront committed by Ledru-Rollin.[100] Stereotypes presented the French as highly strung, the Germans as dirty, the Italians as underhand, and Poles as somewhat immoral revolutionaries, joining in other peoples' revolutions out of pleasure rather than principle.[101] For Bernard Porter, British public opinion tolerated refugees only because people's aversion for regulations was stronger than their xenophobia, thus solidarity with refugees provided a way of sustaining national political struggles. For Caroline Shaw, Britons tended to have a shared narrative of refuge or a morality tale inviting them to view themselves as the protector of foreigners. Taking in exiles, who for that matter were not differentiated from foreigners in general, was not a matter of disinterested generosity or solidarity, but primarily a way of displaying Great Britain's moral and political superiority over a European continent overrun by despotism.

Many historians consider that Britain was not an isolated case. Idesbald Goddeeris thus reckons that Belgian pro-Polish sentiment was a myth: "the Polish cause served as an excuse to internationalize Belgian ideology and as a means of mobilizing the population" – in 1831–1832, it was a matter of patriotism, and in 1833–1834, of radical democrat opposition denouncing the conformism of the new Belgian state.[102] Gérald and Silvia Arlettaz, in the wake of others, assert that the Swiss tradition of taking in exiles was "a mythical characteristic throughout the nineteenth century".[103] In France, pro-Polish sentiment was in many cases primarily a way of displaying one's patriotism and support for the July Monarchy.[104] Lastly, Ester De Fort has extensively nuanced the image of Piedmont as a land of hospitality dispensing abundant subsidies and

---

99 De Fort, "Esuli, migranti, vagagondi nello Stato sardo dopo il Quarantotto," in *Rileggere l'Ottocento. Risorgimento e Nazione*, ed. Maria Luisa Betri (Turin: Comitato di Torino Dell'Istituto per la storia del Risorgimento italiano, 2010), 227.
100 A few weeks after arriving in London, Alexandre Ledru-Rollin published *La Décadence de l'Angleterre*, in which he expressed his hatred for the country that had taken him in.
101 Benard Porter, "The Asylum of Nations: Britain and the Refugees of 1848," in *Exiles from European Revolutions*, 48.
102 Porter, "The Asylum of Nations," 251.
103 *La Suisse et les étrangers. Immigration et formation nationale (1848–1933)* (Lausanne: Antipodes, 2004), 37. See too Lorena Parini, ""La Suisse terre d'asile': un mythe ébranlé par l'histoire," *Revue européenne des migrations internationales* 13/1 (1997): 51–69.
104 Valentin Guillaume, "L'autre exil," 122.

employment to exiles, highlighting instead that the latter often found themselves in deplorable circumstances.[105]

Indifference and mistrust could at times tip into open hostility. While there are fairly few traces of violence committed against exiles, there are many marks of rejection. The Carlists were not always well received, as one of their leaders consigned to his diary:

> The inhabitants of the villages through which we pass look at us in brutal and insolent manner, stinging us to the quick with their vulgar taunts and ironic laughter. Along our journey very many women came out to meet us and, taking advantage of the occasion, sold us food at exorbitant prices.[106]

At roughly the same period, Joachim Lelewel, in a letter sent to Henri de Brouckère, deplored the "aversion" for Poles stirred up among the population by Belgian elites, concluding: "I am certain that Belgian, once we are part of history, will be considered an enemy country".[107] In Cahors, Spaniards were suspected in 1833 of marauding and even of murder.[108] Fernand Rude notes the Besançon conservative bourgeoisie's "surly" attitude towards Germans in 1848.[109] More generally, exiles were criminalized. In Piedmont, émigrés from Lombardy were accused, often wrongly, of theft, pillage, and fraud.[110] The expression *fratelli lombardi* (Lombard brothers) was nearly always used ironically and with contemptuous overtones. The population became increasingly irritated with these guests who were outstaying their welcome. Reactionaries and conservatives continued to vent their hostility in the clerical press and in pamphlets, accusing exiles of being a clique of profiteering ruffians, thus turning them into convenient scapegoats for the rise in criminality. Only the *Gazzetta del Poppolo* came to their defense, denouncing the brutalities and abuses public officials inflicted on them, and bringing discrimination against them to light.[111]

In London, many exiles felt humiliated, abandoned, and unappreciated. As noted by the radical Julian Harney: "the exile is free to land upon our shores, and free to perish of hunger beneath our inclement skies".[112] In 1850, the Bou-

---

105 De Fort, "La Mecca d'Italia".
106 Pedro Rújula, "Exiliados carlistas," in *Exilios*, 180.
107 Goddeeris, *La Grande Émigration*, 78.
108 Archives nationales de France, BB[18] 1329, "Troubles commis par des Espagnols à Cahors".
109 Fernand Rude, *Les Réfugiés allemands à Besançon sous la Deuxième République*, (Besançon: Millot, 1939), 10.
110 De Fort, "Esuli", 228.
111 De Fort, "La Mecca d'Italia", 70.
112 Porter, *The Refugee Question*, 22.

ches-du-Rhône prefect established a direct link between the arrival of Italian political refugees and an increase in the number of thefts and other crimes, stating that this insecurity "upset" the population. He thus recommended removing and expelling democrat political refugees.[113] The days of fraternity, solidarity, and charity thus gave way to times of rejection and expulsion.

3 The rejection and expulsion of refugees

"Welcome or deport" sums up the ambivalent position of European states whose borders were crossed by exiles throughout the nineteenth century.[114] The tradition of taking in exiles in Belgium, France, and Switzerland tends to make us overlook the many individual and collective expulsion measures against refugees living in these countries.[115] Faced with the growing number of foreigners seeking asylum, states passed ever more sophisticated legislation over the course of the century to monitor, dissuade, and increasingly expel exiles.[116] As explained above, the authorities sometimes made residence conditional on not going to certain places viewed as politically sensitive (borders and towns), backed up by various forms of internment. In the event of more extreme threats, the authorities also resorted to expulsion, extradition, and deportation of refugees previously granted residence, or else quite simply blocked them from entering the territory.

Refusing asylum

The history of asylum in nineteenth-century Europe is also a history of refusal, punctuated by many episodes in which land and sea borders were closed. Governments feared "mass" displacements and the attendant troubles to public

---

113 Delphine Diaz, "La figure de l'étranger en France de la monarchie de Juillet à la IIe République: de la tête de Turc au bouc émissaire," in *Boucs émissaires, têtes de Turcs et souffre-douleur*, ed. Frédéric Chauvaud et al. (Rennes: Presses universitaires de Rennes, 2012), 133–144.
114 The formulation is borrowed from Alexis Spire, *Accueillir ou reconduire. Enquête sur les guichets de l'immigration* (Paris: Raisons d'agir, 2008).
115 As Janine Ponty was already arguing in 1996: Janine Ponty, "Réfugiés, exilés, des catégories problématiques," *Matériaux pour l'histoire de notre temps* 44 (1996): 9–13, 10.
116 Paul-André Rosental, "Migrations, souveraineté, droits sociaux. Protéger et expulser les étrangers en Europe du XIXe siècle à nos jours," *Annales. Histoire, Sciences Sociales* 2 (2011): 335–373.

order. Thus to prevent a group of Piedmontese liberals arriving in the wake of uprisings in Turin and Alexandria in 1821, Emmanuel-Armand du Plessis's ultra-royalist government sought to block the insurgents trying to reach Liberal Triennium Spain.[117] Many of them managed regardless, before heading into a second exile after the French expedition to Spain headed by the Duc d'Angoulême. Ten or so years later, 480 Polish refugees seeking asylum were turned back at the French border to Switzerland, which was obliged to grant them temporary residence.[118] In 1871, Belgium closed its border to all French communards not sentenced to banishment.[119] The desire to "contain", "filter", and "control" refugees from the moment they arrived at the border was a permanent feature, though often ineffective despite developments in police techniques to identify and keep records on individuals.[120]

Turning back refugees at the border also raised the question of their destination, giving rise to consultations between states and between various tiers within an administration. Certain states forbade refugees enjoined to return to their country of origin from crossing their territory, while others refused to accept those who had been turned back by a neighboring state. In August 1849, the French legation at the Grand Duchy of Baden reported that Poles turned back by France had not been allowed to re-enter the territory of this German state, despite being recognized as "former refugees".[121] The minister for foreign affairs, Odilon Barrot, initially proposed that prefects intern them in depots, before deciding to direct them to the Channel ports where they embarked for Britain. Exchanges between the center and peripheries of executive power reveal a strategic dimension to the coercive measure of collective deportation. When in February 1836 the French minister of the interior, Adolphe Thiers, decided to deport subjects from Italian states, he issued prefects with instructions for precise expulsion itineraries: those from Parma, Modena, and Lombardy-Venetia being expelled to the Kingdom of Piedmont-Sardinia were to be conducted to Pont-de-Beauvoisin, while those from Rome, Tuscany, and Naples were to be sent to

---

117 Bistarelli, *Gli esuli*.
118 Archives de l'État (Chancellerie d'État), Canton de Berne, KS 20.87, circular to the states of the Confederation, Berne, May 26, 1834. See Diaz, *Un asile pour tous les peuples*, 183.
119 Coupain, "L'expulsion des étrangers," 30.
120 Ilsen About and Vincent Denis, *Histoire de l'identification des personnes* (Paris: La Découverte, 2010).
121 Archives du ministère des Affaires étrangères (AMEF), 38 M D35, letter from the Baden legation to the minister for foreign affairs, August 26, 1849.

Saint-Laurent-du-Var.[122] This sketches out the "roads of exile" presented in the following chapter, a territory with its own timeframes, border crossings, and protagonists to which we shall return later.

In the absence of any inter- or intra-state framework, the choice of expulsion destinations could also result from negotiation between exiles and local authorities. In the wake of events in Milan on February 6, 1843, during which workers and patriots rebelled against the Austrian occupier, the Piedmontese authorities proceeded to arrest and expel 150 insurgents. The sentenced insurgents and their families entreated the authorities for a more lenient sentence and sought to negotiate their exile destination. Very few of them saw their wishes granted, however, with the choice of destination resulting from diplomatic, political, and economic circumstances largely outside their control.[123] Similar negotiations occurred in the kingdom of Belgium in 1843 when the security authorities expelled a group of refugees deemed to be "subversive", escorting them to the port of Ostend and paying their sailing to England.[124]

When it was not possible to turn back groups of refugees to other countries, certain states relegated them to colonial territories at varying remove. Under the July Monarchy, Algeria was used to take in foreign refugees deemed turbulent or too numerous to accept in mainland France.[125] Though they were initially perceived as potentially "useful" auxiliaries for agricultural colonization, this practice was progressively abandoned in favor of immigration by nationals. Ersilio Michel has examined the path taken by the great figures of the Italian *Risorgimento* traveling to Algiers, Oran, and Annaba in the 1830s and 1840s, most of whom enlisted with the Foreign Legion.[126] In addition to these "voluntary" or "official" exiles, some of whom had previously obtained the "status" of refugee, those sent to Algeria also included "political criminals" who had entered the French mainland clandestinely. Thus certain *briganti* having left the Papal States to find refuge in France in the mid-1860s were then deported to Algerian departments rather than extradited to their land of departure.[127] Bilateral extradition

---

[122] Archives départementales du Bas-Rhin, 3 M 526, from the under-secretary of state to the prefect of Bas-Rhin, February 6, 1836.
[123] Durand, "Éloigner les Barabbas," 119–136.
[124] Caestecker, *Alien Policy*, 23.
[125] Diaz, "Indésirables en métropole", 187–204.
[126] Ersilio Michel, *Esuli italiani in Algeria* (Bologna: Cappelli, 1935).
[127] See the Crocco, Pilone, and Viola affair in Ministero degli Affari esteri, *I documenti diplomatici italiani, prima serie: 1861–1870* (Roma, Istituto poligrafico e zecca dello Stato, 1987), vol. 9. On their involvement in the taking of Trivigno and other towns, and the complicated relations they had with certain Carlist generals exiled in Italy, such as Borges, see Simon Sarlin, *Le*

treaties in the nineteenth century between various European states in principle protected political refugees from being sent back to the country where they were wanted or had been sentenced.[128]

Political exiles were often obliged to undertake hazardous peregrinations on being deported, or in the event of a string of refusals by neighboring states to take them in. The episode of the ship *Gian Matteo* provides a good example.[129] On May 19, 1849, the Austrian government expelled 188 Polish refugees, who embarked at the Adriatic port of Duino on the merchant ship *Gian Matteo* headed for New York. On arriving at Cagliari in southern Sardinia, the refugees rebelled and demanded to go to Marseille. When the ship arrived there, they were not allowed to disembark, and the somewhat frightened captain had to sail to Algiers. On being received by the Algerian governor-general, the latter criticized the mainland authorities for having assured the refugees, without consulting him first, that they would be "hospitably received" in Algeria.[130] Paying for refugees' needs represented a significant state expenditure, and this often determined the decision to accept or send back political refugees. In Algeria once again, when the ship *Numancia* arrived in 1874 with 1,647 Spaniards on board fleeing Republican Cartagena, the local authorities, being unable to take in the whole group, were obliged to select those they could receive.[131] Refusing to conduct a collective extradition as requested by the republican government, the Algerian authorities turned to three types of treatment – extradition, internment, and expulsion –, transforming this territory of refuge into a land of relegation. The sources contain many other accounts of "exiles adrift", where their drifting generally resulted from having been turned back in Europe due to diplomatic friction generated by these intense flows of people.[132]

In addition to the collective turning back of refugees arriving at borders, or the deporting of those who had already entered the territory, the authorities of

---

Légitimisme en armes. Histoire d'une mobilisation internationale contre l'Unité italienne (Rome: École française de Rome, 2013), 234 *et seq.*
128 Philippe Rygiel, "Une impossible tâche? L'Institut de Droit International et la régulation des migrations internationales (1870–1920)", (habilitation à diriger les recherches thesis, Université Paris 1 Panthéon-Sorbonne, 2011), 87.
129 Diaz, "Indésirables en métropole".
130 Archives du ministère des Affaires étrangères, La Courneuve, 38 MD 35, letter from the minister of foreign affairs to the minister of the navy and colonies, June 28, 1849.
131 Jeanne Moisand, "Les réfugiés du *Numancia*. Le traitement des cantonalistes espagnols en Algérie française (1874)," *Diasporas. Circulations, migrations, histoire*, 33/1 (2019): 159–172.
132 Delphine Diaz, "Exilés à la dérive: l'Affaire des 'Polonais du Havre', 1834", accessed April 11, 2021, https://www.retronews.fr/conflits-et-relations-internationales/chronique/2018/07/03/l-affaire-des-polonais-du-havre-1834.

various states also expelled individual political refugees, an unusually difficult phenomenon to quantify. Expulsion is a highly particular and discreet administrative procedure, whose legal codification was devised in various European states during the nineteenth century, and repeatedly revised to enhance its effectiveness.[133] For protagonists of the period, and historians of today, it may be mistaken with other procedures to remove individuals, such as deportation, extradition, or simply turning back at the border, as provided for in the penal codes of various states.[134] In theory, expulsion concerned foreigners who had received a conviction and were not allowed to remain in the territory, but this procedure could not be used against political refugees. In Belgium, the law of September 22, 1835, included measures to remove foreigners jeopardizing public order.[135] In France, the law of December 3, 1849, the first to regulate the expulsion procedure, did not apply to refugees, whose status was defined by the laws of April 20, 1832, and May 1, 1834. The former provided for an obligation to "leave the territory" for refugees representing a threat to internal security, and the latter introduced a sentence of imprisonment in the event of failure to respect the decision.[136] Refugees were nevertheless implicitly targeted by those devising this law in 1849. A few months after Italian revolutionaries were chased from Rome, the rapporteur responsible for the draft law, Mr. de Montigny, branded political exiles an insurrectional threat from which French territory needed protecting.[137] As of 1848 Switzerland also reserved the right to expel foreigners "endangering the Confederation's internal and external security".[138] Britain was the only country to guarantee in all circumstance that political refugees could remain on

---

[133] For discussion of this procedure and how it was used in nineteenth-century Europe, see Delphine Diaz and Hugo Vermeren, "Éloigner et expulser les étrangers au XIXe siècle," *Diasporas. Circulations, migrations, histoire* 33/1 (2019): 159–172.
[134] Hugo Vermeren, "L'expulsion des étrangers, une procédure ajustable pour l'exercice d'un pouvoir discrétionnaire," *The Conversation*, accessed April 11, 2021, http://theconversation.com/lexpulsion-des-etrangers-une-procedure-ajustable-pour-lexercice-dun-pouvoir-discretionnaire-87637.
[135] Coupain, "L'expulsion des étrangers", 22 *et seq.*
[136] Diaz, "Les expulsions de réfugiés étrangers", 19–33.
[137] Élie-Benjamin Loyer, "Expulser les indésirables: un aspect de la gestion des populations immigrés sous la Troisième République (1880–1939)," *Diasporas. Circulations, migrations, histoire* 33/1 (2019): 55–72.
[138] Alfred Erich Senn, "Les révolutionnaires russes et l'asile politique en Suisse avant 1917," *Cahiers du monde russe et soviétique* 3–4 (1968): 324–336, 326.

its territory, making it the sole country of "impregnable asylum in Europe",[139] in the words of Louis Blanc.[140]

Expulsion: a selective procedure

Examination of individual cases of French, Belgian, and Swiss expulsion shows that the procedure was mainly used against political refugees sentenced for common offences (vagrancy, theft, etc.).[141] However, the latter received what may be described as privileged treatment. For while convicted foreigners were, on being released, subject to an expulsion order and nearly always forcibly conducted towards their home country, refugees, like deserters, were free to choose their destination. Many opted for Switzerland, Britain, or the United States. The ministerial authorities ensured the essential principle of asylum was guaranteed by not sending refugees back to their country of origin. For, in the words of the head of French general security inculpating prefects who had been sending refugees back to their country of origin: "that would amount to serious disregard for the right of asylum".[142] The other mark of preferential treatment was that, on being expelled, refugees had the right to freely leave the territory, with the authorities assigning an obligatory route and providing a subsidy. In this, they were unlike foreigners found guilty of a criminal offence, nearly all of whom were accompanied by the forces of law and order, by foot, on horseback, and increasingly in horse-drawn or railway cell carriages. Thus the Polish refugee Elias David, on being amnestied from transportation in June 1848, was issued with a passport to be signed by the authorities in the thirty-five localities he was obliged to travel through on his way from Landernau to Strasbourg.[143] In France

---

139 Preface to the English edition of his history of the 1848 revolution, *Historical Revelations* (London, 1858).
140 There are, however, records of some cases of refugees being removed, such as when 650 Jewish Romanians disembarked in England, most of whom were sent on to Canada and the United States: Christiane Reinecke, "Governing Aliens in Times of Upheaval: Immigration Control and Modern State Practice in Early Twentieth-Century Britain, Compared with Prussia," *International Review of Social History* 54 (2009): 39–65, 55.
141 On this point, see work carried out by the ANR AsileuropeXIX team, and particularly the online database ExpulsionsXIX, accessed April 11, 2021, https://asileurope.huma-num.fr/base-de-donnees-expulses.
142 Archives départementales des Bouches-du-Rhône, 3 M 526, circular from the minister of the interior to the prefect of Bas-Rhin, January 22, 1852.
143 Delphine Diaz, Hugo Vermeren, "Itinéraire de transportation et d'expulsion du réfugié polonais Elias David, transporté amnistié de juin 1848", map section on the AsileuropeXIX website,

as in Belgium, refugees were sometimes escorted alongside common-law criminals to the border by squadrons of gendarmes, causing the minister of the interior to upbraid his prefects.[144]

The expulsion of foreign refugees, far from being motivated solely by criminal convictions, could also be grounded in political reasons. Many exiles who had transgressed what the historian Greg Burgess has referred to as the host country's "tolerance threshold" were expelled "for political reasons".[145] Though the legal definition of "political crime" was not clear-cut at the time, it covered a set of subversive acts representing a direct or indirect threat to the established order and to "public order".[146] Many famous exiles were sentenced to expulsion from their host country for political activism: Joachim Lelewel and Peter Kropotkin from France, Giuseppe Mazzini, Felice Orsini and Eduard Bernstein from Switzerland, and Victor Considerant, Félix Pyat, and Victor Hugo from Belgium.[147] The latter, after taking refuge in Brussels after Louis Napoléon Bonaparte's coup in December 1851, returned there in March 1871 during the Paris Commune. He was expelled two months later for "disturbing the peace" after he had published a letter in the *Indépendance belge* newspaper denouncing the way Brussels treated exiled communards:[148] "no one wishes exile", he observed in his poem "En quittant Bruxelles", published one year later.[149] Admittedly, official statistics do not indicate extensive usage of political expulsion. For example, between 1860 and 1869, Second Empire France only expelled 66 foreigners for political offences, a very low percentage of the total number of expulsions pronounced during this period.[150] However, in times of crisis, there was

---

accessed April 11, 2021, https://asileurope.huma-num.fr/cartotheque/itineraire-de-transportation-et-dexpulsion-du-refugie-polonais-elias-david-transporte-amnistie-de-juin-1848.)

144 Archives départementales des Bouches-du-Rhône, 3 M 526, circular from René de Thorigny, minister of the interior, to the prefects, October 31, 1851. On the Belgian case, see Torsten Feys, "International railroads and human mobility controls at the Franco-Belgian border (1840s–1860s)," *Diasporas. Circulations, migrations, histoire* 33/1 (2019): 35–54.

145 Greg Burgess, *Refuge in the Land of Liberty. France and its Refugees, from the Revolution to the end of Asylum, 1787–1939* (New York: Palgrave, 2008), 51.

146 Philippe Rygiel, "Le réfugié dans le droit international durant la seconde moitié du XIXe siècle," in *Arrachés et déplacés. Réfugiés politiques, prisonniers de guerre, déportés (1789–1918)*, ed. Nicolas Beaupré and Karine Rance (Clermont-Ferrand: Presses Universitaires Blaise Pascal, 2016), 63–79, 74.

147 Many French examples are discussed in Diaz, *Un asile pour tous les peuples?*, 184 et seq.

148 Jules Garsou, "L'expulsion de Victor Hugo en 1871," *Revue catholique des idées et des faits* (1930). See too Aprile, *Le Siècle des exilés*.

149 Victor Hugo, "En quittant Bruxelles", *L'Année terrible* (Paris: Michel Lévy frères, 1872), 234.

150 Archives départementales des Bouches-du-Rhône, 3 M 661–664, ministry of the interior, particulars of foreigners expelled from France (1860–1869).

an increase in the number of expulsion orders decreed for political reasons, with refugees being the hardest hit. In 1876, as 15,000 Spanish Carlists were preparing to head for France, the French authorities announced a series of expulsion orders against partisans of Don Carlos said to be "agitators". The latter were escorted by the gendarmerie to the Italian border. A few months later, they were expelled from Italy and interned in France.[151]

In Algeria, one of the French departments to make greatest use of expulsion procedures during the nineteenth century,[152] several leading Spanish Zorrillist refugees were expelled in the early 1880s for their "propaganda in Spanish circles", at a time when France feared an increase in colonial separatism.[153] Peaks in political expulsion were thus closely linked to the social, economic, and political context. The great fear of anarchism in the 1880s and 1890s triggered a wave of expulsions of anarchist militants who were "hunted" throughout Europe,[154] very frequently leading them to go into exile in England or the United States.[155]

Public opinion about the expulsion of refugees

In periods when many refugees were expelled, civil society sometimes spoke out to denounce the brutality of these procedures to remove them, and the political refugees were at times able to draw on large solidarity networks within host societies. The caricature published by Chagot in October 1851 in a satirical Parisian

---

151 Alexandre Dupont, "Répression et déplacements contraints: les exilés face aux États d'après le récit d'un officier carliste (1876)," accessed April 11, 2021, https://asileurope.humanum.fr/cartotheque/repression-et-deplacements-contraints-les-exiles-face-aux-etats-dapres-le-recit-dun-officier-carliste-1876.
152 Hugo Vermeren, "Pouvoirs et pratiques de l'expulsion des étrangers en Algérie au XIXᵉ siècle: un outil colonial de gestion des flux migratoires," *Le Mouvement social* 258 (2017): 13–28.
153 In January 1888, the governor-general of Algeria ordered the expulsion of three editors of local Spanish-language newspapers with links to the Zorrillist committee in Oran, composed of Spanish refugees who supported the republican opponent Manuel Ruiz Zorrilla: Jean-Jacques Jordi, *Espagnols en Oranie. Histoire d'une migration (1830–1914)* (Nice: Éditions Jacques Gandini, 1996), 131.
154 Stéphane Mourlane, "Les anarchistes italiens dans les Alpes-Maritimes et le Var à la fin du XIXᵉ siècle: le choix de la marginalité," *Cahiers de la Méditerranée* 69 (2004): 189–198.
155 See in particular Constance Bantman, *The French Anarchists in London, 1880–1914: Exile and Transnationalism in the First Globalisation* (Liverpool: Liverpool University Press, 2013).

weekly, "Les peuples sont pour nous des frères",¹⁵⁶ is evidence of public support. It shows a discontent foreign figure driven out of the French republic, while the truncheon held aloft by the policeman symbolizes the stricter administrative measures against foreigners under the Second Republic. The expulsion of political refugees was part of public debate, and sometimes debated in assemblies. In Switzerland in 1836, the executive council of the canton of Berne issued circulars reporting on "guilty political schemes" and "abuses" of the right of asylum by certain foreign refugees as justification for the need to deport exiles who continued their political activity in their host territory.¹⁵⁷ This triggered open criticism by liberals in cantonal assemblies and in the press. In the early 1880s, when France expelled a Russian revolutionary refugee, Pierre Lavroff, to England, this occasioned sharp exchanges in the chamber of deputies between French ministers and the radical left.¹⁵⁸ The socialist parliamentary deputy Clovis Hugues was angered by the discretionary and antidemocratic nature of this expulsion, criticizing the many measures taken for political reasons against foreigners involved in the Paris commune in 1871.¹⁵⁹ Protest was at times international. Thus in November 1849, Lord Dudley Stuart in London protested against the French decision to expel Polish democrats, while the foreign office complained that these expellees were systematically sent to England.¹⁶⁰ Forty years later, the absolute right of foreigners to come and remain in England was debated once again when General Boulanger came to take refuge there on being expelled from Belgium.¹⁶¹

In addition to administrative expulsions conducted by state agents within a legally determined framework, there were also various other extralegal ways in

---

156 Delphine Diaz, "Chagot, les peuples sont pour nous des frères", image bank of the AsileuropeXIX website, accessed April 11, 2021, https://asileurope.huma-num.fr/ressources-iconographiques/les-peuples-sont-pour-nous-des-freres-comment-la-police-francaise-entend-la-fraternite-legalite-et-la-liberte-caricature-de-chagot-le-journal-pour-rire-10-octobre-1851.
157 See for example Archives de l'État de Berne, KS 22.96, circular of July 16, 1836.
158 Lavroff was accused of having opened a subscription to support poor nihilist families. Gérard Noiriel, *Immigration, antisémitisme et racisme en France (XIXᵉ-XXᵉ siècle). Discours publics, humiliations privées* (Paris: Fayard, 2007), 162.
159 *Journal officiel de la République française. Débats parlementaires. Chambre des députés* (Paris: Imprimerie du Journal officiel, 1882), session of May 11, 1882.
160 Diaz, *Un asile pour tous les peuples?*, 190.
161 William Feilden Craies, "Le droit d'expulsion des étrangers en Angleterre," *Journal du droit international privé* 16 (1889): 24.

which expulsions took place. There were cases of "disguised extradition",[162] in which foreigners were taken to the border and placed in the hands of the authorities of the destination country instead of being released freely. For example, Gustave Jeanneret, who took refuge in Morteau in September 1856 after the Neuchâtel uprising, was illegally handed over to the Swiss authorities. After requests for his extradition to the French government had failed, because the political nature of his "crime" protected him from this procedure, the Neufchâtel authorities got the Morteau police commissioner to hand Jeanneret over via the intermediary of the lieutenant of gendarmerie at La Chaux-de-Fonds. This stirred unrest among Swiss refugees, and the event was condemned by the keeper of the seals. In a letter sent to the latter on November 21, 1856, the Besançon public prosecutor explained that "what makes this act odious is that the superintendent's motive was less to act as a good neighbor towards the Swiss authorities, than to personally receive a bonus of Fr.300 promised by the federal authorities".[163] Although denounced in this instance, the French prefectural authorities frequently turned a blind eye to such "disguised extraditions", which particularly concerned foreigners condemned for vagrancy. Instead of being freely released on the border, the expellees were handed over to the authorities of the bordering state to prevent their immediately returning to France.

States were ultimately unable to absolutely guarantee the right of asylum for refugees. First, because they reserved the right to remove those considered "dangerous", "agitators", or "vagrants", frequently invoking it at times when there were larger numbers of political exiles, at times in disregard of international undertakings.[164] Second, because of irregularities in the various procedures for removing individuals, particularly expulsion, due to the inexperience or lack of knowledge of the local authorities in charge of carrying them out.[165] Lastly, because governments did not always intervene when popular movements led to foreign refugees being conducted to the border. These spontaneous expulsions, occurring particularly during labor conflicts in the second half of the nineteenth

---

[162] On disguised extraditions and public opinion about the expulsion of foreign refugees, see Torsten Feys, "Riding the Rails of Removal: the Impact of Railroads on Border Controls and Expulsion Practices," *Journal of Transport History* 40/2 (2019): 189–210.
[163] Archives Nationales de France, BB/18/1558, letter from the public prosecutor of Besançon to the keeper of the seals, November 21, 1856.
[164] Noiriel, *Réfugiés et sans papiers*, 114.
[165] Stéphane Duroy, "Le contrôle juridictionnel des mesures de police relatives aux étrangers sous la Troisième république," in *Police et migrants. France, 1667–1838*, ed. Marie-Claude Blanc-Chaléard et al. (Rennes: Presses Universitaires de Rennes, 2001): 91–104.

century,¹⁶⁶ could also involve political refugees. Thus, for example, a popular assembly in Berne in November 1850 called for the expulsion of foreign refugees, of whom there were about 500 in the city.¹⁶⁷

European exile in the nineteenth century thus constituted a major threefold social, political, and cultural reality with far-reaching consequences for the evolution of European societies. Through their number and frequency, they formed a social reality with tens of thousands of men and women obliged to leave their country over the course of the century to take refuge abroad, posing the question, for the states and societies to which they traveled, of how to take them in. In particular, exile gave rise to practices of both public and private origin to assist refugees, contributing to the transition from forms of charity and traditional assistance to solidarity based on the principle of shared humanity. This gave rise to the first forms of humanitarian assistance for refugees.

Exiles were also a political reality, for states had to draw up legislation and set up schemes to control and regulate their presence on their territory. This saw the transnational creation of a law of asylum and refuge with very different facets depending on the country and moment. These exile policies had a repressive aspect when it was a matter of refusing entry or even expelling unwanted outcasts. They also had a liberal aspect, consecrating the fact that it was incumbent on states to take in political outcasts. In that, the phenomenon of nineteenth-century European exile played a part in the construction of administrative states, by confronting the powers of the period with questions relating to controlling movement, to law for foreigners, and to sovereign powers in societies issuing from the Atlantic revolutions. The question of refugees also played a role in international relations of the period, given the differences in legislation from one country to another – not all adopted the liberal position of Britain, far from it – and the tensions between country of departure and host country generated by the presence of banished individuals.

---

166 See in particular Fabrice Bensimon, "'À bas les Anglais!' Mobilisations collectives contre les Britanniques dans le nord de la France en 1848," *Diasporas. Circulations, migrations, histoire* 33/1 (2019): 75–90; Bastien Cabot, *"À bas les Belges!". L'expulsion des mineurs borains (Lens, août-septembre 1892)* (Rennes: Presses universitaires de Rennes, 2017); Laurent Dornel, *La France hostile. Socio-histoire de la xénophobie (1870–1914)* (Paris: Hachette, 2004); Marc Leleux, "Fraternisation et concurrence: liens et limites d'un rapport au travail. L'exemple des ouvriers belges dans le département du Nord du milieu du XIXᵉ siècle à l'entre-deux-guerres," *Revue du Nord* 372 (2007): 837–855.

167 Archives du ministère des Affaires étrangères belge, Correspondance politique sur les réfugiés, vol. 1 (1841–1851), letter from the Belgian legation in Berne to the minister for foreign affairs in Brussels, November 30, 1850.

Finally, exile was also a cultural reality in that Europeans gradually became accustomed to the presence of foreigners in their cities who had fled their country for political reasons. Reactions were not always favorable, and host societies sometimes rejected these émigrés, for various reasons. But on the whole, what transpires is the support, in many forms, for refugees, both due to political proximity – and exile was undeniably instrumental in forging internationalism – and out of compassion and humanitarianism. These social and cultural factors that became embedded over the course of the nineteenth century largely shaped how refugees from around the world were received in Europe during the twentieth century, from the White Russians of the 1920s to the left-wing Latin American militants of the 1970s.

Sylvie Aprile, Alexandre Dupont and Hugo Vermeren
Chapter 3 Travel and transit

In autumn 1838, Maria Teresa of Braganza, Princess of Beira, left her exile in Salzburg, Austria to travel to Spain, where her husband, the Spanish pretender Don Carlos, Duke of Madrid, had since 1833 been leading the Carlists in a civil war against the Liberals who supported the regency of Maria-Christina of the Two Sicilies. Due to the French authorities' hostility towards the Spanish absolutist movement, the princess's departure for Spain was conducted in secrecy, overseen by a French nobleman devoted to the counter-revolutionary cause, Count Robert de Custine. This voyage from Austria to the French Basque country relied on false documents, concealed identities, and support networks. Increased police and military surveillance of the border with Spain caused the princess and her guide to use other expedients for the final stage of their journey.

The princess set out to cross the Pyrenean border guided by a local smuggler, Ganich de Macaye. The accounts of their venture reveal the broad range of stratagems and knowledge he deployed to enable this illustrious exile to join her husband. By following the mule trails long used by smugglers, crossing rivers, donning disguises, and hiding from the authorities, the travelers managed to reach their destination despite the French authorities' efforts to arrest them. This impressive clandestine operation is suggestive of the difficult circumstances in which people headed into exile in the nineteenth century, at a time when states were progressively tightening their control over their territory and borders, making it harder to circulate from one country to another. At the same time, this illustrious escapade illustrates outcasts' capacity to elude security surveillance and slip across borders. The ordeal tended to alter their perception of traveling, frequently associated with earlier trips for learning or leisure. Henceforth the departure and traveling of exiles were subject to a whole set of complex socio-political processes.

About to head off

The moment of departure and time spent traveling and settling into a new place was not just a brief tipping point along the path of exile, but a complex and often lengthy stage which needs to be apprehended in all its multifaceted substance. We need to pay attention to the preparations, the material conditions of traveling, and the ways of passing from one country to the next if we are to reconstitute the complexity of the paths taken and account for the migratory experience in its observable detail.

Departures as a matter of choice?

Going into exile resulted from defeat. This defeat, be it political or military, led to those one had opposed, be it overtly or discreetly, taking or strengthening their grip on power. This threatened the security of their opponents (or those viewed as such) and often of their entourage, forcing them to leave.[1] Political exile followed from the close links between violence and politics during this century. Admittedly, the gradual emergence of liberal and democratic regimes heralded, to a certain extent, the pacification and codification of politics, with political disagreements being increasingly voiced and resolved in the public sphere as defined by the authorities. The famous engraving by Louis-Marie Bosredon, known as "The vote or the rifle" (1848), showing a worker abandoning his rifle in favor of a voting slip to settle internal political matters, is a clear illustration of the pacifying virtues this socialist artist attributed to universal suffrage.[2] Nevertheless, such processes were the exception in the first half of the nineteenth century, and spread only gradually in the second half. Political change was still largely brought about by revolution, insurrection, war (in some cases civil war), or a coup.[3] France continued to be affected by such processes through to the end of the century: the defeat of Napoléon in 1815, the July Revolution in 1830, the February 1848 revolution, the coup of December 2, 1851, and defeat at the hands of Prussia were all key moments punctuating the political life of the country, not to mention other movements which did not come to fruition.

In nondemocratic regimes, the use of violence and armed action was a privileged or even necessary means to assert one's ideas and place them in the public sphere. Hence nineteenth-century political confrontation was marked by vio-

---

[1] Delphine Diaz, "Pour une histoire européenne de l'exil et de l'asile politiques au XIXᵉ siècle: le programme de recherche AsileuropeXIX," *Diasporas. Circulations, migrations, histoire* 28/2 (2016): 163–173.
[2] Alain Garrigou, *Histoire sociale du suffrage universel en France, 1848–2000* (Paris: Éditions du Seuil, 2002); Olivier Ihl, "Louis-Marie Bosredon et l'entrée dans le 'suffrage universel'. Sociogenèse d'une lithographie en 1848," *Revue d'histoire du XIXᵉ siècle* 50 (2015): 139–163.
[3] Jean-Clément Martin, *Violence et Révolution. Essai sur la naissance d'un mythe national* (Paris: Éditions du Seuil, 2009); Jean-Claude Caron et al. (eds.), *Entre violence et conciliation: La résolution des conflits sociopolitiques en Europe au XIXᵉ siècle* (Rennes: Presses universitaires de Rennes, 2008).

lence, with political opponents seen as enemies to be destroyed. Holding or conquering power thus provided the opportunity to deploy state repression and coercion against those one had fought. This threat, whether real or imagined, caused individuals to head into exile. When in 1848 Alphonse de Lamartine addressed parliament in favor of the abolition of the death sentence, he called on his colleagues to abolish it at least for political matters. His speech presented this as marking the new republic's decision to put an end to cycles of oppression against opponents: "I would thus disarm the people of a weapon that has ceaselessly been turned against them in all revolutions; I would reassure fearful imaginations who dread the era of new proscriptions in the republic".[4]

Fairly significantly, Lamartine took the people to be responsible for earlier waves of repression triggering political exiles. This was also the point of view of the Spanish liberal, Sebastián de Miñano, who a few years earlier had written in a Spanish journal published in Paris: "were the people, or, so to say, the plebs not to take part, as they usually do, in political dissent, acting as judge and executioner over those of whom they know nothing and have no wish to know whether they are criminal or innocent, whether they were right or not, on the point which gave rise to the discord, then emigrations would be far less frequent, less numerous, and of course less long".[5]

Indisputably, revolutions and counterrevolutions by the people did cause a large number of exiles in the nineteenth century. Nevertheless, state repression played a far more decisive role. The term used by Lamartine, "proscription", was very little used by the authorities in the nineteenth century because it referred to measures taken in ancient Rome to banish and repress political opponents.[6] Yet it was the reason driving many departures: the authorities thereby sought to conceal the nature of these measures to remove individuals. Proscription measures, though not the subject of this chapter, are central to understanding the dynamics of exile in the nineteenth century. On many occasions, departures were not initiated by those going into exile but stemmed from procedures to remove, expel, banish, or even deport them. The state opted to use police measures to force a certain number of its nationals to leave the territory. Joint committees set up by Louis Napoléon Bonaparte in the wake of the coup of December 2 provide

---

4 Alphonse de Lamartine, *Histoire de la révolution de 1848*, vol. 1 (Paris: Garnier frères, 1859), 338.
5 Sebastián de Miñano, "Emigraciones, emigrados," *Revista Enciclopédica* 6 (1843): 177.
6 Sylvie Aprile, "Proscription", lexicon on the AsileuropeXIX website, accessed April 9, 2021, https://asileurope.huma-num.fr/le-vocabulaire-de-lexil/proscription.

one well-known instance.⁷ Proscription, sometimes in the form of "transportation", to use the terminology of the period, when the authorities deported their opponents overseas to keep them at far remove, was a well-tried practice of France,⁸ Spain,⁹ Portugal,¹⁰ Great Britain,¹¹ and even Russia, which relegated its opponents to Siberia in a form of internal deportation.¹² Transportation was the political version of the deportation of common prisoners, and those condemned, after serving a fixed sentence, sometimes remained in permanent exile.

At a general level, Delphine Diaz has shown that these statuses and experiences were constantly changing under the July Monarchy in France. It is hard to distinguish between those undergoing expulsion, transportation, "voluntary" exile, or even leaving their country for non-political reasons.¹³ What was voluntary about an exile which occurred under the threat of being arrested, thrown into prison, or killed? What difference was there once abroad between those who had left of their own initiative and those banished by court ruling? The only real difference was no doubt the moment of departure: while expulsion and, even more obviously, transportation, were governed by an administrative or judicial procedure,¹⁴ there were many ways of heading into exile, most of which were characterized by ill-preparedness and urgency. For most exiles, their flight and crossing the border were preceded by days of wandering and laying low. The following pages focus on these moments of departure and arrival on foreign soil when exiles were looking for their first place of residence. How did the urgency affect their departure, the choice of the country they were fleeing to, the items they took with them, and the people they left with? What were the main factors influencing the conditions of their departure into exile?

---

7 Sylvie Aprile, Nathalie Bayon, and Laurent Clavier, *Comment meurt une République. Autour du 2 Décembre 1851* (Paris: Créaphis, 2004).
8 Louis-José Barbançon, *L'Archipel des forçats: Histoire du bagne de Nouvelle-Calédonie, 1863–1931* (Lille: Presses Universitaires du Septentrion, 2003).
9 Romy Sánchez and Juan Luis Simal, "Lexiques et pratiques du *destierro*. L'exil politique espagnol en péninsule et à l'Outre-mer, de 1814 aux années 1880," *Hommes & Migrations* 1321/2 (2018): 23–31.
10 Timothy Coates, *Convict Labor in the Portuguese Empire, 1740–1932* (Leiden/Boston: Brill, 2014).
11 See the cases mentioned in Miles Taylor, "The 1848 Revolutions and the British Empire," *Past and Present* 166/1 (2000): 146–180.
12 Saint-René Taillandier, "La Sibérie au XIXᵉ siècle," *Revue des Deux Mondes*, vol. 11(1855): 602–642.
13 Diaz, *Un asile pour tous les peuples*, 30–42.
14 The reader is referred back to chapter 2 in this book.

Candidates for exile

When people headed into exile, their social situation was primordial, for it determined how they traveled. Nineteenth-century literature and illustrations include a canonical image of heading into exile, namely the engraving published in the book by Jessie W. Mario, *Della vita di Giuseppe Mazzini*, depicting the Italian republican preparing to cross the border at an unspecified date. It shows Mazzini on a country road, standing near the carriage taking him abroad (no doubt in secrecy), gazing regretfully back at his homeland.[15] A man in bourgeois dress heading alone into exile, accompanied by those taking him through the mountains which henceforth stand between him and his country – such is the romantic and highly traditional portrayal of exile. But the sociology of nineteenth-century outcasts was in fact much more varied and complex. We shall try to nuance this portrait, which undeniably reflects one reality, by setting out a brief and no doubt incomplete typology of those departing.

The main difference among outcasts as they headed into exile was no doubt whether they had belonged to the military or had taken up arms. Soldiers often sought to procure civilian clothing, to hide or get rid of their arms, and sometimes their horses even, in order to conceal their military status from the authorities in the land of departure, as well as from those in the land of arrival who tended to look askance at the advent of armed men who might well sow political unrest. In the case of soldiers, departure was in no way a choice: they were pushed into exile by government troops and could not choose the country they fled to. In particular, after large-scale uprisings, entire military corps were sometimes pushed to cross the border. This was the case of the Polish officers who headed into exile on being defeated by the Russian army after the 1830–1831 revolution, most of whom settled in Western Europe, particularly in France and Belgium. In the latter country,[16] Jean-Baptiste Madou's engravings, far from showing them renouncing the attributes of their office, depict them still sporting their uniforms.[17] Equally, the thousands of Polish and Hungarian soldiers taken in by the Ottoman

---

[15] Antonin Durand, "Giuseppe Mazzini verso l'esilio", AsileuropeXIX website image bank accessed April 11, 2021, https://asileurope.huma-num.fr/ressources-iconographiques/giuseppe-mazzini-verso-lesilio-giuseppe-mazzini-sur-la-route-de-lexil.

[16] Delphine Diaz, "Exil et circulations politiques autour de 1830: les réfugiés étrangers en France," in *La Liberté guidant les peuples: les révolutions de 1830 en Europe*, ed. Sylvie Aprile et al. (Seyssel: Champ Vallon, 2013), 226–240; Goddeeris, *La Grande Émigration*.

[17] Delphine Diaz, "Madou, souvenirs d'émigration polonaise", AsileuropeXIX website image bank, accessed April 11, 2021, https://asileurope.huma-num.fr/ressources-iconographiques/jean-baptiste-madou-souvenirs-demigration-polonaise-1834.

Empire after the Russian army put down the Hungarian Revolution of 1848–1849 were not obliged by the Sublime Porte to disarm or demobilize. In exchange for converting to Islam, some continued their career as soldiers henceforth for the Ottoman Empire, such as the Polish general Józef Bem (1794–1850).[18]

The other case of mass military exile in nineteenth-century Europe was that of Spanish Carlists endeavoring to restore the ancien regime monarchy in Spain. On two occasions they conducted what amounted to a civil war against the Liberal government in Madrid. Their successive defeats, in 1840, then in 1876, led to the exile of the full-scale armies formed for their cause. It is estimated that 40,000 men arrived at the French border in 1839–1840, and 15,000 in 1876. Once again, it was uniformed, armed troops crossing the border, presenting formidable difficulties for the French authorities on how to manage them, and particularly how to disarm them, triggering tensions with Madrid.[19] In 1874, the French authorities had to face an influx of Spanish soldiers heading into exile along an ill-defined sea border: the region of Oran became a refuge for hundreds of cantonalists, supporters of a federal republic, who had embarked on a military vessel, *Numancia*, after their insurrection in south-eastern Spain was put down.[20] The great waves of republican exiles in 1939 were thus only the latest instance in a phenomenon tracing its roots back to the early decades of the nineteenth century.[21]

Heading into exile was an ambivalent experience for soldiers: if traveling alone or in a small group, they had to conceal their status and pass themselves off as civilians; if traveling as a military corps, they formed a mass migration, states' handling of which needs to be examined. Their case leads us to nuance the classical image of the refugee, often described as a political opponent obliged to flee his or her country alone and in secrecy. There were fewer comparable cases of mass civilian departures, except when forced to leave by govern-

---

18 Katarzyna Papież and Hugo Vermeren, "Itinéraire collectif des réfugiés polonais dans l'Empire ottoman après la révolution hongroise, 1849", map section on the AsileuropeXIX website, accessed April 11, 2021, accessed April 11, 2021, https://asileurope.huma-num.fr/cartotheque/itineraire-collectif-des-refugies-polonais-dans-lempire-ottoman-apres-la-revolution-hongroise-1849.
19 Alexandre Dupont, "Entre exil et emprisonnement, l'originale expérience des carlistes en France (1868–1876)," in *Arrachés et déplacés. Réfugiés politiques, prisonniers de guerre et déportés (1789–1918)*, ed. Nicolas Beaupré and Karine Rance (Clermont-Ferrand: Presses de l'Université Blaise Pascal, 2016), 145–164; Tronco, *Les Carlistes espagnols dans l'Ouest de la France, 1833–1883* (Rennes: Presses Universitaires de Rennes, 2010).
20 Jeanne Moisand, *Les Fédérés du Numancia. Une Commune espagnole et ses mondes* (Paris: Libertalia, 2021</litr>, forthcoming).
21 Jordi Canal (ed.), *Exilios. Los éxodos políticos en España, siglos XV-XX* (Madrid: Sílex, 2007).

ments, such as when the Austrian authorities forcibly embarked Poles on the *Gian Matteo* heading for the United States in 1849.[22] Civilians generally left on their own or in small groups, not least as a way to slip undetected past the authorities.

This should not lead us to adopt too uniform a picture of civilians forced to leave their home country in nineteenth-century Europe. For many of the men were often accompanied by women and/or by children. As a matter of fact, this was also a major factor influencing departure, for leaving with a family entailed a more complex organization, together with greater thought about the destination and about settling there. More time was thus needed to organize the trip, which could not be clandestine.[23] If the family in exile is still a quite new topic of research, various studies have shown how such collective departure could fundamentally alter the conditions of exile.[24]

This book contains a specific chapter on the topic of female exiles,[25] but we may already note the important role they played when heading into exile.[26] Because women were reputed not to be involved in politics, they attracted far less suspicion from the authorities, and could thus leave a country more easily. On being exiled in London after the coup of December 2, 1851, Victor Schœlcher could count on the devotion of his housekeeper, Madame Constance, who shuttled back and forth between Paris and London to meet her master's material needs.[27] Wives often accompanied their husbands into exile, or else joined them there, and were sometimes accompanied by children, making it a family experience. The 1876 painting by the Carlist José Rodríguez Gil showing a Carlist family exiled in Orleans illustrates this, depicting three Carlist officers, visibly of different generations, accompanied by a woman and a child.[28] Although this was very much a minority phenomenon, it acts as a reminder that exile in nine-

---

22 Diaz, *Un asile pour tous les peuples*, 7.
23 As the letters of Jenny Marx illustrate: Karl Marx et Jenny Marx, *Lettres d'amour et de combat*, translated into French and presented by Jacques-Olivier Bigot (Paris: Payot et Rivages, 2013).
24 Tóth, *An Exiled Generation* (New York: Cambridge University Press, 2014); Delphine Diaz, Antonin Durand et Romy Sánchez, "Dans l'intimité de l'exil," *Revue d'Histoire du XIXe siècle* 61 (2020).
25 The reader is referred to chapter 6 in this book.
26 Sylvie Aprile, "De l'exilé à l'exilée: une histoire sexuée de la proscription politique outre-Manche et outre-Atlantique sous le Second Empire," *Le Mouvement Social*, 225/4 (2008): 27–38.
27 Letter 54, Brussels, January 4, 1852, *Correspondance de Victor Schoelcher présentée par Nelly Schmidt* Paris: Maisonneuve et Larose,1995), 200–201.
28 Alexandre Dupont, interpretation of "Emigración carlista par Jose Rodriguez Gil", AsileuropeXIX website, accessed April 11, 2021, https://asileurope.huma-num.fr/ressources-iconographiques/emigracion-carlista-par-jose-rodriguez-gil-1876.

teenth-century Europe has links with the history of gender and the family, with women and children following men into exile, after a certain time lag in some cases, when it was not the women who were obliged to leave because of their own political activities.

Fig. 2. José Rodríguez Gil, *Emigración Carlista*, 1876. Private collection, Biarritz.

Lastly, in addition to gender as a factor, we need to add the social dimension. While the position of those hit by proscription was undeniably upended, different social classes were affected differently. Most of those heading into exile in the middle decades of the nineteenth century came from the elites, or at least from the wealthy classes. Three reasons explain this: departure required financial means, at least while traveling; repression mainly affected leading political figures, often from the bourgeoisie and the educated classes; and the confrontation between liberalism and counterrevolution shaping European politics at least through to the middle of the century opposed two political cultures with substantial backing in the wealthier social strata. This elitist nature of political migration in the nineteenth century also led to another form of collectively organized departure: for many members of the aristocracy and the upper-middle class, going into exile involved taking their servants with them. Though appearing infrequently in the sources, they were an integral part of these journeys, which were hence more planned and organized.[29]

As the example of the servants' shows, one should not overlook the fact that ordinary people were also part of the many nineteenth-century waves of exile: first, because certain large-scale uprisings, such as that of the Carlists or Hungarians mentioned earlier, attracted large numbers of the people; second, because the process of democratization at work throughout the century gradually strengthened the role of the general populace in political life; and third, because European politics and the repression brought to bear on it also cast workers out onto the roads of exile.[30]

Preparations

The place of initial residence also played a major role in the conditions shaping departure. Crossing the border was a common occurrence for those living in its vicinity, offering a classical way of taking provisional refuge. There is no need to go as far back as the second half of the eighteenth century when Voltaire famously settled in Ferney, close to Switzerland to find examples of this.[31] Throughout the nineteenth century, a certain number of border zones played a privileged role in political dissent, for the traditional structure of transborder mobility provided protagonists with escape routes to host countries where they could draw on tacit support or assistance. Peter MacPhee's study of politicization processes in the Pyrénées-Orientales at the end of the July Monarchy and beginning of the Second Empire is illuminating in this respect, showing the extent to which the transborder structure of left-and right-wing opposition

---

29 In 1835, the Prefect of the Bas-Rhin thus pointed out that the Princess of Beira, an important figure of the counter-revolution at the time, had passed through Mainz on her journey of exile between the United Kingdom and Piedmont, with "her retinue [...] composed of 45 people, 8 of whom were priests". Archives Départementales du Bas-Rhin – 3 M 62, Letter from the prefect of the Bas-Rhin to the minister of the interior, July 15th 1835.
30 Additionally, several studies suggest we should adopt a more flexible reading of social classifications, and avoid too strict a separation between these exiles and immigrants who left their country to flee poverty during the early decades of the nineteenth century. See José C. Moya, *Cousins and Strangers: Spanish Immigrants in Buenos Aires, 1850–1930* (Los Angeles: University of California Press, 1998).
31 Writing on March 5, 1762 to Cardinal de Bernis "I have one foot in France and the other in Switzerland", *cf. Œuvres complètes de Voltaire. Correspondance, deuxième partie* (Paris: Leroi, 1835), 5134.

to the conservative liberal regimes in both countries was a decisive factor in their effectiveness, allowing protagonists to slip easily over the border to escape prosecution. The existence of a mountain chain that people had crossed throughout the ages, particularly for illegal activities, made it easier for people to pass, and harder for states to monitor them.[32]

For inhabitants living inland, and for those living in towns, surveillance and monitoring together with the lack of transit networks were significant handicaps which often delayed and imperiled their departure. Victor Schœlcher's correspondence, mentioned earlier, provides one example of illicit border crossings no doubt relying on an organization, while also showing how destabilizing such an enforced situation could be. Schœlcher, who was involved in attempts in Paris to resist the coup by Louis Napoléon Bonaparte, was forced to flee the repression put in place over the following days. He crossed the French border to Switzerland at Les Brenets, accompanied by two seminarists, the brothers Simon and Alphonse Blanc, and their uncle Jean-François Blanc, the economist at the seminary on Rue des Feuillantines in Paris where Schœlcher had been in hiding for three weeks. He then crossed into Belgium, wearing a cassock, and settled in London in January 1852 after nearly a month on the roads. In a letter he refers to "this flight, all alone, in the harshest of cold weather, with a disguised name and costume, the need to adapt my language to my clothing, and, all the time, all the time, the prospect of exile ahead of me".[33] Throughout the period, the way people traveled, and even their attitude and clothing, were shaped by this need for secrecy. Victor Hugo assumed the persona of a common man, Victor Schœlcher that of a priest, and Honoré Préveraud disguised himself as a woman.[34] These episodes occurred on the Paris-Brussels train, a main transport route where there was a permanent risk of being checked. Borders became thicker, and stations and ports were watched more closely.[35]

Unlike those living near the border, for whom exile was often brief and close to home, those living inland were obliged to leave their life behind them. In many cases, they had to abandon their friends and family, who did not always follow them into exile. In addition to the attendant isolation, departure could

---

[32] Peter McPhee, *Les Semailles de la République dans les Pyrénées-Orientales, 1846–1852: classes sociales, culture et politique* (Perpignan: Les Publications de l'Olivier, 1995).
[33] Letter 52, Brussels, Tuesday September 30, *Correspondance de Victor Schœlcher*, edited by Nelly Schmidt, 190.
[34] Sylvie Aprile, "Expériences et représentations de la frontière. Proscrits et exilés au milieu du XIXe siècle," *Hommes & Migrations* 1321 (2018): 78.
[35] Torsten Feys, "Riding the Rails of Removal: the Impact of Railroads on Border Controls and Expulsion Practices," *Journal of Transport History* 40/2 (2019): 189–210.

lead to a loss of economic and social position. Women thus regularly found themselves head of the household which had stayed behind, a role they had to assume while working to reunite the family in a single place. This situation explains why certain exiles were so brief, such as that of the Carlists in France, which in most cases, whether in 1840 or 1876, did not last more than a few months. When the harvest season arrived, the peasants – who formed the majority of the Carlist troops – submitted to the Madrid government and went home to work in the fields.[36]

Going into exile also implied leaving behind a social position, job, and home. In addition to the relegations, re-classifications, and ruptures entailed by exile, a topic studied later on, departure could also mean a definitive break with a prior existence. Perhaps the clearest example is that of exiled princes, though this is scarcely representative of the common experience of outcasts. Many ruling families toppled by revolution were forced to live in exile throughout the century.[37] While doing their best after leaving their country to maintain court life and the distinction practices of the European elite, few of these crowned heads were able to draw on the fabulous riches available to Francis V, Duke of Modena, who, on being chased from power by the *Risorgimento* settled in Venice, where he used his fortune to foment counterrevolution throughout Europe.[38]

For most exiles, the economic consequences of departure were less symbolic, and hence more serious. The confiscation and sequestration of nineteenth-century political exiles' assets have been examined in a recent issue of *Mélanges de l'École française de Rome*,[39] and the programmatic value of these articles – all about the Italian peninsula – emphasizes the scale of this continued repression by the authorities, coming on top of banishment or departure. Another practice used by governments to repress political opponents who had left the country was to seize any remaining assets they had in the country of departure. In

---

[36] Sophie Firmino, "*Les Réfugiés carlistes en France de 1833 à 1843*" (PhD diss., Université François Rabelais de Tours, 2000); Dupont, *Une internationale blanche*, chapter 11.
[37] Bruno Dumons (ed.), *Rois et princes en exil: une histoire transnationale du politique dans l'Europe du XIXe siècle* (Paris: Riveneuve, 2015).
[38] Pierre Larousse, *Grand Dictionnaire Universel Larousse* (Paris: Administration du grand Dictionnaire universel, 1878), vol. 16, 847.
[39] Catherine Brice, "Politique et propriété: confiscation et séquestre des biens des exilés politiques au XIXe siècle. Les bases d'un projet," *Mélanges de l'École française de Rome – Italie et Méditerranée modernes et contemporaines*, 129 – 2, accessed April 11, 2021, http://journals.open edition.org/mefrim/3095; DOI: 10.4000/mefrim.3095.

France, the imperial regime also turned to the compulsory sale of assets. Sylvain Fameau, a lawyer at La Flèche in Sarthe, had been unable to sell his practice before going into exile on Jersey, and so it was the state which received the sale price.[40] The case of François Rousseau, a lawyer and briefly mayor of Clamecy in Nièvre, was similar.[41] His practice was sold for Fr.20,000, though he said it was worth four times that amount, and his house was sold for a knockdown Fr.12,000 despite being valued at Fr.150,000. The Rousseaus lived in Brussels in diminished circumstances for ten years, selling their silverware and contracting debts. Being ill, Rousseau was unable to find a paid position and died in 1866. These measures destabilizing exiles' socio-economic position are no doubt crucial for assessing the full impact of departure.

Escapees

Without the situation being strictly one of expulsion proper, leaving the country did not always stem from a voluntary decision or a strategy to flee before repression struck. Many exiles were in fact forced, being the only way to avoid prison or execution, with correspondingly little or no choice about the country and organization of the journey. In certain cases, the authorities themselves suggested exile as an alternative to imprisonment. In February 1834, Étienne Cabet stood trial on criminal charges for publishing two articles in his newspaper, *Le Populaire*, one of which voiced support for Polish exiles expelled to America. On being sentenced to two years in prison, Cabet opted for a revised sentence of five years in exile.[42]

In many other cases, departure was a way of escaping after days or months of incarceration. Some escapes are still famous, these eventful and at times fantastic departures having been cast in heroic terms. Such is notably the case of the flight by the German democrat Gottfried Kinkel, who during the night of November 6 to 7, 1850 managed to escape from what was reputed to be the securest prison in Prussia, assisted by his wife and a young activist, Carl Schurz. The two men took refuge in Scotland, then London, before Kinkel embarked on a tour which took him across the Atlantic. Recent research suggests that the Prussian author-

---

40 Archives nationales de France, F^{15} 4081, Fameau file. He was "reduced" to giving music and French lessons to stave off misfortune.
41 Archives nationales de France, F^{15} 4060, Rousseau file.
42 Jules Prudhommeaux, "Un commis voyageur en communisme icarien. Chameroy, disciple de Cabet," *Revue d'histoire du XIXe siècle* 120 (1927): 25.

ities probably turned a blind eye to his escape and departure, which rid them of a political opponent whose imprisonment had been resoundingly denounced in European public opinion.[43]

There were also less spectacular escapes, such as those of people sentenced to prison or internment and transported to Algeria, who told of their voyage to Spain and Great Britain. Such was the case of Victor Frond, whose perilous escape punctuated by numerous setbacks was recounted by Victor Hugo in *Histoire d'un crime*.[44] On being detained in the small port of Dellys in the company of two other banished individuals, the three of them managed to embark on a Neapolitan fishing boat which took them to Algiers. Once there, after having scraped together the sum of Fr.750, they left Algeria on a French boat which was forced back by a storm. They set off again three days later, disembarking near Alicante in equally complicated circumstances due to customs patrols. The escapees were then taken aboard a third ship, once again clandestinely. They then passed via Gibraltar, Cadiz, and Lisbon, before setting sail for Southampton and then London. These mishaps meant the journey was lengthy, and expensive. At times they had to work to pay their way, at others they received subscriptions from countrymen they met in the various places along their journey, either refugee Frenchmen like themselves or expatriates, who also helped them to travel towards their final destination by writing letters of recommendation.

We thus need to do away with an overly schematic division within proscriptions: while departure was associated for most exiles with the arrival in power of a new regime, with repression of a revolution or civil war, it was not always conducted in haste. It was sometimes deferred and fitted in better with the plans and objectives of the would-be departee. Sometimes departure only took place a few years after being interned or imprisoned, in which case it was easier to join an existing exiled community able to take in newcomers and share its experience. A certain number of detainees requested an "exile permit" to escape the listlessness of internment and a life without professional prospects. Léonard Peyrusson, a confectioner at Saint-Léonard, left for Valparaiso; Charles Leroy opted for California.[45] In his memoirs, Gustave Lefrançais goes over the journey that took him to London, the exiles' capital. On being sentenced to internment in the town of Dijon, he was unhappy there:

---

43 See Sylvie Aprile's introduction to Karl Marx & Friedrich Engels, *Les Grands hommes de l'exil* (Marseille: Agone, 2015). For an account of the escape, see Carl Schurz, *The Reminiscences of Carl Schurz* (New York: McClure Company, 1907), vol. 1, chapter 10.
44 Hugo, *Histoire d'un crime*, 620–623.
45 Archives nationales de France, F^{15} 411 Haute-Vienne, Peyrusson file; AN F^{15} 4111, dossier 12.

The obligation bearing on me to not leave the town at all became so odious that, after one month, unable to bear it any longer, I requested a passport for England. It was granted all the more readily, the secretary at the prefecture told me, as they had been going to offer it to me. No doubt I had thereby found the means not to die of hunger here. My request set everyone at ease. So here I was, armed once again with the famous yellow passport (with an obligatory itinerary) with London as my destination, stipulating I was forbidden from passing via Paris.[46]

Exile was a journey, and whether or not one was prepared for it, whether or not it was planned in advance or conducted in haste, it acted as a reminder both of the considerable distance – often the social distance – and of the new ties built up between those circulating for their trade and those pushed out onto the roads and high seas. Collusion, suspicion, and betrayal were at the heart of a world made up of mountains and shipwrecks, and in which identity papers acted as precious talismans.

On the move

Belongings

Whether their departure was prepared or precipitate, exiles only rarely set out in a state of absolute vagrancy. The time spent traveling and its attendant mishaps, with the ordeal of passing the border, implied taking some personal effects, money, and papers. Nevertheless, for some, exile meant going underground, accompanied by a state of almost complete penury. Victor Frond and his companions traveled without any luggage, carrying only the few francs they had earned or were given.[47] On arriving in Southampton with Fr.125, they had just enough money to eat at the port then head off for London. It was because they were escaped prisoners that they had no luggage and traveled clandestinely. Yet traveling empty-handed could arouse the suspicion of the police and customs officers. When Gustave Lefrançais went into exile for the second time after the Commune, he left his home – where he had been hiding so as not to attract the attention of any informers – without luggage or any other item. Madame B., who he was to join in Geneva using her husband's identity, had taken the precaution of leaving their baggage at the Gare de Lyon in advance. They thus hoped to pass them-

---

[46] Gustave Lefrançais, *Souvenirs d'un révolutionnaire de juin 1848 à la Commune*, (Paris: La Fabrique, 2013) 160–161.
[47] Hugo, *Histoire d'un crime*, 626.

selves off as a couple of tourists going to Switzerland and thus not attract any attention. In the eyes of the police, travelers were defined "by their baggage as much as by their appearance".[48] German forty-eighters, wishing to travel to the United States in the wake of the failed revolution, did not bother taking any luggage but instead took money and papers, hoping to travel unhindered across Switzerland, Belgium, and France before crossing the Atlantic.[49]

In order to go into exile, one had to carry money, especially if one wished to increase the chances of success and avoid being taken for a tramp, a category under increasing surveillance and repression throughout the century.[50] During the journey money was needed to move around, to obtain food, and to negotiate – especially with those helping travelers to cross borders, often smugglers with intricate knowledge of secret pathways away from the watchful eyes of police or customs officers.[51] But also to negotiate an identity, in which there was an illicit trade, which, though difficult to detect, was associated with practices to circumvent regulations already familiar from the time of economic migrations. Once in exile, identity was often borrowed, and sometimes paid for. Lastly, to negotiate secrecy, that of the innkeeper, hotelier, fisherman, or peasant. As Nancy L. Green points out, the role played by secrecy in clandestine traveling increased in step with improvements to border controls.[52]

In his largely autobiographical novel, the Ligurian author Giovanni Ruffini, a member of Giuseppe Mazzini's *Giovine Italia*, tells of his escape to France after being found guilty in 1833 of conspiring against the Piedmontese government. After crossing the border, having been misled by smugglers he encountered on the way, he had to swim across the river Var and fainted during this perilous undertaking. On coming to, on the bank, his hero, called Lorenzo Benoni, feels his pockets and is relieved to notice that "I still had on my person the objects that

---

48 Arnaud-Dominique Houte, "Le migrant du gendarme. Le quotidien de la surveillance dans le département du Nord pendant la première moitié du XIXe siècle," in *Police et migrants*, 240.
49 Hildegard Binder Johnson, "Adjustment to the United States," in *The Forty-Eighters. Political Refugees of the German Revolution of 1848*, ed. A. E. Zucker, (New York: Columbia University Press, 1950), 43–78.
50 See in particular Nicolas Veysset, "La fin des dépôts de mendicité au début de la IIIe République," in *Les Exclus en Europe 1830–1939*, ed. André Gueslin and Dominique Kalifa (Paris: Les Éditions de l'Atelier, 1999) 112–123, and Jean-François Wagniart, *Le Vagabond à la fin du XIXe siècle* (Paris: Belin, 1999), 103–105.
51 Simonetta Tombaccini-Villefranque, "La frontière bafouée: migrants clandestins et passeurs dans la vallée de la Roya (1920–1940)," *Cahiers de la Méditerranée* 58 (1999): 79–95.
52 Nancy L. Green, "Trans-frontières: pour une analyse des lieux de passage," *Socio-anthropologie* 6 (1999): 48.

are most important to me, my purse and my passport".⁵³ What all exiles had in common during their journeying, perhaps to a greater extent than money even, was the need to be able to produce a genuine, fake, or borrowed passport at any given moment. Better not to be arrested for "lack of papers" on being stopped on the road, in a railway station, or at a port. "My first thought [...] was to get my passport inspected",⁵⁴ noted the Roman exile Bartolomeo del Vecchio on leaving the Papal States for Geneva in July 1849. After having been turned down by the French and British legations, he eventually obtained a travel document from the Sardinian consul after much negotiation. A passport – considered by nineteenth-century administrations as irreplaceable as it held out the prospect that the authorities could "watch over" travelers⁵⁵ – was an indispensable document for exiles to prove their identity as an outcast (or else their borrowed identity) and that they came from a proscriptive state. They could cost large sums of money, as in Spain and certain Italian states, making them prohibitively expensive for some.⁵⁶

Passports helped travelers to cross "paper borders",⁵⁷ but were also useful for moving around countries. In France during the July Monarchy, refugees took their passports with them whenever they traveled. They were obliged to have them inspected in each town or village they passed through. Their passport officialized their status as refugees, and proved their right to asylum and the attendant subsidies. Thus the passports of the Carlist exiles in Alençon whom the French government wish to send back to Spain in 1824 bore the mention that the latter were not entitled to subsidies, unlike those in the depot at Le Mans.⁵⁸ But a passport did not guarantee the right to reside in exile. Many Polish refugees who arrived in France after the 1831 Warsaw uprising were not authorized to reside there despite having passports issued by French consulates abroad.⁵⁹

---

53 Giovanni Ruffini, *Lorenzo Benoni. Mémoires d'un réfugié italien* (Paris: Magnin, Blanchard et Cⁱᵉ, 1859), 337.
54 Bartolomeo del Vecchio, *Un voyage de Rome à Genève*, 5.
55 Gérard Noiriel, *État, nation et immigration. Vers une histoire du pouvoir* (Paris: Belin 2001), 311 *et seq*. On changes to passports in nineteenth-century Europe, see John Torpey, *The Invention of the Passport. Surveillance, Citizenship and the State* (Cambridge: Cambridge University Press, 2000).
56 Vincent Denis, "Le contrôle de la mobilité à travers les passeports sous l'Empire," in *Police et migrants*, 85.
57 On exiles' representations of the border in the middle of the nineteenth century, see Aprile, "Expériences et représentations", 78.
58 Jules Mathorez, "Les réfugiés politiques espagnols dans l'Orne au XIXᵉ siècle," *Bulletin Hispanique* 4 (1915): 263.
59 Diaz, *Un asile pour tous les peuples*, 119.

During this century of migrations, there were other types of papers, some assimilated to passports, proving the identity or situation of exiles: visas, safe-conducts,⁶⁰ itinerary documents, and military or workers passbooks, together with letters of presentation and recommendation which were already indispensable in the nineteenth century for facilitating transit. In exile they acted as a form of recognition and identification, making it easier to travel to and then cross the border. Thus in the mid-1870s, Spanish Carlists made excessive use of letters provided by an employee at the Société des Mines de Carmaux giving them access to French territory.⁶¹ There was a gradation among letters of recommendation: support was required for distant travels, particularly across the Atlantic. Amédée Jacques, a philosophy teacher at the Lycée Louis le Grand, whence he was dismissed in 1850, arrived in Montevideo on July 13, 1852, with a small sum of money and, especially, a letter of recommendation from Alexander von Humboldt, an undisputed authority on Latin America who vouched for Jacques' diplomas and ambitions in the field of education.⁶²

The republican journalist Edmond Plauchut, a voluntary expatriate after the collapse of the Second Republic, was saved by an almost involuntary recommendation. It was because he was bearing letters from George Sand, with whom he had corresponded since 1848, that he was taken in by a rich Portuguese gentleman after being shipwrecked on Cape Verde when heading into exile in Singapore. All he managed to save was the casket containing Sand's letters, on which he placed great value, which turned out to be a wise choice earning him this revealing declaration by his benefactor:

> You are French, and shipwrecked; these letters prove that you have been distinguished by the greatest literary author of our period, by a genius for whom my father, who died here after being deported for his republican ideas, professed keen and lively admiration. In taking you in, I honor the memory of my dear father. It is more than sufficient, you may see, for you to deserve my sympathy. Be my friend; as of today, I am honored to be yours.⁶³

---

60 On the origins and similarities of passports and safe-conducts since the ancien regime, see Daniel Nordman, "Sauf-conduits et passeports," in *Dictionnaire de l'Ancien Régime. Royaume de France, XVIᵉ-XVIIIᵉ siècle*, ed. by Lucien Bély (Paris: Presses Universitaires de France, 1996), 1122–1124.

61 Sylvie Premisler, "L'émigration politique espagnole en France (1872–1876, 1894–1912)," *Cahiers du monde hispanique et luso-brésilien* 21 (1973): 121.

62 Patrice Vermeren, *Amédée Jacques, le rêve démocratique de la philosophie d'une rive à l'autre de l'Atlantique*, suivi d'*Essai de philosophie populaire* (Paris: L'Harmattan, 2001).

63 Edmond Plauchut, *Le Tour du monde en cent-vingt jours; Un naufrage aux îles du Cap Vert; Une excursion à la tombe de Magellan* (Paris: Librairie internationale, 1865), 110.

Having letters of recommendation enabled exiles to shrug off their anonymity, to a certain extent, and to win recognition from their political leaders and their sympathizers abroad. As we have seen, at times a letter of recommendation could shade into a relic carried as a proof of one's loyalty to those left behind. The documents found in the possession of the carbonaro Jean Berra in 1824 are an illustration of this: "the effects of Mr. Jean Berra, who says he is Piedmontese, taken prisoner of war in Spain and sent to England, included a voluminous notebook bearing the title: *Manoscritto enciclopedico ad uso di Giuseppe Rossi*, containing a catechism for use by the carbonari. Mr. Berra declared that this notebook had ended up in his possession after the death of Mr. Rossi which occurred in 1823, in the vicinity of Tortosa".[64] In a more personal register, Victorine Brocher (1839–1921), before leaving Paris during the final bloody week of the Commune to go to Switzerland, went to visit her children's grave where she retrieved a small necklace of pearls hanging on their tomb to take with her into exile.[65]

By foot, by boat and by carriage

The engraving by Marie-Cécile Goldsmid, long attributed to Frédéric Sorrieu, called "Faire ses adieux aux exilés", shows a distraught group of women and children surrounding an allegory of the republic. They remain behind as boats sail away. This image is a reminder of how the transport revolution played a key role in connecting sometimes very distant places. It was the development of railways and especially the generalization of steamboats that turned the history of exiles into a mass transcontinental phenomenon, notably towards the Americas.[66] This globalization of exile is the topic of a specific chapter, but it should be pointed out that for many exiles departing meant definitively leaving old Europe behind.[67]

Sea transport also played a key role in intra-European exiles. One major reason for this was the emergence as of 1815 of the United Kingdom as a beacon for

---

[64] Letter from the ministry of the interior to the Sardinian embassy in Paris, July 8, 1824, Archives nationales de France, F7 6748, Jean Berra file.
[65] Victorine Brocher, *Souvenirs d'une morte vivante. Une femme dans la Commune de 1871*, foreword by Lucien Descaves (Lausanne: A. Lapie, 1909), 308.
[66] Torsten Feys, "Bounding mass migration across the Atlantic: European shipping companies between U.S. border building and evasion, 1860s-1920s," *Journal of Modern European History* 14 (2016): 78–100.
[67] See chapter 7 in this book.

freedom in Europe, and place of refuge for exiles irrespective of political tendency.[68] Getting there implied traveling by boat, as illustrated by the engraving published in November 1851 in the *Illustrated London News* on the occasion of Lajos Kossuth's arriving in England. It shows the leader of the Hungarian uprising leaving Southampton, where he had arrived by boat, to the cheers of onlookers.[69] Another famous image is that of Victor Hugo's departure from the port of Antwerp setting sail for England on the way to Jersey. The central role played by the Channel Islands of Jersey and Guernsey in the history of European exile adds another layer to this picture of sailing to even the closest destinations. While the islands famously took in Hugo and French outcasts, there were also many Poles, Hungarians, and Italians present. For the latter, especially for Neapolitans and Sicilians, North Africa was another place of refuge, one that could be easily reached by sea. In the early 1830s, the July Monarchy sent refugees (especially Poles), once again by boat, to take part in the incipient conquering and colonization of Algeria.[70] Coastal navigation often provided a possible means of escape or clandestine departure.

More generally, the geography of exile in nineteenth-century Europe was dominated by islands and ports. The Ionian Islands (particularly Corfu) for supporters of the *Epanastasis*,[71] Malta and the islands in the Strait of Sicily for those of the Risorgimento,[72] Heligoland for German revolutionaries,[73] the Channel Islands for opponents of the Second Empire,[74] Constantinople for revolutionaries across the entire eastern Mediterranean basin,[75] Marseille for Spaniards and nationals

---

68 Porter, *The Refugee Question*.
69 See Fabrice Bensimon, "Kossuth quittant le port de Southampton, 1851", accessed April 11, 2021, https://asileurope.huma-num.fr/ressources-iconographiques/m-kossuth-leaving-the-docks-at-southampton; Frank Tibor, "Lajos Kossuth and the Hungarian Exiles in London," in *Exiles from European Revolutions*, 121–134.
70 Delphine Diaz, "Indésirables en métropole, utiles en Algérie?," 187–204.
71 Andréas Rizopoulos, "Activités maçonniques avec arrière-plan politique – et réciproquement – en Grèce au XIXe siècle," *Cahiers de la Méditerranée* 72 (2006): 203–224.
72 Gilles Pécout, "Pour une lecture méditerranéenne et transnationale du Risorgimento," *Revue d'histoire du XIXe siècle* 44 (2012): 29–47.
73 Jan Rüger, *Heligoland: Britain, Germany, and the Struggle for the North Sea*, (Oxford: Oxford University Press, 2017), chapter 2.
74 Aprile, *Le Siècle des exilés*, 117.
75 See Enrico de Leone, "L'apport des patriotes italiens dans la formation de la Turquie moderne," *Turcica*, Paris, vol. 3 (1971), 181–192; Emine Türk, "Il contributo degli esuli italiani alla modernizzazione dello stato ottomano," in *Gli Italiani di Istanbul: figure, comunità e istituzioni dalle riforme alla repubblica, 1839–1923*, ed by Attilio De Gasperis and Roberta Ferrazza (Turin: Fondazione Giovanni Agnelli, 2007), 287–94.

from the Italian states,[76] and ports on the English Channel for Portuguese liberals at the beginning of the century[77] – all these places illustrate the preponderance of sea transport in the geography of nineteenth-century exile.

Nevertheless, the roads of exile continued to be followed by foot on many occasions, or, if one had the means, on horseback or by carriage. When there was uncertainty about how they would be received on arrival, outcasts often preferred to avoid railways and ships. This was the case for example of the Italian exiles traveling to Albania during the years 1821–1822, who preferred to travel by land, which was "longer and more tiring, but safer".[78] In the winter of 1831–1832, the Poles traveling to France from Warsaw walked across Prussia and then Bavaria. The lithograph by Jean-Baptiste Madou, "Le passage des Polonais par l'Allemagne", shows one of these migrations by foot, emphasizing how locals fraternized with exiles. The French republicans fleeing to Belgium after the coup of December 2, 1851, also traveled by foot, as Hugo notes in the chapter about their departure in *Histoire d'un crime* (1877).[79] The communards fleeing the final bloody week of the Commune twenty years later did likewise.[80] A certain number of itineraries continued to be used for a remarkably long time, as illustrated by the case of the French-Spanish border which was frequently crossed by those going into exile throughout the nineteenth century. A list of the various waves of Spanish exiles provides a telling example: Joseph I's afrancesados supporters in 1813–1814, liberals in 1814–1815, absolutists in 1820 and 1822, liberals once again in 1823, Carlists in 1840, then again in 1849, conservatives in 1854, then progressives in 1856, conservatives again in 1868, then republicans and Carlists 1875–1876. In addition to these large-scale departures, we need to add the many individuals or small groups going into exile throughout the period. French people also left their country to go to Spain. Lastly, in addition to these proscri-

---

76 Delphine Diaz and Hugo Vermeren, "Répartition des réfugiés à Marseille en 1853," map section of the AsileuropeXIX website, accessed April 11, 2021, https://asileurope.huma-num.fr/cartotheque/repartition-des-refugies-a-marseille-en-1853; Éliane Richard-Jalabert, "Marseille, ville refuge pour les libéraux espagnols, 1825–1848," *Annales du midi* vol. 72, fasc. 3, 51 (1960): 309–323.

77 Grégoire Bron, "L'exil libéral portugais du début du xixe siècle (1808–1834)," *Mélanges de la Casa de Velázquez* 48–1 (2018): 315–321.

78 Ersilio Michel, *Esuli italiani in Albania (1821–1859)* (Milan: Istituto per gli studi di politica internazionale, 1940).

79 Victor Hugo, *Histoire d'un crime*, part IV: La Victoire, chapter XII: Les expatriés. See too Aprile, "Expériences et représentations", 75–82.

80 Renaud Morieux, "La prison de l'exil, les réfugiés de la Commune entre les polices françaises et anglaises (1871–1880)," in *Police et migrants*.

bed departures, were the returns in the wake of amnesties or of political changes in the peninsula.[81]

All these comings and goings combine to build up a landscape of the roads of exile. They were still traveled mainly by foot, especially along the French-Spanish border. While certain important figures were entitled to the comfort of a carriage, such as Queen Isabella II heading into exile after the 1860s revolution, or traveled by horseback, such as the pretender Don Carlos in 1876, and while the coastal roads from Figueras to Banyuls-sur-Mer and from San Sebastián to Bayonne were suitable for vehicles and used regularly, the topography of the Pyrenees and the clandestine nature of heading into exile meant that most outcasts decided to walk or else travel by mule, a mode of transport better suited to mountain footpaths.[82] The itineraries they followed were those which had long been used for trade between populations along the border, whose help was often indispensable.[83] Certain crossing points, such as La Junquera in the Catalan mountains, were used once again during the *retirada* in 1939 under Francoism.[84] The persistence of these routes of exile in the Pyrenees is truly remarkable – but then the same observation could be made for the Jura and the Alps.[85] Over the course of the century, the representatives of virtually every political clan followed in each other's footsteps, or else passed each other by on the same mountain roads, at the same cols and crossing points even. These routes were the same as those used by smugglers, and in his memoirs, Ernest Cœurderoy tells of his discussions with his guide who viewed fugitives crossing the border to Switzerland as a hindrance since they attracted the police and interrupted normal business.

Land journeys by outcasts partly followed the course of those made during the early modern period. Thus Pius IX, fleeing by carriage to Gaeta in 1848, encountered the same mishap as Louis XVI nearly half a century earlier: when the pope was approaching the border with the Kingdom of the Two Sicilies, a coachman thought he recognized him from a portrait, even though he was disguised as

---

[81] Canal (ed.), *Exilios*.
[82] Jean-François Soulet, *Les Pyrénées au XIXe siècle* (Toulouse: Eché, 1987).
[83] José Antonio Perales Díaz, *Fronteras y contrabando en el Pirineo Occidental* (Pamplona: Gobierno de Navarra, 2004).
[84] Alain Tarrius and Olivier Bernet, *Mondialisation criminelle. La Frontière franco-espagnole de La Junquera à Perpignan* (Saint-Denis: Édilivre, 2014).
[85] Marie-Cécile Thoral, "Administrer la frontière: les fonctionnaires de l'Isère et la frontière franco-italienne de la Restauration à la Monarchie de Juillet," *Histoire, économie & société* 26/1(2007): 85–105.

an abbot.[86] Nevertheless, the appearance and rapid development of the railways in the second half of the nineteenth century altered the situation, for with the arrival of mass transport travelers were now more anonymous.[87] But this was not always the case. In late 1851 Edgar Quinet took the train from Paris to Belgium, and while his journey went unimpeded as far as Amiens, surveillance increased from that point on, and at Lille, all the carriages were systematically inspected. Quinet was almost arrested and was only saved when his travel companion, Princess Cantacuzino, managed to mislead the police as to his nationality by speaking to him in Vlach.[88] A few years later, the pope was also saved by the woman with whom he was traveling, the Countess Spaur, who managed to deflect the coachman's suspicions by talking to the former as if he were an abbot.

Eluding surveillance

Ruse was part of the ordeal of going into exile, and especially of crossing borders. It required a combination of improvisation and organization, experience and instinct. As Daniel Roche explains, stricter border checks, the increased surveillance of inns and lodgings, improvements to identification tools, and better diffusion of police information all incited people on the move to make use of stratagems to avoid being turned back or arrested. They made ready use of false documents, smugglers, and "strategies of disguise and multiple identities",[89] given that they were seeking to avoid the repression they had already fled by leaving their country. There were many different types of stratagem to avoid surveillance in the "territories of waiting",[90] the world of border checkpoints, ports, railway stations, inns and lodgings, boats, and trains constituting the experience of traveling into exile.

As mentioned earlier, borrowing an identity and using false documents were apparently very common practices for nineteenth-century refugees on the move.

---

86 Jules-Paul Tardivel, *Vie du pape Pie IX: ses œuvres et ses douleurs* (Paris: J. N. Duquet, 1878), 32–33.
87 François Caron, *Histoire des chemins de fer en France* (Paris: Fayard, 1997 and 2005).
88 Hugo, *Histoire d'un crime*, part 4, chapter 12.
89 Daniel Roche, "Contrôle de la mobilité et des migrants: principes et pratiques. Introduction," in *Police et migrants*, 23–32.
90 On this approach, see Laurent Vidal and Alain Musset, "L'attente comme état de la mobilité," in *Les Territoires de l'attente: Migrations et mobilités dans les Amériques (XIXe-XXIe siècle)*, ed by Laurent Vidal and Alain Musset (Rennes: Presses universitaires de Rennes, 2015), 19–28.

They are mentioned both in administrative sources and the various accounts left by exiles themselves, who sometimes tended to overestimate and romanticize their own role (memoirs, autobiographical novels, correspondence, etc.). Lorenzo Benoni, the hero of Giovanni Ruffini's largely autobiographical novel, travels under a false identity using a friend's passport to escape Piedmontese repression.[91] At this period, identity documents did not have photos, but instead contained a description of the individual's face and distinguishing characteristics.[92] It was thus impossible for the authorities who arrested him at Saint-Laurent-du-Var to distinguish him from his friend with an identical description.

Like this character, many exiles crossed borders using someone else's identity. For example, an exile from the Papal States, Angelo Frignani, on disembarking in Corsica in December 1829, passed through customs checks without any difficulty under the name of a young servant from Bologna.[93] While most fake passports were produced secretly by standard forgers, many people working in the administration or public forces also issued falsified documents.[94] For example, the Sardinian consul in Civitavecchia offered to obtain servants' papers to enable the Roman exile Bartolomeo del Vecchio to reach Switzerland.[95] Equally, many Spanish Carlists traveled with valid passports, issued in Andorra or by consuls of the Two Sicilies and of Hamburg, only under a false identity.[96] The use of fake passports was also sometimes "legalized" by host countries' consular authorities.[97]

Although the stratagems used and the passports shown in the 1860s could present many incongruities which did not seem to bother customs officials, as recounted by Amédée Saint-Ferréol[98] communards and anarchists were subject

---

[91] On presenting his passport to the mayor of Saint-Laurent-du-Var, he was told that it was not in order since it did not bear the visa of the French consul in Nice: Ruffini, *Lorenzo Benoni*, 337.
[92] On developments in police identification techniques, see in particular Ilsen About and Vincent Denis, *Histoire de l'identification*.
[93] Delphine Diaz and Hugo Vermeren, "Itinéraire d'Angelo Frignani (1802–1878), exilé des États pontificaux vers la France", map section on the AsileuropeXIX website, accessed April 11, 2021, https://asileurope.huma-num.fr/cartotheque/itineraire-dangelo-frignani-1802-1878-exile-des-etats-pontificaux-vers-la-france. Many examples are provided in Sylvie Aprile, "Expériences et représentations", 75–82.
[94] Vincent Denis, "Le contrôle de la mobilité à travers les passeports sous l'Empire," in *Police et migrants*, 87.
[95] Bartolomeo del Vecchio, *Un voyage de Rome à Genève ou mémoire d'un exilé*, (Geneva: Chez les principaux libraires, 1850), 5.
[96] Jeanine Sogigné Loustau, "Une micro-étude: les Carlistes en région Centre (1833–1876)," *Exils et migrations ibériques au XXe siècle* 5 (1998): 309.
[97] Diaz, *Un asile pour tous les peuples*, 121.
[98] Aprile, *Le Siècle des exilés*, 113.

to closer detection. Gustave Lefrançais dyed his hair white and was afraid of passing customs at Bellegarde where the travelers were taken off the train and subjected to lengthy interrogation. The journalist and socialist activist Louis Dramard, having boarded a train for Geneva, describes what he calls the "reign of the passport" facing communards who sought to avoid the many checks conducted by brigades of gendarmes and customs officials throughout the journey.[99] Disguises were part of this game of cat and mouse between exiles and policemen. As Denis Rolland and Luc Capdevila observe, "exile is a matter of representations".[100]

Over the course of the long nineteenth century, advances in the monitoring of communication channels, first at ports then in railway stations, developed in tandem with the growing number of political and economic migrations, particularly to the Americas.[101] The movements of exiles were closely watched. In June 1833 the French minister of the interior, Count of Argout, exhorted prefects to call on the National Guard, gendarmes, and customs officers to tighten border control and filter refugees entering French territory.[102] It was in fact mainly gendarmes who policed migrants.[103] Agents surveilling those traveling into exile were tasked with distinguishing between political exiles, criminals, deserters, and vagrants. For outcasts it was better to be able to prove their exiled status which prevented their being promptly dispatched back home.[104] Monitoring movements also involved setting up international police cooperation, to varying extents depending on the territories involved, resulting notably in the exchange of police information. From this point of view, the transnational tracking of anarchist militants as of the 1880s played a key role.[105] Surveillance also entailed recruiting spies tasked with watching exiles, both in their land of departure and

---

[99] Louis Dramard, *Voyages aux pays des proscrits: scènes de la vie d'exil* (Paris: C. Marpon et E. Flammarion, 1879), 13.
[100] Denis Rolland, Luc Capdevila, "France et Belgique, terres d'exil?," *Matériaux pour l'histoire de notre temps* 67(2002): 3.
[101] See in particular Céline Regnard, "Le maintien de l'ordre au défi de l'augmentation du transit migratoire. Marseille, New-York, 1855 – 1914," in *Policer les mobilités. Europe-États-Unis, XVIIIe-XXIe siècle*, ed. Anne Conchon, Laurence Montel, and Céline Regnard (eds.), (Paris: Éditions de la Sorbonne, 2018), 87 – 102.
[102] Archives nationales de France, F1a/2089, circular from the minister of the interior to the prefects, June 26, 1833.
[103] Houte, "Le migrant du gendarme," 235 – 249, 237.
[104] The reader is referred to chapter 2 for discussion of the expulsion of political refugees.
[105] Richard Bach Jensen, *The Battle against Anarchist Terrorism: an International History, 1878 – 1934* (Cambridge: Cambridge University Press, 2014).

in the host country. France, for example, used its consulates to build up a spy network in bordering countries. But exiles often managed to elude surveillance by spies, as illustrated by the reports from Jules Vallès in Switzerland, Belgium, and England in autumn 1872.[106]

In periods when larger numbers of people were forced to move, it was hard to avoid checks, be it before, during, or after crossing the border. Like today, the authorities sought to identify the most frequently used circuits to focus their activity on them. Ersilio Michel refers to the rigorous police surveillance in place as of 1849 of ships heading for Corsica from the ports of Livorno and Civitavecchia.[107] The port authorities checked people, their travel documents, and their luggage, trying especially to intercept any correspondence for exiles. As seen earlier, in the weeks following the repression of the Paris Commune by the Versailles army in the spring of 1871, railway stations in the capital and trains heading abroad were under continuous surveillance, to the extent that the travelers, exasperated by the ceaseless checks, reacted to crossing the border as if it were a liberation. Louis Dramard describes how passengers on the Paris-Geneva train roared in unison "Long live the Commune!" on crossing into Switzerland.[108] The tough, humiliating, and sometimes brutal nature of the checks are frequently mentioned in descriptions of political exiles' reactions, and indeed of travelers more generally. In 1823 the Spanish exile Turillos and his companions were humiliated by the French police.[109] During his travel in Spain in 1894, the traveler Guillaume Bernard was shocked by the inquisitorial stare of gendarmes at the Irun border.[110] On being forbidden from disembarking at Livorno then at Genoa, the Roman republicans thronging ships to flee papal repression contrasted their harsh treatment by the Austrian then Piedmontese authorities, with that received from "the ladies of Livorno" offering them flowers and oranges, and the people of Genoa sending them letters and presents.[111] After a humiliating interrogation by the Saint-Laurent-du-Var authorities during which he was accused of

---

106 Renaud Morieux, "La prison de l'exil. Les réfugiés de la Commune entre les polices françaises et anglaises (1871–1880)," 133–150.
107 Ersilio Michel, *Esuli e cospiratori italiani in Corsica (1850–1861)* (Milan: Tyrrhenia, 1929), 10.
108 Louis Dramard, *Voyages aux pays des proscrits: scènes de la vie d'exil* (Paris: C. Marpon et E. Flammarion, 1879), 20.
109 Jules Mathorez, "Les réfugiés politiques espagnols dans l'Orne au XIXe siècle," *Bulletin Hispanique* 4 (1915): 263.
110 Guillaume Bernard, *Quatre ans en exil*, (Lille: Maison de la bonne presse du Nord, 1894), 10.
111 Bartolomeo del Vecchio, *Un voyage de Rome à Genève ou mémoire d'un exilé* (Geneva: Chez les principaux libraires, 1850), 7.

being a deserter and a criminal, the character Lorenzo Benoni goes on to narrate the solicitude of the population, who give him new clothes and footwear.[112]

It was thus sometimes necessary to find a replacement itinerary. It was not that the "unclear borders" of the nineteenth century were already characterized by the materiality they have today.[113] In the late 1870s, the Pyrenean border was still notorious for being "excessively permeable" despite the presence of French troops,[114] as depicted in the novel by Pierre Benoit about the second Carlist war (1872–1876).[115] But with the development of border controls, people increasingly turned to paid guides to minimize the risks of slipping across the border. The figure of the border guide recurs throughout the history of nineteenth-century migrations, without ever coming sharply into focus, ranging from the lowly Pyrenean shepherd or smuggler profiting at times from his knowledge of informal circuits to the *"traficante d'emigrazione"* operating illegally in the ports of the Italian peninsula,[116] or the Marseille *"pisteur"* described by Émile Témime.[117] They were not all experienced professionals, and exiles also called on the assistance of friends and family, as shown by the example of mothers helping young Piedmontese republicans elude the vigilance of the Austrian police to slip across the Alpine border in the late 1850s.[118]

On arrival

Political exile, like any other migratory phenomenon, cannot be resumed to going from point of departure to point of arrival. Economists' attempts to

---

112 Ruffini, *Lorenzo Benoni*, 337.
113 Aprile, "Expériences et representations," 75–82.
114 Vincent Garmendia, "Note sur la présence carliste en Aquitaine à l'époque de la seconde guerre carliste," *Bulletin Hispanique* 96/2 (1994): 437.
115 Pierre Benoit, *Pour Don Carlos* (Paris: Albin Michel, 1920) adapted for cinema by Jacques Lasseyne and Musidora in 1921.
116 Alida Clemente, "Il business del viaggio nella Napoli dell'emigrazione (1887–1925)," in *Il viaggio degli emigranti in America Latina tra Ottocento e Novecento*, ed Giuseppe Moricola (Napoli: Alfredo Guida, 2008), 21–46; Amoreno Martellini, "Il commercio dell'emigrazione: intermediari e agenti in Europa, in Africa e nel Levante," in Piero Bevilacqua, Andrea De Clementi, and Emilio Franzina, *Storia dell'emigrazione italiana, vol. 1, Partenze* (Roma: Donzelli, 2001), 293–308.
117 René Lopez, Émile Temime, *Migrance. Histoire des migrations à Marseille, L'expansion marseillaise et " l'invasion italienne "* (1830–1918) (Aix-en-Provence: Edisud, 1990), vol. 2.
118 *À nos alliés*, Almanach franco-italien illustré pour 1860, Milan: B. Ponti Libraire-éditeur, 1860.

model migratory phenomenon were long limited to balancing push factors explaining departures with pull factors leading to the choice of where to arrive. Whatever the heuristic potential of such models, they neglect the in-between world of border crossings, journeying, and above all uncertainty. This uncertainty is mostly present at the arrival.

New territories

Exile was a time of rupture and disorientation, but we here need to portray the diversity of cases and appreciate that flight or expulsion could often be less traumatic than imprisonment or deportation to another continent, or than distant migration. The elsewhere of exile was not always radically different, and in particular, there was a tradition of cross-border expatriation between France and Spain, and Spain and Portugal, with the county of Nice also being easy to slip in and out of from France. Was one really elsewhere, for that matter, if one left France by crossing the Jura to reside in Switzerland?

Past experience of traveling could be crucial. Members of the elite had often already traveled, and exiles were used to transport, even though the circumstances were now new. Gustave Lefrançais brings out the social differences between those who were aware of geographic distances and other exiles in his account of the arrival in England of a poor elderly peasant called Badin, who, having had nothing to do with resistance to the 1851 coup, wound up in exile by mistake. The boat transporting Badin to French Guiana for his supposed part in resistance was damaged and washed up on the British coast, transforming the poor prisoner into an exile. The French consulate and exiles worked together to enable him to return to France. But the simple peasant did not know that he had to cross the Channel to reach his native land. Lefrançais's memoirs show that Badin's simple-mindedness, who, ignoring the existence of the Channel, thought he could return home by foot, was also a form of political innocence, having been wrongly sentenced after being denounced by a malicious neighbor.[119] Traveling depended closely on the situation of the outcasts, but also on their knowledge of a world which was certainly foreign or at times hostile.

Armed with a few recommendations and addresses, exiles tried to find compatriots in the hotels where they were staying. On arriving in London, Victor Schœlcher, Martin Nadaud, and Pierre Malardier immediately went to a place

---

[119] Lefrançais, *Souvenirs d'un révolutionnaire*, 169–170.

in Soho where they took up residence in a house run by French people who rented rooms to their compatriots on Gerrard Street.

In the British capital, it was often the store run by Jean-Philibert Berjeau – a publisher, bookshop owner, and hotelier who had settled in the United Kingdom in the wake of the events of June 13, 1849 – which acted as the entry point for French outcasts up until the 1870s. Berjeau also had another activity, being an agent for the French police. One of his reports to police headquarters thus mentions Jean-Baptiste Clément, who had no sooner arrived in London than he hurried round to his shop on Frith Street in the heart of Soho:

> Since yesterday we have had J.-B. Clément in London; naturally, he came to me for news from Paris, after informing me of his position which I believe to be most precarious. I put him in a cheap room at no. 35 Fitzroy Square.[120]

Richard's grocery at 67 Charlotte Street was also one of the first ports of call for refugees to obtain information about jobs or rooms for rent, and spies consequently flocked there.[121] The situation was also very different when the exile arrived accompanied by their family. Looking for housing and a job, and choosing a school for the children was obviously essential, as shown by the correspondence.

Exiles did not systematically seek out political or professional support networks, and their memoirs and correspondence contain examples of animosity, and of withdrawing voluntarily to the sidelines. Some stayed well away from their compatriots, and although this was rare there are several cases amongst French outcasts: although Hugo was surrounded by exiles in Jersey then Guernsey, he was careful to avoid them in London where he did not want to be in competition or permanent interaction with leading figures such as Ledru-Rollin and Louis Blanc, who were already resident there and had established political networks. Edgar Quinet, on returning from Brussels, also chose to keep his distance and became "the hermit of Veytaux" in Switzerland. Barbès, on being amnestied in 1854, left the prison where he had been incarcerated on Belle-Île, yet, refusing to return to France and not wishing to join a community of exiles, chose The Hague in the Netherlands as his destination, living there until his death in 1870.

---

120 Archives de la Préfecture de police de Paris, dossier Ba. 427, report dated September 6, 1871, quoted in Renaud Morieux, "Une communauté en exil: les réfugies de la Commune à Londres" (Masters thesis, Université Paris 1 Panthéon-Sorbonne, June 1997), 84.
121 Adolphe Smith, "Political Refugees," in *London in the Nineteenth Century*, ed. Walter Besant (London: Black, 1909), 401.

The arrival of soldiers was often more problematic than that of civilians, for they were sent to camps and places of internment where the living conditions were very different from those of their compatriots exiled in capitals. This is clearly illustrated by two cases mentioned earlier, the Poles of the "great emigration" and Spanish Carlists. In the first case, on arriving in France, the Poles were placed by the July Monarchy authorities in open depots in Avignon and Besançon. The regime was thereby using a policy already applied to other nationalities, with there being a depot for Italians in Mâcon, one for Germans in Langres, and two for Spaniards, one in Bourges and the other in Périgueux.[122] In the latter case, many studies have shown that during the 1830s there were open depots in the center of France for Carlist soldiers. Nevertheless, it should be noted that their fate clearly differed from that of exiled Spanish Republicans in 1939 who were placed in insalubrious prison camps in south-western France, causing well-known and permanent damage to how the Spanish left perceived the French government.[123] In the nineteenth century, despite numerous demands and protests, the time spent in depots was often of brief duration, being an initial response to an emergency rather than places of prolonged detention. This is clearly visible concerning exiled Carlists in 1876. On being confronted with an influx of soldiers crossing the border in late February, the authorities took the decision to place them together in military barracks, particularly in Bayonne. Still, this was a provisional measure which only lasted a few days and the exiles were subsequently dispatched to the towns of internment to which they were assigned, but where they were free to reside, work, and live as they saw fit.[124] Although the authorities undeniably developed ways of constraining and coercing exiles during the nineteenth century, these were rarely as stringent are those of the following century.

Another characteristic territory where exiles arrived in the nineteenth century was that of a colony, an urban, political, and social form with many different roots and meanings by this period. For exiles, this often corresponded to a settlement abroad of an autonomous community of nationals who could live in accordance with their ideas and beliefs, far from the state repression which had forced them to leave. Nineteenth-century exile colonies thus often had marked

---

122 Delphine Diaz, "Un espace alternatif du politique? Les souscriptions au profit d'exilés étrangers accueillis en France, années 1820–1840," in Alexandre Dupont and Rachel Renault, *Les Espaces alternatifs du politique* (*Mélanges de la Casa de Velazquez*, 2021, forthcoming).
123 Geneviève Armand-Dreyfus, *L'Exil des républicains espagnols en France. De la Guerre civile à la mort de Franco* (Paris: Albin Michel, 1999).
124 Dupont, *Une internationale blanche*, chapter 11.

utopian characteristics. But this was not always the case, as illustrated by the Polish colony in Adampol studied by Katarzyna Papież. She has examined the fate of this colony, founded by Poles who had gone into exile in France, on the territory of a Lazarist foundation near Constantinople in the early 1840s. It had a dual purpose: recreating a little Polish homeland in exile which would serve to perpetuate the combat for the nation, and turning the colony's territory to profitable use by farming it.[125]

Exiles, who had often lived in cities when acting as political opponents, and after having been forced to cross spaces with which they were unfamiliar, tended to find asylum and assistance in towns. What is striking is the role that European capitals played in the circulation of nineteenth-century exiles. While the great emigrant destinations were ports and new cities on the American continent, the major capitals of Europe were not just the places exiles left behind but also where they headed (or sought to head) for. The police were well aware of this, which is why they placed their spies there, and the authorities sought to prevent exiles gathering in groups. These capitals were undergoing major changes at this period, drawing the poor looking for work, while also attracting tourists, with the new means of transport and universal exhibitions contributing to the pull they exerted. Nineteenth-century exiles were among the best guides to these modern cities, at times to their dismay: Élisée Reclus and Alphonse Esquiros wrote the Guide Joanne for London, and Victor Hugo left numerous accounts of Brussels and its inhabitants. Less famous but equally prolix were Ernest Cœurderoy's descriptions of the people walking the streets of Madrid, Lisbon, and Turin. Hugo who fled London, was one of the main authors of the *Paris Guide* about the 1867 exhibition, a work of exile in which the banished express their nostalgia for the capital they had known before it was destroyed Haussmann's works.

Those left behind

More than other migrants exiles traveled alone or without their family. Exiles' main worries related to what would happen to their parents, wives and children left behind. Heléna Tóth devotes a chapter of her book to the situation of persecuted families. They were often instrumentalized by the authorities who pub-

---

125 On all the above, see Katarzyna Papież, "Adampol/Polonezköy, refuge et colonie agricole. Un laboratoire de la polonité en exil dans l'Empire ottoman au XIXe siècle," *Hommes & Migrations* 1321 (2018): 65–73.

lished their pleas for clemency.[126] Poles and Hungarians expressed their fear of reprisals, pushing them to leave as a family or else to have their relatives promptly join them

French exiles feared the effects of civil death which would prevent them from accessing or controlling assets. On January 4, 1852, Schœlcher wrote from Brussels to Camille Pleyel, the son of a famous piano maker of Austrian origin, the Pleyels having been entrusted with managing his rents:

> I fully and entirely recognize you in the long observation about how to ward off the effects of civil death and joint sentence. What solicitude, dear friend, and how well you have thought of everything! I will do the power of attorney. I don't hesitate to prefer spending even Fr.3,000 to safeguard what I own, for once organized as you suggest the thing will be unassailable unless they do away with all laws and all judges.[127]

Fearing confiscation, he wrote once again on January 15, 1852: "yes, carry on with the operation about my goods. These gentlemen will stop at nothing and it is to be greatly feared that they proceed fairly quickly".[128] Victor Hugo who was also in Brussels where he arrived in early January 1852, wrote to his wife:

> [...] to answer everything, you can if appropriate and for things that are not very secret write directly to me at M. Lanvin, 16, place de l'Hôtel de Ville. I moved in today and have informed my host that if anyone asks for M. Lanvin, it's me, and that if anyone asks for M. Victor Hugo, it's me. I am thus living here under two names, when Charles comes, he will find me in an enormous room with three windows with a view of the magnificent Place de l'Hôtel de Ville. I have rented essential furniture (for next to nothing), a bed, a table, etc., – and a good stove. I can work here at ease and find it comfortable. If I come across an old carpet for fifteen francs, I'll be perfectly happy. In the meantime, dear friend, fetch from my bedroom my old couch that you had upholstered in red and white stripes, have it wrapped as succinctly as possible, with straw and canvas (no chest, there's no need), put my address on it, Lanvin, 16, Grande Place, Bruxelles, and have it transported to Van Gend messengers, 130, Rue Saint-Honoré (Laffitte et Caillard). There, explain to them that this piece of furniture must be shipped slow. That costs 7 francs for 100 kilos (two hundred pounds). They will ask you for something less than seven francs for the couch, that you will pay and put on my account. Let me know once it has been sent.[129]

---

126 Tóth, *An Exiled Generation*, in the chapter "What good does it do to ruin our family", 78–113.
127 Schœlcher, *Correspondance publiée par Nelly Schmidt*, letter 54, 201.
128 Schœlcher, *Correspondance publiée par Nelly Schmidt*, letter 59, 223.
129 *Correspondance Hugo*, (À Madame Victor Hugo) Madame Rivière 37, Rue de la Tour d'Auvergne, January 5, [1852], Brussels.

These details may make us smile, but they were part of the early moments in exile. Being unable or unwilling to purchase property, exiles, like migrants, were at times victims of ill-disposed compatriots, but at others, they received good financial advice. In 1852 Hugo bought 168 shares in the Banque nationale, making him one of its largest shareholders.[130] The fortune of the Russian exile Alexander Herzen was managed by James de Rothschild, to whom he also entrusted his papers and documents.[131] The company archives also contain many other investments and examples of asset management for exiles, such as for Louis-Philippe and his descendants, as well as for Polish aristocrats such as Count Branicki.[132]

Another leading figure of exile, Ledru-Rollin, who owned many properties in Paris, had to entrust intermediaries to remotely manage his properties, many of which were concerned by Haussmann's renovation of the city.[133] Hugo sold his goods in 1852 when Paul Meurice became the first collector of Hugo's works, acquiring several plays, and especially the drawing *Le Burg à la croix*. Meurice also became the custodian of the furniture and books that the family retained, and later had them shipped to Guernsey.

Departure always entailed a rupture, even though this was often attenuated by maintaining family ties or by the familiar objects that exiles took with them. Like today, it is mainly through accounts by exiles, sometimes heroized or at least rewritten, that we know about these moments of passage and transit. While they obviously need to be read with caution, they are not just the imaginings of exile, but also reflect its realities.

The traces of this rupture tended to leave a deep imprint on the life of exiles in their new place of residence. Their existence, even after relocating, continued to be marked by distance.

---

130 When Hugo became wealthier with the success of *"Les Misérables"*, his earnings enabled him to buy further shares. In 1862 he owned 231; in 1863, 239; in 1865, 271; in 1866, 289, and on September 27, 1867, the figure reached 300. In 1872, after the Banque nationale changed its statutes and increased its capital, he became the owner of 600 shares. He appeared second on the list of shareholders, where one may read *"Victor Hugo, homme de lettres, domicilié à Guernesey"*. At the same time, he subscribed 70 shares in the name of his mistress, Juliette Drouet.
131 Derek Offord, "The correspondence of Alexander Herzen with James de Rothschild," *Journal in Slavic Studies* University of Toronto, Academic Electronic, TSQ, 66 (2003).
132 CAMT (Centre des archives du monde du travail de Roubaix), Archives Rothschild, 132 AQ.
133 Hélène Lemesle, *Vautours, singes et cloportes, Ledru-Rollin, ses locataires et ses concierges au XIXe siècle* (Paris: Association pour le développement de l'histoire économique, 2003); Sylvie Aprile, "Exil et éloignement, la famille comme recours," in *Éloignement géographique et cohésion familiale (XVe-XXe siècle)*, ed. by Jean-François Chauvard and Christine Lebeau (Strasbourg: Presses universitaires de Strasbourg, 2006), 31–49.

Sylvie Aprile and Delphine Diaz
Chapter 4 Living far away

In the wake of the 1851 coup in France, Victor Frond (1821–1881), a sub-lieutenant with the Paris fire brigade, was arrested, and then imprisoned in Algeria. He escaped and joined the circle of outcasts in England. He was sent to collect money and weapons in Lisbon, where he discovered a new trade, as a photographer. In 1855 he set sail for Brazil, and, together with another exile, Charles Ribeyrolles, became the first to produce a photo reportage about the country. This example is far removed from the plaintive and dramatic portraits of life in exile, sustained by police reports and the accounts and correspondence left by exiles. These sources have often led historians to corroborate the formula of historian Adrien Dansette, for whom the life of an exile abroad "may be resumed as poverty, bitterness, and lack of realism".[1] This tragic vision has recently been explored in greater nuance by many studies of exiles' trajectories, as well as by contributions from the social history of migration, raising the question of the connections exiles had with their place of origin and land of residence.

We may thus distinguish between migrations in which ties with the country of origin disintegrated, and in which the host country became the realm exiles connected with, and migrations in which the country of origin remained the reference framework in which the exile still wished to fulfill his or her objectives, with the host country acting simply as provider of resources. Still, the situation of many exiles did not neatly fit this dichotomy: after fighting on the barricades in Paris, how did one go on to become a bison hunter in America, a swimming teacher in Brussels, a traveling salesman in wines and spirits in England, or a general in the American Civil War?

This diversity means we need to reinterpret the issue of political exile in the light of the many paths taken, without isolating it from other questions about building migrant communities, about cultural exchanges, and any possible transfers and legacies.

1 Social trajectories

In nineteenth-century Europe, exile was a common fate of men and women from across the social spectrum. The varied social and professional origins no doubt

---

[1] Adrien Dansette, *Le Second Empire. Du 2 décembre au 4 septembre* (Paris: Hachette, 1972), 125.

influenced their experience of being forced to reside abroad. The life in Paris of the Polish prince, Adam Czartoryski, whose family had bought the Hôtel Lambert on Île Saint-Louis in 1843, had nothing in common with that of an obscure Spanish Carlist farmer, called Canudes, whose name figures on the 1836 list of those receiving assistance in the Dijon refugee depot, even though both resided in the same country of asylum and lived under the same political regime.[2] Our view of exile needs to take into account the social classes to which exiles belonged, together with their finances, assets, and the symbolic capital they could or could not draw upon while abroad. While nineteenth-century Europe saw varied groups of refugees, exile was still a socially selective phenomenon in the wake of the Congress of Vienna. Fewer workers, tradesmen, farmers, or servants were affected by forced migration than politicians, magistrates, officers, journalists, and students, even though the social composition of refugee groups gradually altered after the 1848–1849 revolutions.

Was exile an elite phenomenon?

Exiles during the first half of the century were largely made up of political, merchant, industrial, and cultural elites. During the 1820s, those forced out by the revolutions in the Italian and Iberian peninsulas were predominantly elites. Agostino Bistarelli has studied the group of Italian liberal exiles from the Kingdom of the Two Sicilies and Piedmont-Sardinia who left the Italian peninsula in 1821. He has managed to identify a cohort of about 1,000 Italian exiles, 737 of whom are of known profession: 59.4% came from the military,[3] a clear majority attributable to the conditions triggering uprisings in Naples during 1820–1821, but also to recruitment by secret societies conveying liberal ideology through the peninsula. Among the civilians identified in this group (299 people in all), a core was formed of students (31 individuals) and members of the professions.[4]

Sociological analyses of the waves of exiles in the following decade confirm the predominance of elites. The majority of the "great Polish emigration", numbering over 8,000 people after the winter of 1831–1832,[5] were members of civil and military elites. Among those to take refuge in western France, studied by Valentin Guillaume, many specified their rank when registering at the prefecture.

---

2 Archives départementales de Côte d'Or, 20 M 1259, register of the Dijon refugee depot, 1836–1837.
3 Bistarelli, *Gli esuli*, 78.
4 Bistarelli, *Gli esuli*, 79.
5 *Cf.* chapter 1 for the context.

Still, not all had pursued a military career before arriving in France. On the contrary, as the refugee Théophile Jarecki explained in October 1833, if the majority of Poles were "classed [...] as non-commissioned officers or soldiers", this situation was "purely accidental", given that they had "joined the military in the wake of the revolution and as part of the general impulse which had led the entire population to take up arms", and that "prior to this, they had been landowners or students".[6] This "accidental" situation could nevertheless last, particularly for Polish refugees settled in France who joined the Foreign Legion, founded in 1831 for overseas service. The case was similar for those who settled in Belgium: Idesbald Goddeeris has demonstrated that for the 128 Poles from the "great emigration" still present there in 1837, 32 were enlisted in the newly formed Belgian army.[7] Countries other than France and Belgium also offered exiles the possibility of a military career, in, for example, the Ottoman Empire from the early nineteenth century onwards, as illustrated by the example of the Frenchman Antoine Juchereau de Saint-Denis (1778–1850), studied by Ali Yaycioglu,[8] a phenomenon which only increased during the Tanzimat.

While Belgium and the Ottoman Empire provided officers from the Polish "great emigration" with many possibilities to assume positions in their respective armies, the situation in France was more socially sensitive given that those who wanted to join the Foreign Legion could only serve overseas, in Algeria, an obligation which soon came to be perceived as a second banishment. For Polish soldiers who refused to join the Legion, this raised even more acutely the question of what they were to become in their land of asylum. This is perfectly encapsulated in the complaint by the refugee Stanislas Odelski, who in 1835 acted as the spokesman for Polish soldiers who had settled in western France:

> What is proposed to us? What means are we offered to improve our existence, as soldiers brought up in camps and cast out on a land whose language and customs we ignore, having no knowledge other than how to wield a horse and lance?[9]

---

6 Guillaume, "L'autre exil," 240.
7 Goddeeris, *La Grande Émigration*, 114–115.
8 Ali Yaycioglu, "Janissaires, ingénieurs et prédicateurs. Comment l'ingénierie militaire et l'activisme islamique changèrent l'ordre ottoman," *Revue d'histoire du XIXe siècle* 53/2 (2016): 28–29: his father had been executed during the French Revolution, and he was brought up and educated by his uncle in Canada. Juchereau returned to France after the Treaty of Amiens, and shortly after entered the service of the Ottoman Empire.
9 Archives départementales des Côtes-du-Nord, 4 M 261, individual file on Stanislas Odelski, letter from Stanislas Odelski to the prefect of Côtes-du-Nord, April 1835, quoted in Guillaume, "L'autre exil," 239.

While a majority of the refugees in the "great emigration" were soldiers, there were still many civilians among them, as indicated by the ranking of professions in the rates of assistance granted at the time by the French ministry of the interior to refugees officially recognized as such. In 1833, at a date when France was providing assistance to 6,939 refugees,[10] predominantly Poles, the rate was divided into five classes combining "civilian and military positions": the first was for ministers and lieutenant-generals, the second for "camp marshals, MPs, and prefects", the third for colonels, magistrates, and senior administrative officials, the fourth for captains, lieutenants, mayors, judges, lawyers, and doctors, with a final class at the bottom of the scale for "non-commissioned officers, soldiers, tradesmen, and farmers". This ranking placing civilian and military positions on the same echelon indicates the great social diversity of refugees receiving assistance in France.

1848, a turning point in the social background of exiles

In 1848–49, as Europe was going through further revolutionary upheavals, repression caused soldiers and civilians alike to go into exile. There was once again great social variety among the latter, though intellectual elites were particularly affected. As Christophe Charle points out, repression of revolutions in Germanic states triggered the exodus of an estimated 15,000 intellectuals in the space of five years, which he describes as the "first major brain drain in German history".[11] Despite this, exile in 1848–1849 primarily affected members of the working classes, driven out by poverty as much by political circumstances.[12] Apparently more civilians than soldiers were forced to leave the Italian peninsula in 1849.[13] Even for those from the army, the boundary between them and the civilian world was increasingly porous. Fabrice Jesné has discussed the trajectory of Gaspare Genna, a Sicilian from Trapani, who "served as a lieutenant in the Neapolitan army and had to go into exile in 1848".[14] On settling to Gallipoli in the

---

10 *Archives parlementaires*, 2nd series, vol. 81, 613.
11 Christophe Charle, "L'Europe des intellectuels en 1848," in *1848. Actes du colloque international du cent cinquantenaire tenu à l'Assemblée nationale à Paris, 23–25 février 1998*, ed. Jean-Luc Mayaud (Paris: Créaphis, 2002), 441.
12 Charle, "L'Europe des intellectuels en 1848".
13 Domenico Giurati, *Memorie d'emigrazione* (Milan: Treves, 1897), 80: "La emigrazione del '49, tolte alcune famiglie della nobiltà lombarda, si compone di gente in massima parte civile [...]".
14 Fabrice Jesné, "Les colonies italiennes d'Orient et la fraternité. Solidarité d'exil, sociabilité locale et sentiment national," in *Exil et fraternité*, 188.

Ottoman Empire, he went into trade and acquired "a certain degree of wealth and an influential position there",[15] becoming the agent for French messaging services, then for Piedmont-Sardinia's consular delegate.

There was thus a dual shift in the exiles of 1848–1849, with larger numbers of civilians and more people from the working classes. The proportion of elites decreased further over the course of the second half of the nineteenth century. The many former communards who spread out across Europe after the final events in May 1871 included many workers and employees.[16] In the case of communards who settled in Switzerland, Marc Vuilleumier has argued that it is particularly difficult to establish their professional background given that the lists available indicate either the original job of the refugees or the job they found in exile. Despite methodological obstacles hindering any clear attribution of refugees to given professional categories, what emerges for the group of communard refugees settled in Geneva is the "crushing majority of employees" (72% in 1873, 68% in 1879). Workers and manual trades make up nearly half the professions indicated in the lists for Geneva in 1873 (49%) and 1879 (47%).[17] Nevertheless, this preponderance did not prevent there being "a non-negligible number of men of letters and journalists" among the ranks of former communards.[18]

With anarchist exiles at the end of the century, the proportion of workers and employees increased further. Constance Bantman has identified about 450 French-speaking anarchists living in exile in London during the period 1880–1914.[19] Among them, most were adult men in their 30s or 40s, employed in skilled and unskilled manual trades. The professions of 180 of these 450 French-speaking anarchists are known, and they were mostly skilled craftsmen working as tailors, shoemakers, mechanics, and so on.[20] A small group was made up of individuals in the intellectual professions: two jurists, two engineers, one lawyer, one accountant, and one medical student. The working classes, who were now predominant, were thus juxtaposed with a small group of members from the middle and upper classes. The situation was the exact opposite of

---

15 Jesné, "Les colonies italiennes," 189.
16 *Cf.* chapter 1 on the context to this exile.
17 Marc Vuilleumier, "Les exilés communards en Suisse," *Histoire et combats. Mouvement ouvrier et socialisme en Suisse, 1864–1960* (Lausanne: Éditions d'en bas & Collège du travail, 2012), 245.
18 Vuilleumier, "Les exilés communards".
19 Constance Bantman, *The French Anarchists in London, 1880–1914. Exile and Transnationalism in the First Globalisation* (Liverpool: Liverpool University Press, 2013), 45.
20 Bantman, *The French Anarchists*, 58.

the social composition observed among groups of liberal exiles at the beginning of the century.

2 Maintaining or breaking homeland ties

Migration studies have paved the way to new ways of examining how exiles related to their place of origin and host country. On the one hand, there were situations in which migrants' links to their countries of origin became looser and the place of arrival became the framework with which they established lasting connections, and, on the other, migrations where there was no such putting down of roots. The two were not necessarily contradictory: clearly, certain exiles were obliged to resort to expedients after initially thinking that they would only reside briefly in the host country. At first, it was mainly a matter of mobilizing financial means. Looking for a job, either taking up a previous career or else turning to a new activity, was thus often of secondary importance. Correspondence by those freshly arrived in exile is full of very prosaic financial details, as we saw in the previous chapter: they had to sell belongings, get revenues transferred, and find friends or relatives to ask for money.

The time of exile comes across primarily as one of rupture, in which those affected left their country, their occupations, and their standard of living. Yet in this exceptional situation, certain people managed to carry on with their prior existence to a certain extent: exile could be a time of returning to prior professional activities or of rapidly rebuilding ties and sociability networks in the host land. Though time in exile has often been described as conducive to idleness, particularly as depicted by the administrative authorities,[21] it could also trigger exiles to promptly resume a prior activity. The Piedmontese liberal exile François Capellini (as his name is spelled in French police sources), a printer by profession, arrived in Chalon in France in August 1821, after briefly passing through Spain during the liberal triennium. On arriving in the town he went to see Mr. Dejussieu, a printer, "to ask for work".[22] Rapidly resuming employment also depended on solidarity networks, helping exiles able to benefit from chain migration effects: a Frenchman living in Lausanne, Charles Bergeron (1808–

---

21 A circular from the French ministry of the interior dated December 12, 1837 (Archives départementales de la Vienne, 4 M 165) recommends that prefects ensure that refugees "held back by a misplaced sense of self-worth" do not persevere "in idleness".
22 Archives nationales de France, F7 6652, letter from the Saône-et-Loire prefecture, August 1821, addressee not indicated.

1883),[23] one of the elite foreign engineers building the first railways in Switzerland, helped many French exiles find jobs there.[24] Bergeron also used the ease with which he could travel to circulate exiles' manuscripts, including writings by Quinet.

In terms of professional practices and skills, we may distinguish three general cases: either exiles continued with the same activity in their place of asylum as prior to their departure, or they drew on skills they already had, particularly linguistic skills, to build a new profession or at least a new source of revenue, or, finally, exile provided an opportunity to acquire entirely new skills.

An example from the early 1870s of the first case is the exiled communard André Alavoine, deputy director of the Imprimerie Nationale in Paris in 1871, who managed to set up a print workshop in Switzerland where he produced "many of the publications by exiles and the Geneva workers' movement".[25] The second case is illustrated by the many exiles and refugees who became language instructors on settling abroad. Sylvie Aprile has shown that certain French republicans, cast into political exile after the 1851 coup, settled for many years in non-French-speaking countries (Great Britain, Flanders, the United States, etc.) where they learned the language while teaching theirs.[26] Learning the host country's language could be a long and arduous undertaking, as illustrated by Alexandre Ledru-Rollin's notebooks from 1857 containing his English exercises.[27] Banished French republicans perceived teaching their own language as a "provi-

---

23 Jean-Claude Sosnowski, "Charles Bergeron", *Dictionnaire biographique du fouriérisme*, entry placed online in May 2009, accessed April 11, 2021, http://www.charlesfourier.fr/spip.php?article668: "Under the Second Empire, [Charles Bergeron] used his position in Switzerland to help French exiles. His frequent travels enabled him to act as an intermediary between France, Belgium, and England. He provided them with work or else accommodated them in his chalet at Les Plans-sur-Bex outside Lausanne. Thus in 1862, no doubt following a recommendation by Jean-Baptiste Charras, who at the time was the main financier of the Freiburg *Confédéré*, he obtained a position for his friend François-Auguste Brückner, a former parliamentarian for Bas-Rhin who had sat in the Constituent and Legislative assemblies, as head of material in charge of the Lausanne-Freiburg-Berne line".
24 Marcel Dupasquier, *Edgar Quinet en Suisse (1858–1870)* (Neuchâtel: À la Baconnière, 1959). A similar opportunity working on the railways was available after the Paris Commune, when many Frenchmen were employed building the line over the Gotthard Pass.
25 Vuilleumier, "Les exilés communards," 246.
26 Sylvie Aprile, "L'expérience de l'étranger: vivre et enseigner en exil après le 2 décembre," *Documents pour l'histoire du français langue étrangère* 32 (2004).
27 Bibliothèque historique de la Ville de Paris, Papiers Ledru-Rollin, MS2028, études de langue, quoted in Aprile, "L'expérience de l'étranger".

sional" activity undertaken for want of anything better to put food on the table.[28] French language instructors in exile in Britain either taught as private tutors or else in private academies, but also on occasions in more prestigious schools and universities.

Although working as a language instructor was generally viewed as an unattractive prospect, it nevertheless enabled certain exiles to make a livelihood and, in certain cases, work their way up the academic echelons. One instance is the career of Pierre Barrère, studied by Sylvie Aprile: before 1848 he had been a tutor, and on being banished he settled with his family in London in 1853. He became a French teacher in Wimbledon, before being appointed Professor of French at the military academy and then a lecturer for officers at the Royal Artillery Institute. His son, Albert, followed in his footsteps: he was involved in events of the Paris Commune, and also went into exile in England, becoming a teacher at the Merchant Taylor School in 1877 and then at Cheltenham College, before joining the Royal Artillery Institute.

As certain among them were winning academic recognition, French teachers in Britain increasingly managed to coordinate their activities, as illustrated by the rapid development over the course of the 1880s of the National Society of French Teachers in England, founded in London in 1881, which even published its own journal, *Le Français*. The members of this society were, according to Sylvie Aprile, a "teaching elite" who were active in prestigious institutions, including reputed public schools and Oxford University.

Thus the case of language instructors illustrates how situations in exile could lead expatriates to draw on skills they already had to embark on a new career, or simply to assure their livelihood. Knowledge of languages and a taste for adventure or foreign climes also led certain exiles to embrace more distant careers. Charles-Edmond Chojecki became Prince Napoléon's courier during the Crimean War thanks to his skills as a horseman and his knowledge of Russian and Arabic.[29]

But we also need to look at the case of exiles for whom heading abroad meant acquiring totally new professional skills, or unexpected career changes. For the Blanquists Clermont and Eugène Fouet, two former students who had been respectively "head of personnel and director of the depot at police head-

---

28 Bibliothèque historique de la Ville de Paris, Papiers Ledru-Rollin, MS2028, études de langue, quoted in Aprile, "L'expérience de l'étranger".
29 *Charles-Edmond Chojecki, L'oeuvre et la vie*, une biographie d'après Emmanuel Desurvire, (Éditeur Emmanuel Desurvire: 2014), 88–95.

quarters during the Commune",[30] their political exile after spring 1871 provided an opportunity for a complete career change, which turned out most successfully. Together they founded a prosperous perfume business in Geneva, whose name and reputation persisted through to the late twentieth century. In England, Tristan Duché, a former solicitor, founded a prosperous gelatin company and opened subsidiaries in Glasgow and Manchester, followed by establishments in Buenos Aires, New York, and Paris. His son, Marius Duché, set up a gelatin factory in Vilvoorde, to the north of Brussels, then two others in Pont Brûlé and Grimbergen.

Whilst it is known that a certain number of illustrious photographers in the twentieth century were exiles, photography was from its origins an artistic activity and livelihood that particularly attracted exiles. It was not yet codified professionally and lay somewhere between a hobby and trade. The photo projects of Victor Hugo and his sons on the Channel Islands are well known, as are the magnificent prints of the "rocher des proscrits" testifying to the artistic success of this new medium.[31] As mentioned earlier, Victor Frond, after learning the new technique of photography in Portugal, set sail for Brazil and opened one of the first photo workshops in Rio, benefiting from the benevolence of the king and court whose portraits he took.[32] Frond paid the travel expenses for a journalist, Ribeyrolles, with whom he wanted to produce a book on the history of Brazil, commissioned by Pedro II. This written and visual reportage was published in a bilingual French and Portuguese edition. The photographs taken for it were sent to Paris, to the Lemercier workshop, which turned them into lithographs to accompany the text and above all to demonstrate its veracity. Brazilian newspapers of the period frequently commented on the importance of this publication, which was part of a campaign to encourage immigration. But Ribeyrolles did not enjoy this success for long, dying of yellow fever in 1859, a few days before he was due to sail back to Europe.

---

30 Vuilleumier, "Les exilés communards," 246. The Clermont and Fouet company only went bankrupt in the 1990s, after trading for over one century.
31 Sylvie Aprile, "Victor Hugo dans le rocher des proscrits," AsileuropeXIX website image bank, accessed April 11, 2021, https://asileurope.huma-num.fr/ressources-iconographiques/victor-hugo-dans-le-rocher-des-proscrits.
32 Between 1847 and 1862, 58 photo studios opened in Rio de Janeiro. Between 1857 and 1860, Victor Frond received more commissions from La Mordomia Imperial than any of the other photographers. He photographed the imperial family in April 1857, just after arriving in Brazil, endowing his studio with immediate prestige. See Lygia Segala, "Prescriptive Observation and Illustration of Brazil: Victor Frond's Photographic Project (1857–61)," *Portuguese studies* 23/1 (2007): 55–70.

Setting aside the most famous authors, the situation of artists cannot be treated in generic terms due to the diversity of their careers and the degree of notoriety attached to exile. It was often essential to travel to win artistic recognition. In the 1850s and 1860s, the violinist Eduard Reményi performed in traditional concert venues and won the patronage of such important figures as Queen Victoria, yet equally displayed his attachment to his friends in refuge, coming to play for them in Guernsey. Artists chose London on political grounds, but also for economic reasons. After fleeing Paris for Bougival in summer 1870 at the beginning of the Franco-Prussian war, Claude Monet placed his canvases in safekeeping with Pissarro before heading to London in September, where the art merchant Paul Durand-Ruel was seeking to introduce the British public to works by French artists. This was no guarantee of success for Monet: other artists were more successful, such as James Tissot, who had already exhibited in London and altered his French forename Jacques-Joseph to James prior even to fleeing Paris in May 1871.

Although the few success stories bring out how exile in nineteenth-century Europe could be the opportunity for a change in career, we should not downplay the number of professional failures affecting those forced to leave. As Marc Vuilleumier has noted about the communards in Geneva, "alongside the successes, alongside those able with considerable effort to eke out a mediocre existence, what poverty there was!".[33] In her study of anarchists in London, Constance Bantman goes over the path leading Aristide Gardrat (also known as Garderat) into exile in the British capital. He was a man of letters and former editor of the *Père peinard* who had fled Paris in the early 1890s. On going into exile in London, he took a job washing dishes, and ended up sleeping on the streets, contracting consumption in Hyde Park. On returning to France he was imprisoned in Sainte-Pélagie and died of his illness there.[34] Even in the United States, where one may spontaneously imagine it was easier for exiles to find work, Joseph Déjacque (1821–1865) was unable to find stable employment. He worked on building sites, and complained that he was at the mercy of wages fixed by the French community. He wrote to Pierre Vésinier telling him that he wished to return to Europe to escape the French bosses in New York, who were "neither the most numerous, nor the least exploitative".[35]

---

[33] Vuilleumier, "Les exilés communards," 246.
[34] Bantman, *The French Anarchists*, 57.
[35] Arthur Lehning, "Une lettre de Joseph Déjacque à Pierre Vésinier du 20 février 1861," *Bulletin of the International Institute of Social History of Amsterdam*, 1 (1951): 16–19.

3 Learning to live in exile

Family horizons

When their exile lasted, nineteenth-century European outcasts were led to face the question of their professional activities, especially when their social origins or initial capital did not enable them to live in idleness. But staying in exile often entailed building or rebuilding family life. Many of the men seeking refuge in Europe were separated from their wives and children: like many other nineteenth-century migrations, exile split families. Yet some exiles traveled with their families. They were thus led to provide for the education of their children accompanying them in their migration or else born abroad, and also to provide for young adults. This was the case of Victor Hugo, who was constantly preoccupied with meeting the needs of his wife, his daughter, his mistress, and his sons who, he feared, might fall into idleness. The preface to Hugo's *William Shakespeare* includes a rather emphatic dialogue which clearly illustrates the perplexity of father and son concerning their future:

> One morning in late November, two of the inhabitants of the place [Marine Terrace], the father and the youngest son, were sitting in the lower parlor. They were silent, like shipwrecked people meditating.
> Outside, the rain fell and the wind blow, and the household was as if deafened by the roaring. Both were thinking, perhaps absorbed by this coincidence between the beginning of winter and the beginning of exile.
>
> All at once the son spoke out, asking his father:
>
> "What do you think of this exile?"
> "That it will be long."
> "How do you count on filling it?"
>
> The father answered:
>
> "I shall look at the ocean."
> There was a silence. The father resumed:
> "And you?"
> "I shall translate Shakespeare", the son said.[36]

François-Victor did indeed throw himself into this task, learning English to do so. While this example is rather unique, it nevertheless raises the broader question

---

36 Victor Hugo, *William Shakespeare* (Brussels: A. Lacroix, Verboeckhoven et Cie, éditeurs, 1864), XIV, translated by Adrian Morfee.

of the generational issues at stake in exile, in which an elderly man was accompanied by younger people and others drawn along in their wake.

How were exiles to envisage their children's education in a context in which they were cut off politically, linguistically, culturally, and generally from their country of origin? Were they to accept to raise their children in the culture of the country or successive countries, or should they seek to maintain their language of origin together with the worship of their ancestors and lost homeland? As we shall see, the options available to exiles were no doubt far less binary than this question suggests, and no doubt they practiced forms of cultural hybridization. Without counting that the presence of children in exile also resulted in the founding of singular educational establishments, employing teaching methods of varying degrees of audacity. For certain children living in exile, expatriation barely interrupted the education received in their native land: the children and grandchildren of kings and queens in exile were largely unaffected in this regard when they went abroad. No sooner was Louise d'Artois settled with her grandfather Charles X in Holyrood Castle in Edinburgh in summer 1830, than she resumed her habitual activities under the instruction of her governess:

> When the vessel carrying us there reached the land of exile, especially when we were established in Holyrood, we had to accept our misfortune in its entirety.
>
> In just a few days each had been given new occupations, and Princess Louise was the first to resume her lessons.[37]

Louise continued her instruction under the Duchess of Gontaut-Biron (1773–1857) in Holyrood, then in the Netherlands and Prague where she continued to reside in exile.[38]

But for other émigrés and exiles, it was far from obvious how to resume or commence elementary education, including for members of elites. For the counterrevolutionary émigrés who settled in London in the 1790s, educating their children was already a major preoccupation. Madame de Ménerville, who had left Paris for Brussels in October 1791 before settling in London, records her worries about her two daughters' studies in her memoirs:

---

37 Marie Joséphine Louise de Gontaut-Biron, *Louise* (Paris: A. Guyot, 1832), 168.
38 Marie Joséphine Louise de Gontaut-Biron, *Mémoires*, 384: "Mademoiselle was fourteen, her education was finished. [...] I had fulfilled my task, I was free, I was pleased with the result of my care, of these years pursuing a single thought".

> My daughters were getting older; their education was a source of worry; their precocious intelligence reacted so well to it! I sent the two eldest to a small school, and they soon spoke English such as to be my interpreters.[39]

Nevertheless, this concern for the education of children and young adults in exile was not the preserve of princely and aristocratic elites. The rupture triggered by exile was also a source of concern for liberal exiles during the first half of the nineteenth century, generating anxiety amongst parents and children alike. At the beginning of the July Monarchy, under a policy to encourage young refugees to resume their studies in France, fees were waived for those deemed the most deserving and who wished to continue a course in law or medicine, for which there were scholarships to buy the requisite material and books.[40] This did not prevent refugee students benefiting from this waiver from undergoing hardship, should the subsidy be paid late, for example. The resumed medical studies of the Italian liberal refugees Vitellini, Ricci, Simi, and Bianchini, granted special authorization by the ministry of the interior to reside in Montpellier, were abruptly interrupted in 1833 when their subsidies were paid several months late. In their distress, they turned to the chamber of deputies to express their disarray:

> Mr. President, please consider our position; how are we to live in a foreign country without money and without credit? Thus we hope, Sir, that the Chamber will consider this petition whose sole purpose is to render less arduous the life we are forced to eke out away from our homeland. We thus venture to beg that you grant a supplement to our pension, for as students it is impossible to meet all the expenses that our status occasions in terms of books, instruments, etc. with the forty-five francs given to us.[41]

This French policy of assisting refugee students was no doubt limited in scope. A few years after being trialed, it was progressively brought into question: a circular from the ministry of the interior dated August 10, 1843 requests prefects to be severe in investigating refugees who, "on the pretext of studies that they neglect or for which they have no aptitude, manage to obtain assistance above the ordi-

---

39 Madame de Ménerville, *La Fille d'une victime de la Révolution française. Souvenirs d'émigration, 1791–1797* (Paris: 1934), 170.
40 Archives départementales de la Vienne, 4 M 165, circular from the ministry of the interior, February 18, 1835: "refugees studying law or medicine, on whose behavior I have only good marks to send to the minister of public instruction, shall in all cases be exempted from enrolment fees, exam fees, et cetera".
41 Archives nationales de France, C 2124, petition no. 1181 from Italian refugees to the chamber of deputies, Montpellier, March 3, 1833.

nary rate".⁴² The figure of the refugee student, more readily accused of idleness than their compatriots with paid employment, was becoming increasingly suspect.

Schooling in exile

Exile prevented certain children and young adults from pursuing their studies, or else made it more complicated, at a moment in their life when such education seemed indispensable. But the constraints of expatriation also generated experiments and ideas about learning throughout the century. Several schools or academies were thus specially founded by exiles to meet the educational challenges facing the children and young adults in their ranks, offering various learning methods and courses. Among these schools, we may mention several in very different contexts, open to boys but also to girls.

In Britain, counterrevolutionary émigrés founded several schools including one for girls opened by Marquise MacNamara. This school in Hammersmith was set up with the financial support of the British Relief Committee, which granted assistance to French émigrés. It sought to help girls in need and enable them, thanks to its education, to go on to become good wives:

> Housed in a spacious dwelling in Hammersmith, these young ladies received a most careful and complete education. Attention was paid to prepare them to be virtuous Christians and practical, educated mothers: grammar, English language, geography, and a few pleasant arts such as drawing, music, etc. were included alongside useful skills.⁴³

The school took in girls for six years before closing in 1801. Nevertheless, the purpose was not so much the intellectual instruction of its pupils as their capacity to become good wives and Christians, and so avoid via a good marriage becoming a financial burden on the exile community.

Four decades later, an establishment for girls opened by members of the aristocratic elite in the great Polish emigration had the same objective. The Saint-Casimir institute, which opened in 1846 on Rue d'Ivry in Paris, with the assistance of Princess Anna Czartoryska, provided accommodation and education for needy young Polish girls, "orphans or abandoned without assistance and

---

42 Archives nationales de France, F1a* 44, circular from the ministry of the interior, August 10, 1843.
43 Abbé de Lubersac, *Journal historique et religieux de l'émigration et déportation du clergé de France en Angleterre* (London: Cox, 1802), 87.

mostly without family on foreign soil".⁴⁴ The fifty pupils still attending in 1852 devoted most of their time "to sewing, embroidery, and various household tasks". The objective in the case of destitute exiled girls, a major preoccupation for groups of exiles whose time abroad was lasting longer than initially expected, was to provide them with elementary instruction and give them the means to "support themselves" in later life.⁴⁵

Founded five years before the Saint-Casimir institute, the Polish School for boys in Paris, whose name soon became associated with the premises it eventually moved into in the suburb of Les Batignolles in 1844, had a very different purpose, namely "the moral and intellectual education of children and orphans of Polish refugees".⁴⁶ The "Batignolles Polish school" became a prominent establishment, and in April 1865, under the Second Empire, it was recognized as being of public utility. Teaching was based on virtually military rules seeking to equip pupils from exiled families with "an education such as to develop their moral, intellectual, and physical faculties, and prepare them to serve their homeland". While defending the Polish nation was the principal basis of this education, it was also grounded in Catholicism, as indicated in the brochure presenting the establishment in 1858.⁴⁷ The school was intended for the sons of those banished in the "great emigration", and in addition to attracting pupils from families settled in France, it was also attended by sons of those residing in Belgium and Britain. The school lasted longer than initially foreseen by its founders, whose sole goal was to prepare pupils to (re)build the Polish homeland.

The teaching in schools founded by Republican exiles and communards in London in the second half of the nineteenth century, with varying degrees of success, was totally different, being devoid of any patriotic objective. The socialist Jeanne Deroin, who went into exile in England in 1859 after two years in prison in France, tried to open a school in London in 1861 specifically for young working-class girls, but it finally failed due to lack of capital and the very low fees.⁴⁸

---

44 Archives nationales de France, F¹⁷ 12536, letter from Mme Suchet de la Redoute, president of Saint-Casimir, to the minister for public instruction, January 13, 1849.
45 Archives nationales de France, F¹⁷ 12536, letter from Princess Anna Czartoryska to the minister of public instruction, Parieu, December 22, 1849.
46 Archives nationales de France, F¹⁷ 9084, deed founding the Polish School, May 22, 1841.
47 Archives nationales de France, F¹⁷ 9084, L'École polonaise des Batignolles, 1848.
48 Adrien Ranvier, "Une féministe de 1848: Jeanne Deroin," *Revue d'histoire du XIXᵉ siècle* 26 (1908): 495.

Later on, in 1874, Napoléon La Cecilia (1835–1878)[49] managed to found a school for the children of exiles.[50] The establishment emphasized its nonreligious nature and was intended for exiles without any resources, with fees of sixpence per week and loans available for those unable to pay them. The school, which unlike that opened by Jeanne Deroin sought to provide a "virile education", closed likewise for lack of revenue. Lastly, the former communards who went into exile in London in 1890 wanted to establish a new school, the "international socialist school". Its governing body included well-known political figures such as the Italian anarchist Errico Malatesta. Schooling was of course free. Most of the pupils, reckoned to be forty or so initially, were the sons and daughters of anarchists passing through London (from Russia, Poland, Germany, France, Italy, and Spain). The teaching was grounded in the principles laid down by Mikhail Bakunin: rational methods, respect for individual dignity, and personal independence.[51] The school was closed down in 1892 after a bomb was discovered in the cellars where it had been placed by a spy.[52] Though the schools founded by French republicans and communards in London were very short-lived, some were nevertheless very novel in their response to a major challenge for political émigrés, namely the presence of children and young people among their ranks, concentrated in Paris and London, the great capitals of exile throughout the nineteenth century.

4 Mobility and sociability

Seeking to explain exiles' professional activities and educational undertakings brings out how they had to accommodate a factor they had not initially anticipated, that is, that their time in exile might last and endure even. As exile lengthened over time, émigrés became more fully inserted in the places where they resided, a phenomenon we shall now examine by looking at where their daily life unfolded.

---

49 He was born in France and the son of another exile, Giovanni La Cecilia (1801–1880), who had been an associate of Giuseppe Mazzini and then Giuseppe Garibaldi.
50 Paul K. Martinez, "Amis éprouvés et sûrs: les réfugiés blanquistes en Angleterre, 1871–1880," in *Blanqui et les blanquistes*, ed. Philippe Vigier (Paris: Société d'histoire de la Révolution de 1848-SEDES, 1986), 164.
51 Constance Bantman, "Louise Michel's London years: A political reassessment (1890–1905)," *Women's History Review* 26/6 (2017): 1003.
52 Xavière Gauthier, *La Vierge rouge. Biographie de Louise Michel* (Paris: Les Éditions de Paris, 2013), 290.

Exile districts?

The purpose of this section is not to go over assigned places of residence, in the administrative meaning of the term, affecting certain refugees when such a category was defined or used by a state,[53] but rather to look at the reasons pushing exiles to group together geographically in districts, streets, or even buildings, focusing on towns. It is useful to recall how Chicago school sociologists, especially Louis Wirth, analyzed migrant ghettos as a way of seeking protection and integration.[54] Wirth has given the following definition: "the ghetto is a cultural community that expresses a common heritage, a store of common traditions and sentiments".[55] Wirth does not associate ghettoes solely with their obvious function of withdrawal to protect an identity, instead detecting other possible dynamics of disintegration, due to the increasing number of contacts with the dominant culture, and the arrival of new waves of migrants in a city's poor districts.

This pattern, while clearly not applicable *stricto sensu* to the world of exiles, nevertheless provides many analogies and lines of inquiry. The Chicago of black and Jewish communities in the early twentieth century might not offer any direct similarities, but it was a migrant town, and exiles in the nineteenth century were often confronted with comparable spatial constraints, choices, and strategies to those identified by American sociologists. Exiles lived mainly in cities marked by demographic growth and the transformations resulting from industrialization. It is clearly difficult to find in present-day Paris or Brussels the places and houses where they resided, which were often razed in the middle or end of the century. Nevertheless, two distinct examples may serve to illustrate a large number of cases. First, Soho, in London, the prime example of an exile district, and second, Brussels, where they tended to live in scattered areas, though the places where they socialized tended to be grouped.

In many ways, Soho is key for a history of where outcasts from across nineteenth-century Europe resided. It took in successive waves of émigrés from the French Revolution, the regicidal members of the Convention under the Bourbon Restoration, followed by the 1848ers, the communards, and then anarchists at the end of the century.

In the 1790s, London was already the largest city in Europe, with one million people, and émigrés were concentrated in two districts. After Marylebone, Soho

---

[53] The reader is referred to chapter 2 of this book.
[54] Louis Wirth, *The Ghetto* (Chicago: Chicago University Press, 1928).
[55] Wirth, *The Ghetto*, 289.

Fig. 3. Map of exile districts in London in the nineteenth century.
Background map: "Tallis's illustrated plan of London and its environs", John Tallis, London, 1851. Map by Hugo Vermeren.

had the greatest density of French émigrés during the French Revolution: 18 % of émigré families – lay people – whose addresses are known lived there at this period.[56] The district acted as a place where French people met and also gathered to read the press and ask for news from across the Channel.[57]

Between 1848 and 1880, French republican and communard refugees settled mainly in an area between Covent Garden, Seven Dials, and especially Soho where most of the poorest refugees were drawn by the cheap accommodation, the main reason why foreigners were attracted to this district.[58] Soho, known

---

[56] Kirsty Carpenter and Philip Mansel (eds.), *The French Émigrés in Europe and the Struggle against Revolution, 1789–1814* (Basingstoke: Macmillan, 1999), 50.

[57] Kirsty Carpenter, "The novelty of the French émigrés in London in the 1790s," in *A History of the French in London*, ed. Debra Kelly and Martyn Cornick, 87.

[58] Stanley Hutchins, "The Communard Exiles in London," *Marxism Today* 15 (1971): 180–186: "the almost automatic venue for exiles since the 1848 revolutions was a well-established custom for French immigrants and continental exiles in general".

for being a refugee hub, was the first place of call for many arriving in London.⁵⁹ Between 1880 and 1914, French-speaking anarchist refugees settled in Soho once again, and, to a lesser extent, around Euston Street in Fitzrovia. New arrivals could hope to meet acquaintances and draw on support networks, even though these hopes were often largely disappointed in the first weeks of exile.⁶⁰ In Soho, residence in areas and buildings tended to be based on national grouping. But other residential strategies emerged at the end of the century: for instance, Constance Bantman has discovered that there were Franco-Italian houses where anarchists from both countries lived.⁶¹

Leaving Soho often indicated greater wealth or fuller integration. The Marx family, Louis Blanc, and the Duché-Chevassus family moved away from the city center, just like Londoners from the wealthy or middle classes. Conversely, moving out could also be indicative of a severe setback. Despite the solid revenue Arnold Ruge enjoyed in Paris and Brussels, he found himself without the means to live in London and settled in Brighton, where he tried to set up a photographic business with his wife, before returning to an activity more in line with his previous experience in teaching. Leaving the city could also be part of a political project. Such was the case of Struve who found in exile an opportunity to found a vegetarian community in Yorkshire, "the colony of renunciation" which soon entered rapid decline, not without provoking Marx's delighted criticism in his book *Heroes of the exile*.⁶² This failure led Struve to leave Europe for the United States.

While Soho was the emblematic district of exile in nineteenth-century Europe, Brussels and certain of its suburbs, such as Ixelles, were also privileged places of residence. There were many reasons for settling in Belgium for French exiles, including its proximity to France, and the fact that it would be easier for them to adapt. Discounting those assigned a fixed residence, exiles were concentrated in Brussels. The same street names and same hotels often crop up when researching where they lived. An undated document found among police surveillance documents from 1834 contains a dozen Polish names with place of resi-

---

59 Thomas C. Jones and Robert Tombs, "The French left in exile: *Quarante-huitards* and Communards in London, 1848–1880," in *A History of the French in London*, 172.
60 Constance Bantman, *The French Anarchists in London*, 54: "Soho was the place where one hoped to find old acquaintances and support networks upon arriving, although one informer's remark that 'any companion, any deserter arriving in London will immediately find brotherly assistance, an abode, a table and a job the very next day' was exaggerated".
61 Bantman, *The French Anarchists*, 56.
62 Karl Marx, Friedrich Engels, *Heroes of the Exile* (1852) (CreateSpace Independent Publishing Platform: 2012).

dence given as the Rue Haute district.[63] In February 1834, at least seven Poles were staying at the Hôtel L'Olivier, on Rue d'Or. The same establishment was described by Szymon Konarski on September 6, 1833, as "the famed hotel with the filth of our gentlemen".[64] However, such grouping did not last, and once permanently settled Poles spread out across the city. Some of the politically active among them lived in the center. Such was the case of Joachim Lelewel who as of 1845 lived at no. 58 of what is now the Rue des Éperonniers. Mlodecki moved into Rue de Ruysbroek with his printshop. Ludwik Ozeasz Lubliner lived on Rue du Marché-aux-Herbes, and Jan Ignacy Moll on the former Rue du Marché-aux-poulets.[65] Polish émigrés moved frequently. Wincenty Tyszkiewi, who reached Belgium in November 1833, lived at nine different addresses in Brussels and its environs between his arrival and 1848. This no doubt reflected opportunities to change accommodation, but also often resulted from chaotic material conditions. Marx, who lived in Brussels for three years, also moved on eight occasions.[66]

During his time in Brussels, Marx stayed on three occasions at the *Le Bois Sauvage*, guesthouse next to the Cathedral of Saint Gudula. He tended to stay there when in transit between two different places of residence. In 1845 the Marxes lived for a few months on Rue Pacheco, in a house occupied by the German poet Ferdinand Freiligrath until he left for Switzerland. They then lived in Saint-Josse for a year through to May 1846, in a building belonging to a German doctor, Breyer. Engels lived a few doors down on the same street, Rue de l'Alliance (with the Marxes at no. 5, and Engels and Mary Burns at no. 7). As for no. 3, it was home to the German philosopher Moses Hess. This grouping was very short-lived. After residing once again at *Le Bois Sauvage*, the Marxes moved to 42, Rue d'Orléans, in Ixelles, where they stayed until February 1848. On March 3, they were informed of their expulsion from Belgium at *Le Bois Sauvage*, where they had once again taken refuge.

Exiled communards were also apparently prone to disperse. Their social homogeneity, being mainly skilled laborers, could have led them to settle along

---

[63] Idesbald Goddeeris, "Des révolutionnaires polonais à Bruxelles (1830–1870)," in *Le Bruxelles des révolutionnaires, de 1830</litr> à nos jours* (Brussels: CFC-Éditions, "Regards sur la ville" collection, 2016), 35.
[64] Goddeeris, "Des révolutionnaires polonais", 35.
[65] Goddeeris, "Des révolutionnaires polonais", 34–35.
[66] Jean Stengers, "Du nouveau sur Marx à Bruxelles," *Bulletin d'information de l'association belge d'histoire contemporaine* 21/2 (1999): 21–22.

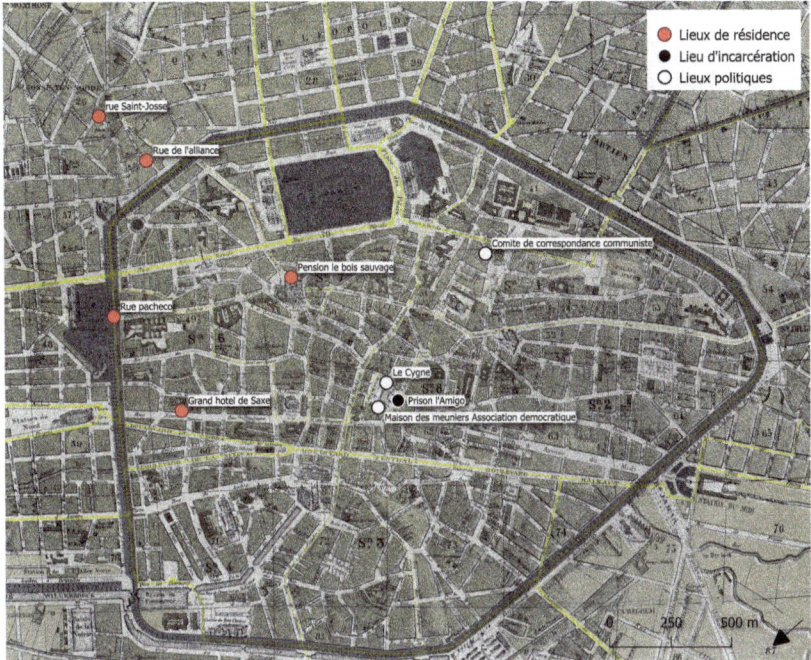

Fig. 4, translation: Red: Places where Marx lived; Black: Places where Marx was imprisoned; White: Political places.
Pension le bois sauvage: Le Bois Sauvage boarding house; Maison des meuniers Association democratique: House of the Democratic Association of Millers; Comite de correspondance communiste: Communist correspondence committee.

community lines in workers' districts and suburbs.[67] But there is no significant evidence of this in the in-depth studies carried out by Francis Sartorius.[68] Of the 750 people for whom precise information has been found, dispersal predominates. The 500 identified for Brussels lived in 220 different streets. In Molenbeek-Saint-Jean there were fifty outcasts living in thirty or so streets, and the situation was similar in Saint-Josse and Ixelles. Only seven communards lived in Laeken, in five different streets, despite its being a workers' district.

If we compare the residential distribution of communards in the 1870s with that of members of German associations in the 1840s, a certain number of roads

---

[67] Not all were skilled workers and the urban development works at Brussels attracted unskilled general laborers.
[68] Francis Sartorius, "Des communards exilés (1871–1879)," in *Le Bruxelles des révolutionnaires de 1830</litr> à nos jours*, ed. Anne Morelli (Brussels: CFC éditions, 2016), 72–81.

appear in each case, but this was primarily due to where furnished accommodation was available rather than to strategic or political choice. This spatial dispersal after the Paris commune is even easier to explain given that exiles did not experience any particular animosity from the local population, meaning they did not tend to withdraw in on themselves, and there was no language barrier to encourage communities to focus inwards. They were perhaps even less inclined to think of their exile in Brussels as something that would last than their Polish and German predecessors had been. Conversely, and perhaps even more so than for Soho, we may identify closely grouped meeting places mostly in the immediate vicinity of the Grande Place. These places are well-known thanks to accounts left by exiles and reports by secret agents, and included the Galerie du roi, the Passage des Princes, and the Petite rue des Bouchers. Four bars in Anderlecht were nevertheless identified as places where communards met.

As shown by this presentation of Soho and Brussels, emblematic places of exile in the nineteenth century, émigrés grouped together with varying degrees of density in districts which brought them together independently of differences in nationality. Nevertheless, this study of sedentary phenomena anchoring exiles in given cities should not eclipse the fact that the latter were constantly inclined to move and travel while in exile. This encouraged exiles wishing to attenuate their feelings of nostalgia to travel and meet old acquaintances, thus injecting some gaiety into a present that was dull and overshadowed by distance.

Exile as a time for traveling and tourism

The identity of the exile could often shade into that of the "tourist" at a time when a sudden increase in leisure traveling made this term popular. The opening lines of a poem in "Une voix de l'exil" by Étienne Arago blend these two identities:

> "You travel a lot." "I am often obliged to.
> The wind blows on me, I have to yield to the wind."
> "How say you that?" "It is because it saddens me."
> "But you see countries" "As one banished" "As a tourist"
> "It's all one".[69]

---

69 Étienne Arago, "Dialogue", *Une voix de l'exil* (Geneva: Blanchard, 1860), 215.

Many memoirs and correspondences depict how exiles voluntarily moved around to escape surveillance, or to reunite for those who found themselves isolated. They thus performed a tourist ritual predating exile, as was the case of Victor Hugo who left Jersey then Guernsey each year, accompanied by Juliette Drouet, to go to the banks of the Rhine. There was no political dimension to this, other than the desire to be free of the social and family control that formed part and parcel of an exile's daily life. Other examples illustrate such habits. Bertrand Barère, who was banished during the Bourbon restoration under the January 12, 1816 law against the regicides, settled in the southern Netherlands. During his time in Brussels, he lived "very frugally", according to Maïté Bouyssy, but this did not prevent him from going on a "late-season trip to Spa."[70] Another member of the regicidal Convention, Pierre-Anselme Garrau, likewise banished in 1816, took refuge in Wiesbaden, where he took the waters to get over the fatigue due to his peregrinations.[71] A few decades later, many exiles were present in Spa once again. Like Arago, they disapproved of the immorality of gambling, but could meet more freely in the gaming rooms than in the cafés and bars in capital cities, thus partaking in an activist form of elite sociability.

To turn exile into a personal or collective opportunity, it was necessary, when not working, to pass the time, maintain political or friendly ties, and educate oneself. The households of exiles thus became places of international sociability: one of the many people who visited Hugo in Guernsey was Démesvar Delorme, the journalist, writer, and politician from the first independent black republic, Haiti. Hugo received him at Hauteville House in September 1861, and the visit took a diplomatic turn since Hugo entrusted him with a letter addressed to the Haitian president, Fabre Geffrard.

Places of sociability

Places of sociability, whether clandestine or not, were essential to exiles' condition. Though often known for the presence of policemen and informants, they provided a crucial way of gathering information, of gauging the number of other exiles, and of hatching plans for journals, plots, or even assassinations on occasions.

---

70 Maïté Bouyssy, "Barère, exilé exemplaire," in *Déportations et exils des Conventionnels. Actes du colloque de Bruxelles, 21–22 novembre 2016*, ed. François Antoine et al. (Paris: Société des études robespierristes, 2018), 34.
71 Gonzague Espinosa-Dassonneville, "Pierre-Anselme Garrau, l'ermite d'outre-Rhin," in *Déportations et exils*, 102.

The regicides of the French Revolution created exile practices and usages by setting up an assistance fund, presided by Cambacérès. In Brussels they met up at the Café des Mille Colonnes where, according to the accounts they have left, the former members of the Convention listened to the silver-tongued former rapporteur of the committee of public safety, Barère. The other main place where they socialized was the Parc de Bruxelles, where former revolutionaries went on lengthy walks out of the earshot of informants. Throughout the century the bars in central Brussels played a leading role in the sociability of exiles there. The owners of these places were glad to rent out their rooms to associations, not all of which were political. Associations also used these premises as their registered addresses and housed their archives there. With the exception of La Bourse, at 19 de la Grand Place, run by Gustave van Soen, their owners were rarely activists. Instead, the choice of bar was often based on the price or quality of the beer. At the Maison du Cygne, also on the Grand Place, the owner rented out a room where the International Workingmen's Association held the meetings of its general council, and which also served as an office, archive area, and library. The IWA moved to La Bourse, then to the Armes d'Allemagne at no. 11. In 1875, it was back at the Maison du Cygne.

Other associations, often trade unions, were also to be found in the same establishments: the wood gilders association was at the Tête d'Or. The Café des Mille Colonnes, on the Place de la Monnaie, was one of the main places where French exiles met in Brussels, as recorded by Saint-Ferréol: "nowadays, the room for the meetings attended by so many exiles and politicians from all countries is called the *blaguorama* [joke-arama]".[72] Still, it was abandoned in the 1840s in favor of the more fashionable Café les Trois Suisses, where Victor Considerant played chess with Félix Cantagrel. According to the newspaper *Le Diable à Bruxelles*, Italian and Polish refugees were also present. When the Saint-Hubert Galleries were built in 1851, this venue made it easier for exiles to meet; according to Saint-Ferréol, "from 9 o'clock to midnight, one may especially encounter those known as the Girondins".[73]

In Geneva, cafés also acted as a vector for exile sociability. In the town which "attracted the largest number of 1871 [communards] refugees", it was "primarily at the Café du Nord that arriving exiles met and gathered. Then in the wake of

---

72 Saint-Ferréol, *Les Proscrits français*, 20.
73 Saint-Ferréol, 310.

the 'Razouza affair', they abandoned this place, deeming it to be a hotbed of spies from Versailles, and instead frequented the Café du Levant".[74]

Fig. 5. "Refugees of the 1871 Commune at the Café du Levant in Geneva", *Le Monde illustré*, April 27, 1872, Paris.

The 1872 image, commented here by Laure Godineau, shows how the Café du Levant had become a place of communard sociability known to all, including journalists, spies, and the police. Unsurprisingly for this period, it depicts a meeting attended solely by men, even though there were female activists exiled temporarily or more permanently in Geneva, such as Victorine Brocher, Victoire Tinayre, and Paule Mink from Paris, or Virginie Barbet from Lyons.

In addition to cafés, libraries were another vector for exile sociability. In London, a good number of the city's residents, from Marx to Vallès, frequented the British Museum. In his newspaper column published under the title "La Rue à Londres", Vallès wrote:

---

74 Laure Godineau, "Les réfugiés de la Commune de 1871 au café du Levant, à Genève", AsileuropeXIX website image bank, accessed April 11, 2021 https://asileurope.huma-num.fr/ressources-iconographiques/les-refugies-de-la-commune-de-1871-au-cafe-du-levant-a-geneve.

> The British Museum is filled with France. Anyone wishing to study the French Revolution, go over the ashes of civil wars, filter their blood, will find more traces of these struggles here than in the galleries, in Rue Richelieu, or even in the theater of these battles. I have been able to live amidst my national land for nine years of exile thanks to this attic stuffed with books redolent of our pitch and our gunpowder. It is a counterweight to the Bible, and the head librarians speak French.[75]

Louis Blanc's *L'Histoire de la Révolution française* confirms this observation, and also pays homage to the wealth of the English collections.[76] French exiles not only found books there, but also, given the many workers present, a practice of popular reading which was entirely new to them. Libraries also acted as a warm comfortable refuge for exiles fallen on hard times, providing an alternative to apartments or furnished rooms. Once again, it was all a matter of means, and certain private residences were on the contrary places of regular sociability outside police surveillance.

Places of sociability attended by exiles in towns could nevertheless be more structured and formalized. A certain number of exiles were freemasons. In Britain, masons residing there for political or professional reasons had free access to lodges.[77] A French-language lodge, *La Tolérance*, several of whose members issued from a Parisian lodge bearing that name, was even established in London, on January 22, 1847, under the authority of the United Grand Lodge of England. It took in exiles on their arrival, including, after the 1851 coup, Louis-Aimé Bourra, a former member of the revolutionary *Les Amis de la vérité* lodge and member of the Society of the Rights of Man. Another refugee, the pastel artist Charles Louis Gratia, joined the lodge and became its master in 1857. In Jersey, masonic lodge no. 590, the French-speaking *La Césarée,* opened in Saint-Hélier in 1851 under the authority of the United Grand Lodge of England. It took in many exiles thanks to its modest membership fees. French exiles also joined another rite, the *Rite de Memphis*, introduced to France by Samuel Onis, from Cairo, who had been initiated in Egypt in 1799. Though dormant in the early 1840s in Paris, the rite resumed operations on March 5, 1848, when three lodges were resuscitated: *Les Disciples de Memphis, Les Sectateurs de Mênes*, and *Les Philadelphes. Le rite de Memphi*s was forbidden after the coup but survived clandestinely in France. A refugee in London, Jean-Philippe Berjeau who had belonged to this

---

[75] Jules Vallès, *La Rue à Londres* (Paris: Éditions de la Pléiade), 1306. He also wrote: "All outcasts are regulars. It is because they find France there, the history of the first Republic, the history of our republic takes up a place as tall and wide as a barricade".
[76] Louis Blanc, *Histoire de la Révolution française* (Paris: Pagnerre, 1861), vol. 11, 73.
[77] André Combes, "Les francs-maçons réfugiés en Angleterre (1850–1880)," *Chroniques d'histoire maçonnique* 33/34 (1985).

rite, acted as an intermediary between France and Britain. It was under his authority that a grand lodge of the *Sectateurs de Mènes* was set up in London, adopting the distinctive name of the earlier Parisian lodge. Berjeau was a central figure in London exile circles. He ran a bookshop which acted as a meeting place for outcasts and was a member of the *Société fraternelle des démocrates socialistes*, which already included many masons such as Bourra, its treasurer. In addition to the *Sectateurs de Menes*, which became the *Philadelphes*, Berjeau set up another lodge, the *Gymnosophistes*, becoming its master, with Boichot becoming master of the *Philadelphes*. The membership of the two lodges included the most influential men in the republican community in London, such as Louis Blanc.

The activity of these lodges was not purely masonic – *Les Philadelphes*, for instance, founded a hospice for its members. They also spread out across the country, opening a lodge in Birmingham, probably under the influence of Chevassus, an industrialist in the city, and another in Brussels, with the *Invisible* lodge, in May 1854. *Le Thabor* was founded in New York by Claude Pelletier, and *Les Amis de la vérité* by Pierre Malardier in Geneva in 1856. There was also *Le Rameau d'or d'Eleusis* at Ballarat, in Australia, founded by Jean-Marie Ballaguy. But these initiatives were mainly short-lived due to a lack of initiates.

5 Boredom and death

Sociability in exile is a key factor for understanding exiles' daily life. But the glorious accounts of exile and memoirs seeking to present the political significance of societies founded abroad, or of simply frequenting reading rooms and bars, often glossed over an important dimension to this existence: enforced residency abroad was also archetypally a time of boredom and inactivity, neither of which are systematically emphasized in the texts left by exiles. Exile is sometimes described as an epic gesture, but it could also be described far more prosaically as a moment of inactivity, aimlessness, or simply a waste of time.

As noted by Sylvie Aprile in *Le Siècle des exilés*, two recurring themes in accounts by French émigrés and exiles in England are the London climate and the dreariness of Sundays.[78] The Duchess of Gontaut-Biron, who arrived in London in spring 1794, wrote that she understood "what the French feel on arriving in London on a Sunday", this "attack of spleen which is only dissipated on Monday by

---

78 Aprile, *Le Siècle des exilés*, 92.

the sunshine in Hyde Park".[79] The duchess – subsequently appointed governess to the above-mentioned Louise-Marie-Thérèse d'Artois, born in 1819 to the Duke and Duchess of Berry, and granddaughter to Charles X – lived through a second period of exile after the July Revolution. After July 1830, the little Louise, accompanied by her governess, followed her grandfather into exile in England, then to Holyrood in Scotland. Once again, the description in her memoirs of their arrival in Edinburgh evokes a renewed onset of spleen during the Scottish stage of her travels:

> Shortly after our arrival in Holyrood, I fell ill. All the emotions I had felt, the chagrin I had experienced on leaving my children behind had shaken my health. I fell into a state of languor which alarmed those around me; it was felt I could not safely look after Mademoiselle's education. The king granted me leave.[80]

A similar oppression emerges from writings by outcasts of a wholly different sort in the second half of the century, such as the exiled Charles de Rémusat. As a representative in the national legislative assembly under the Second Republic, he had signed the decree deposing Louis Napoléon Bonaparte to leave France, but soon returned to the country, in the summer of 1852. A decade later, in the memoirs of his exile; he describes daily life in Lynmore, in the English countryside, where he had settled during 1852 after spending time in Brussels then London:

> The early moments of my stay in Lynmore were [...] fairly sad. The bad weather continued, and a wave of boredom washed over me at the sight of the still misty horizon, the still overcast sky. Yet there is nothing in the world that so angers me with myself as feeling in the grip of boredom. It is, to my mind, the most humiliating thing that can befall us [...]. However, the exile must drain this cup to the dregs. How is he not to feel all the bitterness when he suddenly finds himself transported far from his native land, and, separated from all his past life, becomes as a stranger to his own existence. Without any attachment to his surroundings, without the ties to his old habits, his dear interests, all severed in a single day, he is like the trunk of an old tree cut down by a logger, whose mutilated roots are no longer cooled by the dew nor warmed by the sun.[81]

The boredom and spleen of exile were not the preserve of kings, queens, and their retinue. Many republican outcasts who left France in the middle of the cen-

---

[79] Marie Joséphine Louise de Gontaut-Biron, *Mémoires de la duchesse de Gontaut, gouvernante des enfants de France pendant la Restauration, 1773–1836* (Paris: Plon, 1891), 29.
[80] Gontaut-Biron, *Mémoires*, 377.
[81] Charles de Rémusat, *La Vie de village en Angleterre. Souvenirs d'un exilé* (Paris: Librairie académique, 1863), 2nd ed., 68–69.

tury describe spleen as one of the great ills of exile, with the monotony of their repetitive daily existence punctuated solely by waiting for correspondence and reading the press. Étienne Arago's (1802–1892) *Une voix de l'exil* (1860) contains a poem called "Les sept plaies de l'exil" (The seven scourges of exile), written in Geneva. Among the many maledictions besetting outcasts, he places "inactivity" second, after "isolation", with the former making "the richest nature" barren, and dulling "the subtlest mind".[82] Of course, outcasts' attentive descriptions of the pathos of exile placed them in a literary tradition stretching back through the centuries, echoing the *lamento* in Ovid's *Epistulae ex Ponto* or Dante's complaints about "the bitter bread of exile". Conversely, the melancholy of exile was rarely expressed by French-speaking anarchists in London at the end of the century, as noted by Constance Bantman, arguing that this is attributable to their ideas about nations and attachment to a homeland, though it may in certain cases also be explained by their ignorance of the literary codes and legacies associated with exile. In *Les Joyeusetés de l'exil* [The fun of exile], Charles Malato (1857–1938), a French anarchist and son of a Neapolitan combatant in the 1848 revolutions and then the Paris Commune, describes busy days filled by writing correspondence, grammar lessons, and more nourishing activities such as kneading bread, thus warding off inactivity, described as "depressing and fatal".[83]

The reparation files gauging the trauma of exile after the 1851 coup refer to a fairly large number of situations in which exiles did not return as they had committed suicide. In the file of the widow of Paul Chazeaud, the prefect refers to him as having "chosen Lake Geneva as his final confidant". On May 6, 1846, *L'Écho du Nord* published this enigmatic report:

> On Sunday, the body of a Polish refugee called Marcinoï Doboreski was recovered from the Canal de la Moyenne-Deule, and borne to the morgue in Lille. A knife was embedded deep in the throat. The body had been in the water for a long time and was in an advanced state of putrefaction. A large number of papers were found on the body which were used to ascertain the identity. Yesterday morning, a compatriot, decorated with the Polish Cross, came to claim Doboreski's body, and offered to pay for the burial. It is not known what caused this violent death, but the indications are it was suicide.

---

[82] Étienne Arago, "Les sept plaies de l'exil", *Une voix de l'exil* (Geneva: Imprimerie Blanchard, 1860), 211.
[83] Charles Malato, *Les Joyeusetés de l'exil* (Paris: Stock, 1897), 45.

Violent death resulted from the particular psychology of exiles who were apparently sensitive to rumors and gossip. As Hugo writes in *Les Misérables* of one of the outcasts, Emmanuel Barthélemy:

> Later, fatefully, in London, where both had gone as outlaws, Barthélemy killed Cournet, in a deadly duel. Some time after, caught in the machinery of one of those mysterious adventures involving passion, disasters in which French justice sees extenuating circumstances and British justice only death, Barthélemy was hanged. The somber social edifice is so constructed that thanks to material deprivation, thanks to moral darkness, this hapless being, with his undoubtedly sound, perhaps even great, intellect, started out in a penal colony in France and ended on the gallows in England. Barthélemy, whatever the occasion, flew only one flag – a black flag.[84]

Descriptions of daily life in exile would be incomplete without reserving a place for death abroad, whether this was something exiles feared or an at times brutal reality for the men and women living far from their homes. While the exiles traveling around Europe in the first half of the nineteenth century tended to be young and relatively less exposed to the risk of dying abroad, certain groups had a larger proportion of men of advanced or elderly years, as was the case for former members of the Convention. Bettina Frederking has studied references to their fate in the articles published in the Catholic newspaper *L'Ami de la Religion et du Roi*. She has demonstrated that of the 202 members of the regicidal Convention subject to the "amnesty law" of January 12, 1816, 152 died during the Restoration.[85] This very high mortality rate is attributable to the already advanced age of these outcasts, who had started their political careers during or even prior to the French Revolution. As François Antoine notes, "the members of the regicidal Convention affected by the amnesty law [...] had an average age of sixty when they went into exile".[86]

Wim Lemmens, in his study of the death of Jacques-Louis David in Brussels on December 29, 1826, explains how difficulties arose over organizing the painter's funeral. Villèle was opposed to the body being repatriated to France. The still lively memories left by the funeral procession which had followed the hearse of General Foy a few months earlier no doubt explain this reticence towards the re-

---

[84] Victor Hugo, *Les Misérables* (Paris: E. Hugues, 1879–1882), cinquième partie, Jean Valjean, Livre premier, "La guerre entre quatre murs", 12–13 Hugo is referring to Cournet's stating Barthelemy's companion was a prostitute.

[85] Bettina Frederking, "Qu'est-ce qu'un 'Conventionnel (régicide)'? La construction d'une catégorie dans la presse catholique sous la Restauration," in *Déportations et exils*, 20.

[86] François Antoine, "Les liens entre les spéculations sur les biens nationaux en Belgique et les Conventionnels exilés," in *Déportations et exils*, 71.

quest by the painter's heirs.[87] David's pupils in Belgium wished to hold a requiem mass in Brussels, but this ran up against the fact that the painter had died without the assistance of the church. Finally, negotiations by Louis de Potter resulted in a funeral being held on January 7, 1827. After temporarily conserving his mortal remains, these were buried in Brussels, initially at the cemetery in the Léopold district. The heart of the deceased was then conveyed to the family tomb at the Père-Lachaise cemetery, where a marker was erected in memory of the painter. The body of the painter was thus dispersed between France and Belgium, materializing the aporias and sufferings of exile, who even after death was torn between his country of origin and country of asylum. The outcasts of 1851 who followed in the footsteps of the members of the Convention sought for the traces of their predecessors in the cemeteries of Brussels.[88]

Nevertheless, death in exile was not the fate solely of the relatively elderly exiles who had been members of the regicidal Convention and who spread across Europe during the period of restorations. In France under the July Monarchy, the question of the death of refugees in receipt of assistance was regularly raised in instructions from the ministry of the interior. In those issued on July 31, 1839, it was specified that for refugees who died in France with no direct heirs, any subsidies due could be allocated, on the grounds of extraordinary assistance, to a compatriot in charge of settling their debts and paying their funeral expenses. While the payment of funeral fees was a source of concern for the ministry of the interior, the people accompanying the deceased refugee were also a major preoccupation for the executive. A circular from the ministry of the interior dated September 16, 1840, thus stipulates that the wives of Spanish Carlist refugees who died on French soil should be granted a passport after the funeral to return to their country as quickly as possible.[89]

The harsh living conditions of refugees in the second half of the nineteenth century no doubt explain why death in exile was apprehended by increasingly young refugees, who also feared for the health and survival of their children. In this respect, the case of the Marx family, cast out as of 1843 onto the roads of exile and traveling between Paris, Brussels, London, is emblematic of a concern for the survival of offspring, which unfortunately was well-founded. Once

---

87 Wim Lemmens, "Amor patriae. Immortaliser les fléaux de France: Jacques-Louis David à Bruxelles," in *Déportations et exils*, 50 *et seq.*
88 Sylvie Aprile, "Le proscrit pèlerin: le voyage de l'exilé sur les traces de ses prédécesseurs," in *Le Voyage et la mémoire au XIXe siècle*, ed. Sarga Moussa and Sylvain Venayre (Paris: Éditions Créaphis, 2011), 194.
89 Archives départementales du Rhône, 4 M 406, circular from the ministry of the interior dated September 16, 1840.

settled in London, initially in insalubrious furnished lodgings in Soho, Karl and Jenny Marx lost two children: Heinrich Guido in 1850, born the previous year, then two years later their daughter Franziska, born in 1851. But no doubt it was the death of their "lively, deeply loved" son Edgar, in London, which was the most difficult for Karl and Jenny Marx, as Jonathan Sperber explains:

> The death of this son was the greatest tragedy in Marx's life. At Edgar's funeral, his friend and political associate Wilhelm Liebknecht attempted to console him, reminding him of his wife, daughter, and friends, but Marx, close to losing control, just groaned in reply: "all of you cannot give me my boy back". Edgar's death left Marx depressed and dispirited for the next two and a half years. If he did not give in completely to despair, it was only, as he told Engels, because of the "thought of you and your friendship... And the hope that together we can still do something sensible in the world".[90]

If death in exile was a family affair, it also affected comrades and companions. French republican outcasts thus clubbed together in Belgium to organize funerals, especially as for them it was a matter of civil funerals. Amédée Saint-Ferréol has thus pointed out how in Belgium at this time "hearses, cemeteries, gravediggers, everything concerning burials belonged to the manufactories, to the clergy who used them as they saw fit".[91] Priests' opposition to civil burials even obliged exiles to "dig the soil with picks and place the coffin in the grave" at Dubief's burial.[92] This tussle with the political and clerical authorities encouraged the outcasts to organize themselves, and in 1854, the *Affranchissement* was founded, which on March 15 conducted the burial of the young son-in-law of Edgar Quinet, Georges Mourouzi.

Burials provided an opportunity to display political and anticlerical solidarity in the case of French republicans, and were preceded by rituals which generated political and personal tensions. Certain were most upset when barred from speaking at burials. In July 1853, Déjacque confronted Hugo at the burial of Louise Julien in Jersey, as he records:

> In Jersey, I gave another speech protesting a decision taken by the outcasts in a general assembly granting Victor Hugo the sole mandate to speak, in the name of all, at the funeral of Louise Julien, an outcast. That Victor Hugo speak in his own name, as a simple individual, under his own responsibility, nothing could be better; but in my name, and despite me,

---

90 Jonathan Sperber, *Karl Marx: A Nineteenth-Century Life* (New York: Liveright, 2014), 294.
91 Amédée Saint-Ferréol, *Les Proscrits français en Belgique ou la Belgique contemporaine vue à travers l'exil* (Brussels: Muquardt, 1870), 103.
92 Saint-Ferréol, *Les Proscrits*, 103.

what is more, is a right he does not and cannot have, no more than I have that speaking in the name of others, even should they be cretinous enough to mandate me to do so.[93]

During the funeral of the outcast Henri Beaugrand in January 1853, the rivalries were not expressed through speeches but through flags: the flag of the *Société de la Révolution* was placed at one end of the grave, that of the *Société Fraternelle* at the other.[94]

Irrespective of the social heterogeneity of refugees in nineteenth-century Europe, irrespective of the great variety in their personal trajectories, life in exile was often grounded in an idea of community, whether real or imagined: the community of those who had fought, the community of those who had left under constraint, but also the community of those who were living elsewhere, living in exile and living through exile. The plaintive portrayals sustained by the outcasts themselves also speak of the search for a common destiny. The analysis conducted in this chapter shows that nothing was that simple, and that they oscillated between professional continuity and rupture, successful reconversions and material difficulties, cultural exchanges and focusing on their lost country, insertion in places of strong sociability and individual travels, multiple activities and inactivity, solidarity and rivalries or conflicts. The collective destiny was also often that of relatives, companions, and children. Certain outcasts returned to their country of origin, while others never made the journey back. Irrespective of individual cases, the transmissions and legacies are to be sought within families, perhaps particularly among exiles' children. Unfortunately, the sources are sometimes incomplete, but enquiring into the experiences of these children and what they became during long-term exile provides a way of emphasizing the lasting aspects of life in exile, even when it ended in return – or death.

---

93 Joseph Déjacque, *Les Lazaréennes*, (New Orleans, 1857), second edition, 186, footnote 7.
94 Philippe Faure, *Journal d'un combattant* (Jersey: Lefevre éditeur, 1859), 217.

Constance Bantman, Catherine Brice and Alexandre Dupont
Chapter 5 Politics in exile

The Creole José Antonio Saco (1797–1879), expelled from Cuba in 1834 for his "liberal ideas", spent his life in exile, calling for reforms for his native island. Funded by a planter friend who had stayed behind in Cuba, he traveled around Europe, which was in a state of political ferment, spending time in Paris, Genoa, Montpellier, and Seville, and taking part in debates on the status of the Spanish colony. In the 1870s, he received delegations of Cubans exiled in New York come to Paris to collect donations from compatriots settled in Europe to help fund the patriot camp's war against Spain which had started in 1868. A few months before his death, once Cuba and Spain had signed a truce, he was even elected deputy for his island to the Cortes in Madrid. Saco – itinerant polygraph, nomadic polemicist, and political representative – was an indefatigable apostle of prudent colonial reformism during this "century of exiles".[1]

Saco's intense political activity in exile contrasts with the traditional image of nineteenth-century political exiles, such as Victor Hugo withdrawing to his rock in the Channel Islands, splendidly refusing any dealings with the power that had banished him, awaiting to be summoned back to his homeland by regime change. In her benchmark study of nineteenth-century French exiles, Sylvie Aprile emphasizes how certain exile groups could be affected by the very real processes of depoliticization, inertia, and internal conflict. The reality of their situation was that they were cut off from activist networks, geographically and linguistically isolated in a foreign country, obliged to prioritize matters of daily survival due to lack of money, and weighed down by police surveillance of political exile milieus – all of which no doubt favored depoliticization. Yet Aprile proposes another more dynamic interpretation of exiles' activity, focusing on how they pursued their combat, thus deconstructing the traditional image of impotence.[2] This approach has come to dominate over recent years, with the literature increasingly insisting on how activism mutated in exile, and on the vast repertoire of activism which, though fashioned by circumstances, exiles were able draw upon.[3]

---

1 On José Antonio Saco, see Romy Sánchez, *Quitter Cuba. Exilés et bannis au temps du séparatisme, 1834–1879* (Rennes: Presses Universitaires de Rennes, "Les Amériques" collection, 2021, forthcoming).
2 Aprile, *Le Siècle des exilés*.
3 For example, the 150th anniversary of the Franco-Prussian War and the Paris Commune have led to a re-reading of these episodes, highlighting their transnational character and the place

In an important book published in the 2000s, the sociologist and political scientist Stéphane Dufoix put forward a neologism to designate this activity in exile, "exopolitics".[4] Dufoix uses this term to refer to political action conducted by exiles (in his case, Eastern bloc émigrés) to continue playing a role in the politics of their land of departure. Nineteenth-century exiles were likewise actively involved in exopolitics. In addition to political activity targeting their land of departure, they were also often involved in the political life of their host country. Exile thus functioned as a crucible for political circulations in nineteenth-century Europe.[5]

Studying exiles thus provides a privileged observatory of these circulations. They had already been involved in revolutions, revolts, and conspiracies in their countries of origin, and over the course of their lives and through their socializations often came across and took up alternative models of government. In traveling around Europe and the Americas, they drove the circulation of political ideas and models. Recent works have demonstrated how "internationals" were created in exile, be they liberal, socialist, or even "white".[6] Independently of the circulation of ideas which tended to undergo transformation within host countries, the intensity of exiles' involvement could either wane as a function of the distance and time spent away from their country of departure, or, on the contrary, be "recharged" on successive occasions.

This chapter will also look at the circulation of activist practices in exile. Such an approach focuses on ways of doing politics, on the circulation of "techniques", and on the transfusion of constitutional engineering. It thus examines the action of exiles in their place of asylum, with particular emphasis on the types of mobilization, which changed extensively over time: conspiracies and insurrections; political financing (raising funds, organizing subscriptions, purchasing arms, etc.); and the activist dimension to cultural activities (commemorations, journalism, etc.).

---

held by exiles and international political activists: Nicolas Bourguinat, Alexandre Dupont, and Gilles Vogt, *La Guerre de 1870, conflit européen, conflit global* (Montrouge: Les Éditions du Bourg, 2020); Quentin Deluermoz, *Commune(s) 1870–1871* (Paris: Éditions du Seuil, 2020), see 29–44 especially; Michel Cordillot, *La Commune de Paris. Les acteurs, l'événement, les lieux* (Paris: Les Éditions de l'Atelier, 2021), see the contributions by Jean-Louis Robert and Olivier Peynot for example.

4 Stéphane Dufoix, *Politiques d'exil: Hongrois, Polonais et Tchécoslovaques en France après 1945* (Paris: Presses universitaires de France, 2002).

5 Catherine Brice (ed.), *Exile and the Circulation of Political Practices in the 19th century* (Cambridge: Cambridge Scholars, 2020).

6 Éric Anceau, Jacques-Olivier Boudon, and Olivier Dard (eds.), *Histoire des internationales. Europe, XIXe-XXe siècles* (Paris: Nouveau Monde Éditions, 2017).

1 Combats and beliefs tested by exile

Press, tracts, and pamphlets

Writing was the main force informing, structuring, and sustaining exile communities. Writing and publishing memoirs, accounts, essays, and pamphlets was the first echelon of political activity in exile. It was a response to economic necessity (and the exiles were hard-nosed when negotiating their fees), but also driven by a need to inform and a wish to portray their experience and status as exiles.[7] Chancelleries alerted each other to the publication of a work, while consuls reported back on a text's arrival in the "colony", thus revealing the expected impact of such writings.[8] The circulation of writings, particularly pamphlets, also drove debates and built up genuinely transnational fields. This is one of the major points made in Maurizio Isabella's *Risorgimento in Exile*, analyzing how the writings of pro-unification Italian liberal exiles helped publicize their cause, making exile a place of transnational debate partaking in political construction from abroad.[9]

The press was by far the main medium outcasts used. It functioned at various levels: locally, within exile groups, but most of the time in dialogue with other groups and above all the country of origin. Reflecting the actual or wished for internationalism of exile circles, newspapers were sometimes written in several languages, such as the *El Correo Atlántico* founded in 1835 in Mexico by a refuge from Molise, Orazio de Attellis, Marquis de Sant'Angelo,[10] or the Carlist *La Voz de la Patria*, published in Bayonne by Carlos Benítez Caballero in French and Spanish in 1874.[11] Others included many translations, such as *The Torch*, published in London in the 1890s, with British, Italian, and French contributors

---

7 Aprile, *Le Siècle des exilés*; Delphine Diaz, "The Risorgimento Italians' Journeys and Exile Narratives: Flight, Expedition or Peregrination?," in *Carrying Italy in their Suitcases: Migration, Circulations and Italianness (19th–21st centuries)*, Céline Regnard et al. (eds.) (New York: Palgrave Macmillan, 2022, forthcoming).
8 As illustrated by the case of Luigi Carlo Farini's *Lo Stato romano dal 1815 al 1850* published in Turin in the early 1850s.
9 Isabella, *Risorgimento in Exile*.
10 Bénédicte Deschamps, "Echi d'Italia. La stampa dell'emigrazione," in *Storia dell'emigrazione italiana*, ed. Piero Bevilacqua, Andreina De Clementi, and Emilio Franzina (Roma: Donzelli Editore, 2002), 316.
11 Dupont, *Une internationale blanche*, chapter 7.

and a clearly multilingual "voice".[12] There was nothing new about such an undertaking: from 1853 to 1856 a social democrat newspaper, *L'Homme*, had been published which, despite being exclusively in French, had the stated purpose of being an internationalist publication. Those working on it translated articles by leading European exiles, such as Mazzini, Kossuth, and Herzen.[13]

Production conditions could be very complex. Distribution strategies were devised for various scales, sometimes resorting to unconventional stratagems to circumvent censorship and surveillance, such as the entirely antiphrastic writing used by London anarchists in the period 1880–1914, or the dissimulation of censored journals in more "respectable" publications.[14] Journalistic and political practices were also exchanged and circulated, generating hybridizations which justify viewing the press as the crucible for a transnational public sphere during the nineteenth century.[15] Writing about Cuban exiles, Romy Sánchez has brought to light the transnational circulations and appropriations of news circuits and newspapers, be they produced by exiles, published in host countries, or issuing from lands of departure. Sánchez emphasizes the practice of press cuttings, arguing that it acts as an observatory for how exiles viewed events. In addition to circulating in the press, information could be taken up by exiles and reused in various circumstances.[16]

Prior even to newspapers, which required money, pamphlets were a means of political communication, both within exile groups and between outcasts and their country of origin; like private correspondence, they were circulated intensely and clandestinely.[17] Some exiles were also able to publish newspaper columns in their host countries to share their opinions or give their point of view on an aspect of foreign policy, often placing themselves in a complicated position, particularly in states which practiced censorship. Francesco Crispi, for instance, was expelled from Malta where he had been in exile since 1853 for having written

---

[12] Pietro Di Paola, "The Italian Anarchist Press in London: A Lens for Investigating a Transnational Movement," in *The Foreign Political Press in Nineteenth Century London. Politics from a distance*, ed. Constance Bantman and Ana Cláudia Suriani da Silva (London: Bloomsbury Academic, 2017), 17–119.

[13] Thomas C. Jones, "Rallier la République en exil. *L'Homme* de Ribeyrolles," in *Quand les socialistes inventaient l'avenir: presse, théories et expériences, 1825–1860*, ed. Thomas Bouchet, Vincent Bourdeau, Edward Castleton and al. (Paris: La Découverte, 2015), 348–360.

[14] Thomas C. Jones and Constance Bantman, "From Republicanism to Anarchism: 50 Years of French Exilic Newspaper Publishing," in *The Foreign Political* Press, 99.

[15] Constance Bantman, "Introduction," in *The Foreign Political Press*, 10.

[16] Romy Sánchez, *Quitter Cuba*.

[17] AAV (Archivio Apostolico Vaticano), SS, anno 1849, rubrica 165, fascicolo 7-console pontificio – Atene, folio 7–10761–7 August 1849.

and published in newspapers, something foreigners were banned from doing.[18] As for Charles Malato, an Italian anarchist activist expelled to Britain from France in 1892, he published in the prestigious *Fortnightly Review* in 1894.[19]

Work by Bénédicte Deschamps on the Italian press in the United States brings out the structural role newspapers played for exiled communities, and how journalistic techniques evolved as exiles learned a "new journalism" through their practice abroad.[20] The function of newspapers was not in fact strictly political, and they acted as a link between various outcasts: they were used to organize and inform about cultural activities and events, and included announcements and advertisements about the social and professional organization of the exiled community.

In a period predating political organization, newspapers fulfilled the function of "parties". Thus in 1859 Francesco Crispi wrote to his correspondent in Lisbon, Simeone Gattai, to complain that readers of the Mazzinian *Pensiero e Azione* had to pay another nine month's subscription to the newspaper: "I do not see why the party should lose these sums", he wrote, insisting on the fact that in capitals elsewhere, readers, in addition to paying their subscription, had also organized collections for the Mazzinian party.[21]

Circulating models

Another form of publication with a political function and addressing the exile community and governments was the compilation of laws and regulations, together the most exhaustive documentation possible to do justice to a political regime which had failed at a given moment, and whose exiled leaders now sought to demonstrate its legitimacy. One such project was Francesco Crispi's *Archivio storico contemporaneo italiano*, to which he and Carlo Cattaneo devoted considerable energy in 1850.[22] A call for documents about Italian events from the advent of Pius IX in 1846 to the fall of Venice went out to those who had brought with them into exile newspapers, extracts of proceedings, legal compendiums,

---

18 Francesco Crispi, *Lettere dall'esilio 1850–1860, raccolte e annotate da T. Palamenghi-Crispi* (Roma: Casa editrice Tiber, 1918), 94.
19 Charles Malato, "Some Anarchist Portraits," *Fortnightly Review* 333 (1894): 327–328.
20 Bénédicte Deschamps, "Dal Fiele Al Miele: La Stampa Esule Italiana Di New York e Il Regno Di Sardegna (1849–1861)," *Annali Della Fondazione Luigi Einaudi* 42 (2008): 81–98.
21 Crispi, *Lettere dall'esilio*, 130.
22 On the Tipografia elvetica undertaking, see Rinaldo Caddeo, *La Tipografia elvetica di Capolago* (Milan: Alpes, 1931).

and suchlike. Crispi collected nearly all the newspapers published in Sicily during the sixteen months of the Sicilian revolution, the *Comitato generale*'s official legal acts, the *Atti autentici del Parlamento editi per ordine delle Camere*, and nearly two hundred original documents. For Sicily alone, the Tipografia Elvetica de Capolago went on to publish twenty-six volumes covering domestic affairs for the period 1848–1849. As Francesco Crispi wrote, "Against the Bourbons [...] we have erected a monument that bombs cannot destroy".[23] This monument was ultimately incomplete, but "paper monuments" were an editorial, memorial, and political characteristic of Italian exile.[24]

Certain exiles, finding themselves in a state of enforced inactivity, devoted their energies to an exhaustive study of the country where they were residing, looking for models, comparisons, and examples for their own political project. Writing from exile in Malta in 1853, Francesco Crispi announced his wish to draw up a history of Malta through to 1798, working in the archives and researching municipal laws in the Papal States and the Kingdom of Naples. He corresponded with another exile, Pietro Maestri, in Paris, who was conducting similar research on Lombardy.[25] Paul Gerbod's *Les Voyageurs français à la découverte des Iles britanniques*, and the example of Louis Blanc's *Lettres sur l'Angleterre* reveal the interest French[26] republicans had for the model of Westminster.

More generally, exile played a major role in thought about reforming state and society in nineteenth-century Europe. Residing abroad made it possible to compare different political models and legislations, while providing an opportunity to call for foreign systems to be imported to exiles' land of origin, or for these models to be used as a source of inspiration and adapted.[27] In this respect, exile played a leading role in the circulation of political models. Without having to wait to return home to put their intended reforms into action, exiles could address compatriots through writing to advocate solutions of foreign inspiration. Thus Mustafa Fazıl Pasha, an Egyptian prince exiled in Paris in the 1860s, wrote an open letter to Sultan Abdulaziz in 1867, which was published as a pamphlet and soon circulated clandestinely in Constantinople. In this letter, Fazıl

---

[23] Crispi, *Lettere dall'esilio*, 21.
[24] Catherine Brice, "Les monuments de papier. Exil, archives et politique après le Quarantotto," in *La Repubblica per passione. Studi dedicati a Marina Tesoro*, ed. Arianna Arisi Rota and Bruno Ziglioli (Pisa: Pacini Editore, 2020), 66–79.
[25] Brice, "Les monuments de papier", 77–78.
[26] Paul Gerbod, Les voyageurs français à la découverte des îles britanniques du XVIIIè siècle à nos jours (Paris: L'Harmattan, 1995).
[27] Simon Schaffer (ed.), *The Brokered World: Go-Betweens and Global Intelligence, 1770–1820* (Sagamore Beach: Science History Publications, 2009).

Pasha proposed reforming the Ottoman state in accordance with principles and plans inspired from what was being done in Europe, further presenting the empire as partaking in the trajectory of a shared European history.²⁸ In the same year, Fazıl Pasha also helped three Ottoman intellectuals to travel to Paris, Namık Kemal, Ziya Bey, and Âli Suavi, who had been relegated to internal exile by the sultan. Via their works in exile, these three men contributed to the development of the Young Ottomans' constitutionalist movement.²⁹

Additionally, exiles could also draw on their technical and scientific expertise to advise governments in their host countries, or to transfer political and scientific models and knowledge in both directions. The case of José María de Lanz y Valdívar is instructive. Born in New Spain in 1764, Lanz was a reformer specialized in public engineering and marine affairs. After serving the Spanish monarchy, he became actively involved in the Napoleonic administration in Spain from 1808 to 1814, overseeing public works. The defeat of the Napoleonic troops forced him into exile, along with other *afrancesados*. He divided the rest of his life between Paris and the newly independent Latin American republics, especially Argentina and Gran Colombia, drawing on the knowledge he had acquired during the reign of Joseph I to develop military and scientific structures in these new states. These republics tasked him with negotiating their international recognition, particularly with mainland Spain, and in the 1830s he returned and settled in Paris, remaining there until his death in 1839.³⁰ In Tunisia, where reforms were under way, Italian exiles among the entourage of the beys held a notable place in government spheres, as illustrated by the cases of Giuseppe Raffo and Gaetano Frediani. The latter, a Mazzinian exile, arrived in Tunis in 1834,

---

28 Andrew Arslan, "The Strange Lives of Ottoman Liberalism: Exile, Patriotism and Constitutionalism in the Thought of Muhammad Fazıl Paşa," in *Mediterranean Diasporas: Politics and Ideas in the Long Nineteenth Century*, ed. Maurizio Isabella and Konstantina Zanou (London: Bloomsbury, 2015), 153–170.

29 Şerif Mardin, *The Genesis of Young Ottoman Thought: A Study in the Modernization of Turkish Political Ideas* (Princeton: N. J., Princeton University Press, 1962); Nazan Çiçek, *The Young Ottomans: Turkish Critics of the Eastern Question in the Late Nineteenth Century* (London and New York: I. B. Tauris, 2010).

30 Manuel Lucena Giraldo, *Historia de un cosmopolita. José María de Lanz y la fundación de la Ingeniería de Caminos en España y América* (Madrid: Colegio de Ingenieros de Caminos, Canales y Puertos, 2005</LITR>); Darina Martykánová, "La movilidad en la circulación de conocimientos en el espacio atlántico: La excepcionalidad significativa de José María Lanz (1764–1839)," in *Trayectorias trasatlánticas (Siglo XIX), Personajes y redes entre España y América*, ed. Manuel Pérez Ledesma (Madrid: Ediciones Polifemo, 2013), 15–44.

where he combined business, cultural, and political activities.[31] Such life courses indicate the extent to which exile was a place for political reflection and rebuilding, with repercussions not just for discourse but also for the circulation of knowledge and models.

Becoming politicized in a foreign context

Exile also provided an opportunity for outcasts to familiarize themselves with new ideas, struggles, and issues with which they had not been confronted prior to their departure. It thus acted as a forum for recomposing and reworking discourse, when it did not mark a break in the intellectual and political course taken by exiles. In most cases, exile led those involved to accustom themselves first and foremost to the political situation and issues in their host states. In that respect, exopolitics was not limited to action seeking to change the circumstances in the land of departure, for it also engendered familiarization with the situation in the host country. Thus Victor Hugo spoke out from Guernsey to denounce the death sentences following the Fenian revolt in Ireland in 1867. He wrote his text in defense of the Fenians after being approached by the women of those sentenced to death, indicating that illustrious exiles could also become a figure of authority in their host country, to whom people turned to intervene with the authorities. The definitive edition of his collected *Actes et paroles* attributes the British authorities' decision not to go ahead with their execution to this intervention. But the text is of further interest, contrasting Britain's liberal attitude towards outcasts from across Europe with the repression it conducted in Ireland, demanding that the British leaders conform to the image they presented: "No; the political scaffold is not possible in England. When England hailed Kossuth, it was not that she might imitate the gibbets of Hungary; it was not for the purpose of renewing the hangings of Sicily that England glorified Garibaldi. Else what would signify the hurrahs of London and Southampton? Put an end, if it was so, to all your Polish, Greek, and Italian committees."[32]

Examination of *Actes et paroles* for the period when Hugo was in exile additionally reveals the extent to which he was involved from exile in many political combats not concerning France or Britain. He gave particularly strong support to

---

31 See Ersilio Michel, *Esuli italiani in Tunisia 1815–1861* (Milan: Istituto per gli studi di politica internazionale, 1941), and Leila Adda, "Les apports culturels des réfugiés politiques en Tunisie au XIXᵉ siècle," in *Da maestrale a scirocco. Le migrazioni attraverso il Mediterrano*, ed. Federico Cresti and Daniela Melfa (Milan: Giuffré, 2006), 65–81.
32 Victor Hugo, *The Freeman's Journal from Dublin*, June 3, 1867.

various representatives of the nationality movement: Poles, Italians, Greeks, and even Cubans in revolt against Spain were able to count on his constant backing in their struggle for independence and unification. Victor Hugo also took advantage of the 1868 revolution in Spain, which opened a period of liberalization and democratization, to call on Spain's leaders to abolish slavery, a call which ultimately went unheeded.[33] While Hugo had long been involved in the combat against slavery,[34] for many others it was exile which triggered their politicization on the issue. Particularly in the mid-nineteenth century, exiles in the United States, on being confronted with the slave-owning society of the South, adopted the fight against slavery as their new cause.[35] Many enlisted in the Northern Army during the American Civil War, motivated by the fight for abolition. Although the Quaker Benjamin Lay had not emigrated for political reasons, it was when he was living in Barbados in 1718 and observed the reality of slavery that he became the first abolitionist in the Atlantic world.[36] Politicization on this issue thus reached back a long way.

More generally, exile was an opportunity to become involved in other fields. Nineteenth-century political protagonists thus thought of their struggle on an international scale and wished to pursue their political commitment in other realms. This was the case for example of the Italian exiles from the 1820–1831 revolutionary cycles studied by Grégoire Bron. On being forced into exile in France after the failure of their pro-liberal movement in the Italian peninsula, they followed the passionate debates in France about the situation in Portugal, where liberals, gathered around the young Queen Maria II and her father Pedro I, Emperor of Brazil, clashed with counterrevolutionaries supporting King Miguel I, who had usurped the throne in 1828. These Italian liberals were moved by a conflict that seemed to resemble the one which had led to their exile in France, and they mobilized in favor of Portuguese liberals, mounting an armed expedition to come to their assistance.[37]

Lastly, it should be noted that the forms of politicization possible during exile and the exposure to new issues did not always fit coherently with an indi-

---

[33] Hugo, *The Freeman's Journal From Dublin*, 147–149.
[34] Léon-François Hoffmann, "Victor Hugo, les Noirs et l'esclavage," *Françofonia*, 16/30 (1996): 47–90.
[35] Sylvie Aprile, "Exil et exilés français sous le Second Empire," *Hommes & Migrations* 1253 (2005): 88–97.
[36] Marcus Rediker, *The Fearless Benjamin Lay. The Quaker Dwarf Who Became the First Revolutionary Abolitionist* (Boston: Beacon Press, 2017).
[37] Grégoire Bron, "The exiles of the Risorgimento: Italian volunteers in the Portuguese Civil War (1832–34)," *Journal of Modern Italian Studies* 14/4 (2009): 427–444.

vidual's prior course. On the contrary, in a certain number of cases, exile led to spectacular *volte-faces*, illustrating how complex political landscapes were at the period. These discontinuities transpire particularly in those traveling across the Atlantic, with a certain number of champions of liberalism and democracy in Europe becoming partisans of slavery and imperialism once in America.[38] Though little studied, there were also exiles from the 1848–49 revolutions who enlisted in the Southern Army during the American Civil War, or who joined William Walker's expeditions to Central America in the 1850s with the goal of subjecting populations to this adventurer.[39]

2 The circulation of political practices

The terminology of transfers has been very fruitful in literature about exiles, with attention also being paid to the material aspects making such circulations possible or, on the contrary, hindering them. The perspectives provided by transnational history have led to various new frameworks of interpretation being devised, bringing out the many modes of political life in exile and the forms it could take on various scales. The timeframes for transfers generally exceeded that of exile itself, encompassing the time of return when dissemination could take place. Circulation was also frequently multipolar, connecting up numerous sites of exile in addition to the straightforward pair of origin/host country, and linking up different exile communities present in the same place in the great capitals of exile such as London and Paris. This activism was for that matter complex in its targets. While it certainly addressed the land of origin, it could also be transformed under the effect of dynamic productive exchanges. Writing about France, Delphine Diaz has thus emphasized "exiles' aptitude to intensely experience their social relations in the land of asylum", together with the "permeability of their practices".[40] These observations could be extended to other places of exile.

---

38 Ronald Takaki, *A Pro-Slavery Crusade: the Agitation to Reopen the African Slave Trade* (New York: Free Press, 1971).
39 Michel Gobat, "The Invention of Latin America: A Transnational History of Anti-Imperialism, Democracy, and Race," *The American Historical Review* 118/5 (2013): 1345–1375.
40 Diaz, *Un asile pour tous les peuples*.

A shared political sphere?

Exile milieus provided a sphere for reinventing and reconfiguring politics, along with the organizations and factions involved on occasions. But this sphere was far from uniform. It was mainly characterized by division and dissent, and by the hardening of positions held prior to departure, even though parallel trends may be observed, for example, a move towards depoliticization or the moderation of earlier political stances.

Spanish exiles in France throughout the nineteenth century illustrate the complex dynamics making it more complicated to establish a shared political sphere. During the reign of Ferdinand VII (1814–1833), exiles were able to take political advantage of their presence in exile in what Irene Castells has called an insurrectional utopia.[41] Nevertheless, exile based around clearly identified political leaders also helped profoundly reshape Spanish liberalism: while the divide between exalted liberal (as they were known) and moderate liberals became accentuated, the latter became more aligned with the *afrancesados*, who, despite having supported the pro-French regime from 1808 to 1814, nevertheless shared many ideological premises with the moderates' conservative liberalism.[42] Conversely, during the reign of Ferdinand VII's daughter Isabella II (1833–1868), and especially in the 1860s, centrifugal forces led various groupings from the Spanish left, forced to leave their country by the growing repression exerted by the regime, to come together in shared opposition. Unionists, progressives, democrats, and republicans even ended up joining forces in the Ostend pact signed in 1866, which set out a mission for this exiled left to work together to overthrow the regime in place, while putting off policy disagreements to a later date.[43]

The organization of these exile communities around a few charismatic figures inevitably complicated matters. This additional personal dimension meant that many strategies were more individual than collective, often triggering con-

---

[41] Irene Castells Oliván, *La utopía insurrecional del liberalismo. Torrijos y las conspiraciones liberales de la década ominosa* (Barcelona: Crítica, 1989). See too Juan Luis Simal, *Emigrados. España y el exilio internacional, 1814–1834* (Madrid: Centro de Estudios Políticos y Constitucionales, 2012).
[42] María Cruz Romeo Mateo, "'Nuestra antigua legislación constitucional'¿modelo para los liberales de 1808–1814?," in *Guerra de ideas. Política y cultura en la España de la Guerra de la Independencia*, ed. Jordi Canal and Pedro Rújula (Madrid: Marcial Pons, 2011), 75–103.
[43] Jorge Vilches, *Progreso y Libertad. El Partido Progresista en la Revolución Liberal Española*, (Madrid: Alianza Editorial, 2001); Christophe Chevalier, "Acteurs non étatiques et relations internationales au XIXe siècle: le cas du comité d'Ostende (1866–1870)," *Relations internationales* 174/2 (2018): 722.

flicts and disagreements. Admittedly, this polarization of the exile community could have positive effects and maintain group cohesion. That is what may be observed in the 1870s and 1880s for two very different political groupings, namely Spanish republicans and Carlists: while the former rallied around the charismatic figure of Manuel Ruiz Zorrilla, the latter benefited from the vertical structuration of nineteenth-century counterrevolutionary currents around a dynastic figure, in their case Don Carlos, Duke of Madrid. Nevertheless, this strength could become a weakness if the dominant figure was caught out. Prince Don Carlos's repeated antics throughout the 1870s and his scarcely concealed liaison with the young Hungarian Paula de Samoggy, all far removed from his supporters' image of a Christian prince, earned him the nickname "King of the Hungarian women", and significantly discredited him among Carlist exile circles.[44] Italian exile communities were also divided along political lines, between those in favor of an Italy headed by Piedmont and those opposed to this, often Mazzinians, or between federalists and those supporting unification. Furthermore, arrangements between groups based on regional origins could be fragile.[45]

In her discussion of French outcasts in Britain during the Second Empire, Sylvie Aprile analyzes the difficulties they encountered in constituting a shared political sphere in exile. French republicans in Britain, constrained part of the time to remain within the circle of their community, had to manage the political consequences of disagreements and rivalries often rooted in very personal affairs: for instance, quarrels might arise due to a given refugee's adventures with another refugee's wife. Individual ambitions and hostilities between exiles were such that Victor Hugo steered clear of London, always refusing to reside there for fear of having to associate with the figureheads of the French exile community. These complex social dynamics were compounded by the well-founded fear of informants recruited by the imperial government to report on the activity of their companions in exile. The most spectacular instance of this distrust of informants was no doubt the setting up of veritable tribunals, in which exiles sat in judgment on those accused of spying: an illustration of this is the affair in Jersey in October 1853 when the outcasts charged a certain Hubert with being an informant, sentencing him to death at the issue of the trial. Hubert was saved when Hugo refused to see this sentence carried out. In general, rather than being traitors who had gone over to the side of the imperial authorities, inform-

---

[44] See the chapters by Jordi Canal and Fernando Martínez in *París, ciudad de acogida* (Madrid: Marcial Pons, 2010).
[45] See Ester De Fort, "Une fraternité difficile: exil et associationnisme dans le Royaume de Sardaigne après 1848," in *Exil et fraternité*, 143–161.

ants tended to be particularly impoverished and isolated exiles, driven by necessity to relinquish their political beliefs and accept paid employ.[46]

Places of politicization

But one should not overstate these disagreements and quarrels, or the powerlessness of exiles. On the contrary, nineteenth-century exile was characterized by the intense political social interactions it gave rise to and by the ties it generated between outcasts, both with refugees of other countries and with political protagonists in the host country. In the wake of pioneering propositions by Maurice Agulhon on the significance of sociability in politicization processes,[47] this section looks at the role this played in establishing a shared political sphere conducive to the circulation of activist practices.

The simplest and most classical form of sociability in exile consisted in the fact of gathering, which in practice took very varied forms. Meetings could be highly informal and take place in the home of a given individual, making them difficult for historians to document. In general, the mixing of the public and the private sphere was a major characteristic in the life of nineteenth-century exiles, one consequence of which was that women played a leading role in exopolitics, as we shall see in the following chapter. In a certain number of cases, the wealth or political or symbolic importance of the person hosting these gatherings lent a more markedly public dimension to gatherings in their home. This was the case for the social interactions among Polish exiles at the Hôtel Lambert in Paris, acquired in 1843 by Zofia Anna Sapieha, the wife of Prince Adam Jerzy Czartoryski, the leader of the Polish party in France.[48]

It was also the case of salons hosted by women (also discussed in the following chapter), where exiles socialized with artistic circles. Princely courts in exile were also leading places of sociability for counterrevolutionaries throughout Eu-

---

[46] Aprile, *Le Siècle des exilés*, 154–165.
[47] Maurice Agulhon, *La République au village: les populations du Var de la Révolution à la Seconde République* (Paris: Plon, 1970); Maurice Agulhon, *Le Cercle dans la France bourgeoise. Étude d'une mutation de sociabilité* (Paris: Armand Colin, 1977).
[48] Katarzyna Papiez, "La Grande Emigration polonaise: bals à l'hôtel Lambert à Paris, 1844–1846," accessed on April 11, 2021, https://asileurope.huma-num.fr/ressources-iconographiques/la-grande-emigration-polonaise-bals-a-lhotel-lambert-a-paris-1845.

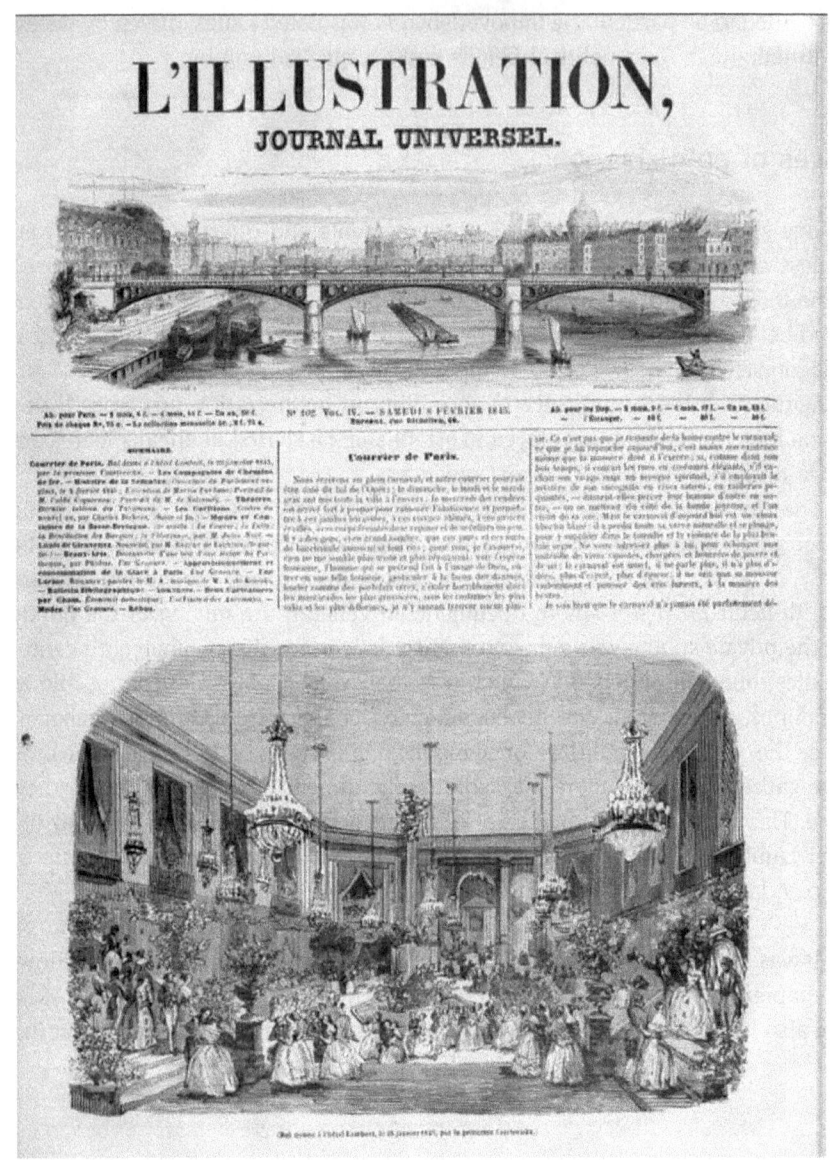

Fig. 6. "Bal à l'hôtel Lambert", *L'Illustration*, February 8, 1845.

rope, such as the court held for decades by the Count of Chambord, the legitimist pretender to the French throne, in Frohsdorf Castle in the Austrian Empire.[49]

Nevertheless, most of these gatherings remained anonymous, a phenomenon concerning all exile communities. Thus Spaniards in exile in Paris during the reign of Ferdinand VII imported the practice of the *tertulia*, a sociability circle halfway between a private reception and a public meeting. This social and political cultural practice met with great success in Paris.[50] Spanish exiles also got into the habit of gathering in a certain number of cafés in the French capital, a practice which lasted throughout the century. Once again, cafés were a traditional meeting place in exile circles, and subject to active surveillance by the authorities, being the place where informants operated.

Sociability in exile must not be reduced to frequenting particular places. In addition to ties of informal acquaintanceship, a certain number of more structured networks could be used for political purposes, such as professional associations and masonic lodges, which played a major role in establishing transnational solidarity as they extended beyond national boundaries. Delphine Diaz mentions the important role played by masonic networks as of the July Monarchy in France.[51] In the 1870s, the Spanish republican Manuel Ruiz Zorrilla was able to draw on his masonic background – he had been Grand Master of the Gran Oriente Español from 1870 to 1874 – to join the Grand Orient de France, where he built up solid friendships with French republicans, who gave him their support and protection.[52]

The British model, no doubt the most complete in terms of party organization in the mid-nineteenth century, influenced many exiles. In addition to studying the Whig and Tory parties or the trade unions, they also observed and followed the great mobilization movements drawing on all vectors of political communication, lobbying, and nationwide organization. Whether it was Chartism or the Anti-Corn Law League cited in 1857 as a model by Giuseppe La Farina for the *Società nazionale italiana* – "Like the famous corn league [...] we intend to propagate our principles by speeches, by studies, by writings, by gatherings, by

---

49 Jean-Paul Bled, *Les Lys en exil ou la seconde mort de l'Ancien Régime* (Paris: Fayard, 1992). On nineteenth-century princely courts in exile, see Bruno Dumons (ed.), *Rois et princes en exil: une histoire transnationale du politique dans l'Europe du XIXe siècle* (Paris: Riveneuve, 2015).
50 Rafael Sánchez Mantero, "París, el exilio liberal," in *París, ciudad de acogida*, 41–54.
51 Diaz, *Un asile pour tous les peuples*, 244.
52 Fernando Martínez López, "La 'corte revolucionaria'. Ruiz Zorrilla en París," in *París, ciudad de acogida*, 113–158.

all honest means at our disposal"[53] – exiles managed to appropriate the nascent forms of organized party politics.

For exiles it was always a matter of what form of organization would bring them together, enable them to be heard, financed, and hence act, either locally or at a distance. This capacity was obviously largely dependent on the laws in the country where they were, and whether groups, gatherings, and organizations were freely authorized, as in Britain or, on the contrary, severely restricted, as in France under the Bourbon Restoration and the July Monarchy, or even in Victor Emmanuel II's Piedmont. Tolerance of exiles' political activities also fluctuated: for instance, the reaction of the British governor of Malta went from being relatively tolerant to increasingly severe after 1849, while the Greek government, which had initially welcomed Italian exiles, changed policy after 1850, yielding to pressure from Austria and Russia.

Mobilization in exile depended largely on an intense politicization of daily life. Cultural events conducted by exile groups often had a political element, as did collective affective rituals such as funerals.[54] These aspects were strongly determined by the social and cultural contexts, that is to say by the political culture of the host and departure milieus. Delphine Diaz has studied how Polish exiles in France in the early nineteenth century appropriated republican practices pertaining to banquets and burials.[55]

Exiles often used commemorations relating to the regime they had fought as a pretext for protests, while the commemorations forming their "shared memory" were built up, at times fairly slowly, given the extent to which they were divided politically. In Athens on November 8, 1849, during celebrations to mark the election of Pius IX to the papacy in 1846, several exiles protested publicly.[56] Equally, religious services were an important moment in exile sociability for Catholics and royalists, as illustrated by the cries of "Long live Pius IX, long live the Pope King" which resounded as the Carlist general, Josep Borges, embarked at Malta to go and reconquer Calabria, or by the masses celebrated in memory of Louis XVI and Marie-Antoinette, attended by the great French legitimist families and exiled royalists across the continent at the end of the nineteenth century, coming together to denounce the impious revolution. As the pontifical consul to Athens noted in 1850 about a Mazzinian commemorative ceremony: "it is

---

53 Giuseppe La Farina, *Programma e Dichiarazione della SNI*, see MRCC, b. 721, fasc. 8, doc. 2.
54 On funerals as a political practice, see Emmanuel Fureix, *La France des larmes. Deuils politiques à l'âge romantique (1814–1840)* (Ceyzérieu: Champ Vallon, 2009), and Avner Ben Amos, *Le Vif saisit le mort. Funérailles, politique et mémoire en France (1789–1996)* (Paris: EHESS, 2013).
55 Diaz, *Un asile pour tous les peuples*.
56 AAV, SS, anno 1849, rubrica 165, fascicolo 7, f°26.

easy to understand that they wish to commemorate their deceased companions, but alongside the romanticism and buffoonery there is clearly always a political goal and an endeavor to maintain a level of awareness".[57] These seemingly anodyne social interactions in fact played a major role in establishing political solidarity in exile.

Manufacturing internationalism

Thus in the nineteenth century exile became a crucible for political internationalism. Over the past ten years or so, scholars have pointed out that transnational solidarity phenomena were central to the political history of Europe at this time, emphasizing that internationals were formed in all political cultures on the continent, even though they tended not to attain the degree of formalization and organization characterizing the socialist internationals at the end of the century.[58] All these internationals were based on contacts established by outcasts with their political brethren from or residing in the host country. The emergence of genuine capitals of exile (Paris, London, New York, São Paulo, etc.), where activists from the same political current but different countries lived alongside each other, also needs to be viewed as an opportunity for activists to establish concrete transnational solidarity practices.[59]

It is no doubt worth going over the various occurrences of such internationalisms in the nineteenth century, for it can help us apprehend a zeitgeist in which exile played the same role in manufacturing internationalism across all political cultures. Liberals were the first to establish such links in Europe during the period of restoration, when Spaniards, Italians, Poles, and Germans formed the main exile cohorts in France and Britain. The Spaniards studied by Juan Luis Simal also took refuge across the Atlantic, in the United States, or in recently independent Spanish-American republics,[60] where many former officers from the Grande Armée saw an opportunity to pursue their liberal combat in the many wars of independence dislocating the Spanish empire through to the mid-1820s.[61] While there is debate among historians on how the concept of an inter-

---

[57] AAV, SS anno 1850, rubrica 165, fasc 14, Atene – Corfu-Malta-Marsiglia, folio 72.
[58] Éric Anceau, Jacques-Olivier Boudon, and Olivier Dard, *Histoire des internationales*.
[59] Delphine Diaz, "Paris, capitale de l'exil intellectuel européen au cours du premier XIXe siècle," in *La Vie intellectuelle en France, XIXe-XXIe siècles*, ed. Christophe Charle and Laurent Jeanpierre (Paris: Éditions du Seuil, 2016), 308–314.
[60] Juan Luis Simal, *Emigrados*.
[61] Walter Bruyère-Ostells, *La Grande Armée de la Liberté* (Paris: Tallandier, 2009).

national may refer to all the ties these liberal exiles were able to establish, the existence of many joint combats through to the revolutions of 1848 indicates that a genuine internationalism arose within this political culture. The same was true, at the same period, for counterrevolutionaries defending a political project inspired by the ancien regime. Building on links established by émigrés during the revolutionary decade, a veritable "white international" was established in the 1820s, whose first combats were focused on the Iberian peninsula, during the Portuguese Civil War (1828–1834) and then the First Carlist War (1833–1840) in Spain.[62]

The changes which occurred during the 1848 revolutions consecrated the pan-European emergence of a democrat republican political culture, the prime victim when authoritarian control was reasserted in the second half of the year. Exiles from across Europe had to take refuge in Britain and Belgium, giving rise to a transnational democrat political culture, as Florencia Peyrou has demonstrated in the case of Spaniards.[63] The Central European Democrat Committee, bringing together this democrat republican current in London, briefly directed this internationalism.[64] The degree of formalization was of course most pronounced in the socialist current. Early contact between socialist activists and leaders and workers in Western Europe in the 1830s and 1840s gave rise to an internationalism that was constitutive of this political culture, embodied as of 1864 in the International Workingmen's Association based around two leading exiles, Karl Marx and Mikhail Bakunin.[65]

These forms of internationalism and political circulation enabled by exile were viewed unfavorably by states, which soon sought to curb them to various degrees. Even very liberal Britain could not accept that exiles openly conspire against foreign governments on its soil. In France at the beginning of the century, practices were extensively shaped by the restrictions imposed on the right to gather by the Napoleonic Penal Code (article 291 forbidding associations of more than twenty people without the agreement of the authorities), which tended to encourage informal and dispersed practices. By the end of the century, the circulation of police practices and the exchange of information had become wide-

---

[62] Jordi Canal, "Guerres civiles en Europe au XIXe siècle, guerre civile européenne et Internationale blanche," in *Pratiques du transnational. Terrains, preuves, limites*, ed. Jean-Paul Zúñiga (Paris: Centre de Recherches Historiques, 2011), 57–77.
[63] Florencia Peyrou, "The role of Spain and the Spanish in the creation of Europe's transnational democrat political culture, 1840–70," *Social History* 40/4 (2015): 497–517.
[64] Georges Bourgin, "Mazzini et le comité central démocratique en 1851," *Il Risorgimento italiano. Rivista storica* 6 (1913): 366–375.
[65] Bensimon, Deluermoz, and Moisand, *"Arise Ye Wretched of the Earth"*.

spread, showing how exile accelerated the circulation of biometrics, identification methods, and administrative practices and terminology across Europe,[66] with the codification of the right to asylum circulating between nations and around the world.[67] Methods to recognize individuals had improved markedly during the Napoleonic period, particularly with the centralization of control mechanisms and the introduction of individual identity documents.[68] Each episode of political unrest during the nineteenth century was followed by stricter control of individuals, whether they were nationals, foreigners, or of course exiles.[69] The increasing number of lists of "suspects" was the fruit of intensive work to collate information from police forces, ministries of the interior, and consular reports, which focused increasingly on exiles' political behavior. The function of consuls became largely a matter of exerting virtually police-type surveillance in places where exiles gathered. Consuls were attentive to the forms of organization adopted by these populations deemed dangerous, and reported on political structures within the refugee community.[70] All forms of public or private gathering appeared suspect, giving rise to reports, and to pressure on host countries to outlaw them. The outcome depended of course on the attitude of host countries. The many amnesties granted by states during the period also provided a way of purging these lists. But while there were increasing appeals to international opinion, any concrete results were in fact few and far between. Nevertheless, throughout the period, origin and host states feared that exiles might form political parties, and wherever outcasts were to be found, police and con-

---

[66] Delphine Diaz, "Les réfugiés en France au prisme des circulaires du ministère de l'Intérieur (1830–1870): pour une étude conjointe des discours et pratiques de l'administration," *Hommes & Migrations* 1321 (2018): 33–40.

[67] Edward Blumenthal, "Les mots de l'exil dans le droit international du XIXe siècle, entre Amérique Latine et Europe," *Hommes & Migrations* 1321 (2018): 43–51.

[68] Ilsen About and Vincent Denis, *Histoire de l'identification*. See too Jean Vidalenc, *Les Passeports : une source d'histoire économique et sociale, problèmes d'utilisation, limites et lacunes* (Paris: Bibliothèque nationale, 1971).

[69] For the kingdom of Naples, see Laura di Fiore, "Documentare il dissenso. Sistema identificativo e controllo politico (1815–1860)," *Meridiana* 78 (2013): 53–75, and Marco Meriggi, "Come procurarsi un passaporto: il caso di Napoli a metà Settecento," in *Gens de passage en Méditerranée de l'Antiquité à l'époque moderne, Procédures de contrôle et d'identification*, ed. Claudia Moatti and Wolfgang Kaiser (Paris: Maisonneuve & Larose, 2007), 399–412. See too Chiara Lucrezio Monticelli, *La polizia del papa. Istituzioni di contollo sociale a Roma nella prima metà dell'Ottocento* (Rubbettino: Soveria Mannelli, 2012).

[70] Silvia Marzagalli, "Études consulaires, études méditerranéennes. Éclairages croisés pour la compréhension du monde méditerranéen et de l'institution consulaire à l'époque moderne," *Cahiers de la Méditerranée* 93 (2016): 11–23; Silvia Marzagalli (ed.), *Les Consuls en Méditerranée, agents d'information, XVIe-XXe siècle* (Paris: Classiques Garnier, 2015).

sular authorities compiled numerous alarmist, though largely fantastical, reports.

3 Exopolitics and illegal practices

At the intersection between writing and transnational sensibilities developed abroad, the implementation of political practices in exile to favor a return to power was a salient feature of nineteenth-century exopolitics. Stéphane Dufoix has demonstrated that such practices nearly always target the land of origin, and frequently seek the overthrow of an existing regime responsible for the exiles' banishment or departure.[71] These considerations also apply to the nineteenth century, and are part of a tradition stretching even further back. In the previous century, in particular, the Jacobites, swept from power by the Glorious Revolution, sought to regain control of Britain from their exile in the courts of Europe, until the 1746 Battle of Culloden definitively put paid to their hopes of reconquering the kingdom.[72]

In the nineteenth century, exiles' political action to reconquer power had to contend with the strengthening of European states and the implementation of surveillance measures and structures of oppression. Scheming to overthrow governments being a highly subversive form of exopolitics, states were confronted with two series of problems and imperatives. First, action by exiles placed host countries in an awkward position vis-à-vis countries of origin, in a century when the normalization and codification of diplomatic relations theoretically forbade such actions to destabilize internationally recognized states.[73] Second, while these exiles could represent a threat to the internal stability of the host regime, particularly when they had ties with political opponents, their presence could in certain cases be a boon for discreetly weakening a foreign regime.

Exiles' action in the nineteenth century thus needs to be read in the light of these various preoccupations. Though mainly secret, a factor which considerably influenced its forms and conditions, it could also be conducted openly. Exile gave rise to an exopolitics in which traditional political activity was bound up with subversive insurrectional activity, with these two forms of action transpiring

---

[71] Dufoix, *Politiques d'exil*.
[72] Eveline Cruickshanks and Edward Corp, *The Stuart Court in Exile and the Jacobites* (London-Rio Grande: Hambledon Press, 1995).
[73] Stanislas Jeannesson, "Le concert européen," *Encyclopédie pour une histoire nouvelle de l'Europe* [online], 2016, placed online on November 19, 2015, accessed April 11, 2021, https://ehne.fr/node/97.

in several different repertoires: conspiring, funding, or preparing an uprising by recruiting men and smuggling weapons, or outright insurrection itself.

Plotting in the age of Romanticism

After having long been disdained by historians, the political tool of plotting or conspiracy has recently resurfaced in several groundbreaking studies about the political history of the nineteenth century.[74] Specialists agree that plots are difficult for historians to apprehend, not least because the secrecy defining them means they leave few traces in the archives, and those that exist are mainly police documents. Additionally, the virtually systematic failure of actions decided upon as part of plots means that this political practice amounts to an avowal of impotence, the vain pursuit of a combat in the absence of any other means. This image inherited from the nineteenth century long dominated with regard to the activity of political exiles: far from their country, without any means or prospects, divided and under police surveillance, plotters rarely went progressed beyond the stage of sterile discussions in the back room of some inn, leading to nothing, or else disclosed by spies who had infiltrated the group of conspirators.[75]

Yet recent research paints a different picture of plotting in exile, relegating the question of its success or failure to the background, instead of focusing on focusing as a political form, and on its significance in nineteenth-century Europe, together with the practical conditions for carrying it out. These conditions are central to what follows: planned insurrections often started with a plot. The other typical manifestation of plotting is of course an assassination attempt, the best-known example in the nineteenth century – prior to the propaganda of anarchist acts at the end of the century – being that carried out by Orsini in 1858, which almost cost Napoléon III his life. This well-studied episode has its place within the history of exopolitics for two reasons. First, it was carried out by exiled Mazzinian networks present throughout Europe, who often had a background as conspirators, such as Orsini who had already fought against the Austrian presence in the Italian peninsula, and whose goal was to oblige Napoléon

---

[74] Much of the following discussion is based on Jean-Noël Tardy, *L'Âge des ombres: Complots, conspirations et sociétés secrètes au XIXᵉ siècle* (Paris: Les Belles Lettres, 2015); Gilles Malandain, *L'introuvable complot. Attentat, enquête et rumeur dans la France de la Restauration* (Paris: EHESS, 2011); Karine Salomé, *L'Ouragan homicide. L'attentat politique en France au XIXᵉ siècle* (Paris: Champ Vallon, 2011).
[75] On this image of exiles, see the analyses in Aprile, *Le Siècle des exilés*.

III to step up his support for the *Risorgimento*. Second, because assassination attempts were facilitated by the exile of many inventors in the field of chemistry, whose experiments, patents, and sociability networks were extremely useful in constructing "infernal machines", as shown in a recent article by Sylvie Aprile.[76]

Nevertheless, by the 1850s and 1860s conspiracies were on the wane, having been primarily a political form of the first half of the nineteenth century. In 1797, Spanish republicans imprisoned at La Guaira near Caracas, for having taken part two years earlier in the San Blas conspiracy in Madrid, played a decisive role in triggering the Gual y España conspiracy which convulsed the Captaincy General of Venezuela for two years.[77] Plotting in exile and plotting in the country of origin were not thought of as two separate actions in early nineteenth-century Europe, characterized by secret organizations linked at various different scales, locally, nationally, and transnationally. This was the case of the Carbonari, whose members were among the most radical liberals in Europe. Though it was primarily a national organization, this should not lead blind us to the many acts of cooperation between Carbonari from different countries, thanks especially to exile. The trajectory of Guglielmo Pepe (1783–1855) – who was exiled after the failed Neapolitan revolution of 1820 and passed via Spain during the *Trienio liberal* where he founded a "Society of European constitutionals", before taking refuge in London, Brussels, and then Paris – is emblematic of the transnational itineraries of these Carbonari.[78] Plotting and exile were also characteristics of the following generation, that of revolutionary romanticism: the *Giovine Europa* set up by Mazzini in 1834 in the wake of the *Giovine Italia*, in 1831, had plotting and conspiracy in exile at the heart of its political practice.[79]

If plotting in exile peaked in the period going from the Congress of Vienna to 1848, it was also associated with certain specific places. Cities of asylum were the natural cradles for plotting, since they were places where exiles socialized and came into contact with nationals from other countries, particularly from the host country. These well-known political centers – first and foremost London and Paris, but with New York, Brussels, and Constantinople also playing a role – should not however eclipse other places where political activity in exile, in this instance plotting, also flourished. This was, first, the case of border areas, with towns near the country of origin often seeing many plots hatched, which could

---

[76] Sylvie Aprile, "Déposer un brevet sans déposer les armes? Exilés et inventeurs français durant le Second Empire," *Revue d'histoire du XIXe siècle* 53/2 (2016): 79–96.
[77] Clément Thibaud, *Libérer le nouveau monde. La fondation des premières républiques hispaniques. Colombie et Venezuela (1780–1820)* (Mordelles: Les Perséides, 2017).
[78] Bruyère-Ostells, *La Grande Armée*.
[79] Giovanni Belardelli, *Mazzini* (Bologna: Il Mulino, 2010).

develop all the more readily given that they took place within traditional cross-border sociability and circulations. Juan Luis Simal has emphasized this fact regarding liberal plots against the absolute monarchy of Ferdinand VII: Bayonne and Perpignan were towns of choice for exiles.[80] Equally, Marseille and Nice, on either side of the border between France and Piedmont, were centers where exiles from the Italian peninsula conspired. Nor should we forget places of passage and circulation, such as islands, straits, ports, and enclaves, which were places where one could be discrete and more readily escape surveillance. In the Mediterranean in the nineteenth century, the *Risorgimento* was prepared in Constantinople and in Tunis, in Barcelona, Malta, and the Ionian Islands,[81] while Spanish exiles plotted in Marseille, Oran, and Gibraltar.[82] The geography of exile thus shaped the map of conspiracies.

Financing struggles

Assisting outcasts included collecting the money they needed to live in acceptable conditions while in exile, often a time of precarity.[83] The charitable dimension to the financial assistance they received should not be dissociated from more direct political motivations: giving money to refugees also meant enabling them to act in exile. Further, the humanitarian argument could be used to conceal the real purpose of a financing operation, with charity providing a cloak of respectability when collecting funds for far more subversive purposes.[84]

Financing their actions was a major issue for nineteenth-century refugees, particularly when they aspired to overthrow the government in their country of origin. Their capacity to collect funds to pay for the functioning of organizations in exile, to purchase material and arms, or to recruit men to take part in an insurrection was a decisive element in exiles' agency. In a recent article chart-

---

80 Juan Luis Simal, "El exilio en la génesis de la nación y del liberalismo (1776–1848): el enfoque transnacional," *Ayer* 94 (2014): 23–48.
81 Gilles Pécout, "Pour une lecture méditerranéenne et transnationale du Risorgimento," *Revue d'histoire du XIXᵉ siècle* 44/1 (2012): 29–47.
82 Jeanne Moisand, "Les exilés de la 'République universelle'. Français et Espagnols en révolution (1868–1878)," in *Exils entre les deux mondes*, 161–187.
83 The reader is referred to chapter 2.
84 Alexandre Dupont, "Soignantes et consolatrices? Femmes contre-révolutionnaires dans la Seconde guerre carliste (Espagne, 1872–1876)," *Genre & Histoire* [online], 19, spring 2017, placed online July 01, 2017, accessed April 11, 2021, http://journals.openedition.org/genrehistoire/2695.

ing a new line of research, Juan Luis Simal and Juan Pan Montojo have demonstrated that financial and economic matters were key to actions by Spanish liberal exiles during the absolutist reign of Ferdinand VII in the 1820s. From their place of refuge, particularly London and Paris, these exiles, often from Spain's economic elites, established close ties with international financial circles, enabling them to combat Ferdinand VII's monarchy on two fronts: first, their insertion in the financial circuits of nascent capitalism meant they could finance operations against the regime; second, speculating against Spanish Treasury bonds provided a way of weakening the Spanish monarchy and its capacity to obtain funding on financial markets.[85] In confronting these attempts to destabilize the monarchy, Ferdinand VII drew on the services of another exile, Alejandro María Aguado, a supporter of Joseph I who had taken refuge in France in 1815 and who, from fear of seeing the popular will subverted, came to terms with the absolutist regime he had fled ten years earlier.[86] As yet no systematic study has been made of how Italian exile was financed, but the influence of such figures as Adriano Lemmi may be detected, who financed Mazzinian military operations and became known as the "banker of the Italian revolution".

Political financing in exile was thus partly dependent on the development of transnational financial structures in the form of capital markets, together with the strengthening of capitalism more generally throughout the century. Research by Arthur Hérisson into international financial assistance to the papacy has brought out the importance and scale of operations such as bank loans and other forms of borrowing in transnational practices to finance exopolitical activity.[87] Of course, the Papal States were until 1870 a state actor able to legitimately draw on financial circuits. Nevertheless, it was a borderline case in that the increasing discredit of the temporal power of the popes during the 1860s and the young Italian state's designs on Rome considerably undermined papal finances; operations to raise papal funds were economically risky, and only attracted bankers and lenders wishing to assist for political reasons. Attempts to finance this disappearing state thus differed little from contemporaneous efforts by King

---

[85] Juan Pan-Montojo and Juan Luis Simal, "Exil, finances internationales et construction de l'État: les libéraux et "joséphins" espagnols (1813–1851)," *Revue d'histoire du XIXe siècle* 53/2 (2016): 59–77.
[86] Jean-Philippe Luis, *L'Ivresse de la fortune. A. M. Aguado, un génie des affaires* (Paris: Payot, 2009).
[87] Arthur Hérisson, "Une mobilisation internationale de masse à l'époque du Risorgimento: l'aide financière des catholiques français à la papauté (1860–1870)," *Revue d'histoire du XIXe siècle* 52/1 (2016): 175–192.

Francis II of the Two Sicilies, who had lost his throne and seen his state disappear a few years earlier in the wake of the Expedition of the Thousand.[88]

In both cases, turning to capital markets to finance the cause rapidly failed to suffice. Calling on the generosity of political supporters from all countries was thus decisive. The success of "Peter's pence", an immense international subscription to defend the temporal power of the popes, is now well-known. Throughout the nineteenth century, subscription was the privileged means for financing political action in exile, particularly for political currents without access to financial markets, such as democrats or socialists.[89] Subscription presented the additional interest of "displaying" the support exiles enjoyed within the host society, or across Europe even. The subscriptions to finance military operations to bring about Italian unification in the 1850s are a clear illustration of this.

The same was true of the formidable mobilization in 1860 to finance Garibaldi's undertaking in Sicily. It was frequent, however, for rival collections to be set up, as had been the case a few years earlier in 1857: Daniele Manin and Giorgio Pallavicino had backed a collection in Paris for the "100 canons of Alessandria" to arm the Piedmontese stronghold, at the same time as Mazzini had launched a campaign to purchase 10,000 rifles for "the first Italian province to rise up". The former implicitly supported a monarchic solution as a possible outcome to the Italian question, something that Mazzini and the action party rejected outright.

Wherever such rival subscriptions were set up – there being up to five subscription lists in Britain – this heightened conflict and confusion. Thus at a worker meeting in Newcastle, speeches by Manin were read out before opening the subscription for the 10,000 rifles. It is worth noting that on occasions these large-scale subscriptions could lead local trade union organizations to work more closely with exile associations.[90] The results were disappointing for Mazzini. As for the subscription for the 100 canons, it met with great success in Piedmont itself and in towns on the Italian peninsula; it received money from exiles in Algeria, Constantinople, Barcelona, and the Cyclades; and in an illustration of the transnational nature of these financial mobilizations, exiled Romanian stu-

---

88 Simon Sarlin, *Le Légitimisme en armes: histoire d'une mobilisation internationale contre l'unité italienne* (Rome: Presses de l'École Française de Rome, 2013), chapter 3.
89 More generally, subscription was central to nineteenth-century repertoires of political action: Alain Garrigou, *Mourir pour des idées. La vie posthume d'Alphonse Baudin* (Paris: Les Belles Lettres, 2010).
90 Elena Bacchin, *Italofilia. Opinione pubblica britannica e Risorgimento italiano 1847–1864* (Turin: Carocci, 2014).

dents in Lyon also contributed.[91] Similarly, at the end of the century, international speaking tours were organized to raise funds for the anarchist movement, in which Peter Kropotkin and Louise Michel were due to travel to the United States. International campaigns supporting Spanish refugees in Britain were also organized in 1895, as part of campaigns against the oppression of anarchists in Spain.[92] Financing oppositions was a central part of mobilization, and exiles' states of origin were quick to intervene. The sequestration of exiles' assets was widely used, for example, in Lombardy-Venetia and the Kingdom of the Two Sicilies, to prevent fortunes being used to finance revolutions and plots, a measure which was in many respects fairly effective.[93]

Preparing insurrection

Manin's 100 cannons and Mazzini's 10,000 rifles provide a reminder of a key dimension in preparing expeditions to overthrow government in the land of departure, namely purchasing the arms needed to carry out an enterprise that was part political, part military. As shown by a recent dossier in *Annales Historiques de la Révolution française* and the book by Éric Fournier on weapons culture in revolutionary circles, nineteenth-century societies were armed societies, and political activity was closely linked with bearing arms.[94] It is thus not surprising that political action by exiles involved procuring arms. In a Europe where states' monopoly on legitimate violence was still being established, armed action was a privileged form of political action for outcasts, explaining for that matter why career officers played a leading role in transnational exile networks, as illustrated by the Spanish generals issuing *pronunciamientos* to call upon the population to

---

91 Vincenzo Pacifici, "La sottoscrizione per i cento cannoni di Alessandria," *Rassegna Storica del Risorgimento* (1984): 173–196.
92 Constance Bantman, "Louise Michel's London years: A political reassessment (1890–1905)," *Women's History Review* 26/6 (2017): 994–1012.
93 Catherine Brice, "Confiscations et séquestres des biens des exilés politiques dans les États italiens au XIXe siècle. Questions sur une pratique et projets de recherches," *Diasporas. Circulations, migrations, histoire* 23/24 (2014): 147–163, and Catherine Brice, "Politique et propriété: confiscation et séquestre des biens des exilés politiques au XIXe siècle. Les bases d'un projet," *Mélanges de l'École française de Rome – Italie et Méditerranée modernes et contemporaines* [online], 129–2, 2017, placed online April 03, 2018, accessed on April 13, 2021: http://journals.openedition.org/mefrim/3095
94 "La révolution par les armes," *Annales historiques de la Révolution française* 393/3 (2018); Éric Fournier, *La Critique des armes. Une histoire d'objets révolutionnaires* (Paris: Libertalia, 2019).

rise up against the authorities,[95] the Polish officers of the great emigration in refuge abroad,[96] or the Hungarian military in 1848–1849.[97]

In Victorian Britain, as in Belgium and the Netherlands, the free trade in firearms was a significant advantage for exiles, who could purchase them openly without triggering any response from the states concerned. These countries were an exception, explaining why they lay at the heart of exiles' arms trafficking, as shown by the example of Spanish Carlists who, in the 1870s, were able to rely on maritime smuggling networks to Spain, where they were combating the liberal government in Madrid. Under these circumstances, the presence of long-established exiles in contact with arms merchants and gunsmiths was crucial.[98] Additionally, these networks enabling exiles to purchase arms were used by the Confederation during the American Civil War,[99] before North America became in turn a field of action for Irish exiles in the late 1860s. In the years following the Civil War, members of the Fenian Brotherhood in the United States were able to draw on the stock of firearms which had lain unused since the war to prepare raids against British Canada, hoping to thus pressure the British government into conceding Irish independence.[100] Similar projects also existed in Britain, in view of a Fenian uprising which occurred in 1867.[101]

Thus purchasing and smuggling arms was a crucial exopolitical mission in the nineteenth-century Atlantic world. But while liberals were able to count on certain highly liberal arms trade legislations, the advance of free trade around the world, and the increasing strength of the arms industry in industrialized Europe, they also had to contend with states' attempts to prevent such operations. The free port of Livorno, studied by Samuel Fettah, provides a striking example. As a free port it had long been a place of fraud and smuggling. The first decades of the nineteenth century turned it into a hub for purchasing and smuggling weapons, attracting exiles from across the Mediterranean basin in search of sup-

---

95 Castells Oliván, *La utopía insurrecional del liberalismo*.
96 Goddeeris, *La Grande Émigration*.
97 Kemal H. Karpat, "Kossuth in Turkey: the Impact of Hungarian Refugees in the Ottoman Empire 1849–1851," in *Studies on Ottoman and Political History. Selected Articles and Essays*, ed. Kemal H. Karpat (Leiden-Boston-Köln: Brill, 2002), 169–184.
98 Alexandre Dupont, "Les États européens au défi de la contrebande maritime. La contrebande d'armes depuis Anvers, Newport et Marseille dans les années 1870," in *Fraudes, frontières et territoires*, ed. Béatrice Touchelay (Paris: IGPDE, 2020), 303–316.
99 Warren F. Spencer, *The Confederate Navy in Europe* (Tuscaloosa and London: University of Alabama Press, 1997).
100 Peter Vronsky, *The Fenians and Canada* (Toronto: MacMillan, 1978).
101 Laurence Marley, *Michael Davitt: Freelance Radical and Frondeur* (Dublin: Four Courts Press, 2007).

plies: Greeks during the war of independence, Algerians during the period of conquest, Spanish Carlists during the war of 1833–1840, and so on. But the combined effects of Tuscany's attachment to the kingdom of Italy in 1861, customs reforms, and above all the abolition of free ports in 1868 dealt a fatal blow to its central role in supplying arms to exiles.[102]

Purchasing arms in the nineteenth century was accompanied almost consubstantially by recruiting the men to use them. Mounting a military operation against the land of departure presupposed having troops ready to fight the armed forces of the regime targeted. The history of outcasts here intersects with the well-known history of transnational military volunteering.[103] Recruitment was of course primarily among the diaspora in situ: this was how the Fenian Brotherhood functioned, in which it resembled many other exile groups. Still, throughout the century such groups could count on the enlistment of foreigners determined to fight for their ideas in another country. From the volunteers recruited by philhellenic committees to fight for Greek independence in the 1820s, to the Garibaldians who went to fight in Crete in 1897,[104] the history of exile was intimately bound up with that of international military volunteering throughout the century. The Italian liberal exiles in Paris in the 1830s studied by Grégoire Bron provide a particularly clear illustration of this: having been banished for their involvement in revolutionary movements disturbing the peninsula in 1820–1821 and then in 1831, their presence in Paris brought them into contact with Portuguese liberals struggling against the absolutist regime of Dom Miguel, leading the former to go and fight in Portugal.[105] Once there, they could find themselves facing exiles from the Vendée forced to leave France after a failed counterrevolutionary uprising in 1832, and who had found a new land of exile and combat in the Iberian peninsular.[106]

The myths surrounding volunteering should not blind us to another central fact in the recruitment of men in exile, namely that exiles, when they had the means, paid mercenaries to fight alongside them. This recruitment – in the most prosaic meaning of the term – illustrates the extent to which exiles' polit-

---

102 Samuel Fettah, "Les consuls de France et la contrebande dans le port franc de Livourne à l'époque du Risorgimento," *Revue d'histoire moderne & contemporaine* 48/2 (2001), 148–161.
103 Gilles Pécout, "The international armed volunteers: pilgrims of a Transnational Risorgimento," *Journal of Modern Italian Studies* 14/4 (2009), 413–426.
104 And even later: Enrico Acciai, *Garibaldi's Radical Legacy. Traditions of War Volunteering in Southern Europe (1861–1945)* (London: Routledge, 2020).
105 Bron, "The exiles of the Risorgimento".
106 Guy Coutant de Saisseval, *Les Légitimistes vendéens au Portugal, la chouannerie portugaise, 1832–1834* (Fontenay-le-Comte: impr. de P. et O. Lussaud frères, 1954).

ical action depended on their financial wherewithal, hence on their skill in raising money. The hiring of mercenaries was generally regarded unfavorably by the authorities in the countries concerned, who established various mechanisms to try to prevent it – except, that is, when it served their interests.[107] Garibaldi's recruitment of over 1,000 volunteers, including exiles from the *Mezzogiorno* and foreigners – although most of the troops came from Piedmont-Sardinia – to go and conquer the Kingdom of the Two Sicilies received the surreptitious support of Cavour and the Piedmontese monarchy, viewing this attempted invasion and uprising as an opportunity to move decisively towards the political unification of the peninsula.[108]

Taking up arms

One of the rooms in the Prado Museum in Madrid devoted to the nineteenth century is dominated by an imposing canvas, six meters by four, by the liberal painter Antonio Gisbert (1834–1901), commissioned by the liberal government of Práxedes Mateo Sagasta and called *Fusilamiento de Torrijos y sus compañeros en las playas de Málaga* (1888).

Considered one of the masterpieces of nineteenth-century Spanish painting, this canvas was intended, in the mind of the government of the period, to depict the combat for freedom in favor of future generations. There was nothing coincidental about the subject selected, namely the execution in 1831 of General José María de Torrijos and his companions by the troops of Ferdinand VII on the beaches of Málaga. A former leading politician of the *Trienio Liberal* (1820–1823), Torrijos had had to go into exile in London once absolutism was re-established by the expedition of the One Hundred Thousand Sons of Saint Louis in 1823. From London, he had organized several attempted insurrections against Ferdinand VII's regime, and finally that of 1831 in which, having been misled by the governor of Málaga, he set sail from Gibraltar heading towards the capital of Andalusia, but was arrested at sea with his men, sentenced to

---

[107] Alexandre Dupont, "L'impossible déchéance de nationalité. L'État français face au volontariat militaire pro-carliste (1872–1876)," *Le Mouvement Social* 2 (2017), 99–110.
[108] Gilles Pécout, *Naissance de l'Italie contemporaine: 1770–1922* (Paris, Armand Colin, 2004); Catherine Brice (ed.), *Frères de sang, frères d'armes, frères ennemis: la fraternité en Italie (1820–1924). Actes du colloque, École française de Rome, Rome, 10–12 mai 2012* (Roma: École française de Rome, 2017).

Fig. 7. Antonio Gisbert, *Fusilamiento de Torrijos y sus compañeros en las playas de Málaga*, 1888. Museo del Prado, Madrid.

death, and executed on the beach. This attempted uprising by liberal exiles became a metaphor for the struggle against the ancien régime in Spain.[109]

It is true that the kingdom of Spain was the theater for many attempted insurrections conducted by exiles from abroad throughout the nineteenth century. Initially, during the two decades of Ferdinand VII's reign from 1814 to 1833, it was the liberals who hatched multiple plans to invade the kingdom from France or Britain,[110] such as the 1819 conspiracy studied by Claude Morange in which exiles residing in Marseille, Bayonne, and Bordeaux, in contact with clandestine liberal networks in Vitoria, Galicia, and Andalusia, prepared an insurrection while drawing up a liberal constitution for the country.[111] After a constitutional regime was established in Spain on the death of Ferdinand VII, it was the turn of Carlists, supporters of the ancien régime, together with democrats and republi-

---

[109] José Luis Díez García and Francisco Javier Barón Thaidigsmann (eds.), *El siglo XIX en el Prado* (Madrid: Museo Nacional del Prado, 2007), 266–272; Castells Oliván, *La utopía insurreccional del liberalismo*.

[110] Simal, *Emigrados*.

[111] Claude Morange, *Una conspiración fallida y una Constitución nonnata (1819)* (Madrid: Centro de Estudios Políticos y Constitucionales, 2006).

cans, to deploy this mode of action from exile,¹¹² echoes of which may be found in the events of 1944–1945 when republican exiles tried to invade Franco's Spain by the Val d'Aran to continue their fight against fascism.¹¹³

It would be mistaken to see this as specific to Spain, as a characteristic of a country marked by instability and military coups. Insurrectional techniques circulated throughout Europe. One such was the barricade, copied and institutionalized as a military means in the period of revolutions, but also as a social practice. When republican Rome came under assault from French troops in 1849, a Barricade Commission defended the town, providing low-paid employment for the city's population.¹¹⁴ In the nineteenth century insurrection was a privileged form of action for exiles, and the best proof that they retained a genuine capacity to act from abroad. The Expedition of the Thousand, although a borderline case, was also an expedition from exile for the nationals taking part from the Kingdom of Two Sicilies. This followed on from other less fortunate attempts, such as that by the Bandiera brothers who, in 1844, left Corfu for Calabria, or that by Carlo Pisacane, an associate of Mazzini, who left Genoa for Campania in 1857.¹¹⁵ During the revolutions of 1848, Belgian exiles in Paris formed a "Belgian Legion" which undertook to cross the Quiévrain to establish a republic in Belgium.¹¹⁶ Similarly, a "Legion of German Democrats" invaded the Grand Duchy of Baden in March 1848 before being crushed by the Württemberg troops.¹¹⁷ The Fenian uprising in Ireland in 1867 was also backed by a ship of American Irish who landed near Cork.¹¹⁸ Insurrection was likewise the means used by Cuban exiles who

---

112 Jordi Canal (ed.), *Exilios. Los Éxodos políticos en la historia de España, siglos XV-XX* (Madrid: Sílex, 2007); Peter McPhee, *Les Semailles de la République dans les Pyrénées-Orientales, 1846–1852: classes sociales, culture et politique* (Perpignan: Les Publications de l'Olivier, 1995).
113 Diego Gaspar Celaya, *La guerra continúa. Voluntarios españoles al servicio de la Francia libre. 1940–1945* (Madrid: Marcial Pons, 2015).
114 Mark Traugott, *The Insurgent Barricade* (Berkeley: University of California Press, 2010), and Catherine Brice, "La Commission des barricades de la République romaine (1848–1849) : une 'technologie politique'? Réflexion sur les contextes mouvants de l'innovation ," *Diasporas. Circulations, migrations, histoire* 29/1 (2017): 131–153, https://doi.org/10.4000/diasporas.791.
115 Renata de Lorenzo, *Borbonia Felix, Il regno delle Due Sicilie alla vigilia del crollo* (Roma: Salerno editrice, 2013).
116 Louis-Antoine Garnier-Pagès, *Histoire de la Révolution de 1848* (Paris: Pagnerre, 1866), vol. 4, vol. 2, p. 263–273; Kenneth Lasoen, "185 years of Belgian Security Service," *Journal of Intelligence History* 15/2 (2016), 96–118.
117 Ulrike Ruttmann, *Wunschbild – Schreckbild – Trugbild. Rezeption und Instrumentalisierung Frankreichs in der deutschen Revolution von 1848/49* (Stuttgart: Franz Steiner Verlag, 2001).
118 Lucy E. Salyer, *Under the Starry Flag. How a Band of Irish Americans Joined the Fenian Revolt and Sparked a Crisis over Citizenship* (Cambridge (MA): Harvard University Press, 2018).

had taken refuge in the United States in their bid to win independence for the Ever-Faithful Island.[119]

Except for the Expedition of the Thousand, all these attempts met with varying degrees of failure. Many factors explain why such expeditions were rarely crowned with success. Lack of preparation, lack of means, the distance between the lands of exile and departure, difficulties in communicating with networks in situ (when they existed) all no doubt played a major role. Above all, exiles had to face the hostility of states, with the exiles' host country often nipping any such expeditions in the bud. Indeed, the authorities' repression of such movements was often implacable, and many leaders of insurrectional activities joined the pantheon of martyrs to their cause, such as the Irishman Robert Emmet who, after heading the 1803 uprising on his island, was hanged and decapitated by the British government a few months later, [120] or the Cuban Domingo Goicuria who was sentenced to death and garroted in 1870 for his part in the Cuban War of Independence.[121]

Conversely, three elements appear to have been decisive in organizing such expeditions, though without thereby guaranteeing their success: support in the land of departure, the backing of part of the population in situ, and the possibility of retreat in the event of failure. The Expedition of the Thousand provides a clear illustration of the first two points. Carlists and republicans seeking to enter Spain over the French border could count on the backing of Basque and Catalan populations as well as on comparatively safe refuge in the departments of southern France.[122] Supporters of the Bourbon monarchy who organized expeditions from the Papal States in the early 1860s were for their part able to benefit from all three conditions: with the clandestine support of the papacy, they could draw on the mistrust of part of the *Mezzogiorno* towards the young Italian state, while the papal lands afforded a haven in the event of strategic withdrawal.[123] Their southern *brigantaggio* was a failure, as were many attempts at insurrection by nineteenth-century exiles. Insurrection as a form of action thus brings

---

119 Sánchez, *Quitter Cuba*.
120 Marianne Elliott, *Robert Emmet: The Making of a Legend* (London: Profile, 2003).
121 Manuel Moreno Fraginals, *Cuba–España, España–Cuba. Historia común* (Barcelona: Grijalbo Mondadori, 1995).
122 Lluís Ferran Toledano González, "Refugio militar y santuario político: el exilio carlista en los Pirineos Orientales," in *Exilios en la Europa mediterránea*, ed. Julio Hernández Borge and Domingo González Lopo (Santiago de Compostela: Universidad de Santiago de Compostela, 2010), 131–161.
123 Sarlin, *Le Légitimisme*, chapter 5; Laura di Fiore and Chiara Lucrezio Monticelli, "Sorvegliare oltre i confini. Il controllo delle polizie napoletana e pontificia dopo il 1848," *Passato e Presente* 101 (2017): 47–70.

out all the ambiguity of exopolitics: while revealing the extensive agency exiles enjoyed in this century of state-building, it also reveals how hard it was to alter the course of history in a country where they no longer lived, and rendered all the more foreign by distance.

Hence exile no doubt encouraged the circulation of insurrectional practices, the generalized borrowing of small-scale warfare techniques, and even the theorization of these practices, particularly what has been referred to as "guerilla" warfare. Nevertheless, such attempts were rarely crowned with success, causing exiles to adopt more state-focused solutions, such as recognition for the kingdom of Piedmont, deemed best-placed to complete Italian unification. Despite this, the transnational practices of volunteering and subscription played a role in organizing exiles into political bodies ready for a return to their land of origin. Furthermore, these practices also influenced political developments in Europe, in at least two ways. Although of only limited immediate effect, they helped influence the course of events by giving a certain number of struggles international visibility, whose outcome might well have been different had they remained circumscribed within national borders. Many insurrectional and revolutionary movements would not have prospered, for that matter, without the support they received abroad, or without political exile, communities structured and connected by networks of acquaintanceship and correspondence. In this respect, while exopolitics did not in itself suffice to bring about the political transformation of Europe, it undeniably played a role.

Another crucial contribution by nineteenth-century exiles was their elaboration of a transnational pan-continental grammar of politics which contributed to the emergence of a European sphere. Exile was the crucible for the internationalisms which appeared as of the early decades of the century, becoming a major reality in late modern Europe. Additionally, it enabled watchwords, political forms, and activist practices to circulate, resulting in borrowings, hybridizations, and mutual influences causing repertoires of collective action to undergo decisive transformations. Lastly, since they sought to project a voice and a combat abroad, exiles were vectors in the emergence of European public opinion, which could be mobilized against the government being combated, with such mobilization rapidly emerging as a fundamental aspect of political action. It is thus perhaps no exaggeration to consider that exopolitics in nineteenth-century Europe was a privileged locus for the birth of political modernity, irrespective of the limited effectiveness of the struggles of the day.

Sylvie Aprile, Delphine Diaz, Alexandre Dupont and
Antonin Durand

Chapter 6 Gender and exile

In 1849, under the Second Republic, the socialist and feminist Jeanne Deroin (1805–1894), a seamstress by profession, stood for election in Paris in support of women's suffrage. After Napoléon III's coup on December 2, 1851, she was forced into exile, reaching London in August 1852. She crossed the Channel alone, without her husband or children. Once in the British capital, she ran a newspaper, *L'Almanach des femmes*, in which she championed the emancipation of women and workers. It ceased publication in 1854, when her political activity diminished, though without ever entirely ceasing for the rest of her life in London until her death. The case of Jeanne Deroin acts as a reminder that the experience of exile was not the exclusive preserve of men during the nineteenth century. Still, the male monopoly on political activity, thought of as being wielded unchallenged in Europe at this period, would appear to have led far more men than women to leave their homeland and become expatriates. Hence the history of political refuge has confined the role of female exiles and refugees' partners to that of passive companion.

This chapter critiques such a vision, bringing out the presence of women within various exile contingents in the nineteenth century, despite the silence or discretion of the sources traditionally used for the history of these unusual migratory movements. It seeks to shed light on the family contexts in which exiled men operated, insisting on their ties of dependency on their companions, sisters, or mothers, while also discussing the female care on which these refugees depended, which could decisively shape their ties within host societies. In addition to these women who have remained in the shadows, there are a certain number of authentic female exemplars of political exile whose courses are charted here. This reappraisal of the place of women in exile is accompanied by reflection on the gendered division of roles in the event of forced migration, together with analysis of the masculine imaginary of exile and its role in constructing masculinity in Europe.

1 Visible and invisible women

As Anne Morelli has observed, while the expression "political exile" can refer equally to a woman or man, "the image that springs to mind is most often of a man. The image of the political exile is, like that of the activist, built on the model of masculinity. Its archetype is a man, with woman being an 'anomaly'".[1] Yet while exile or forced migration befell men, who outnumbered female outcasts throughout the nineteenth century, it was also experienced by women and children. This chapter examines the place women held in exile groups traveling the continent, bringing out the gendered roles assigned to them or from which they managed to distance themselves. While labor migration has been studied since the 1990s, it is only more recently that this has fed into analysis of political exile. Yet recent studies have sought to resituate women in forced nineteenth-century migrations, such as Sylvie Aprile's study of the lives of republican outcasts during the Second Empire,[2] Heléna Tóth's research into the wives of German and Hungarian exiles after 1848,[3] or Alexandre Dupont's work on Spanish Carlists in France during the Second Carlist War (1872–1876).[4]

Do administrative and police sources have nothing to say?

If the figure of the nineteenth-century exile was long associated with men, this is no doubt due to the main sources used by historians to study these unusual migratory movements. Among the archives which may be used to explore the lot of women in exile, first place goes to identity and travel documents in the form of passports. Yet these do not necessarily provide any details about female travelers. In France, passports were meant to be individual, but the head of the family often managed to get his wife and minor children included on his passport. Women traveling alone were however issued with a passport in their own name. This was the case of the widowed Polish countess, Klaudyna Potocka (1831–1836), whose journey from Poland in 1831 is narrated in two works, the memoirs by her compatriot Józef Tanski, and Józef Straszewicz's *Les Polonais et les Polonaises*, a gallery of biographical portraits published in France.[5]

---

[1] Anne Morelli, "Introduction. Exhumer l'histoire des femmes exilées politiques," "Femmes exilées politiques. Exhumer leur histoire," *Sextant* 26 (2009): 7.
[2] Sylvie Aprile, "De l'exilé à l'exilée: une histoire sexuée de la proscription politique outre-Manche et outre-Atlantique sous le Second Empire," *Le Mouvement social* 225/4 (2008): 27–38.
[3] Tóth, *An Exiled Generation*.
[4] Alexandre Dupont, "Soignantes et consolatrices? Femmes contre-révolutionnaires dans la Seconde guerre carliste (Espagne, 1872–1876)," *Genre & Histoire* [online] 19 (2017), placed online July 01, 2017, accessed April 13, 2021, http://journals.openedition.org/genrehistoire/2695.
[5] Joseph Tanski, *Cinquante années d'exil* (Paris: Lalouette, 1880), 77, and Joseph Straszewicz, "Claudine Potocka," *Les Polonais et les Polonaises de la révolution du 29 novembre 1830* (Paris: Beaulé et Jubin, 1839), 2: "Having more easily obtained a passport, as a woman, she

These accounts shed light on her departure from Warsaw, where she managed *in extremis* to obtain a passport for Prussia. Apparently benefiting from the less stringent administrative checks on women and members of elites, she got the names of one female and three male servants placed on this document, though they were, in fact, people who had been severely compromised during the revolution whom she thus helped save. Still, this is an exceptional case, with it being more normal for women to be invisible or discreetly present on such verification documents.

But these are not the only sources to gloss over the role of women, for the administrative and police documents providing information on refugees' treatment by states and their relays at lower echelons did likewise. Circulars about foreign refugees, general administrative correspondence, "depot" registers, and refugee certificates all provide detailed information about these populations, being even more precise in states which granted them assistance or assigned them to a place of residence. Nevertheless, these administrative sources, which have been extensively used to examine how refugees were treated, often leave wives and daughters in the shadows, even though they could make an equal claim to being exiles or refugees.

French nineteenth-century administrative documents for refugees illustrate this relative blindness regarding women. The first laws on "foreign refugees", passed under the July Monarchy (the laws of April 21, 1832, May 1, 1834, and July 24, 1839, initially enacted temporarily but rolled over by the regime from one year to the next), were supplemented by numerous administrative circulars subsequently issued by the ministry of the interior. This extensive regulation helped progressively define refugees as individuals who had severed all ties with their land of origin, had come to France for exclusive political reasons, and who were obliged to rely on government assistance to subsist. Two hundred and forty-one circulars sent out by the ministry of the interior to departmental prefects have been collated and transcribed for the period 1830 to 1870.[6] Of these, only thirteen refer in any detail to the case of women in exile. The few circulars to mention them systematically associate them with children, another group of more vulnerable refugees, and another blind spot in administrative sources on refugees present in France. Additionally, these texts from the ministry of the interior seek at all costs to ensure that isolated women be prevented from

---

used it to save, at her own peril, people who had been most compromised during the revolution".

6 These 241 circulars have been collected from the many archives in France explored by Delphine Diaz and Hugo Vermeren. The entire corpus may be consulted online on the AsileuropeXIX website, accessed April 13, 2021, https://asileurope.huma-num.fr/circulaires-sur-les-refugies.

entering France, or else from remaining in the country without their husbands' financial assistance.

As for the national groups targeted in these texts, the ministry of the interior was more sensitive to the fate of Spanish women, with seven of the circulars studied pertaining to this socially and ideologically heterogenous group (as composed during the 1830s and 1840s). The wives, sisters, and daughters of Spanish Carlist refugees were the group of women most frequently invoked in French administrative circulars between 1830 and 1870, which may be explained by two factors. First, the keen interest in Carlist women may be explained by the large number of refugees arriving in France after the end of the First Carlist War (1833–1840): in September 1841 there were still 7,500 Spanish legitimists in France, even though the war was over and most had been granted amnesty.[7] Second, this Carlist political emigration was socially heterogenous, including in its ranks many peasants, servants, and day laborers without resources. The fact that these refugees – and particularly their women – might end up being a lasting burden on the monarchy thus emerged as a source of acute concern for the French authorities. After spring 1848, national groups other than Spaniards were also a source of lively preoccupation, especially Italians and Poles, since many male refugees from these countries had set off alone from their country of asylum to join other theaters of revolution.

Analysis of administrative circulars shows the ministry of the interior was uninterested in refugee women. When they did attract its attention, it was because of the financial burden they might represent for the executive should they no longer be supported by their husbands, brothers, or sons. Above and beyond what these French regulatory texts reveal about how women refugees were viewed (or should one say the women of refugees), one may also enquire into how they were treated at the lower tier of the department or refugee depot. In France, refugee depots enabled the prefectural authorities to gather a population placed under their surveillance in a single place.[8] Depending on the time and place, these depots were used to provide foreigners with accommodation, mostly in empty barracks, or else acted as places where refugees had to regularly come and gather to answer a rollcall to receive their monthly subsidy.

For each refugee depot, the prefect had to draw up a monthly register of names listing in alphabetical order all the foreigners in their jurisdiction.

---

[7] Archives départementales de la Somme, confidential letter from the ministry of the interior to the prefect of the Somme, September 13, 1841.

[8] On this point, see Gérard Noiriel, *Réfugiés et sans-papiers. La République face au droit d'asile, XIXe-XXe siècle* (Paris: Hachette, 2006), 51, and Diaz, *Un asile pour tous les peuples*, 122.

These administrative documents of vital importance for overseeing refugees may also be examined for references to women, though the conservation of these handwritten registers, and the way they record information, varies greatly from one departmental archive to another. For instance, the register of refugees residing in Tours on December 31, 1833, indicates that twenty-eight refugees were present.[9] In accordance with ministerial regulations, the register gives their name, first name, rank, and nationality. Additionally, alongside each entry is a column headed "women" and another headed "children", without any names or first names. We know for example that among the twenty Spanish refugees present in Tours was a certain Jean Barcelona – in the partially French spelling of his name – a financial administrator, and that he was accompanied by his wife and five children, for which he received the highest rate of subsidy in the whole group (5.5 francs per day). While this heterogenous group of foreign refugees residing in Tours in 1833 certainly included women – eight in all, according to the figures given in the relevant column – their names are never listed, unlike those of their husbands.

Moving from the level of refugee depot to the individual level of surveillance documents refugees carried on their person, we may make the same observation. In France, the certificates issued by prefects to refugees in receipt of assistance as of the July Monarchy also occluded from view any women accompanying the named individuals. The back of these refugee certificates could be used to list any information deemed essential, such as civil status, summary physical description, and allocated rate of assistance, and was stamped by the prefects each time the subsidy was paid out. Although their format changed over the course of the period under study, their objective remained unaltered, namely identifying foreigners and attesting to their status as "refugees" in the administrative meaning of the term.

But French administrative documents about individual refugees were not the only ones to hide women from view. In the new kingdom of Belgium, the *Sûreté publique*, set up in 1832 as part of the ministry of justice, and entrusted as of 1839 with conducting surveillance of foreigners, complied thousands of individual files recording information about vagrants and refugees. The Belgian authorities gradually started keeping individual files on each foreigner. These files systematically contained a document specifying place of birth, profession, and marital status. The *Sûreté publique* endeavored to monitor documented foreigners throughout their stay in Belgium, which explains why certain files, in addition

---

9 Archives départementales d'Indre-et-Loire, 4 M 503 and 4 M 506.

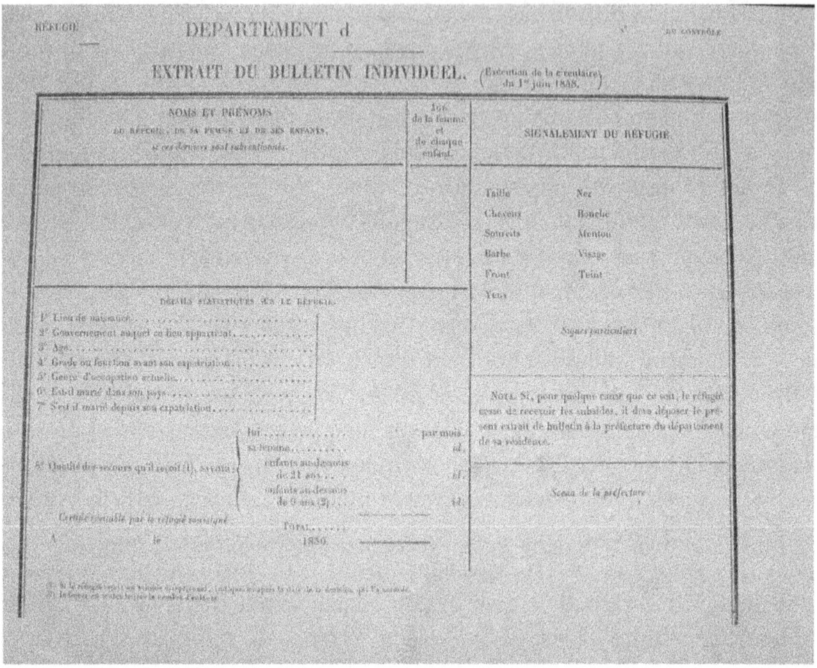

Fig. 8. Refugee certificate from the Second Republic.
Source: Archives départementales des Bouches-du-Rhône, 4 M 956.

to this information sheet, contain passports, expulsion orders, correspondence with the authorities, or more personal letters seized on these foreigners. A file was opened for each foreigner arriving on Belgian soil, with only few exceptions. Nevertheless, the administration decided not to allocate a specific file to married women and children, but to include any documents about them in the file of the father of the family, making it difficult to quantify and study the two categories in question.[10]

---

[10] On the reception of foreign women in nineteenth-century Belgium, see Hilde Greefs and Thomas Verbruggen, "Foreign domestic servants in Antwerp: a comparative regional approach on female migration trajectories to nineteenth-century European cities" in *Gender and migration: a gender-sensitive approach to migration dynamics*, ed. Christiane Timmerman et al. (Leuven: Leuven University Press, 2018), 173–194, and Thomas Verbruggen, "Maids on the Move: The Migration of Foreign Domestic Servants to Antwerp and Brussels (1850–1910)" (PhD diss., Antwerp University 2020).

Few written traces

Collective registers and individual certificates are essential administrative documents, but they tend to screen off married women and underage girls. Yet single women, widows, and unmarried women appear here and there under their own name in such sources for the administrative oversight of refugees. Their voices may also be heard in the entreaties sent to host country authorities, predominantly written by women. Single women were more frequently led to take up their pens to write to the authorities and seek to negotiate improved treatment. For instance, certain Polish widows who had settled in France after the "great emigration", on being authorized to return home as of 1842, wrote to the French authorities demanding recognition as political refugees in their own name.[11] Equally, after the displacements triggered by the revolutionary events which broke out across Europe in 1848, the wives of refugees were spurred by moments of isolation to address entreaties. Writing supplications was a common activity for the women of political exiles who had stayed behind in their home country, as shown by Heléna Tóth for the Hungarian refugees scattered around the world after 1849, whose female entourages back home wrote ceaselessly to the authorities requesting their return.[12]

Entreaties to authorities are thus an essential source for studying the agency and leeway available to women in exile and the wives of exiles in nineteenth-century Europe. But more personal letters also provide useful points of entry for examining the daily life of those obliged to live abroad or else separated from their husbands. In her study of republican outcasts from the Second Empire, Sylvie Aprile has drawn on family correspondence by women in exile, looking at the example of the epistolary network built up by Hermione Quinet who accompanied her husband into exile.[13] In addition to such "followers", as Nancy L. Green calls them, certain solitary female exiles also maintained intense epistolary relationships providing detailed information about how their lives unfolded. One such instance is the correspondence by Louise Michel from her exile in London, showing the breadth of her epistolary network, a "cluster with the

---

[11] Delphine Diaz, "Femmes en exil, femmes réfugiées dans la France du premier XIXe siècle. Vers la difficile reconnaissance d'un statut," in *Arrachés et déplacés. Réfugiés politiques, prisonniers de guerre, déportés, 1789–1918*, ed. Nicolas Beaupré and Karine Rance (Clermont-Ferrand: Presses universitaires Blaise-Pascal, 2016), 55.
[12] Tóth, *An Exiled Generation*, 214 et seq.
[13] Aprile, "De l'exilé à l'exilée," 30.

'Grande Citoyenne' as its incandescent center".[14] Such sources, and the perspectives they provide, have enabled historians to examine the agency of women forced to depart in the nineteenth century, shedding light on the leeway available to them and on their participation in genuinely political activities in exile.

2 Politics and women exiles

The literature on the action of women in exile insists on certain characteristics which may be usefully pointed out.[15] First, their agency depended partly on the conditions surrounding their departure: had they followed their husband? Their father? Had they left of their own accord due to their own political activities? Or in the wake of a government decision? Being a woman in exile covered a wide range of situations that should not be too strictly separated from other forms of mobility, particularly emigration for economic reasons,[16] or traveling for studies or leisure.[17] Additionally, these actions by women have been concealed in two different ways: first, sources provide little information about women's political involvement in exile; second, this silence reflects the way representations of the period downplayed their involvement, and the fact that many exiled women were relegated to the private sphere and the gendered activities traditionally performed by women.[18] Lastly, given that there are few archival sources about them, and that historians have until recently neglected these women in exile, there are many gaps in our knowledge and a tendency to emphasize those female figures viewed as heroines by their contemporaries, and thus presented as exceptional in the sources.

Bearing these elements in mind, the following pages seek to emphasize the importance of female exopolitics in the history of nineteenth-century exiles. This importance resides in three factors: first, because it took specific forms resulting

---

14 Michelle Perrot, *Libération*, February 24, 2000, on Louise Michel's correspondence published by Xavière Gauthier under the title *"Je vous écris de ma nuit"*. *Correspondance générale, 1850–1904*, edition prepared and presented by Xavière Gauthier (Paris: Max Chaleil, 2000), 1st ed.
15 See in particular Nancy L. Green, *Repenser les migrations* (Paris: Presses universitaires de France, 2002); Aprile, "De l'exilé à l'exilée".
16 Donna R. Gabaccia, *From the Other Side. Women, Gender and Immigrant Life in the US, 1820–1990* (Bloomington: Indiana University Press, 1996).
17 Nicolas Bourguinat, "Traces et sens de l'Histoire chez les voyageuses françaises et britanniques dans l'Italie préunitaire (1815–1861)," *Genre & Histoire* [online], 9 (2011): placed online June 09, 2012, accessed April 13, 2021, http://journals.openedition.org/genrehistoire/1460.
18 Anne Morelli, "Introduction. Exhumer l'histoire".

from the politicization of a certain number of actions traditionally carried out by women; second, because this politicization paradoxically conferred women with a degree of public agency from which politics debarred them at this period; and third, because this action, whether specifically female or not, meant that these female protagonists in exile were crucial links in the exopolitics of all political groupings, far removed from the women of whom, as Virginia Woolf noted reprovingly about traditional works of history, one "catches a glimpse [...] in the lives of the great, whisking away into the background, concealing, I sometimes think, a wink, a laugh, perhaps a tear."[19]

Politicizing daily life

As seen earlier, women were less suspected of political activism by the state, and hence enjoyed greater freedom of movement, granting them a crucial role in the logistics of exile, in organizing escapes, and in maintaining links with the country of departure once abroad. Still, the literature agrees that once in exile, they were expected to conform once again to the gendered roles assigned to them, running the household and family. This inferiorization also applied in the sphere of work, with exiled women finding it harder than men to pursue a profession fitting their aptitudes – should they not simply be prevented from so doing by having to look after their home. This is the process Carol Diethe describes in her discussion of the London exile of Jenny Marx and Johanna Kinkel.[20] Both were obliged to assume the dual burden of running their households while helping their husbands maintain their political activity. Yet in observing this undeniable situation of domination from another perspective, one could apply to Jenny Marx the remark about Johanna Kinkel by the journalist Edgar Bauer: "Frau Kinkel is in fact the man of the house, the real Herr Kinkel".[21]

Although this quotation deploys the gendered stereotypes of the period, in which action and decision are deemed male attributes, it also emphasizes, albeit unwittingly, the important role women played in maintaining exiles' agency. First, they oversaw the family's material circumstances: managing the budget, running the household, and educating children were just some of the tasks

---

19 Virginia Woolf, *A Room of One's Own* in *A Room of One's Own; Three Guineas*, ed. M. Schiach (Oxford: Oxford University Press, 2000), 58.
20 Carol Diethe, "Keeping busy in the Waiting-Room: German Women Writers in London following the 1848 Revolution," in *Exiles from European Revolutions*, 253–274. However, it is important to distinguish between the two wives, for Johanna Kinkel was an active musician and author.
21 Diethe, 255.

that befell them. In exile, these tasks acquired a political dimension in many respects. One only has to consider the question of educating children: Sylvie Aprile has shown how French republican exiles in London attached great importance to transmitting their political values to their offspring,[22] a phenomenon of equal significance for counterrevolutionary families in exile.[23] In this respect, it is wholly accurate to speak of the politicization of daily life,[24] with activities traditionally performed by women being endowed with crucial political effects in the context of exile.

Women in exile also served, on a daily basis, as a form of protection for exiled men, who might be threatened with expulsion or retaliatory measures by the host country authorities at the request of the land of departure, or else due to their political activities in exile. It is true that Britain was an exception, there being virtually no repression of exopolitics.[25] But in other countries, the presence of a family endowed refugees with respectability which could be used to dissimulate illegal activities. In cases where women in the family continued to be politically engaged, this could be a decisive factor. In March 1870, María de Lirio wrote to the sub-prefect of the Basses-Pyrénées to protest against the expulsion to Spain of her son, Santiago, accused of "Carlist plots". She no doubt played a role in the expulsion order being annulled a few days later, whether through the press campaign she launched against this decision or her letter to the sub-prefect, praying God to grant him "as much health as you have procured displeasure to this disarmed yet proud Spanish woman".[26]

Lastly, the apparently gendered assignation of women to the domestic sphere could conceal the work they did in the shadows to make exile more bearable. Jenny, Karl Marx's daughter, refers to this in a letter to Kugelmann in December 1871, in which she describes her activity to help refugee communards in London: "for the past two weeks I have been running from one suburb of Lon-

---

[22] Aprile, "De l'exilé à l'exilée".
[23] Hélène Becquet, *Marie-Thérèse de France. L'orpheline du Temple* (Paris: Perrin, 2012). For general discussion of the issue of transmission in counterrevolution, see Jeremy MacClancy, *The Decline of Carlism* (Reno: University of Nevada Press, 2002). See too Paul Chopelin and Bruno Dumons (eds.), *Transmettre une fidélité. La Contre-Révolution et les usages du passé (France, Espagne, Italie, XIXe- XXIe siècles)* (Brussels: Peter Lang, 2019).
[24] Laurent Le Gall, Michel Offerlé, and François Ploux, *La Politique sans en avoir l'air. Aspects de la politique informelle, XIXe- XXIe siècles* (Rennes: Presses Universitaires de Rennes, 2012).
[25] Thomas C. Jones, "Définir l'asile politique en Grande-Bretagne (1815–1870)," *Hommes & Migrations* 1321 (2018), 13–21.
[26] Dupont, *Une internationale blanche*, chapter 3.

don to the next (no small feat in this immense town) and then I have often written letters until one in the morning. The purpose of these trips and these letters is to obtain funds to assist refugees".[27] In this case, her involvement was detrimental to her own situation, since she added, referring to the difficulty communards and their wives had in finding work: "I can speak from personal experience. The Monroes, for example, have broken off all relations with me because they made the terrible discovery that I am the daughter of the chief agitator who has defended the ignominious Commune movement".[28] Jenny had been tutor to the children of this Scottish family residing in London.

As we may see, rather than having reduced access to the political sphere, women in exile tended to be faced with a dual role in the nineteenth century. While supporting their family, they were also political protagonists. They sought to reconcile these two spheres by politicizing their daily actions, or by becoming involved in exopolitics via the missions assigned to them within the gendered division of roles in the society of the period. Conversely, certain women managed to exploit their political activity to economic and social ends, as illustrated by the seemingly fairly exceptional case of Mathilde Franziska Anneke (1817–1884). Mathilde was the wife of Fritz Anneke, a liberal Prussian officer alongside whom she had fought in the 1848 revolution, going into exile with him in 1849 in the United States, where she played a key role in her husband's exopolitics. The latter, being unable to profit from his writings on revolutionary events in Germany, had to rely on the shrewder professional activities of his wife. She drew on her success as a journalist, speaker, and translator to finance the *Newarker Zeitung*, a German-language newspaper for exiles founded by her husband in 1853. It was she too who, from her new abode, in Switzerland, saved her husband during the American Civil War: as an officer in the Northern army, he had been arrested for his criticism of the Union's military organization, and was only released after his wife's indefatigable work writing in German newspapers.[29]

Most of the time, however, what we may observe is a politicization of daily activities. Carol Diethe points out that Jenny Marx and Johanna Kinkel both complained about how German refugees abused the hospitality extended in their re-

---

[27] Letter from Jenny Marx to Kugelmann, December 21, 1871, in Karl Marx and Friedrich Engels, *Inventer l'inconnu. Textes et correspondances autour de la Commune* (Paris: La Fabrique, 2011), 268–269.
[28] *Inventer l'inconnu*, 268–269.
[29] Marianne Walle, "'Le pain amer de l'exil'. L'émigration des Allemands révolutionnaires (1848–1850) vers les États-Unis," in *Deutschland – Frankreich – Nordamerika: Transfers, Imaginationen, Beziehungen*, ed. Chantal Metzger and Hartmut Kaelble (Stuttgart, Franz Steiner Verlag, 2006), 140–151.

spective households. It was often within the household that women, via their role as mistress of the house, were led to develop a genuinely political activity.[30] Receiving fellow outcasts was part of this, particularly for women who been established in exile for a long while. But emphasis needs to be placed on salons, another form of political action halfway between the public and private spheres, whose gendered dimension is clearly transparent.

Salons, as a place of cultural and political sociability traditionally organized around a woman,[31] were carried over into exile in varying forms depending on social class. In elite circles, they retained a key function in sociability and exopolitics, particularly among conservatives and counterrevolutionaries.[32] Nor should the phenomenon of salons be distinguished too strictly from that of courts in exile: exiled monarchists strove to recreate in miniature the life of the court they had left behind, which often involved holding balls and receptions in the residences of fallen sovereigns. In Paris in the 1870s, Carlist exiles thus attended the salons of the Duchesse de Chevreuse and of Margherita of Bourbon-Parma, the wife of the pretender Don Carlos, or else gathered from time to time at the Basilewski Palace, home to the deposed Queen Isabella II.[33] These forms of sociability in exile, at the intersection between the public and the private, and placed under the patronage of women, were not the preserve of conservative elites, even though the question of economic resources was absolutely crucial. Florence Loriaux has also identified them among socialist circles exiled in Belgium, likewise during the 1870s.[34]

Caring

One of the best-known nineteenth-century political salons of exile was no doubt that of Princess Cristina di Belgiojoso. She was exiled in 1831 from the kingdom of Lombardy-Venetia after her aligning herself with liberals supporting the *Risorgimento*, and from 1835 to 1842 held a salon at Rue d'Anjou in Paris which at-

---

[30] Diethe, "Keeping busy", 255.
[31] Antoine Lilti, *Le Monde des salons. Sociabilité et mondanité à Paris au XVIIIᵉ siècle* (Paris: Fayard, 2005).
[32] Steven D. Kale, *French salons. High Society and Political Sociability from the Old Regime to the Revolution of 1848* (Baltimore: John Austin University Press, 2004).
[33] Dupont, "Soignantes et consolatrices?".
[34] Florence Loriaux, "Femmes et exil durant la Première Internationale," *Carhop* [online], 8/2008, placed online December 17, 2012, accessed April 13, 2021, https://www.carhop.be/images/femmes_exil_premiere_internationale_f.loriaux_2008.pdf.

tracted artists in the capital, as well as providing a way of influencing French elites towards favoring Italian unification.

Fig. 9. Francesco Hayez, *Portrait of Cristina di Belgiojoso*, 1832.
Private collection, Florence.

Concomitantly, Belgiojoso provided financial support for Italians exile in France, providing them with temporary lodging. That explains why her salon and her lodging of exiles only acquired scale as of 1835, when the Austrian authorities lifted the sequestration on her assets, in place since she had fled Lombardy-Venetia in 1831.[35] This brings out just how significant the financial dimension was in the agency of exiled women. The wealthier among them encountered fewer difficulties in acting, in which they resembled their male counterparts, but perhaps the phenomenon was even more pronounced for women given the specific forms their action took.

In addition to being a place of sociability, salons were also a sphere for transnational politicization, and mobilization even. This may be illustrated by the balls held by the Duchess of Chevreuse in her Parisian residence in spring 1875, with the blessing of Margherita of Bourbon-Parma, and in association with organizations of Spanish ladies present in Paris, presided respectively by the Marquise of Miraflores and the Duchess of Medinaceli. The purpose of these balls was to collect money for Carlist ambulances. Despite protests from the Spanish ambassador to France, the French authorities admitted they could do nothing to prevent them, given their charitable purpose and the fact that these gatherings were held in private places, thus precluding any coercive action.[36] This brings out the full significance of action by women in exile. These had specific forms and spheres of action which transformed gender domination into an advantage, with the emergence of a female exopolitics far less exposed to repression than that conducted by men due to the very forms it took.

The balls in the faubourg Saint-Germain and the reasons behind them illustrate the forms women's actions could take. The alleged reason for collecting money was that it would be used to finance Carlist ambulances, and thus help those wounded in the civil war racking Spain. Female exiles were thus particularly involved in activities relating to care, providing them with a sphere of action which did not transgress gender boundaries. Hence exiled women often helped outcasts reduced to poverty, such as di Belgiojoso's assisting Italian exiles or Karl Marx's daughter succoring communards. Outside exile circles, it was also the women of the host countries who were most involved in assisting refugees.[37] Delphine Diaz has shown the leading role women played in assis-

---

35 Mariachiara Fugazza and Karoline Rörig (eds.), *La Prima donna d'Italia. Cristina Trivulzio di Belgiojoso tra politica e giornalismo* (Milan: FrancoAngeli, 2010).
36 On these balls, see Dupont, "Soignantes et consolatrices?".
37 Pamela Pilbeam, "Jeanne Deroin: French feminist and Socialist in Exile," in *Exiles from European Revolutions*, 275–294.

tance committees helping the various groups of refugees who reached France during the July Monarchy.[38]

Assisting the weak is a classic component of care, and in the nineteenth century, female exiles were thus especially involved in collecting money. Recent research has shown that financing political causes was a privileged field in which women – still deprived of legal political expression – were able to deploy their energies.[39] Once again, the link to the domestic sphere is clear: women exiles were in charge of keeping the household on a stable financial footing, whence there was but a short step to turning to a more overtly political activity, yet without too visibly transgressing gender stereotypes. Furthermore, such activity was part of charitable practices typical of the nineteenth century, in which Catholic women from high society were involved in works to help the poor. In this respect, and while bearing in mind this class aspect, Catholicism paradoxically granted women fairly extensive political agency for the period.[40] Still, fundraising activities, once again involving exiled women alongside women from the host country, could take various forms. Public subscriptions and lotteries were held to assist Poles in France in the 1830s.[41] Princess di Belgiojoso financed refugee assistance out of her own pocket, and in 1834 also gave 30,000 lira towards an attempt by Mazzini and his companions to invade Savoy.[42] Princess Margherita of Bourbon-Parma subscribed to an international Carlist loan in 1869, taken out with a Dutch Catholic banker, Jan Wilhelm Cramer.[43] This field of research, at the intersection between gender and the financial dimension of exopolitics, is no doubt one of the least explored for the nineteenth century, making it hard to move beyond the odd example to paint an overall picture.

One final activity which may be mentioned in these forms of mobilization specific to female nineteenth-century exopolitics was the confection of flags and uniforms to serve the cause. The most remarkable case here comes from outside Europe. In the history of Philippine nationalism, Marcela Mariño de Agon-

---

[38] Diaz, *Un asile pour tous les peuples*, 51.
[39] Arthur Hérisson, "Une mobilisation internationale de masse à l'époque du *Risorgimento*: l'aide financière des catholiques français à la papauté (1860–1870)," *Revue d'histoire du XIXe siècle* 52/1 (2016): 175–192.
[40] Magali Della Sudda, "La politique malgré elles. Mobilisations féminines catholiques en France et en Italie (1900–1914)," *Revue française de science politique* 60/1 (2010): 37–60.
[41] Diaz, *Un asile pour tous les peuples*.
[42] Alessandro Giulini, "Belgioioso Trivulzio, Cristina di", *Enciclopedia Italiana* (1930), accessed April 13, 2021, http://www.treccani.it/enciclopedia/cristina-principessa-di-belgioioso_%28L%27Unificazione%29/.
[43] Dupont, *Une internationale blanche*, chapter 3; Emiel Lamberts (ed.), *The Black International. L'internationale noire (1870–1878)* (Brussels: Presses universitaires de Louvain, 2002).

cillo (1859–1946) holds a unique place. She was exiled to Hong Kong with her husband Felipe Agoncillo for their anti-Spanish activities in the 1890s, and in 1898 was entrusted by the leader of the revolt against Spanish domination and future president of the ephemeral Philippine Republic (1888–1901), Emilio Aguinaldo, with weaving the national flag, which she accomplished with the help of her daughter and another nationalist exile, thus winning a place in the Philippine national pantheon.[44] Such an activity also illustrates how exiled women were able to use the skills attributed to them by European societies of the period to act politically in their own manner.

This leads us to examine the extent to which developments to this specifically feminine repertoire of political action contributed to the emergence of feminist thought in exile. Sylvie Aprile cites the cases of Jenny d'Héricourt, who had gone into exile after publishing her *La Femme affranchie,* and of Marie Huleck, a Reform League activist in the mid-1860s in England, who went on to join the IWA general council before departing for the United States. The latter went to the United States where she established contact with members of the international feminist movement. She thus built up bridgeways between American and French women, even giving a speech to the American Equal Rights Association conference in 1869, in which she proposed setting up an international feminist league.[45] Likewise, a few years earlier, Mathilde Franziska Anneke had set up the *Deutsche Frauen-Zeitung* in the United States, the first feminist press outlet in the country.[46] Florence Loriaux, for her part, has studied the little-known figure of Wilhelmine Müeller (who went under the name of Mina Puccinelli), a Russian who had participated in the Paris Commune before taking refuge in Brussels in 1871, and then joining the IWA, within which she fought more specifically for the cause of women, enrolling many female members.[47]

---

44 Barbara Watson Andaya, *"Gender, Warfare, and Patriotism in Southeast Asia and in the Philippine Revolution,"* in The Philippine Revolution of 1896: Ordinary Lives in Extraordinary Times (Quezon City: Ateneo de Manila University Press, 2001), 1–30; Christine Doran, "Women in the Philippine Revolution," *Philippine Studies* 46/3 (1998): 361–375.
45 Aprile, "De l'exilé à l'exilée". See too Michel Cordillot, *La Sociale en Amérique. Dictionnaire biographique du mouvement social francophone aux États-Unis* (Paris: Éditions de l'Atelier, 2002).
46 Delphine Diaz, "Femmes, genre et exil en Europe à l'époque contemporaine," *Encyclopédie pour une histoire nouvelle de l'Europe* [online], 2016, placed online May 19, 2017, accessed April 13, 2021, https://ehne.fr/node/987.
47 Loriaux, "Femmes et exil".

Actresses in their own right

Let us continue with the mysterious Mina Puccinelli, and the odd snatches of information she provides in the introduction to her only published work, *L'Homme obscur qui ment: roman historique de la France*, brought out in Brussels, and in which she attacks Napoleon III for his wish to return to power.[48] She presents herself as follows: "Mina Puccinelli, director and editor of '*El Leon*' newspaper, captain of the volunteers of death, Spanish legion, honorary member the Congress republican club in Madrid".[49] Comparing this information with the few studies published about her suggests that she may have taken up arms in the 1870 war in the Spanish legion serving in Garibaldi's Vosges army,[50] and may have lived in Madrid, where she may have worked as a journalist while frequenting Republican circles.[51] The repeated use of "may" indicates how little has been established about her. Nevertheless, her life raises questions about the extent to which masculine modes of action were wholly distinct from feminine modes in exile. While female exiles did indeed develop specific forms corresponding to the gender stereotypes weighing on them, they were also fully inserted in masculine forms of exopolitics. In addition to conducting their combat on a transnational scale, there were clear instances of gender transgression.

What first strikes the observer is no doubt their participation in combat. Armed struggle, including within the political sphere, was closely associated in the nineteenth century with the prerogatives of masculinity, with there being a link between masculinity, political affirmation, and bearing arms.[52] An increasing number of studies – about the uprising against Napoléon in Spain, the Paris Commune, and the Russian Civil War – remind us that any such gender-based distinction in the bearing of arms should not be thought to have applied too strictly.[53] But the fact is no doubt all the more remarkable concerning female exiles. For some, it was their part in armed combat which caused their departure, such as Mathilde Anneke after 1848, or Louise Michel, who took

---

[48] Mina Puccinelli, *L'Homme obscur qui ment: roman historique de la France* (Brussels: E. Cheval, undated).
[49] Puccinelli, *L'Homme obscur*, 3.
[50] Alexandre Dupont, "'*Ayudemos a Francia*': les volontaires espagnols dans la guerre franco-allemande de 1870–1871," *Mélanges de la Casa de Velázquez* 45/1 (2015): 199–219.
[51] Manuel Ossorio y Bernard, "Puccinelli (Mina)," *Ensayo de un catálogo de periodistas españoles del siglo XIX* (Madrid: Imprenta y litografía de J. Palacios, 1903), 359.
[52] "La révolution par les armes," *Annales historiques de la Révolution française* 393/3 (2018).
[53] On this topic, see Marie Derrien, Fanny Giraudier and Charlotte Gobin (eds.), "Genre et engagement en temps de guerre (XVIe-XXIe siècles)," *Genre & histoire* 19 (2017).

part in the fighting of the Paris Commune and had her photo taken wearing federal uniform.[54] But in other cases, it was exile which provided the opportunity to take up arms. Such was the case of the Russian exile Elisabeth Dmitrieff, who, after running the women's union for the defense of Paris and caring for the wounded,[55] was also present on the barricades of the Paris Commune, showing that there was only a slight step from care to forms of political involvement deemed more masculine. Such was also the case of Belgiojoso, who in 1848 left her exile in Paris to take part in the revolutions rocking the Italian peninsula, and was involved in defending the Roman Republic in 1849 before going into exile once again in Asia Minor.[56] At the other end of the political spectrum, mention may be made of the legitimist princesses from across Europe who did not shy away from the battlefield – such as the Duchess of Berry preparing a military uprising in the Vendée in 1832 from her exile in Italy, the Portuguese princess, Maria das Neves, who headed the Carlist army in Catalonia alongside her husband Don Alfonso during the 1872–1876 war, and Maria Sophie of Bavaria, the wife of Francis II of the Two Sicilies, and the soul of Neapolitan resistance against unification in Gaeta until she headed into exile.[57]

Independently of these striking examples, it should be emphasized that female exiles did not limit their actions to their household, nor did they hesitate to resort to illegal forms of exopolitics. Christelle Taraud thus explains that Louise Michel, deported to New Caledonia, not only refused to take part in putting down the 1848 Kanak revolt, but even lent her help to the insurgents, advising them for example to cut the telegraph wires to slow communication between the French troops.[58] This is a form of expertise, transmitting in exile the guerilla tactics she

---

54 "Louise Michel en costume de fédéré", cliché Fontange, 1871, Montreuil – Musée de l'Histoire vivante.
55 Gustave Lefrançais, *Souvenirs d'un révolutionnaire de juin 1848 à la Commune* (Paris: La Fabrique éditions, 2013).
56 Delphine Diaz & Hugo Vermeren, "Le dernier exil de la princesse Cristina di Belgiojoso", map section of the AsileuropeXIX website, accessed April 13, 2021, https://asileurope.huma-num.fr/cartotheque/le-dernier-exil-de-la-princesse-cristina-di-belgiojoso-1808-1871-depuis-rome-assiegee-jusqua-lasie-mineure.
57 Alexandre Dupont, "Le genre de la contre-révolution au xixe siècle," *Encyclopédie pour une histoire nouvelle de l'Europe* [online], 2016, placed online January 29, 2018, accessed April 13, 2021, https://ehne.fr/node/1201. It will be noted that this repertoire of action gave these domestic figures a political substance that most studies of them tend to neglect in favor of anecdotal chronicles about the life of these monarchs.
58 Christelle Taraud, "Les bagnes de l'Empire au féminin. Ou comment déporter les opposantes politiques de la métropole dans les colonies françaises au xixe siècle," in "Femmes exilées politiques. Exhumer leur histoire," ed. Anne Morelli, *Sextant* 26 (2009): 17–25.

had no doubt learned during the Paris Commune. Smuggling could also provide an appropriate form of action for women.[59] Such was the case of Florence Willocq, the Belgian wife of the French bookseller François Lemonnyer, who had taken refuge in Brussels in 1872. While the couple's political motives have not been established, Florence's husband entrusted her with discreetly passing prohibited books, especially internationalist works, into France. Accompanied by three other women, she smuggled the books by hiding them under her skirts.[60]

Little is known about such illegal practices in exile, particularly those by women. However, their legal and public actions to pursue their political combat in exile are better known. Literary and publishing activity is no doubt the most interesting to observe, presenting a certain number of cases where ongoing commitment and depoliticization went side-by-side. The case of Jeanne Deroin has been well studied in this respect: her exile in London, during which she published two almanacs defending the cause of women, shows her progressive withdrawal into spiritualism and away from politics.[61] In many cases, for both men and women, exile entailed leaving political action behind.

Nevertheless, many women were involved in publishing or writing, enabling them to pursue their combat by other means. A figure such as Germaine de Staël (1766–1817) built her literary career on the successive exiles marking her life. She spent nearly two decades outside France – in Coppet, in Switzerland, where she held a salon attended by émigrés, and published works which regularly enraged the authorities, as well as in Germany, where her stay in 1803–1804 provided material for her *De l'Allemagne* (1811) – enabling her to forge a crucial body of work in the history of Romanticism.[62] Johanna Kinkel also produced numerous works, such as *Hans Ibeles in London*, part fiction and part autobiography, in which she evokes life in exile.[63] We saw earlier the example of Mathilde Anneke's journalism, who created the first feminist newspaper in the United States. Her many lectures and articles financed her husband's activities, and she went on to become a war correspondent documenting the American Civil War for German newspapers from her residence in Switzerland.[64]

These various elements reposition women within a history of exopolitics in which they played an essential role, not least because they were paradoxically

---

59 Anne Montenach, *Femmes, pouvoirs et contrebande dans les Alpes au XVIIIe siècle* (Grenoble: Presses Universitaires de Grenoble, 2017).
60 Loriaux, "Femmes et exil".
61 Sylvie Aprile, "De l'exilé à l'exilée"; Pilbeam, "Jeanne Deroin".
62 Aprile, *Le Siècle des exilés*, 50–52.
63 Diethe, "Keeping busy".
64 Walle, "'Le pain amer de l'exil'".

freer than their male counterparts who struck the authorities as more suspect. Given the current state of the literature on exile, in which the place of women is no doubt recognized yet insufficiently appreciated, it is unusually difficult to put forward a history of exile presenting male and female exile within a single account. A study such as that by Natalia Tikhonov, looking at female students from the Russian Empire in Switzerland and placing them within the cohort of students who, while abroad, in a sort of exile, gave rise to the Russian social democrat movement, no doubt provides an example of what studies of gender in exile should tend towards.[65]

3 Family disorders

In the wake of observations by Éliane Gubin and Valérie Piette on the particular forms of persecution which could push women to flee their country,[66] it should be pointed out that, in the nineteenth century, there was no specificity comparable to sexual violence, taken into account nowadays in asylum requests. Nevertheless, Gubin and Piette do identify one specific situation, namely forced marriage. While not necessarily related to politics, and not systematically leading to expatriation, the example they choose suggests a particular connection between the situation of young women and exile. Such was the case of the future anarchist Emma Goldman who, on being threatened with a forced marriage in 1886, when just sixteen, fled her country, Lithuania (Russia at the period), for the United States, the first of many exiles in her life. Her case raises the question of the emancipation of young women which, together with the many departures of Russian female students to European universities, particularly in Switzerland and France, may feed analysis of female exile. Research by Irina and Dimitri Gouzevitch has established a clear correlation between calls by women for access to higher education in Russia and their participation in revolutionary combat.[67] For many, emigration was their sole solution. These Russian pioneers went to study abroad mainly between 1864 and 1873, in which year their number decreased dramatically. This drop resulted from the government decree of May 21, 1873, enjoining all female Russian students abroad to return to the national ter-

---

[65] Natalia Tikhonov, "Les étudiantes de l'Empire des tsars en Europe occidentale: des exilées 'politiques'?," in "Femmes exilées politiques".
[66] Éliane Gubin and Valérie Piette, "Sur la singularité de l'exil politique féminin dans une perspective historique," *Sextant* 169 (2009).
[67] Irina and Dimitri Gouževitch, "La voie russe d'accès des femmes aux professions intellectuelles scientifiques et techniques (1850–1920)," *Travail, genre et sociétés* 4/2 (2000): 55–75.

ritory, with the promise that they would be able to take up a place within the Russian system.

Couples at risk

In addition to this specific case of Russian students, the particular position of women also needs examination. Political exile, when it was not the woman herself who was targeted by exile, included many wives, mothers, and daughters. Mention has already been made of the question of couples, whether it be a couple separated by exile, or the wife of a migrant or soldier having to single-handedly manage the family assets and education of children, or that of a woman accompanying or joining a man in exile, a "follower". There is thus little that is specific to their overall situation, but it nevertheless deserves close attention.

Correspondence and memoirs of exile often include amused or indignant commentary on transgressive and immoral situations. Adultery was extensively commented, and rumors spread rapidly within a restricted community in which people lived in sight of others. One may think of the two boats taken by Adèle Hugo and Juliette Drouet arriving one after the other, condemned to live on the same island, first Jersey then Guernsey. Eugène Sue's love life in Annecy was stigmatized because he lived with a younger freer woman who was additionally related to the Bonaparte family. Herwegh and Herzen's friendship led their couples into a state of promiscuity which encouraged the adulterous relationship between Natalia Herzen and Georg Herwegh, a relationship Alexander Herzen sought to have condemned by a tribunal composed of friends in exile, including Pierre-Joseph Proudhon and renowned writers such as Jules Michelet.[68] In London, Emmanuel Barthélemy challenged Cournet to a duel in 1852 because the latter claimed the former's mistress was a prostitute. No biography of Marx could omit discussion of the pregnancy of "Lenchen", a servant working for the Marx family, and Engels's recognition of the child. The Pole Charles-Edmond Chojecki, who likewise recognized a child he had with Countess Laura Czosnowska in 1847, had to fight for many years to prevent the removal of his daughter born outside wedlock.[69]

As Paul K. Martinez has pointed out in his discussion of exiled communards in London, police agents spread rumors about adultery and nonmarital births.

---

[68] Simone Rist, "L'affaire Herwegh," *Revue des études slaves* 78/2–3 (2007): 229–242.
[69] Emmanuel Desurvire, *Charles Edmond Chojecki, l'œuvre et la vie* (publisher and place not indicated, cop. 2014), 4.

They peddled exile gossip, such as Chaboud's adultery with Blond's wife, the liaison between Madame Dubacq and Jean-Baptiste Clément, and then later with Albert Leduc, the adulterous relationship between Leduc's sister and E. Levrault, and the advances made by Poissier towards Martelet's wife.[70]

This could all seem highly anecdotal; yet these facts, like many others, reveal how stifling it could be to live within the confines of an exile community, and how the overthrow of social rules meant that ties which would have remained hidden in other circumstances were forced out into the open. Whether members of the nobility, the bourgeoisie, or the middle classes, most exiles sought to uphold forms of sociability and family codes they did not call into question. Sometimes they no longer had the means to do so, and if they were in business or politics were sometimes unable to attend balls or society gatherings. The correspondence of Laure Fleury and her daughters with Hermione Quinet provides a very precise illustration of the difficulties of women's situation in exile. In 1862 Laure Fleury wrote that she and her daughters no longer attended Mme Didier's salon: "we can no longer go into society: it requires an expenditure we cannot make, even to do so simply".[71]

Conversely, exile provided some with an opportunity to sever ties, to abandon a spouse, or live in a way less bound by norms. The poet Alphonse Esquiros broke off all contact with his wife Adèle with whom he had published several books. After departing, he formed a new couple in England in the late 1840s with a young English woman with whom he had a son. As for Georg Herwegh, his correspondence refers on several occasions to his wish to live a communal life formed by the Herwegh and Herzen couples.

You shall be an exile, my daughter

It was not only wives and couples who could pay the price of burdensome group surveillance. The daughters and sons of outcasts also often fell victim to it, or were at least affected by this situation. Hugo's family provides an illustrious example once again: while Adèle Hugo's madness cannot be attributed solely to exile, there is little doubt that it played a role, and triggered her desire to flee and join her fictitious lover. Alexandre Herzen's daughter also experienced similar episodes.

---

70 Paul K. Martinez, (PhD diss."Paris Communard Refugees in Great Britain, 1871–1880", University of Sussex, 1981), 159.
71 Bibliothèque nationale de France, Manuscrits Naf 20788.

Chapter 6 Gender and exile — 197

Fig. 10. Herzen and his daughters, Olga et Tatiana, photograph, 11 January 1855. ITAR-TASS News Agency / Alamy banque d'image.

More prosaically for exiles, marrying their daughters posed the question of their dowry. This was a concern for Laure Fleury, the wife of Victor Fleury exiled in Belgium, who raised it on numerous occasions in her correspondence with George Sand. Her husband had not managed to find an alternative career, and the family revenues were dwindling. Nevertheless, one of their daughters had declined a marriage proposal made to an "outcast's daughter", preferring to wed another exile, Louis Seinguerlet. Political exile reduced the pool of possible matches and hampered traditional marriage strategies. Mathilde Kestner, the daughter of a republican industrialist from Thann in Alsace, made a fine match in accepting the hand of Colonel Charras. The ceremony, conjoining French and European outcasts, was held in Geneva in 1859; as a wedding gift to meet the couple's needs, the bride's father included in her dowry an industrial establishment near the French border. The imperial authorities viewed this union as a deliberate provocation by the Kestner family:

> Fortunately, such examples only occur very rarely among the upper classes, for they tend to mislead the minds of the masses and pervert their moral sense. Kestner had married his first daughter to a former parliamentarian in refuge in Switzerland named Chauffour, who, as I have already informed Your Excellency on several occasions, is in regular correspondence with republicans in Alsace. The alliance with Charras thus corresponded perfectly to his antecedents, while flattering all the instincts of a girl brought up to worship revolutionary ideas.[72]

The father-son relationship no doubt deserves separate treatment. Many correspondences reveal the disappointment fathers felt when their sons opted to submit to a regime the former had fled. It was often mothers who were moved by this situation. Madame Céleste Madier de Montjau mediated between her husband, who had refused any amnesty, and her son, who had preferred to return to France to pursue his career as a musician, leading him to perform at the opera in the presence of the emperor. As Madier de Montjau's wife wrote, he had the misfortune of not being continued by his son.[73] Yet Raoul Madier de Montjau had received a republican education, with an outcast, Versigny, as his tutor. When Versigny left for Switzerland, Raoul's mother decided to remain in France and concentrate on his education, which filled her every waking hour. Alexander Herzen's situation was apparently fairly similar, for he had placed great hopes in his son, as indicated by the dedication to *From the other shore:*

> You are only fifteen and have already known the rigor of destiny. Do not look for solutions in this book, it contains none; nor does our century. A solution is an end, and we are at the dawn of the revolution of the future. [...] The man of today, sad *pontifex maximus*, can only lay down a bridge. The unknown man of tomorrow shall cross it. As for you, do not remain on the old bank; it is better to founder than to seek one's salvation in the almshouse of reaction. [...] Go, when the hour strikes, and preach this religion at home in Russia. One day my word was loved there, and perhaps I shall be remembered. I bless you for this voyage, in the name of reason, of liberty, and of fraternity.[74]

---

[72] AN, BB 30 376, report by the attorney general of Colmar, January 6, 1859, 194.
[73] Bibliothèque nationale de France, NAF 20792, fol. 95–96.
[74] Jacques Le Rider, "Malwida von Meysenbug et Alexandre Herzen," *Revue des études slaves* 78/2–3 (2007): 210.

But Alexander Herzen's son soon renounced activism to devote himself to scientific works.

Such estrangements between father and son were of course not systematic: François-Vincent Raspail shared his exile with his elder son, while the sons of Pierre Barrère, exiled during the Second Empire, became in turn exiles of the Commune. As for the Russian revolutionary, Herzen, he transferred his ambitions to his daughter Natalia, known as Tata, recommending to her English tutor that she steer her away from the "frenzy for adornments" the "hankering after rags", and the "banal idea of marriage".[75] But Tata had no such ambitions, perhaps due to her incomplete education caused by the family's peregrinations, according to Herzen's biographer, Michel Mervaud.[76] Still, Tata remained sympathetic to the revolutionary ideal throughout her life: the tragic fate of the communards aroused her indignation, and while never becoming an activist she sided with Dreyfus. Herzen's second daughter, was more politically involved, and marked by the ideological estrangement between her father and her governess, subsequently her adoptive mother, a highly renowned German exile called Malwida Von Meysenbug.[77]

Exile did not destroy couples or families, but often weakened them. It could also strengthen ties and turn exile into a way of escaping the world together. Hermione Quinet found it a lot easier to put up with her solitude in Veytaux than the sociability of outcast circles in Brussels. Exile was beneficial to their couple for it created "a sacred island" where she had Quinet all to herself,[78] adding that "since 1851 there has never been a single thought of the master that has not passed through the heart and mind of his companion".[79] The image of the muse, mediator, and consoler also characterizes a final type of women for whom exile was of great importance, though not affecting them directly. These great figures sought to obtain pardons for exiles and to help them to return, or at least to comfort them by regular epistolary exchanges. George Sand and Marcelline Desbordes-Valmore both played this role, the former to Barbès and the latter to Raspail.[80]

---

[75] Michel Mervaud, "Lettres d'Ogarev à Natalie Herzen," *Cahiers du monde russe et soviétique* 10/3–4 (1969): 478–523
[76] Mervaud, "Lettres d'Ogarev," 480.
[77] Le Rider, "Malwida von Meysenbug," 207–228.
[78] Quinet, *Edgar Quinet, depuis l'exil*, 38.
[79] Quinet, *Edgar Quinet, depuis l'exil*, 38.
[80] Correspondance Sand-Barbès, and Jonathan Barbier, "Les Républiques de François-Vincent Raspail, entre mythes et réalités" (PhD diss., Université d'Avignon), 2016, 482–483.

4 Masculinity in crisis?

Thus the implications of exile for women and families – whether dispersed or on the contrary gathered in circumscribed spaces where living alongside one another could be difficult – have long been neglected. If nineteenth-century exile is often associated with essentially masculine figures, that does not mean that masculinity in exile has been thoroughly examined. Nevertheless, recent works on this notion, when taken conjointly with the study of migrations, provide a way of addressing a new facet in the reality of exile and its associated representations.

A canvas by Antonio Ciseri dating from around 1860, *L'Esule* [The Exile], summarizes the representations associated with exile to such an extent that it provides a sort of allegory of this figure. A man dressed in a long worn coat with a large hat pulled down over his long thick hair is sitting on a rock; his cheek rests on his clenched hand as he stares at the horizon in a meditative posture. It is thus a masculine allegory, in itself fairly rare, testifying to the omnipresence of men in political migrations of the nineteenth century. According to calculations by Delphine Diaz, about 90% of refugees in receipt of assistance in France in the wake of the 1830s revolutions were men, illustrating the undeniable predominance of men, in tandem with the authorities' lesser concern with assisting women.[81]

Even more striking is that Ciseri's canvas reveals changes in the bodily and symbolic attributes of masculinity: from the imposing beard to the posture, this portrait contrasts almost point by point with representations associated with the other great masculine figure of the Italian *Risorgimento*, namely the regular or volunteer soldier.[82] This divergence in the path taken by masculinity echoes a broader change in which masculinity expanded beyond the sole territory of virility, leading to an emphasis on masculine characteristics according greater place to sensitivity in the Romantic era.[83]

Beards thus tended to become established as an indissociable attribute of outcasts. From Giuseppe Garibaldi to Giuseppe Mazzini, from Auguste Blanqui

---

81 Diaz, "Femmes en exil, femmes réfugiées," 47–62.
82 On the notion of masculinity and its usages in history, see Raewyn Connell, *Masculinities* (St. Leonards: Allen & Unwin, 1995); John Tosh, *Manliness and Masculinities in Nineteenth-Century Britain* (London: Taylor and Francis, 2004).
83 Anne-Marie Sohn, *"Sois un Homme!". La construction de la masculinité au XIXe siècle"* (Paris: Éditions du Seuil, 2009).

to Victor Hugo, the leading figures of exile gave facial hair its badge of honor.[84] Exiles did not wear the same beard as soldiers: theirs tended to be ill-kempt – though Mazzini took pride in the care he lavished on his –, signaling exiles' deprivation and difficulty in tending to their bodies. In opposition to soldiers' beards, with not a whisker out of place, they no doubt also symbolized the rejection of order and discipline that characterized the most radical exiles. Because a beard covered much of the face, it could also be used as camouflage, as remarked by Victor Hugo about the socialist attorney Noël Madier de Montjau who, to escape repression in France in 1851, had to trim his "very dark and very thick eyebrows" then "cut his hair and let his beard grow".[85] Others, on the contrary, shaved off their beards to pass unnoticed.

In addition to beards, it was the entire set of representations associated with exiles which delineated an alternative figure of masculinity to the older and better established image of the soldier.[86] Exiles and transnational volunteers, two major figures of political "pilgrims" helping spread liberal and conservative ideas alike during the nineteenth century,[87] conveyed markedly different representations of virility.[88] Both were rooted in the shared structuring value of fraternity, which has come in for renewed attention by historians over recent years. Lynn Hunt has thus demonstrated how revolutionary fraternity, reconfiguring the family-based conception of the nation once the paternal figure of the king had disappeared, developed to the detriment of women.[89] The symbolic construction of fraternity in exile was admittedly very different from the brotherhood in arms within soldiers of a regiment,[90] but it also contributed to the association of exile with masculinity, thus removing women from view.

---

84 Jean-Marie Le Gall, *Un idéal masculin. Barbes et moustaches, XVᵉ-XVIIIᵉ siècles*, (Paris: Payot, 2011); Christopher R. Oldstone-Moore, *Of Beards and Men. The Revealing History of Facial Hair* (Chicago: University of Chicago Press, 2016).
85 Hugo, *Histoire d'un crime*, IV, 12, "Les expatriés", electronic edition by Jean-Marc Hovasse and Guy Rosa.
86 Stefan Dudink, Karen Hagemann, and John Tosh, *Masculinity in Politics and War. Gendering Modern History* (Manchester: Manchester University Press, 2004). See too Stefan Dundink and Karen Hagemann, "Masculinity in Politics and War in the age of democratic revolutions," in *Gendered Nations. Nationalisms and Gender Order in the Long Nineteenth Century*, ed. Ida Blom, Karen Hagemann, and Catherine Hall (Oxford-New York: Berg Publishers, 2000), 3–21.
87 Gilles Pécout, "The international armed volunteers: pilgrims of a transnational *Risorgimento*," *Journal of Modern Italian Studies*,14/4 (2009): 413–426.
88 Lucy Riall, "Eroi maschili, virilità e forme della guerra," in *Storia d'Italia. Annali 22. Il Risorgimento*, ed. Alberto Mario Banti and Paul Ginsborg, (Turin: Einaudi, 2007), 253–288.
89 Lynn Hunt, *The Family Romance of the French Revolution* (London: Routledge, 1992).
90 Brice and Aprile, *Exil et fraternité*.

Yet the figure of the exile sporting the bodily marks of his privations offers a very different representation of masculinity to the "heroic virility" which, as George Mosse has demonstrated, influenced European nation-building.[91] Paintings and engravings depicting Victor Hugo in Jersey, or Giuseppe Mazzini crossing the border, draw the representation of national heroes upwards, both literally and metaphorically, to a more advanced age, while also turning away from the idea of the *ephebos* towards that of the wise man. Exiles thus opened a breach in the stereotypical ideal inherited from military societies in which virility was associated with virtue, femininity with fragility.

The risk that these masculine figures lose their virility was sufficiently acute to be a source of concern for host authorities: in certain refugee depots, weapons practice and gymnastics sessions were organized to prevent the physical decrepitude which might accompany the idleness besetting outcasts. The prefect of the district of Morges in the canton of Vaud was thus concerned in 1850 about the twenty or so German refugees in his charge, writing to the department of justice and police to alert them to the need to "pluck them from their apathy, their nonchalance, which after a certain time will mean *they are no longer men*".[92]

This fear that men might lose their virility due to the torments of exile was not limited to the moral preoccupations of host countries: letters addressed to the authorities in charge of foreigners to voice grievances or request pardons reveal a gendered distribution intended to protect the supplicants' virility: it was women who wrote requesting for subsidies or presenting the household's material difficulties.[93] Men, conversely, were meant to remain imperturbable in the face of adversity, and even admonished their wives for soliciting outside assistance. The veterinary surgeon Bergougnioux, exiled in Belgium then Jersey in the wake of the coup by Louis Napoléon Bonaparte, thus wrote to his wife on several occasions to dissuade her from seeking employment, even though he was struggling to survive on his work as a typesetter for Pierre Leroux.[94]

Appearances were thus mainly saved in dealings with the administration, but masculinity did not emerge unscathed from the experience of exile: by introducing weaknesses in the figures of national heroes, it brought into question men's

---

91 George Mosse, *The Image of Man. The Creation of Modern Masculinity* (New York-Oxford: Oxford University Press, 1996).
92 Archives du Canton de Vaud, K VII e 10-B, letter from the prefect of the district of Morges to the department of justice and police of the canton of Vaud, April 16, 1850. Emphasis added.
93 Joanne Bayley, "'Think Wot a Mother Must Feel': Parenting in English Pauper Letters," *Family & Community History* 13 (2010): 5–19.
94 Aprile, "De l'exilé à l'exilée," 28.

capacity to look after their wives.⁹⁵ Additionally, the predominance of men in exiled populations could result in a shortage of men in lands of departure: as the historian Raul Merzario famously observed about the diocese of Como in the early modern period, "men were rare, women abounded".⁹⁶ At the same time, the enforced absence of men and the querying of their capacity to meet their household's needs generated new leeway for women, sometimes obliged to work to make up for uncertain male revenues. This collateral emancipation led to a redistribution of gender functions within the household. It added to the torments of exile, in what Laura Guidi has called a "crisis of masculinity", with men not only being held at a distance from their family, but also prevented from exercising their marital and paternal functions.⁹⁷

This was all the more true when exile was triggered by the woman's political involvement. Such was the case of the couple formed by Jeanne Deroin and the father of her three children, the Saint-Simonian Antoine Ulysse Desroches, who was unable to accompany her in her flight to England in 1852 and died a few months later in a state of great destitution. This situation, which seemed to strip a man of his virility by placing him in the position of follower, traditionally incumbent on wives, did not fail to be turned against men, such as in a caricature published in the Spanish satirical newspaper *El Moro Muza* depicting Emilia Casanova, the founder of the League of the daughters of Cuba, with her husband, the writer Cirilo Villaverde.⁹⁸ She is portrayed sabre in hand, with an authoritarian air and two flags planted in her enormous hair bun, addressing her husband: "I am going to Cuba, Cirillo, to defend our cause. You look after finishing the flags that I have left incomplete, Cirillo". In addition to being part of a satirical tradition of witch-hunts against female separatist activists, as demonstrated by Romy Sánchez, this caricature directly targets the man who, in consenting to this role inversion, seems to be shorn of his virility.⁹⁹

---

95 See for example Paola Corti, "Women Were Labour Migrants Too: Tracing Late-Nineteenth-Century Female Migration from Northern Italy to France," in *Women, Gender, and Transnational Lives. Italian Workers of the World*, ed. Donna R. Gabaccia and Franca Iacovetta (Toronto: University of Toronto Press, 2002), 133–159.
96 Raul Merzario, *Il paese stretto. Strategie matrimoniali nella diocesi di Como, secoli XVI-XVIII* (Turin: Einaudi, 1981).
97 Laura Guidi, "Donne e uomini del Sud sulla via dell'esilio," in *Storia d'Italia. Annali 22*, particularly 227–230.
98 *El Moro Muza*, July 3, 1870.
99 Romy Sánchez, "Quitter la Très Fidèle. Exilés et bannis au temps du séparatisme cubain, 1834–1879" (PhD diss., Université Paris 1 Panthéon-Sorbonne, 2016), particularly "Les femmes et les enfants d'abord?".

Apprehending exile through gender is still a challenge, or an exploratory approach at least. But it is particularly suggestive and, to our mind, offers broader perspectives: one may enquire whether exile, or at least exopolitics, might not provide an entry point to an exploration of gender. It is not simply a matter of bringing a few female figures to the fore, or of emphasizing the important accompanying role they played. Several cases bring out the specificity and depth of female involvement. While the nineteenth century often looks like a century in which women were made inferior, and excluded from politics, exopolitics opened up new spaces. Marriage and maternity in exile also led people to reconsider the place accorded to women and their combats. Apprehending the gender dimension to and in exile may also provide a way of making room for two aspects often absent in works on politics, namely psychology and intimacy. The action of exiles seems deeply linked to the feelings of these men and women in a state of enforced separation and isolation, or, on the contrary, caught in a stiflingly restricted circle. Moving beyond the exhumation of a few powerful female figures for whom exile was a form of emancipation, what we may observe is a complex landscape in which nostalgia, feelings of loss, and sadness were found alongside the solidarity and strong feelings of friendship that replaced family ties which became loosened and stretched by absence over time. Was it possible to be happy in exile? There is no doubt no single answer to this question, but this form of migration necessarily troubled, destabilized, and sapped exiles' lives, where this was felt not solely within the private sphere, but in all likelihood also reverberated throughout how they conceived of and conducted politics.

Were exiles more attentive to women's fate than others? Once again, it would be hazardous to assert so. At the very most, one may note that many of them compared the situation of their female compatriots to that of the women they encountered in their places of exile. This comparison gave rise to at least one form of attentiveness: certain exiles included women in their demands, though without this really amounting to a specificity. Nevertheless, the circulation of European women played a role in the development of early feminism, particularly in the United States, whose pioneering figures then ferried new ideas and experiences back to Europe

Romy Sánchez and Fabrice Bensimon
Chapter 7 European homelands, global vistas

The communist Friedrich Sorge (1828–1906), sentenced to death for his part in the revolutionary combats of 1848–1849 in his native Saxony, was forced to take refuge in Switzerland, Belgium, and then London. In 1852 he emigrated to New York, where he became involved in the movement for the abolition of slavery. A socialist with ties to Marx and Engels, Sorge was active in the International Workingmen's Association (IWMA) and supported the Paris Commune. He was one of thousands of forty-eighters from Germany, Hungary, and France to go the New World, where many were active in democratic and socialist movements. Thousands also left Ireland for exile in America. Others, sometimes the same people, were transported to Australian penal colonies, including thousands of British rioters, trade unionists, and Chartists. Still more emigrated to Canada, the United States, Australia, and New Zealand, where they continued their combats for democracy, workers' rights, and agrarian reform. In parallel to this, Mediterranean Europe also generated exiles, who departed under varying degrees of duress and fanned out beyond the continent. Certain Spanish liberals and Carlists were deported to the West Indies, while "seditious" individuals from the empire were relegated to Ceuta, Melilla, or Fernando Po in the Gulf of Guinea. Italians involved in the *Risorgimento* withdrew to Buenos Aires and Brazil, with some venturing as far as California. After the 1871 Commune, thousands of Parisians were deported to New Caledonia, while others fled to the United States. These European exiles who departed or were expelled far from their homelands sometimes pooled forces to work on the common aspects of their respective causes.

This chapter focuses on the material and political circumstances underpinning these experiences of exile outside Europe. It examines the view that saw colonies as places of relegation, or on the contrary as lands untainted by domination, together with the burgeoning hope that America might be a land of emancipation. In so doing, it sketches out the specific geopolitics of the nineteenth-century world, in which dominated groups crossed oceans to build lands of freedom, sometimes mutating into colonizers trampling the freedoms of others underfoot. This chapter considers diverse forms of exile, including

---

Note: We wish to thank Jonathan Beecher and Thomas C. Jones for their comments on this chapter.

those sometimes deemed to belong to other categories (such as "economic" emigration and deportation). It relies upon narratives of exile that were mostly those of literate men who produced written sources which have reached us. It takes examples among teachers and journalists, rather than among manual workers. Therefore, a large number of anonymous exiles are not explicitly dealt with except when overall flows are assessed.

It starts by examining the factors relating to exile outside Europe: why leave not just one's country but one's continent? It then seeks to circumscribe and quantify groups leaving Europe, before focusing on how the United States, and New York in particular, emerged as a privileged destination for extra-European exile. Despite the distance, exiles continued to be oriented towards their land of departure, towards pursuing their combat, building a memory, and preparing their return.

1 From "Europe's ancient parapet walls of brick" to the boundless ocean

During the half century following the Napoleonic wars, tens of thousands of Europeans left the continent for political reasons.[1] The causes and circumstances of departure were varied. Many exiles opted for neighboring countries, whence it was easy to return (such as Switzerland, Belgium, and Great Britain). But for others – or in some cases subsequently for the same – it seemed more promising to head across the Atlantic due to the United States' capacity to absorb major inflows. Often migrants hoped to be able to become socially and economically integrated, while also aspiring to bring their political ideals to life. Additionally, revolutions in transport and communications were bringing the New World closer to the Old. Far from being a destination with no prospect of return, the Americas often afforded a place of temporary refuge while awaiting more clement political circumstances. They could even act as a political base for building networks, raising funds, setting up organizations, and fomenting revolts.

---

1 Arthur Rimbaud, 'The Drunken Boat', in Wallace Fowlie, *Rimbaud: Complete Works, Selected Letters. A Bilingual Edition* (Chicago and London: The University of Chicago Press, 2005), 129.

Tropisms

There were many reasons for exiles to head for destinations outside Europe. European governments willing to take in exiles were often subject to considerable pressure by home states. The classic destinations of Belgium and Switzerland expelled many refugees for this reason, for example. The only real exception was Britain, for the reasons mentioned earlier. But after 1848, the main assistance it offered refugees, who often had to contend with material difficulties, was a one-way ticket to New York, an offer taken up by 1,500 refugees during the 1850s.[2] Additionally, certain states, such as Habsburg Austria, the duchy of Baden, and the kingdom of Württemberg, preferred to make sure that their opponents were outside Europe, with this being a condition of their release.

For various reasons, it seemed a lesser ill to depart for the United States, viewed by some as a land of milk and honey, and by all as a place of political freedom. Writing in 1854, the refugee Henri Delescluze noted:

> Land of freedom, land of the future, powerful virgin earth, Caesar's exiles and those of Europe salute you! Your hot and fiery sun heats their blood, chilled by the cold of poverty and tyranny. [...] Take in these refugees. They bring you their arms, their courage, and their faith; but forgive them, they have left behind their hearts in their beloved homelands.[3]

In heading for towns and countries where many compatriots had emigrated, political exiles were able to draw on support networks, exploit economic opportunities, find an audience and readership, and perhaps even renew ties with past associates committed to their cause. Despite its specific characteristics, leaving for a destination outside Europe was part of the vast nineteenth-century flow of European migrations. Practical reasons made the New World more accessible. Steam engines, propellers, and iron hulls cut the time needed to cross the Atlantic: for the shortest crossings, from Liverpool, London, Hamburg, or Le Havre, to New York, Boston, or Halifax, travel time was cut from three weeks in 1820 to four or five days by the beginning of the twentieth century; the crossing to Australia was reduced from four months to forty days. The rapid drop in prices, due to ships' increased speed and capacity, also helped bring the New World closer to the Old. The development of railways, like that of the telegraph linking Europe to America in 1866 and to Australia in 1902, also helped shrink the world. As

---

[2] Thomas C. Jones, "Définir l'asile politique en Grande-Bretagne (1815–1870)," *Hommes & Migrations* 1321 (April-June 2018), 18.
[3] Henri Delescluze, *Le Républicain*, 1854, quoted in Michel Cordillot, *Utopistes et exilés du Nouveau Monde. Des Français aux États-Unis de 1848 à la Commune* (Paris: Vendémiaire, 2013), 135.

Lucy Riall has pointed out, the rise of publications, the press, and a literature for the general public helped build up a community of readers (albeit an imagined one) spanning seas and oceans.[4] Mazzini, Garibaldi, and Kossuth were thus famous figures in the United States.

From the Mediterranean to the Atlantic

After having been relatively neglected by research into political exile, Mediterranean Europe has recently come in for closer study.[5] Long considered as endemically "backward" in economic and political terms, southern Europe and its Iberian, Italian, and Balkan peninsulas were home to most of the liberal uprisings in the continent after the Congress of Vienna. Spanish resistance to Napoleonic troops as of 1808 grew into a liberal combat with the promulgation of the Cadiz constitution in 1812. Liberal revolts in Naples, Piedmont, and Portugal took place in 1820, as did the Greek uprising, just as Spain was once again declaring itself to be anti-absolutist. All these hotbeds of revolution, and the subsequent repression they unleashed, caused many to head into exile well before 1848. Additionally, as of the 1790s, the French and Spanish empires were at the heart of this "age of revolutions": from the slave uprising in Saint-Domingue to the founding of independent republics stretching from the Caribbean to the mouth of the Río de la Plata, political upheavals in this Euro-American world engendered ever more transatlantic political migrations.[6]

Those heading overseas from these southern shores were chased out by expulsion orders, or sometimes left semi-voluntarily in anticipation of government reprisals. The reasons for their departure were as varied as their destinations. These Mediterranean refugees came from across the political spectrum, including Carlists, Garibaldian republicans, and "exalted" Spanish liberals of 1820 during the *Trienio Liberal*. The overlap between political and economic migrations only accentuated the variety amongst those heading overseas, well before the large flows of the end of the century embedded "national" migratory routes.[7]

---

4 Lucy Riall, *Garibaldi. Invention of a Hero* (New Haven and London: Yale University Press, 2007), 133.
5 Maurizio Isabella and Konstantina Zanou (eds.), "Introduction", *Mediterranean Diasporas: Politics and Ideas in the Long 19th century* (London: Bloomsbury, 2015).
6 Delphine Diaz *et al* (eds.), *Exils entre les deux mondes...*, op. cit.
7 Sylvie Aprile, "Exilé(e)s et migrant(e)s transatlantiques : histoire entremêlées, historiographies parallèles," in Delphine Diaz *et al* (eds.) *Exils entre les deux mondes*, 267–280; José C.

Migrations associated with the Atlantic revolutions provide a way of contextualizing the flows which marked the history of Europe throughout the nineteenth century.[8] Certain historians have warned against presupposing that the Atlantic sphere saw the largest number of circulations in the nineteenth century, arguing that this downplays Asiatic and African migrations, and institutes an artificial difference between free, supposedly white migrations and forced, supposedly African and Asiatic migrations.[9] Still, the Atlantic world shared a set of common political cultures with Europe, encouraging people to cross the ocean, whether by choice or under duress. From the United States' declaration of independence in 1776 to the issue of the independence wars in Central America, South America, and the Caribbean in the late 1820s, the entire hemisphere drew in and cast out large numbers of individuals. It gave political refuge to the losers in the Napoleonic wars and those banished after failed liberal revolutions in Europe, while British and Spanish loyalists were chased out or else fled of their own accord.[10]

A new sequence in transatlantic political migrations opened in 1808 when France invaded Spain. As of 1813, the tide turned against Napoleonic troops in the peninsula; the *afrancesados*, viewed as sympathetic to the Emperor and his brother Joseph I, now king of Spain, fled. Those heading across the ocean were far fewer than the 12,000 who went into exile across the Pyrenees.[11] Nevertheless, some supporters of the empire headed for the United States, where Joseph Bonaparte himself went into exile, or else to the new republics of Mexico, the United Provinces of the Río de la Plata, or Gran Colombia.[12] In 1823, those regarded as liberals were once again chased out of the Spanish peninsula. Yet in 1834, when Spain had adopted a moderate constitutional charter, most liberal exiles were granted amnesties enabling them to return.[13] It was now the turn of

---

Moya, *Cousins and strangers: Spanish immigrants in Buenos Aires, 1850–1930* (Berkeley : University of California Press, 1998).

8 Janet L. Polasky, *Revolutions without borders: the call to liberty in the Atlantic world*, (New Haven and London: Yale University Press, 2016).

9 Delphine Diaz et al (eds.), *Exils entre les deux mondes*, op. cit., 12.

10 Walter Bruyères-Ostells, "De l'Empereur au Libertador : circulations et exils d'officiers napoléoniens entre Europe et Amérique après 1815," in *Exils entre les deux mondes*, 46; Jesús Ruiz de Gordejuela Urquijo, *La expulsión de los españoles de México y su destino incierto, 1821–1836* (Sevilla: CSIC, Escuela de Estudios Hispano-Americanos, 2006); Maya Jasanoff, *Liberty's Exiles: American loyalists in the Revolutionary World* (New York: Alfred A. Knopf, 2011).

11 The reader is referred to chapter 1.

12 Juan Pro, "Los afrancesados españoles en el exilio," in *Exils entre les deux mondes*, 19–44; Pedro Rújula López, "Los afrancesados," *Ayer*, 95 (2014) 13–22.

13 Simal, *Emigrados*, 19.

the Carlists to go into political exile. In 1833 these legitimists contested the sovereignty of the queen, instead backing the claim of her uncle, Don Carlos. As of the beginning of this conflict, which lasted until 1840, Carlists took refuge mainly in France, although some crossed the Atlantic, whether in the wake of banishment or of their own accord, where they established links with other counterrevolutionaries in the Atlantic world.[14]

Spain was far from being the only liberal hotbed in the subcontinent to cast out exiles to distant lands. A few months after General Rafael Riego restored liberal government in Spain, the province of Salerno in the kingdom of Naples saw an uprising by officers and sub-officers, demanding a constitution and the granting of freedoms. This uprising, initially joined by the troops sent to quell it, was severely quashed by the Austrian troops in spring 1821; several hundred individuals were expelled from the kingdom or else left, fearing reprisals.[15] A re-run of the situation occurred with the uprising in Piedmont and Genoa that same year. Most exiles headed for Catalonia, Gibraltar, or else Marseille, but some ended up in Constantinople, Egypt, Tunisia, and even Buenos Aires, which had just left the Spanish Empire.[16] Still in 1820, part of Portugal rose up in the name of liberal ideals: though few of those persecuted took refuge across the Atlantic, a small number chose Brazil as a place of political fallback, especially after the attempted absolutist restoration of 1828, when several hundred liberals left for the former Portuguese territory which had become an independent empire in 1824.[17] As for the Greeks, the 1820 revolution produced mainly European exiles, although a few individuals hit by the war against the Ottomans were taken in by philanthropists across the Atlantic.[18]

In the decades following the exiles of the 1820s, the Americas became an ever more significant asylum destination. The Carlist war of 1833–1840, and then the Carlist uprisings of 1846–1849, led the Spanish monarchy to relegate

---

14 Emmanuel Tronco, *Les Carlistes espagnols dans l'ouest de la France, 1833–1883* (Rennes: Presses universitaires de Rennes, 2010); Alexandre Dupont, "'L'exil est une dure école, mais c'est une école où l'on apprend bien'. Les carlistes en exil en Europe (1868–1876)," in *Exils entre les deux mondes*, 191.
15 Simon Sarlin, "Une source inédite sur l'exil napolitain de 1821," blog entry *Exil*, accessed April 15, 2021, https://exil.hypotheses.org/123.
16 Bistarelli, *Gli esuli*; Sarlin, "Une source inédite".
17 Numbering about 400 people in all, according to Grégoire Bron. They were poorly received in Brazil, and most returned to France between 1829 and 1831. See Vitorino, *Exilados: (1828–1832): história sentimental e política do liberalismo na emigração* (Lisbon: Portugal: Livraria Bertrand, [undated]).
18 Alexander Kitroeff, "Greek Americans," in *Immigrant struggles, immigrant gifts*, ed. Wayne A Cornelius and Diane Portnoy, (Fairfax, Va.: GMU Press, 2012), 141–157.

several people to Cuba and Porto Rico. In 1836, for example, the Captain General of Catalonia sent Carlist prisoners to Cuba, where they joined the ranks of the military or public works regiments, including those building the island's first railway line.[19] Protagonists in the *Risorgimento* fleeing the peninsula after the failure of renewed uprisings in the 1830s, and then after the Italian *Quarantotto*, also went into exile overseas in a series of steps. The stages of Garibaldi's American exile are well known. The transatlantic dimension to his legendary existence, with his initial exile in Brazil after the failure of the attempted revolt in Savoy and Genoa in 1833–1834, and his first exile in New York in 1849, led to his being known as the "hero of the two worlds", a moniker formerly attributed to Lafayette.[20] Nevertheless, the Garibaldi myth tends to eclipse other transatlantic Italian exiles. From the late 1820s to the early 1860s, Argentina, Uruguay, and Brazil took in many Italian exiles, including intellectuals such as Livio Zambeccari, who arrived in Montevideo in 1826, and, like Garibaldi, took part in the separatist war of Rio Grande Do Sul, which broke out in 1835.[21] Others headed for Mexico, such as Claudio Linati, where, in association with a Cuban exile, he published one of the first literary journals in the independent nation.[22] Lastly, New York continued to be a landmark destination for Italians exiled by the *Risorgimento*, with certain making it as far as California.[23]

The kingdom of Great Britain and Ireland did not resort to proscription or banishment. But it did practice transportation to its Australian penal colonies, including for political and social reasons. Additionally, in the years between the Great Famine (1845–1851) and 1890, 3 million Irish emigrated to North America, mainly the United States. Many did not view themselves as emigrants seeking a better life, but as exiles fleeing a famine caused by the British government, making it hard in their case to distinguish between migrants and exiles.[24]

---

19 Jesús Raúl Navarro García, "Carlistas castellano-manchegos sentenciados a Cuba durante la primera guerra carlista," *I Congreso de Historia de Castilla-La Mancha*, vol. 6, tome 2, (Junta de Comunidades de Castilla-La Mancha, 1988), 67–76.
20 Pasquale Fornaro and Jean-Yves Frétigné, *Garibaldi: modèle, contre-modèle* (Mont-Saint-Aignan: Publications des Universités de Rouen et du Havre, 2011); Howard R. Marraro, "Garibaldi in New York," *New York History* 27/2 (1946), 179–203; Pierre Milza, *Garibaldi* (Paris: Pluriel, 2014).
21 Bistarelli, *Gli esuli*, 138.
22 Bistarelli, *Gli esuli*, 142.
23 Bistarelli, *Gli esuli*, 143–145; Francesca Loverci, *Giuseppe Garibaldi e la comunità Italiana in California* (Roma, Ministero Della Difesa, Comitato Storico per lo Studio della Figura e Dell'epopea Militare del Generale Giuseppe Garibaldi, 1984).
24 Kerby A. Miller, "Emigrants and Exiles: Irish Cultures and Irish Emigration to North America, 1790–1922", *Irish Historical Studies* 22/86 (Sep. 1980), 97–125.

Polish exile to the United States started after the November 1830 uprising against Russia. Austria and then France refused to take in some of the defeated, of whom 234 headed for New York. Between 1830 and 1861, a continuous flow totaling over 800 Poles went into exile in the United States, sometimes after an initial period of exile in France, Austria, or Switzerland.[25]

The nature of departures from France fluctuated with the changes in regime. Under the July Monarchy and the Second Republic, Fourierists and Icarian communists headed across the Atlantic to build socialist communities there.[26] Between 1848 and 1880, several thousand democrats, revolutionaries, forty-eighters, Second Empire refugees, and communards left France for exile in the United States. Though it is by definition impossible to count them exactly, given that family projects were mixed up with political, economic, and social reasons, Michel Cordillot has nevertheless identified 4,650 French-speaking political exiles in the United States between 1848 and 1920, no doubt only part of the total number. Among them, 960 men, 305 women, and 230 children left Britain for the United States, following a classic step-migration process; this was only a fraction of the number of political exiles who left France for the United States.[27]

The regime of the Habsburg Empire used exile as a prime tool to repress its opponents. When Hungarian insurgents were defeated in 1849, some were given the option of leaving definitively with no possibility of return. Over 5,000 of them headed to the Ottoman Empire, whence certain left for the United States. In Austria, opponents were also sometimes offered a "one-way" passport as an alternative to prison.

Concerning the German states, it is once again difficult to distinguish between exile and emigration: tens of thousands of protagonists in the 1848–1849 revolution left their country. The Grand Duchy of Baden and the kingdom of Württemberg, the main German territories from which people went into exile, employed similar practices to the Habsburg Empire. After 1848 the authorities wished their opponents to leave. But in their eyes, the emigration of an opponent to neighboring Switzerland was more a source of anxiety than a solution. In many instances, these states negotiated with their political prisoners and en-

---

25 Florian Stasik, *Polish Political Emigrés in the United States of America, 1831–1864* (Boulder: East European Monographs, 2002).
26 François Fourn, *Étienne Cabet ou le temps de l'utopie* (Paris, Vendémiaire, 2014); Bruno Verlet, *Des Pionniers au Texas 1850–1880* (Paris: Vendémiaire, 2012); Cordillot, *Utopistes et exilés*.
27 Alvin R. Calman, *Ledru-Rollin après 1848 et les proscrits français en Angleterre* (Paris: Rieder, 1921), 135, quoted in Cordillot, *Utopistes et exilés*, 142.

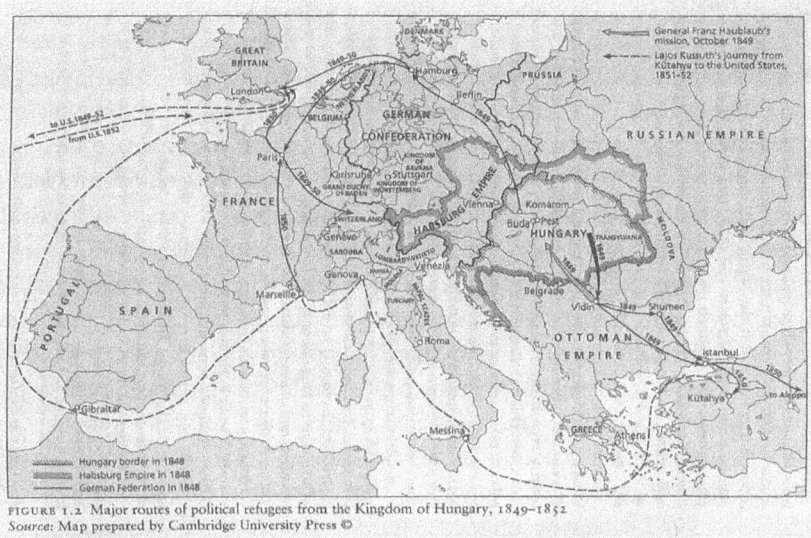

FIGURE 1.2 Major routes of political refugees from the Kingdom of Hungary, 1849–1852
Source: Map prepared by Cambridge University Press ©

Fig. 11: The routes of Hungarian exile, 1849–1852. Map by Heléna Tóth with the assistance of Cambridge University Press (with the authorization of the author and the publisher).

couraged them to emigrate. Some refused, hoping a trial would decide in their favor. Others negotiated, such as a certain J. F. Frank who requested financial assistance from the government to leave for North America, the right to take his family, to leave in the springtime, and to select the destination of this choice.[28]

So while transatlantic exile was a major break in an individual's life, it could also fit in with family or personal reasons. And while exiles to the New World were mainly victims of political repression, they could also exercise their free will, in choosing the moment, destination, and circumstances of their departure.

2 Exiles to the New World

An attempt at quantification

It is impossible to quantify exactly political exile outside Europe in the nineteenth century. The first problem is one of definition; as we have seen, depending on the conceptions of contemporaries and historians, leaving Europe may be

---

28 Tóth, *An Exiled Generation*, 59.

viewed as either political exile or economic migration.[29] Those involved were sometimes hard-pushed to describe the nature of their travels over the course of their life, and it would be foolish to ascribe a fixed category to each voyage. Additionally, nobody really counted exiles. The main sources for quantifying migratory flows in the nineteenth century – states, ports, and shipping companies – did not distinguish between exiles and emigrants. In the case of those traveling to distant and often unknown lands, the lack of documentation may be accentuated by the fact that people traveled with only the bare minimum, and in sometimes precarious conditions: crossing the sea to leave Europe sometimes entailed losing personal effects and documents. Conversely, the fact of having crossed the sea, if not undertaken clandestinely, obliged people to embark with valid documents. While prior to the end of the nineteenth century the notion of identity papers was far from fixed,[30] documents issued by a political authority were needed to officially disembark in a port of arrival. Crossing an ocean thus sometimes necessitated more detailed documentation than traveling around a continent, which was a more frequent occurrence in Europe. Nevertheless, these documents only rarely mention the reason for travel: the only migrations to make explicit their political nature were cases of banishment. The documents of those banished indicate that they had been expelled and were to be placed under surveillance on arrival. It is thus easier to count enforced exiles than voluntary or semi-voluntary departures, which can sometimes look like study or leisure trips.[31]

We may at best distinguish between groups whose numbers are known to varying degrees because their traveling stemmed from political reasons. But these orders of magnitude are themselves to be treated with caution, and do not take into account circulation between lands of exile, or any returns, both of which are even harder to quantify.

Table 1: some figures concerning the main groups of exiles leaving Europe (1815–1880)[32]

Period	Place of departure	Group	Place of arrival	Number of individuals
1798–1803	Ireland	United Irish	United States	2,000[33]

---

29 Aprile, "Exilé(e)s et migrant(e)s transatlantiques".
30 Ilsen About and Vincent Denis, *Histoire de l'identification*.
31 Aprile, *Le Siècle des exilés*, 222–224.
32 These figures are far from exhaustive. Certain groups, such as the Italians who left the peninsular after 1849 and the failure of the Roman Republic, are difficult to quantify and/or sepa-

Table 1: some figures concerning the main groups of exiles leaving Europe (1815–1880) *(Continued)*

Period	Place of departure	Group	Place of arrival	Number of individuals
1788–1862	United Kingdom	Penal deportation	Australia	3,600 deported for social and political reasons (out of a total de 162,000)[34]
1814–1815	France and French Empire	Bonapartists	United States and Spanish America	About 6,000[35]
1814	Spain	*Afrancesados*	United States and Spanish America	Fewer than 100[36]
1814	Spain	Liberals	United States and Spanish America	Fewer than 100[37]
1820	Spain	Absolutists	Cuba, Porto Rico	Fewer than 100[38]
1822–1826	Piedmont-Sardinia	Liberals	North America, former Spanish America: Río de la Plata, Uruguay, Brazil; United States	Fewer than 100[39]
1823	Spain	Liberals	United States, former Spanish America	100[40]

---

rate from so-called economic migrations. On this subject, see *Storia dell'emigrazione italiana. Arrivi* (Roma: Donzelli, 2002); Donna R. Gabaccia, *Italy's Many Diasporas*,. Equally, the findings of ongoing studies of Spanish deportees in the 1860s sent overseas are not yet known. See Jeanne Moisand, *op. cit.*, and Juan Luis Bachero y Bachero, *La neutralización del adversario político. La Deportación en la España del siglo XIX* (Madrid: Ed. Centro de Estudios Políticos y Constitucionales, 2020).

33 David Brundage, *Irish Nationalists in America. The Politics of Exile, 1798–1998* (Oxford: Oxford University Press, 2016), 34

34 George Rudé, *Protest and Punishment: Story of the Social and Political Protesters Transported to Australia, 1788–1868* (Oxford: Oxford University Press, 1978).

35 Walter Bruyères-Ostells, "De l'Empereur au Libertador : circulations et exils d'officiers napoléoniens entre Europe et Amérique après 1815," in *Exils entre les deux mondes*, 46.

36 Juan Pro, "Los afrancesados españoles en el exilio," in Delphine Diaz et al (eds.), *Exils entre les deux mondes*, 19–44.

37 Juan Luis Simal, *Emigrados*, 90 and seq.

38 *Ibid.*, 146.

39 Bistarelli, *Gli esuli del Risorgimento*, 87–88.

40 Simal, *Emigrados*, 235.

Table 1: some figures concerning the main groups of exiles leaving Europe (1815–1880) *(Continued)*

Period	Place of departure	Group	Place of arrival	Number of individuals
1828	Portugal	Liberals	Brazil	Fewer than 500[41]
1830–1861	Poland	Insurgents	United States	800 or more[42]
1833	Piedmont-Sardinia	Mazzinian liberals	Former Spanish America; United States	Fewer than 100[43]
1835–1836	Piedmont-Sardinia	Italian legion of "Garibaldians"	Río Grande Do Sul	535[44]
1837	Papal States	Political prisoners viewed as affiliated to "Young Italy" (deported)	Brazil	73[45]
1848	Spain	"Radical" progressives/Carlists/ 1848 sympathizers: deported	Philippines, North Africa (*presidios*)	About 500 (colonial army)[46]
1848–1857	France	Icarians and Fourierists; democrats, republicans, and socialists	United States	Several thousand (including 2,000 "utopians", of whom 1,000 to 1,500 were Icarians). The names of 850 are known[47]
1848–1849	German states	Forty-eighters	United States	Several thousand

---

[41] Nemésio, *Exilados* (1828–1832).
[42] Stasik, *Polish Political Emigrés*.
[43] Bistarelli, *Gli esuli*, 135-145.
[44] Donna R. Gabaccia, *Italy's Many Diasporas* (Seattle: University of Washington Press, 2000), 49.
[45] Salvatore Candido, "L'emigrazione coatta in Brasile di carcerati politici presunti affiliati alla 'Giovine Italia'," *Rassegna Storica del Risorgimento* 77(4) (1990): 485–512.
[46] Juan Luis Bachero Bachero, "La deportación en las revueltas española de 1848," *Historia Social* 86 (2016): 109–131.
[47] Cordillot, *Utopistes et exilés*, 143.

Table 1: some figures concerning the main groups of exiles leaving Europe (1815–1880) *(Continued)*

Period	Place of departure	Group	Place of arrival	Number of individuals
1849–1850	Hungary	Forty-eighters	Ottoman Empire, United States	5,000–5,500 1,000? (4,000 immigrants in all)[48]
1866–1867	Spain	Democrats and progressives	Philippines and the Mariana islands	Over 500[49]
1871	France	Communards	New Caledonia	4,000[50]
1871	France	Communards	United States	Several hundred[51]
1869–1878	Spain	Cantonalists; exiles and "people of ill repute" (deported)	Algeria, Mariana islands, Philippines.	About 3,500[52]

Banished and deported

Deportation and exile, though not the same thing, were connected. As mentioned earlier, between 1788 and 1868 the United Kingdom transported prisoners to its Australian penal colonies. Of the 160,000 people deported over the course of this long history, George Rudé has counted 3,600 "protesters" (amounting to 2.2% of the total), a term covering trade union activists, Luddites, rioters who attacked toll gates, enclosures, or workhouses, and especially Irish nationalists and insurgents.[53] In this instance, deportation was a policy of social and political regulation, with the colonial empire being used to protect the British landowning classes. Indians were also deported to Burma, the Andaman Isles, Aden, Maur-

---

48 György Csorba, "Hungarian Emigrants of 1848–49 in the Ottoman Empire," in *The Turks*, ed. Hasan Celâl Güzel, C. Cem Oğuz, and Osman Karatay (Ankara: Yeni Turkiye Publications, 2002), vol. 4, 224; Tóth, *An Exiled Generation*, 21.
49 Jeanne Moisand, *Les Mutins du Numancia. Une commune sous la Première République espagnole* (Paris: Libertalia, 2021, forthcoming).
50 Roger Pérennès, *Déportés et forçats. De la Commune de Belleville à Nouméa* (Nantes: Ouest-Éditions et Université Inter-Âges de Nantes, 1991).
51 Michel Cordillot, *Utopistes et exilés*, 266.
52 Jeanne Moisand, *Les Mutins du Numancia*.
53 George Rudé, *Protest and Punishment*.

itius, Bencoolen, and the Straits Settlements in Malaysia, in what resembled an imperial network of penal deportation. While many deportees died before serving their full sentence, and most of the others subsequently stayed, more complex trajectories were not uncommon. For example, one of the leading figures of Irish nationalism, John Mitchel (1815–1875), was initially imprisoned in Bermuda, a penal colony in the Caribbean, after having been sentenced for "felony" in 1848; he was then deported to Tasmania, whence he escaped in June 1853, heading for Sydney, San Francisco, and then New York, where he was welcomed by the Irish diaspora. He edited a newspaper there, *The Citizen*, in which he formulated the most influential criticism of the Irish famine, blaming it on the British. He returned to Ireland in 1875 and was elected to Parliament, though he died before taking up his seat.

France adopted a similar policy of removing "undesirables", sending them as of the late eighteenth century to Louisiana, then to the West Indies or French Guiana.[54] While as of the mid-nineteenth century the United Kingdom progressively relinquished the policy of peopling its colonies by "regenerating" them with those deemed renegades, France on the contrary increased its use of political deportation to its new colony of Algeria: the insurgents of June 1848 were sent there, apart from those from Lyon who were shipped to French Guiana.[55] The Second Empire continued with this policy, applying it to both common and political prisoners, any divide between the two being deliberately muddied by transportation. The Third Republic continued to deport political "troublemakers" and "incorrigible" reoffenders, with the communards being sent to New Caledonia or what was known as the "living hell of Guiana". In the night of March 19 to 20, 1874, six escaped from New Caledonia, including the pamphleteer Henri Rochefort and two elected members of the Paris Commune, Paschal Grousset and François Jourde. News of this escape echoed around the world. They arrived in San Francisco in May 1874, where they were supported by a subscription organized by French activists in California, before heading across the United States. In an interview with the *New York Herald*, Rochefort heaped blame on those who had quashed the Commune amongst great bloodshed, and denounced the conditions of penal deportation.

The Spanish Empire also carried out deportations for political reasons throughout the nineteenth century, with the practice becoming an integral part

---

54 Miranda Frances Spieler, *Liberté, liberté trahie... faire et défaire des citoyens français, Guyane 1780–1880* (Paris: Alma, 2016).

55 Louis-José Barbançon, "Les transportés de 1848 (statistiques, analyse, commentaires)," *Criminocorpus. Revue d'Histoire de la justice, des crimes et des peines* (2008): http://journals.openedition.org/criminocorpus/148.

of the numerous waves of penal exiles. Indeed, certain exiles left Spain for fear of being deported, the most feared sentence being deportation to the Philippines on the outer reaches of the Spanish Empire. Liberals, Carlists, republicans, and cantonalists were thus sent to the same lands of relegation as the Crown had used for its enemies and dissidents. Spain used its "distant" territories, in addition to the Balearics and Canaries, to confine those viewed by the authorities as highly dangerous.[56] Such individuals were sent to the unincorporated territories in North Africa, mainly Ceuta and Melilla, which had been Spanish possessions since the sixteenth century, or to Cuba, despite the need to protect the island from any "political contagion".[57] As of the second half of the century, Spain sought to imitate British and French practices by creating territories for distant deportation, such as the island of Fernando Po in the Gulf of Guinea, or the Marianna islands in the Pacific, whither insurgent Cuban separatists, republicans, and cantonalists were sent in the 1870s.[58] Thus in 1869 the Cuban independentist Carlos del Castillo, the founder of the first savings bank on the island, was deported along with 249 other supposed "rebels", embarking at Havana for the island of Fernando Po off the West African coast.[59] Thanks to his social status and the money he took with him, he managed to negotiate his escape with the local authorities on the island, described by his fellow prisoners as a living hell. With its hostile climate, forced labor, and corrupt captain general, Fernando Po was viewed by the Spanish governments of the period as a penal colony from which people did not return alive. On escaping from this insalubrious island with a few compatriots, Carlos del Castillo stopped over in Southampton on

---

56 Romy Sánchez and Juan Luis Simal, "Lexiques et pratiques du destierro: L'exil politique espagnol en péninsule et à l'Outre-mer, de 1814 aux années 1880," *Hommes & Migrations*, 1321, (2018) : 23; Juan Luis Bachero, "La represión en el absolutismo: entre la ley y la arbitrariedad," in *La represión absolutista y el exilio*, ed. Marieta Cantos Casenave and Alberto Ramos Santana (Cádiz: Universidad de Cádiz, 2015), 71–82.
57 Romy Sánchez, "Ceuta: quand la barrière de l'Europe était un bagne colonial," *Mélanges de la Casa de Velázquez* 48–1 (2018): 331–339; ANC, Asuntos Políticos, 121/30.
58 Pedro Armengol y Cornet, *A las Islas Marianas ó al golfo de Guinea ? memoria... sobre si convendria establecer en las islas del golfo de Guinea, ó en las Marianas, unas colonias penitenciarias... por D. Pedro Armengol y Cornet*, (Madrid: E. Martinez, 1878); Élodie Richard, "La déportation comme alternative à la prison, un concours de l'Académie royale espagnole des sciences morales et politiques (1875)," *Hypothèses* 6–1 (2003): 99–109.
59 Francisco Comín Comín, Angel Pascual Martínez Soto, and Inés Roldán de Montaud, *Las cajas de ahorro de las provincias de ultramar, 1840–1898: Cuba y Puerto Rico*,(Madrid: Fundación de las Cajas de Ahorro, 2010); Romy Sánchez, *Quitter Cuba. Exilés et bannis au temps du séparatisme, 1834–1879* (Rennes: Presses universitaires de Rennes, "Les Amériques" collection, forthcoming).

his way to New York, where he settled, this time as an exile, becoming one of the leading figures in Cuban exile organizations working for the island's independence.[60] As the example of this subject of the Spanish empire shows, deportation and exile sometimes occurred concomitantly in the life of a political "dissident", and it was possible to pass from one condition to the other relatively quickly, and on numerous occasions.

Profession, culture, and gender

The overlap between migrations viewed as economic and those stemming from political reasons adds to the sociological diversity of the group studied here. Certain but not all European exiles who left their continent came from the elites in their land of birth. Others came from modest backgrounds, in which case heading for a distant land fulfilled a dual objective, improving their daily life and offering the prospect of political freedom. Additionally, there could be numerous changes in situation for a given individual: some left wealthy but saw their status decline once abroad, whereas others became notably rich in their land of exile, at times on several occasions in their life.

The United States economic dynamism, labor needs, and the colonization of its interior all acted as powerful factors for integration. Political exiles did not necessarily all work in the same sectors: for example, few Irish nationalists were navvies or farm laborers. However, some may have been laborers and some may even have been rejected by state authorities: in the major American coastal states, tens of thousands of Irish paupers were deported solely because they were poor.[61]

Conversely, the presence of emigrant populations provided a market for those with professional skills. Out of a non-representative sample of 382 Germans in exile after 1849, Adolf Eduard Zucker has counted 74 journalists (19%), 37 doctors (10%), 25 teachers (7%), and 22 lawyers (5%) – all professions in which, on top of individuals' professional knowledge, their mastery of the German language and cultural skills enabled them to work for their compatriots settled in the United States.[62]

---

60 Sánchez, *Quitter Cuba*.
61 Hidetaka Hirota, *Expelling the Poor. Atlantic Seaboard States and Nineteenth-Century Origins of American Immigration Policy* (New York: Oxford University Press, 2017).
62 Adolf Eduard Zucker (ed.), *The Forty-Eighters. Political Refugees of the German Revolution of 1848* (New York: Columbia University Press, 1950), 270.

One profile recurs frequently in sources on the history of exile, namely people of letters, be they teachers, publishers, journalists, or language instructors. Needless to say, these people produced many more documents than poor and illiterate migrants. That being said, writing, translating, or teaching provided a relatively good living for those on the move, provided they could overcome the language barrier. Additionally, these professions could enable exiles to cooperate thousands of miles from their native lands. Thus one of the first literary publications in independent Mexico, *El Iris*, appeared in 1826 thanks to an association between several liberal exiles residing in Central America: the Italians Claudio Linati and Florencio Galli, the Spaniard Ramón Ceruti, and the Cuban poet José María de Heredia y Heredia.[63] This publication, with ties to York rite masonic networks, intended to "civilize the semi-barbarians" of Mexico, which had recently been freed from Spain. This project, though short-lived, brought together former Carbonari, an engraver, and a poet to work on a Mexican national project, showing that the political and literary circulations of European liberalism could echo strongly in independent South America in the 1820s. Spanish was these men's *lingua franca*, while liberalism provided a shared political basis.

While it was commonplace for political exiles to be language instructors,[64] this could lead them to travel far beyond the confines of Europe and the Atlantic world. The Pole Michel Alexandre Kleczkowski, listed by the Paris police as a political refugee in October 1842, studied Chinese in the French capital, probably at the school of oriental languages.[65] Looking for a livelihood, he turned to a career in diplomacy when Guizot's France decided to set up permanent diplomatic posts in China. He was appointed interpreter to the French consulate in Shanghai in March 1847. In 1854 he became secretary-interpreter to the French legation at Macau, going on to hold the equivalent post at Peking in 1861. On returning to France in 1863, he worked to promote the study of Chinese in Parisian universities, and taught at the Sorbonne as of 1869, and then at the school of oriental languages as of 1871. It is hard to tell to what extent his career as a diplomat and Sinophile stemmed from his status as a political exile; nevertheless, his role as a cultural relay between France and China was sometimes brought into question by his status as a "foreigner" in his two countries of adoption.

---

63 Isabella, *Risorgimento in Exile*, 51 *et seq.*; Bistarelli, *Gli esuli*; Simal, *Emigrados*, 244-246.
64 Aprile, *Le Siècle des exilés*, 218.
65 Marianne Bastid-Bruguière, "L'origine polonaise de l'enseignement universitaire du chinois moderne en Europe: Michel Alexandre Kleczkowski (1818–1886)," *Ex Oriente Lux. Księga Pamiątkowa dla Romana Sławińskiego* (Krakow: Krakowska Szkoła Wyższa, 2005), 29–59.

Another recurrent profession was soldiering, particularly for those preparing a future uprising. Adolf Eduard Zucker's German sample, for example, includes 67 soldiers (17%). In addition to soldiers were all those with experience of war, particularly during the American Civil War. Many French exiles enlisted in the Union Army, especially in the Lafayette guards, such as Charles Navière, who had taken part in the events of February and June 1848, been involved in resisting the coup of December 2, 1851, and went on to distinguish himself through his bravery at the battle of Fair Oaks in 1862.[66] Two other units were formed in New York, while dozens of Icarians based in Saint Louis also enlisted. Even the former Fourierists in slave-owning Texas adopted an openly Unionist position. French exiles' involvement in the war, and the Union victory, led them to integrate American politics. About 150,000 Irish and Irish Americans also enlisted in the Northern army. Thomas Francis Meagher (1823–1867) had been one of the leaders of the Young Ireland movement quashed in 1848; after being deported to Tasmania he escaped, and set up an Irish Brigade for the Union, numbering up to 4,000 men – Lincoln's administration encouraged Fenians to organize within the army. But not all Irish nationalists enlisted for the North, certain being steadfast supporters of slavery and the Confederation, such as John Mitchel, whose three sons served in the Southern army. Equally, certain French exiles who had settled in South Louisiana chose the Confederate camp. Such was the case for example of Camille de Polignac, the son of Charles X's minister and grandson of Marie Antoinette's favorite. De Polignac was brought up in exile as of 1832, and took part in the Crimean War, before enrolling with the Southern troops and distinguishing himself during the Red River campaign in 1864.[67]

Many former Irish combatants in the American Civil War subsequently joined the Fenian movement, which counted nearly 50,000 members in the United States by the late 1860s. Many took part in a failed anti-British expedition to Canada in 1866. John Devoy (1842–1928) had served in the Foreign Legion in Algeria in 1861, returning to Ireland for the Fenians, where he infiltrated the British Army; he was arrested in 1866, and released in 1871 on condition of never returning to the United Kingdom; he went to the United States where he became one of the leaders of the American Fenians. In 1875, he organized the escape of six Fenians from a prison in Western Australia; he later raised funds for the Easter 1916

---

66 Navière Charles [Biographical dictionary of the French-speaking social movement in the United States] by Michel Cordillot, September 26, 2014, accessed April 16, 2021, http://maitron-en-ligne.univ-paris1.fr/spip.php?article164910.

67 Jeff Kinard, *Lafayette of the South: Prince Camille de Polignac and the American Civil War* (College Station: Texas A & M University Press, 2001).

uprising in Dublin and for the Irish War of Independence (1919–1921). His career thus illustrates how the Fenians were a transnational movement spanning the Atlantic, with each branch of the organization sustaining the other from the 1860s through to 1922.

Lastly, certain intellectual and professional projects only came to fruition in exile. Such was the case for the democrat philosopher and freethinker Amédée Jacques (1813–1865). After the coup of December 2, 1851, Jacques left France for Uruguay on the recommendation of Alexander von Humboldt, like many other learned exiles of the period. After having sought to reorganize the university there, he left for Argentina, where he decided to work as a photographer and surveyor, before teaching physics in Buenos Aires. He wrote many travelogues and manuals of public instruction for the Argentine republic, where he died, but not without having promoted his philosophy of education, a project which had remained embryonic in France. In his case, the distant elsewhere detailed in his *Excursion au Río Salado et dans le Chaco* (1867) fed into his intellectual reflection, leading him to take part in his host country's national project, in his instance Argentina's public instruction.[68]

To close this section, mention may be made of one example of linguistic exile. In 1865 the Welsh non-conformist preacher Michael D. Jones (1822–1898), concerned by the progressive eradication of his native tongue, organized an emigration of Welsh people to Patagonia, in Argentina. Jones had noted with regret how his compatriots had rapidly integrated in the United States, and so for him, it was a matter of setting up a little Wales outside Wales, far from any major population centers. Between 1865 and 1912, several hundred Welsh people settled in scarcely populated Patagonia, on lands granted by the Argentine government. They formed a Welsh-speaking community which has survived, with between 1,500 and 5,000 Patagonians still speaking Welsh to this day.

The vast majority of these exiles were men, reflecting the world of European politics whence they came. Certain wives played a leading political role, such as Matilda Tone (see below), the widow of the Irishman Wolfe Tone, the main leader of the 1798 uprising against British domination which left between 10,000 and 50,000 dead. Additionally, after having played a political role during spring 1848, several women were obliged to go into exile. This was the case for example of Jenny d'Héricourt (1809–1875). A homeopath, woman of letters, Icarian communist, and feminist, she settled in Chicago in 1864 where she joined the Amer-

---

[68] Patrice Vermeren, *Le Rêve démocratique de la philosophie: d'une rive à l'autre de l'Atlantique; suivi de textes choisis de Amédée Jacques: Lettre inédite à Victor Cousin (1837); De l'enseignement public de la philosophie (1848)* (Paris: L'Harmattan, 2001).

ican movement for women's rights. She was involved in establishing links between American and French feminists, and a translation of her book, *La Femme affranchie* (1860), was published in the United States. Finally, American activists played a significant role in exiles' activities and communities, as we shall see with the internationalist Victoria Woodhull and her sister Tennessee Claflin.

3 Centers of exile in the United States

Though not the only destination for exiles, the United States played a central role. First, the country welcomed exiles. Admittedly, Congress had passed a resolution in 1788 making it possible to turn back undesirable immigrants, but it was hard to apply and was not in fact implemented. As we have seen, several European states, when they wished to be rid of political opponents, saw the distant United States as a better option in comparison to European destinations. In the United States exiles were not subject to any particular surveillance, unlike in Belgium for example. Michel Cordillot, who has studied the French-language socialist and republican press in the United States, numbering forty to fifty newspapers between 1848 and 1880, notes that these not only published signed correspondence, but also included countless lists of names (for subscriptions, petitions, and those attending meetings), suggesting activists considered they could act safely.[69]

Additionally, over the course of the century, the United States became the main destination for European migrants. Between 1821 and 1932, the country took in about 32 million migrants – perhaps 70 % of the total number leaving Europe. Political exile and emigration, when it is possible to distinguish between the two, were mutually sustaining. During the seventeenth and eighteenth century, the North American colonies had been built on the promise of religious freedom, under assault in Europe. This promise was enshrined in the constitution, and reasserted in the nineteenth century, even though it was often not fully upheld: Irish Catholics, for example, were discriminated against, and targeted by riots and nativist parties. Freedom of expression was also protected by the constitution, something which attracted many exiles, even though it did not apply equally once again: for instance, in the southern states before the Civil War, it could be difficult – not to say dangerous – to criticize slavery.

---

69 Cordillot, *Utopistes et exilés*, 140.

The only real exception appears to be New Orleans, where there were several thousand French exiles, including several socialists and republicans, such as the Fourierist Ernest Valeton de Boissière, the neo-Babouvist Jules Juif, and the radical anarchist Joseph Déjacque, a declared abolitionist.[70] But not all exiles were abolitionists, or else did not remain so. And the slave-owning states only took in a minority of exiles, who were more numerous in New York and New England.

The new Jerusalem: utopian socialists in the United States

British socialists were the first to venture to America to found ideal communities. In 1825 Robert Owen (1771–1858), a reformer and enlightened manufacturer from New Lanark in Scotland, acquired a town in Indiana, and invited people to join him there to build a "new moral world". His four sons, one of his daughters, and several hundred people recruited in the United States settled in New Harmony, where Owen himself spent only a few months. Its population soon reached 700 or 800 inhabitants, but it lacked skilled workers, and the community was riven by divisions, and undermined by Owen's projects which often contradicted American usages. It split in 1827, and Owen returned home.[71] Other Owenites subsequently set up communities in Britain and the United States. The most ambitious initiative was no doubt Thomas Powell's Tropical Emigration Society, established in 1844. This company sold shares to about 1,600 people. It wanted to settle on lands in Venezuela, and its project was for an agrarian and technological utopia, with one of those behind the project, the German John Adolphus Etzler, wishing wind and solar power to be accorded a significant role. A first group of colonists left for Trinidad in 1845, followed by another 193 people; only some reached Venezuela, and few remained there. The colonists were undermined by conflicts, desertions, and deaths due to tropical fevers and the heat; the remaining members regrouped at Erthig in Trinidad, and the company was dissolved.[72]

During the period 1848–1880, several waves of political emigrants and exiles left France for the United States, including utopians and Icarians wishing

---

[70] Marieke Polfliet, "Émigration et politisation: les Français de New York et La Nouvelle-Orléans dans la première moitié du xixe siècle (1803–1860)" (PhD diss., Université de Nice Sophia Antipolis, 2013), https://halshs.archives-ouvertes.fr/tel-00880222.
[71] John Fletcher C. Harrison, *Robert Owen and the Owenites in Britain and America. The Quest for the New Moral World*, (London: Routledge and Kegan Paul, 1969).
[72] Malcolm Chase, *Chartism: A New history* (Manchester: Manchester University Press, 2007), 87–94.

to build communities abiding by their principles in a country viewed as receptive to such undertakings. In *The Voyage to Icaria* (*Voyage en Icarie*, 1840), Étienne Cabet (1788–1856) sketched out his ideal city. His project took the form of a settlement in a wholly unpopulated region, thus untainted by the vices of French society, hence in the United States. His disciples, the first Icarians, set sail from Le Havre on February 3, 1848, and arrived in Texas. This was the beginning of an ordeal in which the heat, a cholera epidemic, and malaria decimated most of the members of this initial wave. Cabet first left France in December 1848, when 485 of his supporters had already crossed the Atlantic. Then, after returning to France, he headed off for Texas once again in March 1852, expelled by the Bonaparte authorities. In the United States he convinced about 400 colonists to pursue their goal of a community. They settled at Nauvoo in Illinois, founding a community which enjoyed a certain degree of prosperity and lasted until 1856. Faced with a revolt against his authority, Cabet, accompanied by 100 or so Icarians and their children, left for St Louis in Missouri, where he died. Over the next four decades, the remaining members of the various clans continued the venture – punctuated by splits and moves – at Nauvoo in Illinois, Saint-Louis and Cheltenham in Missouri, Corning in Iowa, and Icaria-Speranza in California where the last community was not dissolved until 1886.

The Icarians were ill-prepared for the rigors of the climate. They were confronted by a duplicitous property speculator and the problems raised by a state of virtual economic autarky. Though Cabet was recognized as a republican socialist leader in France, he was not thereby endowed with the practical capacity needed to run a community. He soon came to be seen as an authoritarian chief, and contested as such. The Icarians sought to live in egalitarian fashion, with community refectories and living spaces, plus family lodgings composed of two sparsely furnished rooms. Children were brought up in community creches by adults who were not necessarily their parents. Nauvoo had two schools, two infirmaries, a well-stocked library, a laundry, a baker's, a butcher's, farmed lands, a coal mine, and so on. Although gender-based labor specialization remained the rule, with women working as seamstresses or in the laundry, and men as carpenters or stonemasons, divorce was authorized, and women took part in community assemblies and various elections as of right.

A second wave of departures from 1847 to 1854 was composed of Fourierists led by Victor Considerant (1808–1893). They had twice attempted to found a phalanstery in France under the July Monarchy, but without success. The coup of December 2, 1851, and proclamation of the Second Empire precluded any further attempts. In the United States, the socialist author of *Social Destiny of Man* (1840), Albert Brisbane, had developed a dynamic Fourierist movement with a specific American form. With up to 100,000 members and supporters, and thirty or so phalansteries home to 7,000 or so participants, it influenced the labor movement and certain early feminists.[73] This explains Considerant's interest. The account he wrote after his first voyage reveals just how captivated he was.[74]

Hundreds of Fourierists signed up to create a colony. The 200 who founded the community of Reunion in Texas ran into the same difficulties as those which had plagued the Icarians: the climate, the challenge of making their community economically viable (including in times of crisis), internal conflicts, and the limitations of their leader, Considerant, who was depressed by these difficulties. They additionally confronted problems raised by Texan society, increasingly mobilized to defend slavery in the face of advances by the abolitionist movement. By 1860, over half the colonists had returned to France, the others having integrated American society. Several continued with their political projects, such as the leather currier Charles Capy who founded an IWMA section in Dallas, the jeweler Christophe-Désiré Frichot who, after taking part in an attempt to create a phalanstery in Brazil, also joined the First International, and the farrier Louis "Lewis" Louis who settled in New Orleans, where he likewise founded an IWMA section. Several Fourierists enlisted for the Union, but others fought in the ranks of the Southern army.

To a certain extent, the saga of the Icarians and Fourierists was the final great adventure of "utopian" socialism. These were not forced exiles, for the socialists left of their own accord to found a better world. Like very many nineteenth-century emigrants, they ran into the classic difficulties encountered by town dwellers with no farming skills. Looking back, it is easy to mock their failures. But these communitarian experiments, bred of a revolt against the French political and social order, fed into the thought of all socialists of the period.

New York, the capital of European exile?

As we have seen, the map of exile is vast and scattered across many places. But New York was its center, or at least its crossroads, a sort of capital for exiles across the Atlantic, comparable to London in Europe. As the main port of entry to the United States, the city became the destination for many exiles, some of whom went no further.[75] It was also a cosmopolitan city, a melting pot absorbing new arrivals. Former insurgents, brothers in arms, and combatants

---

73 Carl J. Guarneri, *The Utopian Alternative. Fourierism in Nineteenth-Century America*, (Ithaca and London: Cornell University Press, 1991).
74 Victor Considerant, *Au Texas* (Brussels: Au siège de la société de colonisation, 1854).
75 Cordillot, *Utopistes et exilés*, 144.

for various causes met up there, regrouped, either remained or headed for other destinations, and sometimes set off back home. This was clearly the case after 1848, with New York being home to over 50% of French refugees between 1848 and 1851.

It was also where Garibaldi disembarked after the collapse of the Roman Republic in July 1849. After seeking to take refuge in Tunis, Gibraltar, and Tangiers, he set sail from Liverpool for the United States on June 27, 1850.[76] The *New York Herald* stated that "Few men have achieved so much for the cause of freedom and no one has accomplished so many heroic acts for the independence of a fatherland".[77] On arriving, Garibaldi found certain companions in arms among the Italians living in the city, now pursuing careers in business, journalism, or else teaching Italian. Together with French republicans and German refugees, they organized a reception committee for the "hero". The Sardinian consul in Washington reported back to his minister that the reception committee was composed "of the most violent and biggest demagogic hotheads of the community".[78] He noted that "the color red" was apparently "indispensable for admission to the ranks of the demonstration", and that "numerous German workers and tailors [were] irritated [...] by the leadership assumed by the socialists", suggesting this was a factor in Garibaldi's decision not to attend the event. He added that the *Giovine Italia* clubs in New York were highly active, an additional reason, to his mind, to keep a close watch on Garibaldi's activities in the Americas.[79] Garibaldi worked for nearly a year in a candle factory on Staten Island belonging to his friend Meucci. But when Francesco Carpanetto suggested to him in January 1851 that he set sail for Central America, where the former was intending to go into business, Garibaldi accepted straightaway. He only passed through New York briefly, in 1853. And in June 1882, a few days before his death, a ceremony attended by thousands of Italians from New York was held in front of the residence where he had lived.[80]

Kossuth's voyage from the Ottoman Empire to England, then the United States, then back to England, and finally Italy, is another classic example. His arrival in New York was preceded in August 1851 by that of a group of forty-three Hungarian émigrés, former soldiers who gave musical performances in uniform in southern Manhattan, before subsequently playing the melodies of their

---

76 Howard R. Marraro, "Garibaldi in New York".
77 "The Expected Arrival of Gen. Garibaldi," *New York Herald*, July 25, 1850.
78 Cordillot, *Utopistes et exilés*, 188.
79 *Ibid.*, 189.
80 *Ibid.*, 201. This house has become a museum managed by an association of Italian-Americans and a masonic lodge. http://garibaldimeuccimuseum.org/

country and their revolution for a broader American public. These evocations of their homeland were supplemented by publications, triggering great interest in Hungary and its national hero. By the time Kossuth arrived in December 1851, the country was in a state of expectation. The outcome of his tour was mitigated, however, with audience numbers tailing off; he disappointed American abolitionists by refusing to condemn slavery. But at the same time, the publicity surrounding his voyage and his person enabled other Hungarian exiles to capitalize on their condition, such as the officer János Kalapsza, who founded a successful riding school in Boston. In American public opinion, the exoticism of the Hungarians derived partly from the fact that they often came from the Ottoman Empire, their initial land of exile, and their nation thus appeared to be a borderland between West and East.[81]

On February 24, 1854, a demonstration by exiles was held in New York by the French members of the Society of the Universal Republic. The march was attended by about 500 people. The abolitionist Cuban newspaper for exiles, *El Mulato*, reported that: "all the nationalities gathered together under the standard of fraternity enthusiastically greeted the inauguration of this republic that Napoléon the little [sic] destroyed with his impious hand". The march was attended by Italians (with their banner "God and the people"), Cubans and their flag bearing a single star, and French carrying the stars and stripes, "then several German and Hungarian commissions, and finally the Poles appeared, brave and exalted as always, whose standard bore the following words: 'Death to tyrants! Poland is not dead!'".[82]

New York acquired a symbolic dimension as a cultural capital. How else can we explain why Karl Marx, exiled in London, and never setting foot in New York, wrote 487 articles for the *New York Daily Tribune* over a twelve-year period (1851–1862), a larger body of writing than the three volumes of *Capital*? Horace Greeley's progressive newspaper admittedly enabled the Marx family to make ends meet, but with its print-run of 200,000 issues in the early 1850s, it was one of the most read newspapers in the world. As the United States came to acquire a leading place in the European imaginary, New York established itself as the horizon on which exiles projected their expectations. Its centrality was even more marked among communards, of whom 83% of those identified as living in New York resided in a dozen streets in southern Manhattan (see below).[83] New York thus asserted its unique role as the main land of exile for European refugees.

---

81 Tóth, *An Exiled Generation*, 128–136.
82 "Celebración del Aniversario de la república francesa," *El Mulato*, no.3, March 6, 1854.
83 Louis Simonin, "New York et la société américaine," *Revue des Deux Mondes* (December 1, 1874), 658–688, quoted in Cordillot, *Utopistes et exilés*, 144.

4 Were distant exiles long-term exiles?

In moving far from Europe and their native land, exiles did not alter their behavior. Instead, they continued to organize themselves, build up networks, think about returning, reflect on the political future of their country, construct a memory, and build up an image of heroic deeds to be appropriated by future generations – those who, they believed, would accomplish the cause for which they had fought and been defeated.

Pursuing a combat

If on starting their new life certain exiles renounced their cause, most continued with their undertaking, though often in refashioned and renegotiated form, depending on the host country and specific circumstances of their exile. Distance from Europe created singularities in comparison to exile on the continent, as we shall now see through a few examples.

Following the failure of the liberal uprisings of 1820–1821 in Naples, Sicily, and Piedmont, certain of those involved left for South America, where emancipation from the Spanish and Portuguese empires had been under way since the 1810s. Such was the case of the former Carbonaro, Livio Zambeccari. After heading into exile in Spain, like many Italian liberals in the early 1820s, he arrived in Montevideo in 1826 in the midst of the Cisplatine War between the United Provinces of Río de la Plata and the Brazilian Empire.[84] The recently formed Brazilian imperial army was composed of European mercenaries and volunteers, but Zambeccari chose the opposing camp whose struggle resulted in the independence of Uruguay in 1830. He then fought against the government of Juan Manuel de Rosas in Argentina, and in the struggle for the independence of Rio Grande do Sul as of 1835. He was captured by the Brazilians in 1836, two years before Garibaldi also threw his support behind this territory in its conflict with Brazil. He was released in 1839, and returned to his hometown of Bologna in 1841, the year Garibaldi and his Italian Legion became involved in defending Uruguay against Rosas' Argentina.[85] For Zambeccari, as for Garibaldi and his "red shirts", South America provided a theater for temporarily transposing causes and struggles, adapted to the local context. It was not simply about supporting independence.

---

[84] Mario Caravale and Istituto della Enciclopedia Italiana, *Dizionario biografico degli Italiani*, (Roma: Istituto della Enciclopedia Italiana, 1960) "Zambeccari, Livio, conte".
[85] *Ibid.*

Above and beyond this, it was a matter seeing what had failed in Europe triumph elsewhere, choosing one or several camps from a spectrum of varied political options, exporting and borrowing combat techniques, and creating solidarities with protagonists on the ground amidst often fluctuating ideals and beliefs. The idea of federalism, for example, so central to political debates about the *Risorgimento*, owed much to the experience of Italian exiles fighting in the Southern Cone in the 1820s and 1830s, according to the historian Maurizio Isabella, and did not simply derive from admiration for the model of the United States.[86]

After being deported, former convicts also resumed their struggle. William Cuffay (1788–1870), whose father Chatham Cuffay was probably a former slave of African descent from Saint Kitts in the British West Indies, worked in London as a tailor. A trade union activist, he became one of the most radical leaders of the Chartist movement. In August 1848 he was arrested and tried for his presumed role in a conspiracy. He was sentenced to penal deportation and spent the rest of his life in Tasmania, lying south of Australia. His wife was able to join him in 1853 thanks to a subscription, and Cuffay was released in 1856. Like most of those transported to Australia, he did not return to Europe. He resumed his combat for the labor cause and for democracy. In one of his final speeches in Hobart, in 1866, he appealed as always to his "fellow-slaves": "I'm old, I'm poor, I'm out of work, and I'm in debt, and therefore I have a right to complain".[87] In other words, in Tasmania, a colony of 80,000 inhabitants, half of whom had been sentenced to transportation there, Cuffay continued the struggle he had conducted on the other side of the world, in London, the largest city in the world at the time with 2.5 million inhabitants. In the United States, Australia, and New Zealand, thousands of émigré Chartists continued with their struggle, inspired by their activity in Britain, calling for democratic reform, universal suffrage, agrarian reform, and workers' and trade union rights.

French exiles, for their part, tended to cherish the republican ideal. In New York, the Society of the Universal Republic was founded in late 1853, based on the Revolutionary Commune set up in Britain by Marc Caussidière and Félix Pyat. It was this society which organized the demonstration of 1854 mentioned earlier. It continued to play a structural role among French exiles, opening a jobs bureau for the unemployed, dispensing French and English lessons, providing legal support, and intervening in conflicts between French residents.

But not all those who had been involved in the European revolutions of 1848 commemorated this event once in exile. On crossing the Atlantic some went on

---

[86] Isabella, *Risorgimento in Exile*, 60 et seq.
[87] Chase, *Chartism*, 303–311.

to live a life far removed from their initial combat. This was the case of those who took part in the expeditions of the Venezuelan adventurer Narciso López in 1851, with the goal of annexing Cuba, removing it from Spanish domination, and turning it into a new US state. On September 6, 1851, the *Gaceta de La Habana* reported that thirteen Germans, ten Irishmen, six Englishmen, nine Hungarians, and two Frenchmen had taken part in the fifth and final attempted invasion by López, a veteran of the Spanish army who had since become the Crown's enemy.[88] Two of the Germans involved in this failed voluntary expedition of 1851 were former combatants of 1848. The first, Louis Schlesinger, was an officer of Hungarian origin, a former companion in Kossuth's struggle, who had taken part in the Viennese revolution. He was known by the Prussian authorities as a "proven demagogue", and listed as "very dangerous" by the Spanish authorities during his exile in the United States.[89] He reached New York in 1850 shortly after the Magyars were defeated at Komárom. He met López in New Orleans and set about recruiting people for his renewed liberation expedition, "a hundred or so Polish and Bulgarian refugees who he felt could be useful to his cause while also showing that his objective was not solely annexationist".[90] The second was Conrad Eichler, a merchant from Mainz, likewise considered by the authorities as a political troublemaker. Among those identified as "Hungarian" on the prisoner list was János Prajay, another "red republican" who had been present in London in 1849 along with other refugees from the Magyar revolt, before traveling to New York in 1850 where he published his memoirs of the rebellion.[91] In parallel to this, a Hungarian patriot wrote to Kossuth in New York in 1852, informing him that many of his compatriots were drawn by the "Cuban agency" lobby, and had been caught up in adventures such as López's for purely monetary motives.[92] A few Frenchmen and some Irishmen were also involved in these expeditions. After having survived the fiasco of López's expeditions, Louis Schlesinger became involved in another attempted annexation, this time by the American filibuster William Walker. From 1856 to 1857 Walker was the president of Nicaragua, where he re-established slavery, with Schlesinger acting as his colonel. But

---

[88] BNJM, *Gaceta de La Habana*, December 6, 1851.
[89] Michael Zeuske, "¡Con López a Cuba!," *Ibero-Americana Pragensia* 27 (1994): 17.
[90] Louis Schlesinger, "Personal narrative of adventures in Cuba and Ceuta," *US Democratic Review* 31 (1852): 211.
[91] Salvador Bueno, *Cinco siglos de relaciones entre Hungría y América Latina* (Budapest: Editorial Corvina, 1977), 114.
[92] Bueno, 115.

Schlesinger disavowed his superior before the latter was defeated and subsequently executed by firing squad in Honduras in 1860.[93]

Under the banner of the International

In the 1850s two organizations were set up by exiles in Britain, with British, French, German, and Polish members: the International Committee in 1854, then the International Association (IA) in 1855. Their purpose was to bring about by social revolution "the universal social and democratic republic". This internationalism appealed to exiles in the United States, many of whom had lived in London, such as the freemason Claude Pelletier who acted as an intermediary. Most IA members in the United States were French or German, such as Sorge. The IA commemorated the anniversaries in the radical calendar. In 1858 it organized demonstrations to the glory of the Italian conspirators Pieri and Orsini, who had been executed in Paris after their assassination attempt against Napoléon III. On September 22, a torchlit march in New York was attended by 5,000 people, sparking the interest of the American press. American topics of debate came to dominate. The vast majority of democrat and socialist exiles hated slavery, the "peculiar institution" contradicting the image of freedom associated with the United States. Increased tension in the 1850s and the Civil War (1861–1865) led them to enlist, particularly in the Union Army. This participation in American debates, including armed involvement, contributed to the exiles' integration.

After the Civil War, the American economy picked up and needed labor, attracting many migrants, including French people. Michel Cordillot has explored the history of the Union Républicaine de Langue Française (URLF), founded in 1868 in Saint Louis, comprising many French speakers, including certain former Icarians who had remained there since the days of Cabet. The URLF rapidly spread to New York, Boston, Paducah in Kentucky, Newark and Paterson in New Jersey, Carondelet in Missouri, then to Kansas, Keokuk in Philadelphia, New Orleans, San Diego, Iowa, and Chicago, where the section numbered 600 or so people. A *Bulletin* linked up these various groups; in late 1870 it had 800 subscribers in nineteen different places, amounting to several thousand readers, held together not only by republican ideas and their opposition to the imperial regime, but also by a certain anticlericalism and various strains of socialism.

---

93 Michel Gobat, *Empire by Invitation William Walker and Manifest Destiny in Central America* (Cambridge: Harvard University Press, 2018).

In 1864 the IWMA was created in London. It developed rapidly as of 1868–1869, particularly in France, through a series of social movements. URLF activists soon became involved, brought on board by exiles such as Claude Pelletier. On June 8, 1870, the first New York French-speaking section was set up. Its members were galvanized by the Franco-Prussian-War, the collapse of the imperial regime, and the proclamation of the republic. Some could no longer bear to remain in the United States, and over the course of September 1870, several hundred French volunteers, sometimes accompanied by Francophile foreigners, left New York and San Francisco for France, to fight Prussia. At the same time, the IWMA's US sections mobilized; on November 9, 1870, two thousand people attended a meeting in New York against the war, with speakers such as Victor Drury for the IWMA French section, Sorge for the Germans, and New Democracy's J.W. Gregory for the English-speaking associates. The Paris Commune unleashed a torrent of denunciations in the United States. French exiles were divided. The New York section of the URLF supported those in favor of the Commune, as did sections with a predominance of Cabetists and Fourierists, while others withdrew their backing.

The IWMA expanded rapidly. The number of sections in the USA rose from 6 in May 1871 to thirty-five by late November, reaching forty-seven in 1872. All in all, the International numbered sixty sections and 4,000 members in twenty-five towns.[94] These sections were composed of three linguistic and/or national groups. About twenty sections, accounting for nearly half the overall membership, were German-speaking, and headed by politicized, often socialist refugees. The 18 English-speaking sections were part of the American reformist tradition, thus IWMA banners were brandished at a demonstration of 20,000 people calling for an eight-hour working day on September 13, 1871. Lastly, there were seventeen French-speaking sections.

These IWMA sections were strengthened by the arrival of communards. Several hundred of them, of whom 106 have been identified with certainty, reached the United States, twenty years after the refugees of December 2, 1851. Certain had already lived there for several years and had returned to France once the Republic was instituted on September 4, 1870, thus finding themselves in Paris on March 18, 1871. They nearly all settled in the great cities on the East Coast, particularly New York. During a demonstration on December 17, 1871, ten thousand people formed a funeral procession honoring the recently executed communards. Amidst the red flags, a banner borne aloft at the head of the procession

---

[94] Michel Cordillot, "Socialism v. Democracy? The IWMA in the USA, 1869–1876," in *"Arise ye wretched of the earth,"* 270–281.

proclaimed "Honor to the martyrs of the universal republic", while many demonstrators followed the banner of section 2 of the IWMA. The French were followed by German, Cuban, American, and Italian societies, together with a delegation of Irish Fenians. The following day the entire country was informed of this red demonstration, without equivalent in Europe. Among the American personalities attending were the sisters Tennessee Claflin and Victoria Woodhull; shortly afterward the latter announced she was a candidate in the 1872 presidential election, with the former slave Frederick Douglass as her running mate, and their ticket was supported by many internationalists.

The IWMA sections were divided between those supporting the leaders of the general council, autonomists who were hostile to it and called for sectional autonomy, and Blanquists who formed their own international confederation within the IWMA ranks. In 1872 the IWMA congress at The Hague voted for the general council to be transferred to New York. The IWMA was suffering from the repercussions of the repression of the Paris Commune, and as of 1873, it went into decline. In 1876 it stopped publishing the *Bulletin*, and on July 15 the (centralist) IWMA voted its own dissolution at Philadelphia. Neo-Fourierist projects and socialist agricultural colonies continued, including in Honduras in 1875 and in Venezuela in 1875–1876. Former exiles now became involved in the burgeoning American labor movement.

Building and maintaining a memory

Pursuing combat in exile across the Atlantic sometimes took more peaceful forms than conspiracies or establishing combat organizations, but which were no less important for all that: building a memory, erecting a paper pantheon, or narrating heroic deeds to be appropriated by future generations.

Matilda Tone (1769–1849) was not yet thirty when her husband, the leader of the United Irish, Theobald Wolfe Tone (1763–1798), committed suicide in prison the day before he was to be executed by the British authorities. Her life was one of exile with no return, first in the United States, then in France, then in the United States again, in Washington. Her three children died of tuberculosis: "Oh don't expatriate yourself, don't expatriate yourself", she said in 1849 to an Irish visitor envisaging exile. "Here I am for thirty years and I have never had an easy hour, longing after my native land". Two weeks later she died, without ever having seen her "poor old Dublin" again. As reported by the historian David Brundage, Matilda Tone nevertheless left a monument, the *Life of Theobald Wolfe Tone*, a *magnum opus* of 1,200 pages published in 1826,[95] a biography sanctifying Tone as a hero and martyr. She said nothing of his personal misdeeds or his acerbic comments about Federalist leaders of the 1790s who had become famous in the United States. Her work, a model of political construction, became one of the handbooks of Irish nationalism; it was a product of exile.

The construction of a memory from exile overseas could also include rewriting a nation's history, particularly in fiction. This was the case of a work by the exiled Spanish liberal, Félix Mejía, who settled in Philadelphia, where he wrote a play in 1824 called *Pizarro or The Peruvians*.[96] It tells of the "conquest" of Peru, examining the idea of a homeland and the consequences despotism may have on a territory. The historian Juan Luis Simal points out that Mejía adopted a broad definition of homeland to include his belonging to Spain, without this conflicting with the little American homelands championed in his play. On leaving the United States to settle in Guatemala in 1827, Mejía honed his definition of the republican "homeland", drawing inspiration from Antiquity. He was involved in the politics of the young Guatemalan nation, and had to prove his new patriotic allegiance through his writing while renouncing his native Spain – just as his character Alonso had done, the ally of the Peruvians who denies his belonging to Spain in order to oppose the despotic Pizarro. In presenting a Ciceronian conception of the republic as an "association of free virtuous individuals wishing to respect the law and perform duties",[97] Mejía's writings preserved his native Spain – in his wishes a liberal land opposed to the black legend of Conquistador Spain – while celebrating new political organizations, such as Guatemala. In his instance, dramaturgy and political writings amount to a profession of faith: by venturing onto institutional terrains far removed from his native land, Mejía established himself as an American public intellectual. Nevertheless, he was chased out of Guatemala when it became a dictatorship in 1838, and took refuge in Cuba where the colonial yoke and absolutist exception still prevailed, before going back to Madrid where he died in 1853.[98] Building a memory on the other side of the ocean was thus subject to variations within an individual's life, making it impossible to fix any political position – however radical – in writing.

---

95 Brundage, *Irish Nationalists*, 1, 48–49, 87.
96 Simal, *Emigrados*, 448 et seq.
97 *Emigrados*, 449.
98 *Emigrados*, 238.

Returning from afar

It is virtually impossible to quantify the number of exiles who returned. Heléna Tóth estimates that up to 10% of German émigrés to the United States returned to Europe.[99] Hundreds of Hungarians also returned. In the late 1850s, several European states (including France, the German states, and Austria) passed amnesty laws or took measures to pardon exiles. Such measures were often accompanied by the requirement that recipients express their regret, something not all exiles were prepared to do. And family, professional, or political reasons could lead exiles to opt to remain in their host countries. Returning to a land they had left, which had already changed, and where old wounds had not necessarily healed, was sometimes a disappointment.

The aspiration to return could also sometimes include the deceased.[100] The most famous and widely read radical in Britain, Thomas Paine (1737–1809), had been forced into exile in the United States. As the Quakers had refused to bury this scandalous deist in New Rochelle cemetery in the state of New York, he was interred in his farm as requested in his will; only six people attended the ceremony. In 1819 the radical journalist William Cobbett set about getting Paine's remains exhumed and brought back to Britain, where he had spent the first thirty-seven years of his life. Although Cobbett succeeded, he was unable to obtain their reburial, and when he died in 1835 he was still in possession of Paine's bones. It is not known what has become of them since.

Certain returns gave rise to combats. In 1834 six farmworkers from southern England were sentenced for "swearing a secret oath" and sentenced to penal transportation to Australia. A vast campaign in England was launched to obtain their release, gathering 800,000 signatures; the trade unions' central committee organized a demonstration in London, one of the first of its kind in Britain. The Tolpuddle martyrs were pardoned and returned to the country as heroes in 1838 and 1839. This successful campaign acted as a trampoline for the Chartist movement.

Subsequently, obtaining the return of deportees and exiles was a frequent objective. For instance, the Irish nationalists staged a successful political demonstration calling for the repatriation of the mortal remains of Terence Bellew McManus, a former 1848 and Young Ireland combatant, when he died in 1861 in San Francisco where he had taken refuge after escaping from Tasmania (see fig. 11).

---

99 *Emigrados*, 214.
100 The reader is referred to chapter 4.

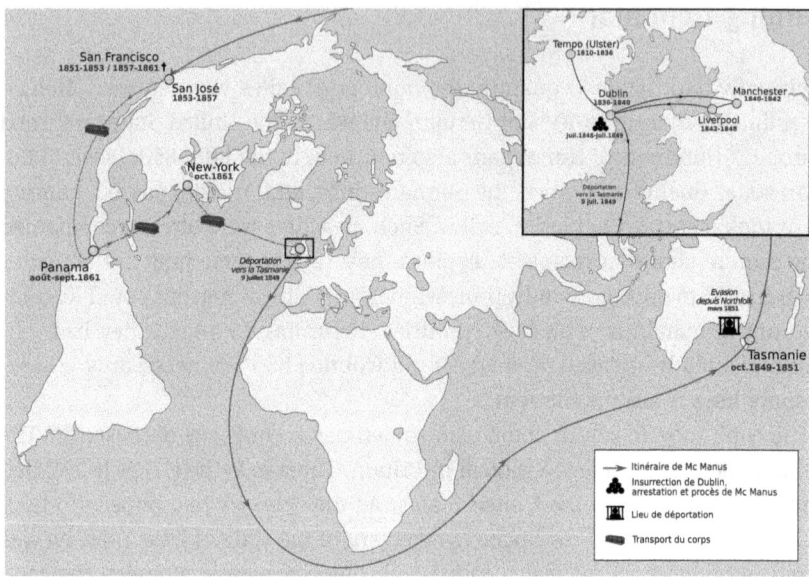

Fig 12, translation: Arrow: Mc Manus' itinerary; Canon balls: Dublin uprising, Mc Manus arrested and put on trial; Prison: Place of deportation; Coffin: Transport of body; *On Australia*: escape from Northfolk March 1851 (map by Hugo Vermeren).

The California Fenians organized to have his body returned to Ireland, via New York. He was buried at the Glasnevin cemetery in Dublin, alongside his former brothers in arms. The eulogy started by describing "the anguish of the exile, doomed to die and leave his bones for ever in a foreign land".[101] This demonstration had a mobilizing effect for the Irish nationalist movement, enhancing the influence exerted by US Fenian leaders in Ireland.

Many French exiles in the United States apparently returned to France after the collapse of the Second Empire in September 1870.[102] But others turned their distant exile into an opportunity for long-term expatriation and decided not to return home. Such was the case of Alexis Peyret, a republican from Béarn who arrived in Montevideo at the age of twenty-five, shortly after the 1851 coup. Six years later he became the administrator of the agrarian colony of San José in the Argentine province of Entre Rios. He married there, and in 1868 was appointed second-in-command of the development junta for the

---

101 Brundage, *Irish Nationalists*, 100.
102 Olivier Brégeard, "Une communauté fragile, les Français de New York au milieu du XIXe siècle," *Annales de démographie historique* (2001): 43–53, quoted in Aprile, *Le Siècle des exilés*.

town of Colón in the same region. In 1870 he decided not to return to France but to pursue his administrative career, becoming a history professor at the national college of Uruguay. He left Uruguay on being criticized for his political stance in favor of autonomy for the provinces, settling in Argentina where he also taught history. In 1889 the Argentinian government sent him to study the agricultural machines on display at the Universal Exhibition in Paris. This return to France was only temporary, however, since he returned to Argentina. In 1893 he became the first president of the French Alliance in Buenos Aires, and acquired Argentinian citizenship. Thus although Alexis Peyret decided not to return, he managed to act as a veritable "cultural hyphen" linking up France and the Americas.[103] In 1871 he wrote a draft constitution, and during his time in France in 1889 was the Argentine delegate to the International Socialist Congress. In South America he wrote down the tales of his native Béarn, while supporting European immigration to his new country of residence. The fact of not returning to France made him a fully-fledged Franco-American, who remained connected with his native land despite the distance at which he resided.

By the end of the century, European states made less use of banishment and proscription, at a time when economic and social emigration was acquiring new scale. Admittedly, new categories of exiles also appeared. Such was the case of the anarchists, many of whom fled their country of origin (especially France, Italy, and Germany) for Britain or the Americas. While economic reasons played a major part in the emigration of nearly 2 million Jews who left Eastern Europe for the United States by the 1920s, Anti-Semitic persecution and pogroms in Russia as of 1881 also played a critical part in this flow.[104] Those deported to Siberia, where Russia relegated large numbers of people, including Polish insurgents, anarchists, populists, and Marxists, should be added. Official statistics for 1898 indicate there were 290,000 deportees in Siberia.

Over the course of the century, destinations outside Europe became increasingly prominent in political exile. Many states casting out exiles were in favor of enforced distance. But for exiles, heading for the Americas could also bring opportunities, and a reunion with associates, family members, or political brethren. As the world shrank during the nineteenth century, the New World became closer to the Old. Exiles sought to exert their own agency and make the best of their distance from their homeland, which was never of course either wholly wished for or wholly imposed – and was never irrevocable. Additionally, as of the

---

103 Aprile, *Le Siècle des exilés*, 245–246.
104 Tara Zahra, *The Great Departure: Mass Migration from Eastern Europe and the Making of the Free World* (London. W.W. Norton, 2016).

1850s, the political migrations leading exiles away from Europe became increasingly mixed up with migratory flows viewed as stemming from economic reasons. Thus, the same transatlantic ships carried candidates for emigration aspiring to a better life and exiles from a European revolutionary cause; on occasions it could be hard to distinguish for a given individual which criterion prevailed.[105]

Political exile to the New World and other destinations outside Europe was a mass experience, sometimes undermined by the better studied and wider mass experience that was economic transatlantic migration at more or less the same period. In fact, it was only via numerous departures that several authoritarian regimes in Europe were able to stabilize themselves in the middle of the century, by displacing those contesting them. These exiles also played a part in setting up many societies, including in the United States. In other words, nineteenth-century European exile to the rest of the world was a key dimension in the formation and globalization of present-day societies.

---

105 Aprile, "Exilé(e)s et migrant(e)s transatlantiques"; Nancy L. Green, *Repenser les migrations* (Paris: Presses universitaires de France, 2002).

Sylvie Aprile and Laure Godineau
Chapter 8 Returns and memories

On July 13, 1880, just a few days after the vote for full amnesty, the former communard Jules Vallès returned to France, after nine years of exile in Britain. He was welcomed at the Gare du Nord by a public of political and literary friends. He had not waited long to leave his country of refuge and return to Paris. While in exile he had maintained extensive contact with France, particularly via the intermediary of Hector Malot, who had interceded with the press and publishing world on his behalf. His return to the French capital paved the way for his sustained activity as a journalist and man of letters, notably launching the newspaper *Le Cri du Peuple* in 1883, whose title recalled the great paper he had directed during the Commune, and publishing *L'Insurgé* in instalments. He returned repeatedly to his experience as a revolutionary and exile until his death in 1885. In the light of his career, this chapter seeks to examine the moment of return to the country of origin. For Vallès, there was apparently no hesitation about returning immediately after the amnesty. But were things so simple for all the many political exiles in nineteenth-century Europe?

It should be pointed out that there are very few monographs about returns, even though the literature on nineteenth-century exile has developed over the past twenty years.[1] Sources on exiles are often partial and scattered, and this is even truer of sources about their return, given that those returning were no longer subject to the same surveillance, especially when they blended into the anonymous mass. Refugees undertook, indeed and in their imagination, at least two trips: their departure, and their return. Departure became part and parcel of their past, and was often narrated as an adventure. They had had to change name, assume a disguise, slip across the border, make their first contacts abroad, both with the land and those living there. Sometimes the trip was one way: when refugees became migrants or else died in exile, what was intended as temporary became their final resting place. But however long they remained abroad, and even though certain came to terms with their new environment, the true voyage was their long-awaited return. Yet they left few accounts, no doubt because it was often a great disappointment, portrayed as a new exile, a

---

[1] Ansgar Reiss, "Home Alone?, Reflections on Political Exiles Returning to Their Native Countries," in *Exiles from European Revolutions*, 297–315. Many of the remarks for the history of exile are also true for migration history in general. See José Moya, "Remigration: Patterns of Leaving and Returning from Prehistory to the Advent of Globalization," in *Return Migration in Romance Cultures*, ed. Andreas Gelz, Marco Thomas Bosshard (Freiburg: Rombach, 2014), 21–44.

theme found in the writings of Georges Renard and Lucien Descaves about refugees from the 1871 Commune, and indeed in those of many earlier authors.[2] This somewhat somber portrayal clearly needs considerable nuancing depending on the nation in question, for it is very different to return as victor or vanquished, as a hero or one forgotten by history.

Those returning had to learn how to live in a country which had changed, both economically and politically. On returning to Paris in the second half of the nineteenth century, French exiles found a cityscape transformed by Haussmann, and a political environment which had in many cases erased their period.[3] Conversely, it is probable that most Italian refugees who returned after Italian unification received a warmer reception, for they were more clearly on the winning side. Nevertheless, we must avoid any overly schematic analysis. A major parameter was any evolution in the country of origin. This varied greatly depending on the nation-building undertaken during the century – see for example the differences between the Italian and German units, the Austro-Hungarian compromise, the political upheavals in Spain, and the repression of various nationality movements. It is nevertheless with a certain irony that Juan Rico y Amat depicts the figure of the returning outcast in his *Diccionario de los políticos:*

> Those without political existence acquire a certain importance on emigrating. They may say that the opposing party wanted to see them dead, and emigration saved their lives: they may repeat to whom they please that they have tasted the bitter bread of the émigré, and been the victim of political consequences. Their fellow believers, now in power, would be cannibals were they not to give them a good slice of turrón to sweeten this past bitterness.[4]

This chapter thus sets out to study the multi-faceted circumstances in which exiles returned, arrived, and resettled in their home country. Different elements could shape the return experience, such as length of absence, geographical dis-

---

[2] Georges Renard, *Un exilé* (Paris: P. Ollendorff, 1893); Lucien Descaves, *Philémon, vieux de la vieille* (Paris: P. Ollendorf, 1913). On representations of communards' return as a renewed exile, see especially Laure Godineau, "Le retour d'exil, un nouvel exil? Le cas des communards," *Matériaux pour l'histoire de notre temps*, 67 (2002): 11–16.

[3] On this subject, see for the 1880s Laure Godineau, "Paris attendu, Paris retrouvé. Les exilés communards et le peuple de Paris, de la nostalgie aux retrouvailles," in *Être Parisien, Actes du Colloque organisé par l'Université Paris 1 Panthéon-Sorbonne et la Fédération des Sociétés historiques et archéologiques de Paris-Ile-de-France* (Paris: Publications de la Sorbonne, 2004), 379–390.

[4] Juan Rico y Amat, *Diccionario de los políticos* (Madrid: Imprenta F. Andrés, 1855), 17, quoted in Laurent Dornel (ed.), *Le Retour* (Pau: Presses universitaire de Pau et des pays de l'Adour, "Espaces, frontières, métissages" collection, 2017), 159.

tance between country of origin and the host country, age, family, and gender. But this is variable, and archives are sometimes lacking, concerning women and families for example. The chapter also examines memories of exile in the land of refuge, become a land of departure, and in the land of origin, home once more. It focuses, first, on what enabled or prevented return, and, second, on the reasons why exiles did or did not embark on this return voyage. But returning was not enough: they also had to find their place once again in a land and society left, for some of them, many years earlier. Independently of their bitter, ironic, or distant personal appraisals of their return, how did they conceive of it in the long term, and by extension view their experience during their years elsewhere? Answering these questions involves looking at the traces of exile in individuals' life courses and in collective memories. The chapter closes on a final question: are traces still to be found in the castles, forts, prisons, cafés, and streets where refugees gathered and drew up their plans? Was the homeland to which they returned, either living or dead, prepared to commemorate the past they embodied?

1 Returning

How many left and how many returned? Just as for departures, the question arises of the numbers involved, though we cannot provide any precise answer. In her study of German and Hungarian refugees, Heléna Tóth arrives at an estimated rate of return of 10% based on figures for émigrés to the United States. In other cases, for French exiles for example, the vast majority returned.

"Remigration" is hard to analyze. Pardons, particularly individual pardons (whether solicited by exiles or not), made it possible to return, as did collective amnesties, political opportunities, and negotiations.

The possibility of return

For certain exiles, such as the Poles of the "great emigration", there was no real possibility of return. For others, on the contrary, the governments which had forced them to leave now sought their submission. In such cases, the exile could receive an individual pardon, implying, at least in theory, an initiative on their part. Sometimes pardons were not solicited, and were issued as a strategy by the ruling power to discredit those who had deserted the combat, had betrayed or fled according to the terminology often used to disgrace them, or else to insist on the pardon granted: "Since we have not been able to be rid of this unbearable individual, let us at least seek to dishonor him. He is as dangerous outside as inside [the country]: if we authorize his return, he will be sunk forever".[5] This line of thinking, attributed to the head of the French government, De Broglie, by the famous polemicist Henri Rochefort, in reference to his case, illustrates a far more general situation. Exiles, even when subjected to at times intense pressure, nevertheless retained the choice of whether to accept a pardon or to refuse it. In the latter case, it was often a matter of opposing a measure they viewed as humiliating, due both to its nature and the implication that they had solicited it, while at the same time refusing to be singled out from a movement or repression which had, in nearly all cases, been collective. Those banished under the Second Empire – Hugo, Quinet, Charras – objected strongly to individual pardons, and to amnesties for that matter, decided on by the emperor, the embodiment of personal authoritarian power.

Lajos Kossuth likewise decided to reject all compromise and hence refused to return. In a letter to Ferenc Deak, one of the main Hungarian architects of the compromise of 1867, Kossuth cast himself in the role of Cassandra, describing it as thankless but falling to the person "who is right".[6] He was begged to return on several occasions, but in vain: 2,000 inhabitants of the town of Scentes sent him a petition in 1875 calling on him to return; in 1877, a committee of a hundred or so inhabitants of the town of Cegled visited him in Shireen, where he lived, once again urging him to return to Hungary.

More humble exiles, such as César Provençal, awaiting an end to his exile in Nice (still an Italian possession), noted the humiliating nature of these personal requests and compromises:

> It was there, amidst the pleasures and the garden parties, that I finally heard of the general amnesty accorded after the battle of Solferino (June 24, 1859) in favor of refugees who, like me, had refused to put in writing any submission which would have been too painful for people who, without being too proud or too susceptible, could not and ought not to do so without abasing themselves.[7]

These examples should not conceal the fact that many pardons were indeed solicited, by families, political friends, or the individuals concerned. Heléna Tóth demonstrates how families could function as an argument, even as a lobby.

---

[5] X, "La grâce forcée," *Les Droits de l'Homme*, May 1·1876. At the time, Henri Rochefort was in exile in Geneva, after having escaped in 1874 from New Caledonia, where he had been deported for supporting the Paris Commune.

[6] Tóth, *An Exiled Generation*, 252.

[7] Léonce Boniface, "Un proscrit varois de décembre 1851 dans le comté de Nice, le docteur César Provençal (1814–1868)," *Provence historique*, 3–14 (1953): 126–130.

Many letters requesting pardons argue that the good son, good husband, or good father, on returning to the bosom of his family – and thereby his reason – would cease all political activity.[8] The mother of Count Gyula Andrássy fought for seven years, providing a detailed analysis of the history of the revolution in Hungary in her letters to Austrian ministers, explaining her son's attitude by the loyalty characterizing his rank, which prevented him from betraying his brethren. Still, it was far more probably his marriage in exile to Katinka Kendeffy, whose family had remained loyal to the Habsburgs, which facilitated his return in 1857. More frequently, a family's financial dependency on an outcast was put forward as an argument for clemency and return. Such requests were subject to procedures, officialized to varying degrees depending on the regime. Studies of Germany and Hungary emphasize the production of collective letters and accompanying petitions. Heléna Tóth has highlighted the place the local authorities played in acceding to returns, for it was they who were approached with requests for information on exiles' personality, acquaintances, and families. When Pal Szakadaty, a former officer in the Hungarian army, applied to return from the Ottoman Empire, eleven people in his place of origin, Nagypalad, were questioned about his character and finances. The replies being favorable, he was allowed to return. In Germany, it was likewise representatives in the town of origin who decided whether exiles could return. It was in the wake of such an inquiry that the Baden forty-eighter Joseph Dietrich was barred from returning to Hilzingen, the town where he had been mayor.[9]

As shown by César Provençal's comments, amnesty was associated with key events in the life of a political regime, and acquired a strong symbolic dimension. Such was the case, for example, in France when the imperial prince was born in March 1856, or in the event of enthronements in Austria or Germany, such as in the Duchy of Baden in 1857 when Grand Duke Frederick married and came to power. Equally, the French republican regime wanted to demonstrate its conciliatory nature in passing the amnesty law for those sentenced in the wake of the 1879–1880 Commune. Still, it was sometimes difficult to distinguish procedures for pardons and those for amnesties, the two being conflated. The imperial decree of August 16, 1859, shows how ambiguous amnesty could be, for it was subject to a discretionary authority. As Stéphane Gacon argues, it was basically a collective pardon granting amnesty.[10] The partial amnesty law of 1879 for communards displays the same ambivalence, despite their being repub-

---

8 Tóth, *An Exiled Generation*, 78.
9 Tóth, *An Exiled Generation*, 232.
10 See Stéphane Gacon, *L'Amnistie. De la Commune à la guerre d'Algérie* (Paris: Éditions du Seuil, 2002).

licans. It provided for granting amnesty to those who had first been pardoned by the president of the republic, thus making it a conditional pardon. Those held to be the leaders of the uprising were excluded from pardon, hence from the amnesty. Consequently, certain of those pardoned/amnestied publicly denounced this measure in their favor, thereby asserting their solidarity with the exile community, embodying their ideal of unity threatened by piecemeal returns subject to personal decision. Thus the geographer Élisée Reclus – imprisoned in 1871, sentenced to deportation to New Caledonia, which sentence was commuted in the wake of a petition by European scholars to banishment from France, on which he settled in Switzerland – objected to the "insult" to his companions in exile: "Among these 'men covered by an eternal blemish' are my noblest friends [...]. Their cause is still mine, their honor is mine, and any insult to them strikes to the depths of my heart", he wrote in 1879.[11] The general amnesty law of 1880, which was collective and did not subject recipients to any private individual pardon, put an end to this ambiguity, and to what could be perceived, or exhibited, as a form of compromise or submission. But despite public protest to the 1879 law, many exiles had already returned under its provisions.

Refusal could be temporary and subject to constraints which evolved with political opportunities and changes specific to the country of origin. Examples abound. Under the Consulate and especially the Empire, French émigrés were able to return without negotiating their being struck off the list of émigrés or taking an oath of loyalty to the government, as had been the case under the Directory. In 1802, the senate decreed a general amnesty; few declined, prior even to 1814, though some remained abroad in various military positions. Under the Second Empire, Victor Hugo announced his refusal to return to France when a general amnesty was declared in 1859, choosing instead to return to great publicity once the republic was proclaimed in September 1870.

Ultimately, irrespective of the range of situations, what these various cases reveal is the extent to which the possibility of returning reactivated fundamental issues associated with exile: return, being subject to national political decisions, lay somewhere between individual choice and a sense of belonging to a community, between combat and compromise or submission even, between past struggles and/or repression and present-day opportunities, between memory and action.

When a land of origin offered the possibility of return, this could be accompanied by measures in the land of refuge. The road of exile discussed in chapter 3, about departures, often mapped the same route as the road of return. In

---

11 *Le Révolté*, April 5, 1879.

the case of the Spanish refugees amnestied in 1840 at the end of the First Carlist War, the French minister of the interior, Tanneguy Duchâtel, sought to exercise close control, via the prefects, over their departures and voyages. They were meant to cross the Pyrenees via just two border towns, Canfranc (the Somport pass) and La Jonquère (the Perthus pass), as stipulated in a circular of December 19, 1840. The decree of September 14, 1841, added the town of Irun, which in 1842 became the only authorized transit point.[12]

Returning Carlists were also subjected to close oversight when Spain was torn by the Second Carlist War (1872–1876). As of 1874, when Alfonso XII acceded to the throne, the regime, wishing to see a return to order and an end to civil discord, sought to get former insurgents to submit. In March 1876, the Spanish government published an *indulto* – a pardon – from which Carlists could benefit providing they explicitly submitted to the new king. In exchange for this submission, to be performed before a Spanish consul in France, former soldiers were allowed to return to Spain. The procedure had long existed at an individual level. Most Carlist exiles were from the working classes, being mainly peasants and craftsmen, and did not have the money or cultural capital required to return to their country by their own means. Wishing to be rid of these financially burdensome refugees as quickly as possible, the French government provided those wishing to accept the *indulto* with a pauper's passport accompanied by assistance along their route to the border. The itinerary of one such soldier, Juan Esquerré from the Catalan province of Lleida, is illustrative of this carefully managed return.[13]

Interned in Périgueux, Esquerré applied to benefit from the *indulto* in mid-February 1876, prior even to the generalization of the amnesty measure in the month of March. He apparently presented himself to the Spanish consul in Perpignan, one of the transit points for Carlist refugees returning to Spain. In journeying from Périgueux to Perpignan, Juan Esquerré received financial assistance from the French state in the form of money dispensed by mayors in various predefined towns along the way. This was not purely a matter of financial assistance, for it also provided the authorities with a way of controlling the movements of refugees. Juan Esquerré thus stopped at sixteen towns, in six

---

12 Delphine Diaz and Hugo Vermeren, "Return routes taken by amnestied Carlists (1840–1841)", map section of the AsileuropeXIX website, accessed April 16, 2021, https://asileurope.huma-num.fr/cartotheque/le-retour-des-refugies-carlistes-vers-lespagne-1840-1841.
13 Alexandre Dupont, "Return from exile and assistance along the route. The journey to Spain by the Carlist Juan Esquerré", map section of the AsileuropeXIX website, accessed April 16, 2021, https://asileurope.huma-num.fr/cartotheque/retour-dexil-et-secours-de-route-le-trajet-vers-lespagne-du-carliste-juan-esquerre.

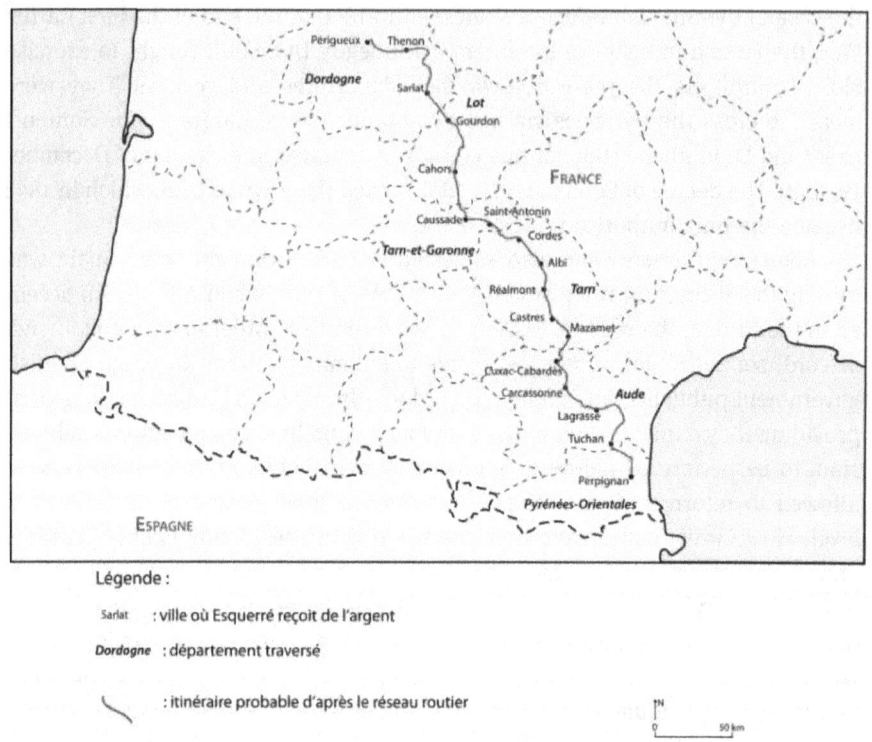

Fig 13, translation: Sarlat: town where Esquerré received money; Dordogne: département Esquerré crossed; Line: Probable route given the road network.

départements, where the mayors checked his passport and gave him small sums (of two francs or less), a way of ensuring that he presented himself at the next town on his route.

The case of the Spanish Carlists shows lastly that exiles sometime sought to return clandestinely to their country of origin, either temporarily or permanently. Returning to Spain was not driven solely by the wish to return to one's homeland, but also by the desire to resume arms in the cause of the pretender. This was the case of the brothers Victoriano and Nicolás Alcoya, who twice sought to return clandestinely to Spain, before submitting, for reasons unknown, to the Spanish consul in Perpignan. The consul got them to recount their journey, and it is this account which has been used to produce the map of their itinerary presented below.

The example of the Alcoya brothers clearly shows the dialectic which existed throughout the war between state repression and clandestine transnational solidarity. The two men, arrested and interned in Lille, escaped in spring 1875, on

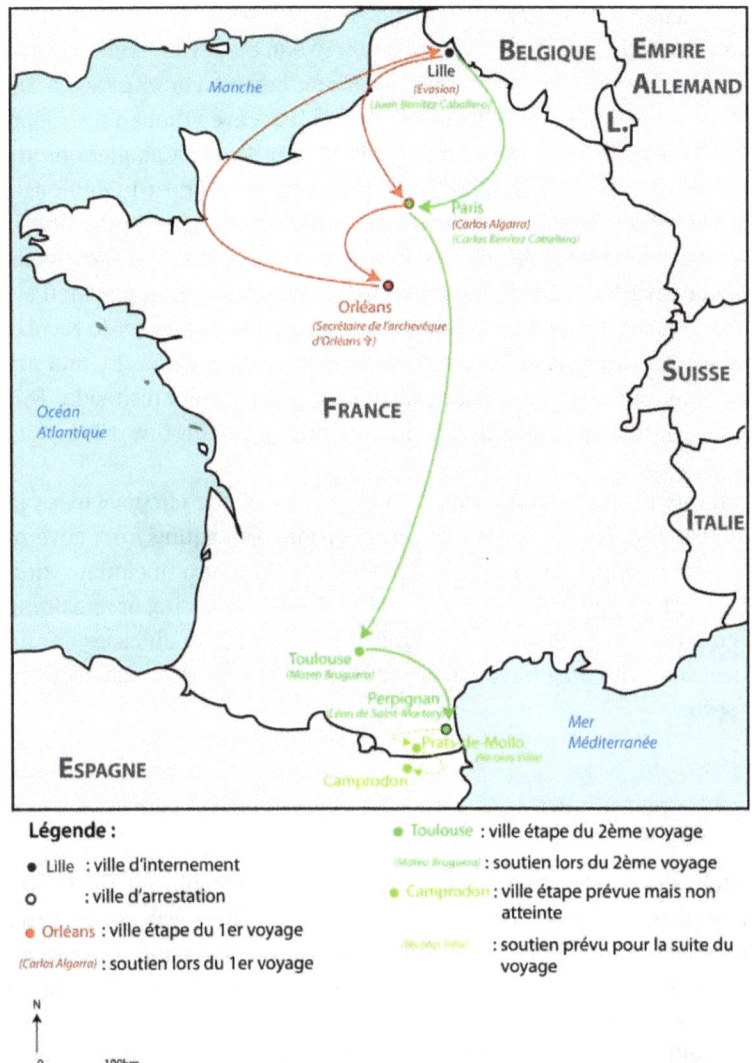

Fig. 14, translation: Black: Town where interned; White: Town where arrested; Red: halt during 1st journey; Red in brackets (Carlos Algarra): help during 1st journey; Green: halt during 2nd journey; Green in brackets (Mateo Bruguera): help during 2nd journey; Lime green: planned halt but not reached; Lime green in brackets (Nicolas Villa): planned help for rest of journey. On map: Evasion: Escape; Secrétaire de l'archevêque d'Orléans: Secretary to archbishop of Orléans.

which they went to see Carlos Algarra in Paris, a Carlist who had settled in France at the end of the 1833–1840 conflict. He gave them a letter of recommendation addressed to the secretary of the archbishop of Orléans. On arriving in Orléans, the brothers were told that their contact there had died. They were arrested by the authorities and interned again in Lille. They then sought to pass via another line of transit to Spain, more successfully this time, even though their journey ended in Perpignan. They were first helped by the Benítez Caballero brothers, interned respectively in Lille and Paris, then sent to a priest in Toulouse, Mateu Bruguera, who was well acquainted with pro-Carlist circles in the border region. Bruguera sent them to Léon de Saint-Martory, a bookseller in Perpignan and mainstay of Carlist support in the Pyrénées-Orientales. He had prepared everything for the rest of their journey, and gave them a letter to present to Nicolas Villa, who helped smuggle people across the border at Prats-de-Mollo, and another for the chief of Carlist customs at Camprodon, on the Spanish side. This French-Spanish solidarity was effective in organizing clandestine transits to Spain.

These various examples bring out the complexity of the circumstances in which exiles returned, independently of any decisions emanating from governments in the land of origin. More generally, being able to return (including without submission) presented exiles with the choice of either returning or remaining in the host country – or perhaps more simply, for it was not in all cases an unshakeable decision, with an alternative which was not always as straightforward as it might seem.

Choosing to stay or choosing to return

Was successful exile one that came to an end? Or was it the contrary? The choice was not always dictated by political or patriotic reasons. There was not necessarily any planned decision in advance, no straightforward separation between returning and remaining. The possibility of returning did not necessarily bring about return, for which it was necessary to have the means, to be the right age, and to be willing to launch into yet another new life. There were various reasons which could lead exiles to return or, conversely, to remain in a land of refuge. Among these were the causes and conditions of their departure, the reception policies and practices in the host country, and, lastly, the relationships exiles had with, on the one hand, their land of origin, and, on the other, their land of refuge. Martin Nadaud, a former mason from the Creuse who had become a parliamentary deputy under the Second Republic, was banished in January 1852, returned in 1859, then left again and spent another eleven years in England. On arriving in Paris, he felt he bothered his former companions in the masons' association he had helped set up, and who now counted ministers and the emperor's family among their clients. His memoirs laconically evoke this failed return:

> My disappointment was not that great, I wrote to my two employers in Wimbledon that they could count on me when their pupils returned. I went back to England, and stayed there until war was declared.[14]

In Britain, Nadaud no longer worked as a mason but as a teacher in a military academy. Exile thus provided him with a wholly different status. A few notes found in the Guéret police archives nevertheless indicate that he did not sever all ties with the Creuse, and that he returned clandestinely to his region of birth in the 1860s. He does not mention this, and such silence frequently surrounds clandestine trips back and forth. Economic integration and the success stories already mentioned explain why some chose to remain in exile. Let us here mention the more singular situation of the Rudolf Meszlenyi's widow, Zsuzanna, Lajos Kossuth's sister, who became the sole support of her family who had taken refuge in the United States. During the revolution, she had set up and run several hospitals in Hungary, and in America became a genuine businesswoman.[15]

Some exiles distinguished themselves by carving out a place in the political life of their host country. The case was fairly rare in Europe, but more common in the Americas, particularly in the United States and Argentina. Two German forty-eighters, among others, drew on their experience to embark on political and diplomatic careers. Carl Schurz, after having helped Gottfried Kinkel make his spectacular escape from Spandau Fortress and reach Britain, emigrated to the United States in September 1852, accompanied by his wife.[16] The Schurzes long resided in New York, before then moving to Philadelphia, and finally settling in Wisconsin in 1856. A member of the local Republican party convinced Schurz to give a speech in German at a meeting. He became one of the architects of German-American support for the antislavery and anti-nativist party. In 1861 he was recompensed by President Lincoln, who appointed him ambassador to Spain. At the time this was a crucial position for it involved blocking the assistance Cuba wished to provide to the Southern forces. However, he did not retain this post, as in

---

14 Nadaud, *Léonard, maçon de la Creuse*, 304.
15 Tóth, *An Exiled Generation*, 110, according to the *Memorial of Madame Suzanne Kossuth Meszlenyi* (sic) published in Boston by N-C Peabody, 1856. In 2017, the Hungarian nurses association held a year of remembrance to mark the 200th anniversary of the birth of Zsuzsanna Kossuth, head hospital nurse during the Hungarian revolution and the 1848–1849 war of independence, and younger sister of Governor Lajos.
16 See Carl Schurz, *The Reminiscences of Carl Schurz* (New York: McClure Company, 1907), vol. 1.

1862 he enlisted in the Union Army with the rank of brigadier general. He was placed under the command of Franz Sigel – another forty-eighter – and took part in the famous battle of Gettysburg (July 1–3, 1863). Carl Schurz then moved to Detroit where he founded a Republican newspaper, the *Detroit Post*, then to Saint Louis where he took over the running of a German newspaper, the *Westlichen Post* (1867). In 1869 he became the first German-American to be elected to the senate, sitting until 1875. His political career did not end there, for he went on to become a government minister as secretary of the interior (1877–1881). He retired to New York where he resumed his journalistic career as editor of the *New York Evening Post*. He remained politically engaged, opposing America's imperial policy during the annexation of the Philippines in 1898.

Another German, Lorenz Brentano (1813–1891), served his host country without losing sight of his land of origin. Born in Mannheim in the Grand Duchy of Baden, Brentano was elected to the second chamber of the Baden parliament in 1845. After the revolution in March 1848, he was elected to the Frankfurt Parliament, sitting on the far left. After the failed republican uprising of 1849, he fled to Switzerland. He went into exile in the United States in 1850, initially working as a journalist in Pottsville in Pennsylvania, then as a farmer in the county of Kalamazoo (Michigan), before returning to his profession as an attorney in 1859, after being admitted to the Chicago bar. He was the editor and owner of a newspaper for German immigrants, the *Illinois Staats-Zeitung*, and joined Abraham Lincoln's Republican Party. He embarked on a career as a diplomat serving his new homeland, becoming Lincoln's ambassador to Scandinavia (1862), and then consul in Dresden (1872–1876). Despite the 1862 amnesty law enabling him to return to Germany, Brentano remained in Chicago, where he died at the age of seventy-seven in 1881.

In Argentina, Alexis Peyret, whose life in Latin America was sketched in the previous chapter, also decided to remain, though without severing ties with France, his land of origin. Other cases may be cited, such as the Italian exiles who settled in the Ottoman Empire. Fabrice Jesné has shown how they joined the Italian colonies there, reinvigorating these diasporas both demographically and culturally.[17] Anacleto Cricca, an émigré of 1849, became the doyen of the Italian community in Smyrna, though he finished his days there in a state of great destitution in the wake of several setbacks. Exiles were not primarily representatives of Italy abroad, but rather immigrants contributing to the development of their host country, which was particularly keen on benefiting from West-

---

[17] Fabrice Jesné, "Les 'colonies' italiennes d'Orient et la fraternité. Solidarité d'exil, sociabilité locale et sentiment national," in *Exil et fraternité*, 185.

ern knowledge as part of the program for accelerated modernization known as the Tanzimat. This welcome, also found in Latin America, no doubt helped political refugees put down roots.

Deciding to remain could thus be occasioned by having successfully integrated the land of refuge, or else result from apprehension about returning to a land of origin left many years earlier. Victor Richard, exiled in London after the Paris Commune, provides an example of success in Britain. He ran a prosperous shop in the capital, specializing in products from the continent. Over the years, he became a leading figure in the exile community, helping needy refugees. He did not return to Paris after the 1880 amnesty, remaining in London for another fifteen years, where he continued to take in refugees. However, in one of his letters to Jules Vallès, he reveals that his decision not to return was not due solely to his success, but also to circumspection at what might await him in Paris, which had changed dramatically during his nearly ten years of absence. It shows the ambiguities, difficulties, and complexity which could arise once it became possible to return:

> As for me, I shall remain in London until further orders, when you go to Paris you see such shops! The small risk being crushed by the large! Have I lost all my energy in exile? I do not think so, but one becomes more circumspect with age, perhaps overly so![18]

In 1868, Barbès, for his part, explained to his friend George Sand why he was staying in the Netherlands:

> You recently asked me anxiously why I do not go elsewhere. Alas, I too often ask myself this question, and the only true reply I can give is that – perhaps more even than suffering and death – I fear moving and the unknown, for nothing holds me here, absolutely nothing other than habit. The Dutch are unfriendly; I know hardly any more people than the day I arrived; but apparently I am made of the same stuff as stones and trees: I remain where I have been planted, or rather, where I fall. I also reckon that should I die outside France, I ought to leave my bones in this country, since I have spent so many years here.[19]

Barbès – admittedly exceptionally misanthropic – expresses a general truth: it was the weariness of old age which could push exiles to put down roots where fate had led them. In his case, the many years spent in prison no doubt also entered into the equation.

---

18 Letter from Victor Richard to Jules Vallès, London, May 5, 1880, in Gérard Delfau, *Jules Vallès, l'exil à Londres. 1871–1880* (Paris: Bordas, 1971), 340.
19 Sand-Barbès, *Lettres d'hier et lettres d'aujourd'hui. Correspondance d'une amitié républicaine 1848–1870*, foreword by Michelle Perrot (Paris: Le Capucin, 1999), 159.

Family situations could also play a decisive role. They were varied, opposed even: while some families followed exiles into unknown lands, others remained in the country of origin, awaiting what they hoped would be a rapid return. Refugees sometimes also embarked on new relationships, modifying their perceptions and expectations, and sometimes engendering children. Sources are often sketchy or silent on the subject as if the person choosing to return or remain were acting solely on a deliberate decision of an individual free of any affective engagement. Yet it is known that these unions could be an important factor in the possibility of return.

Valentin Guillaume's thesis includes a large chapter on Franco-Polish marriages, emphasizing how frequent they were, and how they were far more sought-after by the Polish community in northern France during the nineteenth century than during the twentieth.[20] He points out that a certain number of these marriages took place very shortly after leaving Poland. Such was the case of Marcel Olszewski, who went to the sub-prefect's office just a few days after arriving in Guingamp (in Brittany), to obtain authorization to return to Pontarlier (in eastern France), where he was to join his French wife, Delphine Maire, whom he had married on May 2, 1833, just eight months after arriving in France, in order to find "together with his new family, the resources and means of distraction so necessary in his unfortunate position". In the Orne, in autumn 1834, Michel Konachowski and Jean Rohr, both lieutenants in their thirties, married two young women from Mortagne. Valentin Guillaume notes that fifteen years later, at least 203 of their compatriots had declared that, far from their family and their native land, they had married young women born in western France. It is certain that a "good" marriage could encourage Poles to tie the knot, but they should not be viewed as dowry chasers; though their wives came from highly diverse socio-economic backgrounds, they were mainly orphans and workers. These French women could also no doubt hope to find considerable support from these young Polish refugees, often in receipt of assistance and apt to bring in a salary.[21] Be that as it may, these marriages show that the exiles of the "great emigration" established ties with the local population. As Valentin Guillaume notes:

> These men were no longer foreign refugees; within the space of a few years they had become husbands, sons-in-law, fathers-in-law, just as they had become friends, neighbors,

---

20 Guillaume, "L'autre exil", 280–281.
21 Pierre Gerbet, "La vie des réfugiés politiques à Clermont-Ferrand de 1815 à 1870," *Bulletin historique et scientifique de l'Auvergne* 63 (1943).

and work colleagues, as suggested by the witnesses present by their side when they married at the town hall.²²

This insertion within local society is clearly fairly remarkable for the poorest among them, such as Antoine Minuszyc, who in 1833 arrived wounded in Falaise (in Normandy), where he died in July 1872 at the age of eighty-two. Some received subsidies throughout their lives as refugees. The case of the Poles is slightly unusual since for them there was never any possibility of return, but the number of these unions and the fact that they occurred at so early a stage suggests a clear wish to integrate. Other European exiles married and ended their days in France. After having managed to reach Marseille, Angelo Frignani, a Carbonaro from Forli who had fled from a madhouse where he had been imprisoned by the papal authorities, initially settled in Aix, before reaching the Italian refugee depot at Mâcon in 1832. In September of the same year, he married a Frenchwoman. Apart from a few trips to Paris and Lyon, he spent the rest of his life in Pierreclos, near Mâcon, where he died in 1878.²³

Lastly, for refugees who, for various reasons, had severed ties with their land of origin, or had seen them dry up, it was no doubt far harder to return than for those who had maintained contacts, however fragile. Throughout his absence, Jules Vallès corresponded frequently with his friends in Paris, particularly the faithful Hector Malot who, assisted by Émile Zola, facilitated his dealings with Charpentier for the publication of *Jacques Vingtras I* as a single volume, prior even to returning and pursuing his literary activity. At the same time, Arthur Arnould, who had taken refuge in Switzerland, continued to be in touch with Paul Meurice, working clandestinely as of 1874 on *Le Rappel*, a newspaper which published his novel *La Brésilienne* in installments in 1877, meeting with great success and paving the way to his career as a writer after his return.²⁴ There was nothing comparable between the situation of those with many friends and strong support, and others whose relationships had withered.

Whatever the reasons leading exiles to return rather than to remain, initial contact with their homeland was marked by the reception they received. With the exception of certain figures, or in the infrequent case of large numbers re-

---

22 Guillaume, "*L'autre exil*", 293.
23 Delphine Diaz and Hugo Vermeren, "Itinerary of Angelo Frignani (1802–1878), exiled from the Papal States to France" map section of the AsileuropeXIX website, accessed April 14, 2021, https://asileurope.huma-num.fr/cartotheque/itineraire-dangelo-frignani-1802-1878-exile-des-etats-pontificaux-vers-la-france.
24 See Laure Godineau, "Retour d'exil. Les anciens communards au début de la Troisième République" (PhD diss., Université Paris 1 Panthéon-Sorbonne, 2000), 323–324.

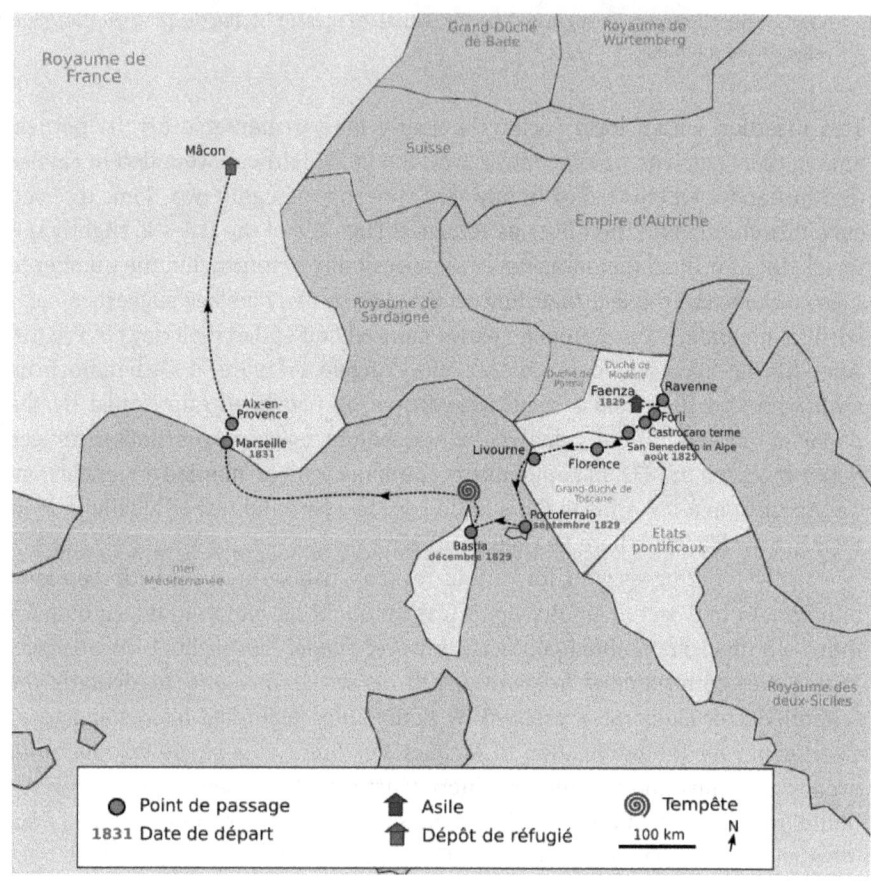

Fig 15, translation: Dot: Place of passage, Date: Date of departure; Arrow Faenza: Asylum; Arrow Mâcon: Refugee depot; Swirl: Storm.

turning en masse,[25] such perceptions have left few traces in the sources. On arriving at the Gare du Nord on September 5, 1870, Victor Hugo declared:

---

25 The case of the return of those deported to New Caledonia after 1871, and who, after being amnestied, returned in convoys in 1879–1880, is unique in that it was a collective repatriation organized by the public authorities. On this topic, see Laure Godineau, "L'arrivée à Paris des premiers déportés communards amnistiés, 1879 (*Le Monde illustré*, 13 septembre 1879)", AsileuropeXIX website image bank, accessed April 16, 2021, https://asileurope.huma-num.fr/ressources-iconographiques/larrivee-a-paris-des-premiers-deportes-communards-amnisties-1879.

> Words fail me to express how moved I am by the indescribable welcome extended to me by the generous people of Paris. Citizens, I had said: the day when the republic returns, I shall return. Here I am.[26]

The crowd had indeed gathered to acclaim Hugo, who symbolized opposition to the Second Empire, and who had now returned to his motherland following the proclamation of the Third Republic. This triumphal return occasioned many comments, appraisals, and images, such as Faustin's caricature, *Victor Hugo*, illustrating the reversal in the trajectories of the republican writer returning from exile and that of the former emperor. The lithograph depicts Napoléon III thrown to the ground, while the great Hugo stands imposingly at the center of the image, holding the "Paris 1870" edition of *Les Châtiments* under his arm, which includes a preface with the title "Au moment de rentrer en France" [On returning to France].[27]

Ten years later, in 1880, Henri Rochefort left Geneva, arriving in Paris on July 12, just after the full amnesty had been passed. Like Victor Hugo, he was welcomed by a large and enthusiastic crowd awaiting him at the Gare de Lyon and in the surrounding streets. The press was quick to report the numerous anecdotes of shop windows broken by the pressure of the throng, and how his carriage struggled to make its way through the sea of people, reaching the Place de la République only with difficulty. Like Victor Hugo, he was a celebrity returning to the fold.[28] The welcome he received was part of the first republican celebration of July 14 as a national holiday. These examples should not, however, mask the fact that European exiles returning singly or in groups – though not en masse – did not trigger any great reaction, and passed the border without any fanfare. And this first contact was only the first step along the road to settling anew.

---

26 Declaration published in *Le Rappel*, September 7, 1870, reprinted in Victor Hugo, *Actes et paroles 3*, rentrée à Paris (Paris: Hetzel, 1880), 47.
27 See Thomas C. Jones, "Faustin, Victor Hugo, 1870," AsileuropeXIX website image bank, accessed April 17, 2021, https://asileurope.huma-num.fr/ressources-iconographiques/victor-hugo.
28 See Roger L. William, *Henri Rochefort: Prince of the Gutter Press* (New York: Charles Scribner's Sons, 1966), 166.

Fig. 16: Faustin, *Victor Hugo*, 1870.
Special collections of the University of Sussex (Brighton). Item SxMs 162/3/9.

2 Back home

Rediscovering one's place

Returning was only one stage, and once back home the path could be promising and unencumbered, rough and rocky, or more banally somewhere between the two. Settling in once again also depended on various factors, such as the time spent in exile, age, the economic and social conditions presiding over return, the original profession, and the profession(s) exercised during exile.

The cases of Jules Vallès and Arthur Arnould illustrate that maintaining ties while abroad made it easier to resettle, independently of the immediate choice to return. Equally, experiences abroad could sometimes become an asset, with exiles continuing a course embarked on elsewhere. When the writer and journalist Noël Parfait returned to France in 1859, he returned with considerable advantages under his belt, having worked in Brussels as Alexandre Dumas's secretary and ghostwriter, and then as Victor Hugo's proofreader. Once in France, he worked for Michel Lévy, and in 1875 became literary editor at Calmann-Lévy. Amiel, another outcast from the Second Empire and a civil engineer who had worked on building the Puerto Real to Cadix railway, took over the concession to a railway line in the Ariège on returning, putting to good use his initial training and professional experience during his years of exile. The sculptor Jules Dalou, whose *La Brodeuse* had been bought by the state in 1870, met with success during his exile in Britain after 1871 where, after having been introduced by the painter and sculptor Alphonse Legros, a childhood friend settled in London, he exhibited his works at the Royal Academy, selling them to the British aristocracy and receiving two major commissions, including *La Charité*, which was subsequently installed at the fountain behind the Royal Exchange. On returning to France with his family in 1879, he became a recognized and well-known sculptor, producing various works including *Le Triomphe de la République* installed on the Place de la Nation.[29]

There are abundant examples of success after return. On returning to Hungary in 1867 after spending nearly twenty years in exile, the engineer and Hungarian patriot István Türr was tasked with planning the canals linking the Danube and the Tisza, going on to become involved in research to cut the Panama Canal, before working with another Hungarian engineer, Bela Gerster, on the possibility of cutting the Corinth Canal. The Italian Gaetano Frediani, born in

---

29 *Le Triomphe de la République* was commissioned by the City of Paris in 1879. The plaster cast was inaugurated on the Place de la Nation in 1889, followed by that of the bronze in 1899.

Genoa in 1811 and a Mazzini supporter who had fled to Tunisia in 1834, turned his time in exile to good use. He built up a prosperous business in trade and finance on either side of the Mediterranean, in Tunis and Genoa. He started as an oil merchant, heading the merchant lobby to the bey, and was then appointed consular officer to Genoa where he represented Tunisia's interests from 1862 to 1881, in close contact with merchant and financial circles in the town.

Théophile Thoré-Burger (1807–1869), still well-known to art historians, is another striking figure in the intellectual and artistic circulations attributable to political exile. A barrister by training who became a journalist and art critic, he went into exile in Brussels on being sentenced in May 1849 for revolutionary activities. He was already a prolific art critic, and on being expelled from France became especially interested in Dutch painting, writing essays and catalogues on private collections. His greatest contribution was clearly his rediscovery of Vermeer, who had fallen into neglect and become one of the "illustrious unknowns" of Dutch art. In exile, Thoré-Burger tirelessly tracked down Vermeer's canvases, which had been scattered, exploring private and public collections throughout Europe. On returning to Paris after ten years away, he continued his research into other Vermeer works, in lesser-known collections or in the possession of art dealers. Most of the paintings attributed to Vermeer at the time passed through his hands; he bought some himself, and helped private collectors acquire others. In 1866 he was the main force behind the first Vermeer exhibition to be held in Paris. This passion for Dutch art was not unrelated to his politics:

> Holland, which had the courage to shake off any religious and political yoke, feeling more at ease than any other people, produced the freest, most original, most varied, most revolutionary, most natural, and most human of schools: it is no doubt that which is freest of the past, which adheres the most to nature, and which thereby best signals one of the trends in subsequent art. [...] That is why I [...] have devoted all my passion to shedding light on one of these schools, that which seems, to my mind, to be the most singular, and the most instructive for innovators.[30]

Yet despite the many successes, writings on exile which describe a return often highlight and lament the professional difficulties encountered, illustrating the disappointment of those who returned. *Un exilé*, a novel by Georges Renard (1847–1930), is revealing in this respect. As a young man, he was secretary to Roseel, the war delegate during the Paris Commune, and fled to Switzerland in summer 1871, where he taught Greek, Latin, and history at the Collège de

---

30 W. Thoré-Bürger, "Le salon de 1861-L'avenir de l'art," *La Revue Germanique*, 15 (1861): 260–261.

Vevey, going on to become professor of French literature at the Académie de Lausanne. On returning to Paris in 1879, he was unable to find an academic post as he had hoped (having attended the École Normale Supérieure which prepared students for a career in teaching). In 1887 he returned to Switzerland where he remained until 1900, without severing all contact with France. Thanks to his political friends he obtained the chair in the history of work at the Conservatoire des Arts et Métiers, in Paris, before being appointed professor at the Collège de France in 1907 where he taught until his death in 1930. Despite this illustrious career, he encountered obstacles on returning from exile, and it is on these misfortunes that his semi-autobiographical novel insists. It tells the tale of young René, faced with the coldness and indifference of his former fellow lawyers, and failing to find a fitting position. "Yesterday we were banished, today and tomorrow we are internal exiles, such is our fate",[31] he concludes bitterly in the name of all. For it was a collective experience that Georges Renard claimed to be depicting, that of his own friends, be they men of letters or manual workers, and more generally that of all exiles. "Yet however true this story of a man may be, I would not have written it were it not of general scope", Renard states in his preface.[32]

His narrator highlights the hostility encountered by former insurgents or those sentenced in a country which had chosen another political path or else wanted to forget its past. Difficulties were in fact linked to many overlapping factors. The case of Eugène Pottier, the author of the words to the "Internationale", who, like Georges Renard, went into exile after the Paris Commune, shows how many variables were in play. Pottier was a highly qualified tracer of patterns on fabric, and at the end of the Second Empire was at the head of one of the most reputed fabric printers in Paris. On returning to France in 1880, aged over sixty, he had to confront ongoing economic transformations:

> I returned [from the United States] with the amnesty, poor and old. I tried to resume my work as a drawer, but conditions in my industry had totally changed: as is the case everywhere, I would have needed some capital.[33]

---

31 Renard, *Un exilé*, 275.
32 Renard, *Un exilé*, 1 ("À Gaston Stiegler").
33 Lettre from Pottier to Paul Lafargue, Paris, May 29, 1884, in Eugène Pottier, *Chants révolutionnaires* (Paris: Éditions sociales internationales, 1937), 266, quoted by P. Brochon in E. Pottier, *Œuvres complètes*, prepared, presented, and commented by Pierre Brochon, (Paris: Maspero, 1966), 217–218.

He was not the only one to be disappointed on returning from exile. Such was also the case of Joseph Déjacque, an opponent of the Second Empire. He worked as a wallpaper hanger, and wrote poetry denouncing the poverty of the proletariat. A socialist and forty-eighter, he refused all forms of exploitation and authority, and went into exile after the 1851 coup, reaching London in 1852, moving on to Jersey and then the United States where, among various activities, he wrote the anarchist utopia *L'Humanisphère* and published the *Libertaire* newspaper, and actively condemned slavery. In 1862 he returned to Paris, in the wake of the 1859 amnesty. "I am nostalgic not for the country where I was born, but for the country that I have only glimpsed in dreams, the promised land, the land of freedom beyond the Red Sea", he later wrote to Pierre Vésinier. He was only just turned forty, but ended his days in 1865 at the Bicêtre Hospice. According to Gustave Lefrançais, poverty drove him to madness and then to his death.[34]

Generally, those returning encountered competition or straightened circumstances, without having envisaged or prepared themselves for these eventualities. Even if the conditions were not the same for exiles who were not manual workers, they nevertheless had to contend with changes in the world of publishing, the press, letters, and the arts, which they had not fully gauged beforehand. Their age and the life they had led in exile were also significant factors, but while we should certainly not downplay difficulties and disappointments, the cases mentioned above suggest we should not give in to generalization either.

Continuing the fight

The range of situations was once again vast. Some discontinued all political activity, while others pursued national or transnational involvement. What were the key variables: age, once again? Activism in exile? Many of those banished under the Second Empire held political office on returning to France. They occupied widely differing points along the political spectrum, as moderate parliamentarians or future supporters of Boulangism. While covering the entire gamut of political affiliations, they tended to be heavily involved in debates about the amnesty law for former communards, and many joined the Republican Union, Gambetta's "party". As parliamentarians or officials in the new republican ad-

---

[34] Dictionnaire Maitron online, entry for Joseph Déjacque [*Dictionnaire des anarchistes*] by Jean Maitron. Revised and supplemented entry by Karine Pichon and Franck Veyron placed online March 19, 2014, last modified on March 28, 2019, accessed April 17, 2021, http://maitron-en-ligne.univ-paris1.fr/spip.php?article154757.

ministration, the former opponents of empire played a role in defining French nationality and the status of foreigners. Their speeches to parliament and publications in the press hint at how their experience of exile played a role in constructing French republican citizenship. But were the former outcasts able to easily assume or resume a national or local career after being decentered from politics? Much ridicule was heaped on this old generation who no longer knew how to make their voices heard. Against this, one could cite Victor Hugo's burial, an official and popular ceremony at one and the same time; yet it was not the exile who was being commemorated, but the grandfather of the Republic.

Many outcasts slipped into the background in their old age, or became an embarrassment if they acted as a reminder of the democratic values for which they had fought and been banished, and which they now saw watered down or flouted. When Gédéon Acs, a former Protestant minister who had spent much of his life in exile in Boston, disembarked at Pest in 1861, shortly after being amnestied, he was immediately confronted with the fact that he was now an outsider. He disapproved of the forms and expressions of Hungarian nationalism, and commented ironically on the silver boots sported by the inhabitants of the capital, and the increasingly affirmed taste for folk songs and dances, which he found ridiculous.[35] In contrast, on returning in 1869, Ferenc Pulszky (1814–1897), a companion of Lajos Kossuth, became director of the Hungarian national museum, then director-general of Hungarian museums and libraries in 1872. Many activists from Baden and Prussia returned to Germany after unification, and some even supported Bismarck's regime, such as Arnold Ruge, who was awarded an annual pension of 3,000 marks by the German Chancellor in 1877, for "services to the cause of German unity".[36] Lothar Bucher went still further in his political realignment. On being amnestied in 1861 he returned to Germany. He started by working in the press, and though now politically distanced from democrats remained in regular contact with the socialist Ferdinand Lassalle. Despite their marked political differences in opinion, Bucher published a text by Lassalle, and Lassalle subsequently named Bucher his literary executor in his will, and left him a pension. In 1864 Bismarck offered him a position in the ministry of foreign affairs; Bucher went on to be one of his most trusted aides. He was involved in drawing up the first draft of the constitution for the German Confederation. After unification he was named *Wirklichen Geheimen Legationsrat*

---

[35] Tóth, *An Exiled Generation*, 249–250.
[36] Lucien Calvié, *Aux origines du couple franco-allemand, critique du nationalisme et révolution démocratique avant 1848* (Toulouse: Presses universitaires du Mirail, 2004), 88.

and appointed to the *Vortragenden Rat* of the German ministry of foreign affairs. In 1878 he was entrusted with drafting antisocialist laws. During the subsequent debates, Karl Marx wrote a letter to the *Daily News*, published on June 13, 1878, disclosing his earlier relations with Lothar Bucher, and the latter's involvement with newspapers close to the International, together with his ties with Lassalle. This caused Bucher to lose all credibility, and he was sidelined from politics. He nevertheless remained close to Bismarck: when the latter withdrew from the chancellorship in 1890, Bucher became his personal adviser, and was involved in writing his memoirs. It would however be mistaken to view all German refugees as subsequently going on to work with the new regime. Wilhelm Liebknecht returned to Prussia from London after the 1862 amnesty. In 1867, with August Bebel, he founded the Saxon Popular Party, then the Socialist Worker's Party of Germany in 1869, which became the Social Democratic Party of Germany (SPD) in 1890. The key role he played in the evolution of the SPD, drafting the 1875 Gotha program, shows the central role played by émigrés' experience.

The experience of repression and exile was also mobilized to maintain links between generations of German Socialists, and between internationalists. Karl Blind, a compatriot of Liebknecht in London, and erstwhile friend of Karl Marx, did not return to Germany, remaining in the British capital from 1849 to his death in 1907. He too remained attached to socialist ideas, teaching them to his family. His stepson, Ferdinand Cohen-Blind, returned to study at Tübingen in 1862. He was close to his stepfather, whose radicalism he shared. He carried out a failed assassination attempt against Bismarck in Berlin in 1866, was arrested, and committed suicide in his prison cell. As Sandrine Kott notes in her biography of Bismarck, Cohen-Blind's act clearly stemmed from his stepfather's influence, to whom he explained in a letter that he had attacked Bismarck because he deemed him a threat to German unity and freedoms. His deed was warmly greeted in southern Germany, particularly in the streets of Stuttgart, where he was feted as a second William Tell.[37]

As these varied examples show, the lasting existence of a "party of exile", or a fraternal alliance even, was not a feasible prospect. The politics of emigration dissolved as soon as exiles grasped opportunities enabling them to return, either by submitting, or else by working alongside new political representatives and taking part in the new political unity of their country, or in the new regime as in France.

---

37 Julius H. Schoeps, *Bismarck und sein Attentatër. Der Revolveranschlag Unter der Linden am 7 Mai 1866* (Frankfurt: Ullstein, 1984), 29–42, quoted in Sandrine Kott, *Bismarck* (Paris. Presses de Sciences Po, 2003), 228.

Making reparation or drawing a veil over the past

To understand the policies implemented over the course of the century to make reparation or else to draw a veil of forgetfulness over the past, we need to return to the experience and aftermath of the French Revolution and Empire. Most émigrés from the revolution returned to France prior to the restoration of the monarchy, granted this possibility by the emperor. But for many, once the monarchy was restored, this awakened hopes (subsequently dashed) that they would obtain revenge and reparation. Aristocratic émigrés hoped to recover their former status, property, and honors, reappraised in the light of their "sacrifices". In fact, certain adapted with great success, such as Hercule de Serre (1776–1824), appointed first president of the Court of Colmar in 1815, then president of the electoral college of the Haut-Rhin, before being elected as parliamentary deputy for the same *département* in 1816. He became president of the chamber of deputies in 1816, and in 1818 was appointed minister of justice, then ambassador to Naples, dying in 1824.

However, the situation of aristocratic émigrés without fortune or support was more arduous, given the drastic reduction in military numbers. But it was above all the Bourbons' attitude which profoundly disappointed their former companions in exile. Louis XVIII's watchword, "union and forgetfulness", was an injunction that Napoléon was the only one to successfully put into practice. The amnesty pronounced by Louis XVIII and the guarantee to those who had purchased goods during the revolution that they could retain them had the opposite effect from that intended: when article 11 of the charter proclaimed that "it is forbidden to seek to discover opinions and votes cast up until the restoration, and courts and citizens are ordered to forget even", the émigrés were indignant to see the king refuse to condemn the revolution, accusing him of ingratitude towards them.

The former exiles regrouped, forming an association in 1821 to defend their interests. Their purpose was to obtain indemnity and condemnation of the revolution. The restored monarchy reawakened the conflict, and the granting of an indemnity – the "émigrés' billion" – approved in 1825 did not bring about any true reconciliation. The émigrés' misfortune was fundamentally rooted in their refusal to integrate post-revolutionary society. This clearly transpires in the memoirs they wrote after returning to France, often published posthumously. In these works, their authors evoke a definitive exile, from the land of their childhood and the customs and values of the aristocracy. François-René de Chateaubriand was one of the most talented writers on the theme of exile, which he presents as stretching from the cradle to the tomb. The experience, which was probably the first collective instance of political exile, reveals that emigration was a process, a phenomenon which never stabilized, a time of conflicts, of adapting to circumstances, reassessing categories, and redefining who one was.

The question of reparation resurfaced with the law of July 30, 1881, known as the law of national reparation, which allocated a pension or life annuity to French citizens who had been victims of the coup of December 2, 1851, or of the law on general security of February 27, 1858 (or, if they had died in the interim, to their un-remarried widows and relatives of the first degree).[38] Exiles were of course among the claimants. The law was not intended solely for them, but the general committee chaired by the minister of the interior was composed of eight parliamentarians who had all been victims of exile: four senators (Victor Hugo, Jean-Baptiste Massé, Elzéar Pin, and Victor Schœlcher) and four deputies (Louis Greppo, Noël Madier de Montjau, Martin Nadaud, and Alexandre Dethou).[39] Those applying for the indemnity had to send their request backed up by information and supporting documentation to the prefect of the *département* where they had been residing when they had been affected. The sub-prefect of the *arrondissement* of residence then drew up a document detailing the applicant's civil status, profession, the nature of the political measures or rulings against them, the duration and consequences thereof, and the resources and political conduct of the applicant. These were then forwarded to the prefecture and examined by a committee composed of the prefect, three members of the general council appointed by the prefect, and three delegates elected by the victims. After deliberating, this departmental committee drew up its assessment and proposed the sum to be allocated. The applications were then examined by a general committee based in Paris, which adjudicated as a final instance. About 25,000 applications were received. As Denise Devos has shown, their purpose was to provide proof of the damage suffered, and they thus painted a dark picture of exile, in which victims and their families tended to go over the conditions of departure, their difficulties in settling, and subsequent impoverishment. There were numerous applications by exiles, a large number of whom had remained abroad, with many applying for compensation in order to pay their journey back to France. Hence the law affected not just memories of exile, but also returns.

---

38 Denise Devos, "La loi de réparation nationale du 30 juillet 1881: source de l'histoire de la répression de l'insurrection de décembre 1851," *Revue d'histoire du XIXe siècle* [online], 1 | 1985, placed online October 28, 2002, acccesed April 2021: http://journals.openedition.org/rh19/3; DOI: 10.4000/rh19.3.

39 Jean-Baptiste Massé was exiled only briefly, in Nice.

3 Traces, memories, and legacies

Once exiles had returned and resettled in their country of origin, what traces were left by their time abroad? Here one may turn to the writings they left as a way of forgetting nothing of "what exile is" (Victor Hugo), and of justifying and glorifying it. The period in exile was abundantly presented in these texts, memoirs, and political reminiscences. It sometimes acquired prominence, underpinning the fame of an author now become one of the "classics of exile", such as Malwida von Meysenbug's memoirs.[40] But it also figured prominently in Giovanni Ruffini's autobiographical novel.[41] Still, there were in fact fewer such works than one might think, and their status is ambivalent, to say the least, when published after their authors' return. Most such accounts were written shortly after. The most fully documented work on the banishment of French republicans after the 1851 coup is that by Saint-Ferréol, published in 1875, five years after the end of the exile of most of those depicted. The preface was written in 1869, "year seventeen of the coup". Saint-Ferréol, an exile himself, had felt the need to collect the history of exile to ensure nothing was lost:

> Time, which carries all before it, the banishers and the banished, the democratic governments and the royal or imperial dynasties, the peoples themselves and religions, will soon have erased the material traces of our passage in exile, driven away like dead leaves by the wind, along with our friends who lived their lives as outcasts together, far from their homeland, and the documents that each could provide about himself, his country, and the events he witnessed or underwent. Before that happens, it is useful to set down on paper the fleeting impressions, to say what we saw, what we know, so that, come judgement day, no proof or piece of evidence shall be missing in the trial to be brought by the revolution against usurpation and despotism.[42]

Saint-Ferréol also published his memoirs in five volumes in 1885. There is only one chapter about exile, and it refers the reader back to the earlier work. The actual return is barely mentioned, at least from a personal point of view, Saint-Ferréol having far more to say about electoral matters in Brioude. Edgar Quinet's book about his time in exile, published after his death by his widow Hermione Quinet, was, as she states in her foreword, actually written in exile, unlike other posthumous texts, and never reread or reworked by its author.

---

40 Malwida von Meysenbug, *Memoiren einer Idealistin* (Berlin/Leipzig: Schuster & Leoffler, 1900).
41 Ruffini, *Lorenzo Benoni*.
42 Saint-Ferréol, *Les Proscrits*, vol. 2.

Martin Nadaud and Pierre Joigneaux, who were likewise banished under the Empire, wrote their memoirs, but exile only formed part of their account. Nadaud discusses his return only briefly, even though it entailed his leaving mediocre lodgings in Wimbledon for the prefect's official residence in Guéret, an imposing Renaissance château in the town center.[43] Joigneaux was less laconic. It is thus difficult to detect a precise attitude even within a given exile community. Further study would be necessary, comparing cases across Europe and analyzing the particular psychology of those who returned. In the wake of James Joyce, Stéphane Dufoix has insisted on the sense of anguish of those who returned home, and the effects of "successful prophecy", that is, the accomplishment of ideas for which they had left their country, whether voluntarily or not.[44] One of the traces Dufoix identifies is the continuing existence of Hungarian and Czechoslovak exile associations after 1989. In his memoirs, albeit in an annex, Saint-Ferréol mentions the existence of an association, the "family of outcasts": but, at least in the case of French exiles, it apparently never played any notable role.[45]

Memories of exile

Refugees created their own places of memory: tombs, residences, and battlefields were a pretext for traveling, and played their part in accounts of exile. Exiles invented a tourism of activism in Europe, organized around geographical curiosity and the historical and archaeological past. Those banished under the Second Empire sought primarily to ward off the oblivion which had befallen the members of the regicidal Convention. While memories of the latter resurfaced spontaneously, discovering their material traces was a laborious undertaking:

---

[43] As pointed out in the biography by Gillian Tindall, *Le Voyage de Martin Nadaud* (Monaco: Anatolia, Éditions du Rocher, 2001), 322.
[44] "A nation exacts a penance from those who dared to leave her – payable on their return", James Joyce, *Exiles*, quoted in Dufoix, *Exopolitie*, 294.
[45] Amédée Saint-Ferréol, *Appendices de mes mémoires* (Brioude: imprimerie D. Chouvet, 1893), 45. This association was no doubt involved in implementing the reparation law. No great figure of exile was involved in its bodies. The president was named for each meeting; secretary Bocquet, treasurer Orry, both members of the fraternal society of 1849, both banished; its executive committee was composed of Minor Leconte, a republican prior even to the revolution, Luguet, a mechanic, Roussel, a tailor, Blot, a cobbler, Pico, a photographer, and Taquet, a tinsmith, *ibidem*. During the 1880s, a "society of 1871 outcasts" was also set up, but its history is chaotic and difficult to follow, see Godineau, "Retour d'exil", 613–617.

> We sons of the revolutionaries of the great Republic, we have vainly sought for their remains in cemeteries, where stand so many sumptuous monuments on which nobody reads the mendacious epitaphs. We have discovered nothing. Not a single stone indicates where these sleeping combatants now lie. The tomb erected to David in 1825, because his politics had been forgotten and only the memory of the painter remained, is now overrun by grass. It is empty, it is true. The body of the illustrious member of the Convention was claimed by his family and transported to Paris.[46]

During their peregrinations around places of burial, "exiles discovered a fragment of sculpted stone framed in a wall on which could be read: 'Cavaignac, banished by an iniquitous government, died in exile. This stone is all that remains of the tomb of the deceased'", according to David d'Angers' biographer.[47] Time and oblivion performed their work, as did counterrevolutionary propaganda. Saint-Ferréol even wondered whether antirevolutionary vandalism had not led fanatics of the restored monarchy or the church to come and smash the gravestones to "throw the remains of the regicides to the winds".

This filial commemoration was ambivalent, for outcasts always feared dying and being buried far from their land on foreign soil. Their first concern, after having taken offense at the neglect of these gravestones, was to carry the remains of Cavaignac's tomb back to France. Tomb worship had become a common component of protest. Since the revolution, and especially since the restoration of the monarchy, funeral rites had been a pretext for political practices, in which the rite of individual passage gave way to public display of a collective statement summoning the past, the present, and the future.

Saint-Ferréol also insisted on the edifying image the members of the Convention wished to give of themselves, forming in Belgium what Abbé Grégoire called a "family". Filiation with members of the Convention at times bordered on caricature: Pierre Barrère, a former representative of the people in 1848, was presented as the descendant of Barère, a member of the Convention whose *Souvenirs* had been published in 1842, despite no family link being established. For his part, Quinet was proud to walk in the footsteps of Marc-Antoine Baudot, a member of the Convention he admired, retracing backward – from Brussels to Vaud – the course the latter had taken into exile. Emblematically, a clock once owned by Baudot measured out the suspended time of exile at the Quinet household in Brussels. The community needed to show forms of consensus, and drawing on the past was one way of doing so.

---

46 Saint-Ferréol, *Appendices de mes mémoires*, 12.
47 Henry Jouin, *David d'Angers, sa vie son œuvre, ses écrits et ses contemporains* (Paris: Plon, 1878), quoted in Luzzato, *Mémoires de la Terreur*, 196.

As of 1851, refugees from the Second Empire who had sought to prevent the members of the Convention falling into oblivion were keen to protect their own deaths from a similar effacement of funerary rites. There were to be no weeds growing on their tombs. Funerary worship was based on placing their sepulchers in groups, such as the square of outcasts' graves in Jersey, on disseminating funeral eulogies, and on keeping memories alive by commemorating anniversaries of death. These funeral rites sometimes gave rise to lengthy voyages. Hugo narrates the ceremony which was held when James Demontry died at Cologne in 1850, and Gindrier went there to exhume the mortal remains:

> He had the heart removed, embalmed, and placed in a silver vessel which he took to Paris. The Réunion de la Montagne appointed him, Cholet, and Joigneaux to transport the heart to Dijon, Demontry's town of birth, and to celebrate a solemn funeral. This funeral was prevented on the orders of Louis Bonaparte.[48]

Memories of banishment under the Second Empire also involved a battlefield, Waterloo, near Brussels, the city of asylum. Visiting or staying at Waterloo was initially mainly a pretext to enquire into and denounce the imperial legend. Edgar Quinet and Colonel Charras went there to work on demolishing Napoléon's tactics. Hugo subsequently visited to complete *Les Misérables* and, as he wrote, to "win the battle once again". Republicans also appropriated this place of memory, which was one of the first tourist sites of the period. This tourism was already modern, that is, commercial, with its share of souvenirs, prospectuses, means of transport, and museum usages. On this subject, Saint-Ferréol wrote:

> Waterloo – we went there often, not like the English to scrape the bark from the trees on which some illustrious general had leant, or to purchase a souvenir of the battle, the trouser buttons and fragments of rusted arms that are made for export in the surrounding villages, making old from new. No! From the top of the tumulus on which the victors placed a lion threatening France, while the heirs to the leaders of the coalition fraternize with another Napoléon, we wanted to see the scene where the great drama was played out, and which we judged in a new way.[49]

Vallès was disappointed to discover but a "rusted field". On the visitor register at the lion's mound he wrote: "on the battlefield of Waterloo we thought only of the defeated from the faubourgs of Paris. Signed Humbert, Callet, Vallès". In *Le Vol-*

---

48 Hugo, *Histoire d'un crime*, 279.
49 Saint-Ferréol, *Les Proscrits français en Belgique*, vol. 1, 239.

taire of August 22, 1878, Vallès also recounted his trip to the Channel Islands, and pilgrimage to Jersey:

> In this island, those defeated in the coup, those banished in 1851 bivouacked and established a colony. I remember with what emotion and respect I pronounced this name under the Empire. [...] I thus went to this corner of the earth which was the place of asylum of my elders, whence Ribeyrolles and Hugo issued their cries![50]

But Jersey had likewise become a counterfeit of exile:

> Are there any outcasts left on this path, I finally asked, thinking of our elders and returning towards the austerity of the past. None here. But look, here is a café where they sometimes went. There are only nobodies here nowadays. Yet in a corner is a man with faded clothing, and a faded and shifty face.

This man, who tried to sell him photos of the island, was no outcast, but a former zouave, Louis Gicquel, guilty of numerous embezzlements and whose case was famous at the time.

Exile as memory

What remains of the presence of exiles in host countries? It is often hard to reconstitute the places where they settled over a century ago. The ports, town centers, and outskirts of capitals have been refashioned or demolished. Present-day Rue Vaneau in Paris has retained scarcely any trace of Marx's time there, and does not resemble the street that he knew: the first house with an upper story where he lived no longer exists, rendering obsolete the habitual description of a building home to several refugee families – the Ruge, Herwegh, and Marx households. The presence of commemorative plaques, when they exist, is no guarantee of authenticity: while Marx and Engels did frequent Le Cygne on the Grand Place in Brussels, they did not write the *Manifesto of the Communist Party* there.

Cemeteries are the places most visited by pilgrims of exile, often imitating the pious practices of the refugees who themselves set out in search of their predecessors.[51] It is also cemeteries which retain their traces, such as Marx's grave at Highgate Cemetery in London (but it is not the original), or the cemetery of exiles

---

50 Jules Vallés, *Le Voltaire* August 2, 1878, quoted in Aprile, *Le Siècle des exilés*, 277.
51 Aprile, "Le proscrit pèlerin", 200.

in Jersey. Since the 1840s, the Champeaux cemetery in Montmorency has been the resting place for the most heroic Poles who died in the French capital or its vicinity. Lying a dozen miles north of Paris, Montmorency owes this particularity to two veterans of the *Grande Armée* who stayed and were subsequently buried there: Julian Ursyn-Niemcewicz, and Karol Kniaziewicz. Since then, many other Polish exiles have chosen this as their final resting place, and it now has over 500 Polish graves. There are also many graves of Polish exiles in Parisian cemeteries. The Polish essayist Marya Kasterka described them in the following terms:

> Many remarkable Poles lie in the Montmartre Cemetery; to name but a few: General Maciej Rybiński, commander-in-chief of the Polish army in 1831; Colonel Karol Rożycki, leader of the revolution in Volhynia in 1831; the painter Wańkowicz, to whom we owe the famous portrait of Adam Mickiewicz; Abbé Duński, known for his activity in the Polish émigré colony in Paris; Théodore Pociej, of the great Lithuanian family, and so on and so forth. The grave of Isidore Sobański, in a state of some neglect, bears a melancholy inscription: "Year 12 of the Polish emigration".

She adds:

> The Polish avenue at Montmartre ceremony is most curious. Here we find mainly collective graves. The first tomb has a high catafalque with a large coffin, surrounded by helmets, rifles, cannons, flags, drums, and so on. This grave was established by Léon Stempowski for General Franz Sznajde, and contains the coffins of twenty Polish exiles, including General Jules Sieradzki, Alojzy Biernacki, minister of finance in 1831, and Abbé Jean-Paul Dąbrowski. The second tomb – a small Greek colonnaded temple with a cross and Polish eagle on the roof – bears the Latin inscription *Exules Poloni Memoriae Suoriimet*. Here lie Polish officers and soldiers of 1831. The third tomb, with a broken column as its monument, is decorated with military emblems and the inscription *Memoriae Polonorum*, and contains eighteen coffins of Polish soldiers of 1831.[52]

Adam Mickiewicz, for his part, has three tombs. He died in November 1855 in Constantinople amidst a cholera epidemic, and his coffin remained for several weeks in the house where he had died. On December 30, a funeral ceremony was held at the Church of Saint Anthony, then the coffin was put on a boat for Marseille. His remains arrived in Paris on January 8, 1856. A second funeral service was held at the Church on January 21, followed by burial at Montmorency

---

[52] Mary Katerska, "Les tombeaux polonais dans les cimetières parisiens," *La Pologne, politique, économique, littéraire et artistique*, November 15 (1926): 722–723.

Fig. 17: Photo of the Polish avenue at Montmartre cemetery in Paris.
Photo published under license CC-BY-NC-SA 2.0 Creative Commons.

Cemetery. On this occasion, his wife's body was placed in the same grave as that of her husband. In 1890, his body was transferred to Kraków Cathedral.

Statues provide indications about complex remembrance strategies. The death of the Venetian Daniele Manin was commemorated in Turin by a subscription and a monument inaugurated in 1861. Ivan Brovelli has revealed the tension which existed at the time between those seeking to salute Manin's republican actions, and the Piedmontese monarchy, who preferred to honor one of the architects of Italian unification.[53] In 1868, his remains were transferred to Venice, where a monument was erected in his honor in 1875. Kossuth's funeral also took place in Turin, on March 23, 1894. The town of Pest immediately declared it was willing to pay for his funeral, transport his remains to Pest, and erect a mausoleum in honor of the great patriot. The role played by the leader of the Hungarian uprising was still a source of concern for the government, and the minister of the interior decided to close national theaters on the day of his burial to prevent protests. Kossuth's body was finally repatriated, and his burial was the occasion for a great ceremony of reconciliation.

In some instances, the passage of exiles has left more significant traces. This depends primarily on the notoriety of the refugee. Would memories of outcasts be so strong in Guernsey without Victor Hugo's house? He turned his residence into a living museum of exile, incorporating inscriptions on this topic in the decor, and displaying objects which had belonged to outcasts. The inscription carved into the wood above the dining room is well known, *Exilium Vita EST*, but it is less known that Hugo used one of the shimmering coats of the Hungarian poet Telecki to decorate the ceiling of the oak gallery, and one of his sashes is still visible today, part of the decor around the fireplace in the red drawing-room. Because of this house, memory of exiles is more present in Guernsey than in neighboring Jersey, despite the latter being home to the *rocher des proscrits* and the cemetery where refugees from across Europe are buried.[54] The house in Guernsey was donated by Hugo's family to the City of Paris, and reopened to the public in April 2019 after major renovation.

Conversely, Frohsdorf Castle has gradually fallen into a state of disrepair, suggesting a very different legacy. The "little Versailles" of the French royal family in exile was long the prime sanctuary of Bourbon remembrance. The Duchess of Angoulême, the only member of her family to be released from the Temple Prison, lived there surrounded by macabre souvenirs, such as the bloodied collar of her father, Louis XVI. On the death of the Count of Chambord in 1883, the castle was partially sold to pay the death duties.

---

[53] Ivan Brovelli, "La figure de Daniele Manin. Une stratégie de l'exil dans le cadre de la fraternité franco-italienne (1849–1880)," in *Exil et Fraternité*, 92.

[54] It is also Hugo's famous photographs which have kept his memory alive in the Channel Islands, see Sylvie Aprile, "Victor Hugo dans le rocher des proscrits", AsileuropeXIX website image bank, accessed April 17, 2021, https://asileurope.huma-num.fr/ressources-iconographiques/victor-hugo-dans-le-rocher-des-proscrits.

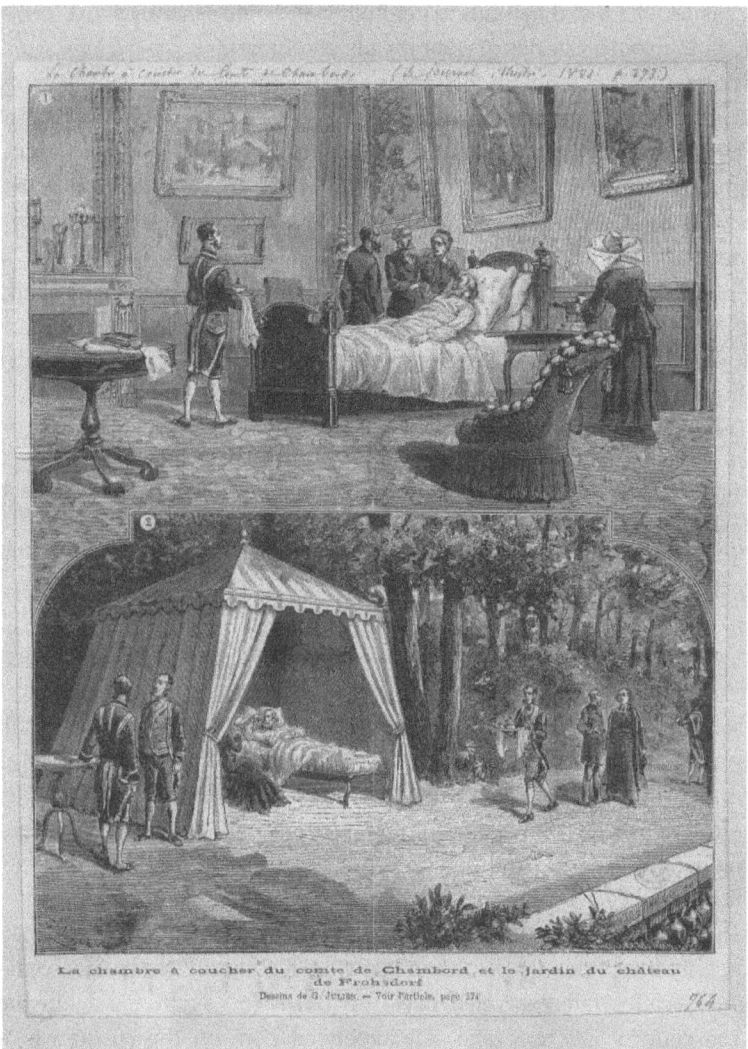

Fig. 18: G. Julien, *The bedchamber of the Count of Chambord and the garden at Frohsdorf Castle*, 1883. Source: Bibliothèque interuniversitaire de Santé, Paris.

It was sold to the Nazi regime on April 22, 1941, which converted it into a convalescent home. In 2005, the Austrian state sold the castle, which in the meantime had become a training center, to a property developer who converted it into a luxury hotel. Princess Béatrice de Bourbon-Massimo settled in a hunting lodge next to the castle, which still belongs to her family and houses many souvenirs of exile, such as the shoes Charles X wore for his coronation.

When not associated with an outstanding figure, the persistence of memory is related to the length of exile and above all the presence of large numbers of refugees. In France, the particular place played by the Poles of the "great emigration", the intense sociability of its members, and above all their desire to transmit a legacy through education and religion have meant their memory is still alive and not relegated to cemeteries.

So the return of exiles was far from being a simple linear phenomenon, and was rather comprised of distinct timeframes. First was the anticipated and planned return, perhaps something all exiles thought about, whether it was a matter of envisaging it as the only possible solution or, on the contrary, rejecting it. As Stéphane Dufoix observes:

> Exile is necessarily oriented towards its end. Its inescapably provisional nature in time and space endows this object of political research with its greatest originality. It is constructed in a spatialization which is not that of the land of origin nor, viewed globally, that of any country in particular, being instead transnational.[55]

Sometimes, over the course of years, refusals and successes, or political changes in the countries left behind or where exiles had settled, caused the imagined end to recede from view. Exiles remained outside their country of origin. Did they still think in terms of exile? Were they still exiles, or had they become someone else? The question is worth raising given that in certain cases there were in fact very few returns if any. For, as we have seen, many parameters came into the equation, relating both to the opportunity for returning and to the possibility of a successful return, finally resulting in highly contrasting life courses.

Returning, just like departing, meant undertaking a voyage with its new rituals and uncertainties. It would be nice to know the feelings of those who, sometimes several decades later, traveled back, of those who saw once again the shores of the country left long ago. All depended here on the substance of exile, on the ease with which borders could be crossed, as well as what was demanded of the refugee on his or her return. For returning was also, finally, a matter of placing oneself in an "after", in both material and moral terms. Those who returned had sometimes become virtual outsiders, or at least sensed the gap opened up by the passage of time. These feelings of unease and incomprehension made reintegration all the more difficult. Age also created a gap, and the

---

[55] Stéphane Dufoix, "Le retour des exilés," *Hommes & Migrations*, "Vers une politique migratoire européenne", 1216 (1998): 82.

pain upon returning was often that of aging. "Politics", which had presided over departures, soon caught up with those who returned. What experience could the exiles draw on, especially if returning to a land which, desiring peace, hence forgetfulness, had institutionalized forms of opposition in a free press, parliament, elections, all of which were unknown and foreign to the returning exiles? In new political contexts, memories of exile might, at best, put to use, or, at worst, progressively abandoned and forgotten. The most visible testaments are no doubt the "monuments of paper",[56] the great publishing enterprises such as the *Martiri della Libertà italiana* published by the Tuscan Patriot Atto Vanucci as of 1848, or the *Documenti della Guerra Santa* compiled by the Italian exiles Crispi and Cattaneo, exploring the lives of the dead, of those who had fought or left to defend freedom. A fragile memory, when all is said and done. For many, once the saga of exile was over, prose re-asserted its rights.

---

56 See Céline Léger and Jean-Marie Roulin, ed., "Retours d'exil," *Autour de Vallès* 50 (2020).

Sylvie Aprile and Delphine Diaz
Conclusion

This book opened on the topicality of exile and on present-day research. This conclusion does not seek to bring the subject to a close, but, on the contrary, to open out onto what was the near future of the "century of exile", namely the twentieth century, as well as onto the more distant twenty-first century.

As Nancy L. Green has pointed out,[1] what characterizes migrants is their taste or at least their aptitude for comparing. The same is true of exiles. This is illustrated by the "success" of Hannah Arendt's reprinted essay, "We Refugees".[2] Twentieth-century refugees have extensively compared their situation with that of their predecessors, and most of their accounts bear the implicit or explicit mark of this search for similarities and dissimilarities. We have proceeded likewise, showing that, above and beyond the violence and statistics of world conflicts and their aftermaths, the questions raised by the reality of everyday life and by public policies were often the same, or could at least be identified in the same manner. Where? How? On what grounds? With whom? For how long? These questions exist for the nineteenth century, but also for the twentieth and twenty-first centuries. Above and beyond this observation, there remains perhaps the question, as yet unanswered, of the specificity of these exopolitics and its protagonists. The enigma resides in the never or only partially resolved gap between the elites and the masses, between the visibility of some men – and some women – and the anonymous mass of exiles. In the absence of votes and parliaments, it is always difficult to detect adherence and support given the divisions, dispersal, and need for secrecy. In the twentieth century, exiled Italian and Chilean intellectuals were no doubt were more successful than the men and women of the nineteenth century in pinpointing this distinguishing social feature. Ian Buruma, writing a few years back in 2001, added fuel to the fire:

> Exile is in fashion. It evokes images of a critical spirit operating on the margins of society, a traveler, rootless yet at home in each metropolis, a tireless wanderer from conference to academic conference, a thinker in several languages, an eloquent advocate for minorities, in short, a romantic outsider living on the edge of the bourgeois world.[3]

---

1 Green, *Repenser les migrations*, 23.
2 Hannah Arendt, "We Refugees," *The Menorah Journal*, January 1943, 69–77, republished in Hannah Arendt, *The Jew as Pariah. Jewish Identity and Politics in the Modern Age* (New York: Grove Press, 1978), 55–66.
3 Ian Buruma, "The cult of exile," *Prospect* March 20 (2001): 23–27. His position has been criticized by Stéphane Dufoix, "Le débat du débat," *Le Débat*, 118/1 (2002): 188–191.

He thereby denounces the neo-romanticism of exile. Nowadays, the situation has changed, migrants flee war and oppression just as much as they seek a safe country where to work and bring up their children. The charge brought by Ian Buruma against intellectuals emulating Saïd seems less acceptable nowadays. His credibility has also suffered a blow for, ironically, Ian Buruma was obliged to resign from the prestigious *New York Review Book* in 2018 for having supported a journalist of Iranian origin, Jian Gomeshi, accused and then cleared of sexual harassment. Gomeshi has since posted on YouTube a short film in English, *Exiles*, full of the good sentiments previously denounced by Buruma, in what may be likened to a form of repentance or penitence. Without here taking sides, it is certain that the violence done to men and women and now considered genuine grounds for exile were not viewed thus in the nineteenth century, at least not as far as we know. The relationship between inclusion and exclusion has no doubt shifted in meaning.

Our study, focused on Europeans but not on Europe, has sought to follow nineteenth-century global political circulations, still under-analyzed in comparison to economic and artistic circulations. Yet artificial distinctions are sometimes made between these circulations, which were in fact mutually sustaining. The refugee from the Duchy of Parma, Claudio Linati (1790–1832), who had fought in the Napoleonic wars before being arrested in Turin and banished after the liberal riot of 1821, went on to introduce lithography to Mexico, where he produced numerous engravings in the late 1820s depicting the costumes and customs of the country. A few years later, as we have seen, the French republican Victor Frond, after drifting from Algiers to Lisbon, studied photography and produced the first major photo reportage on Brazil, winning the support of the emperor, Pedro II. Such examples, which should not be studied from a sole perspective – be it political, economic, or artistic, the three in fact being intertwined – illustrate the merits of decompartmentalizing the history of exile, and drawing on the broader contributions of the history of movements and circulations. At the same time, their itineraries through Europe, Africa, and across the Atlantic remind us how mistaken we would be to restrict our perspective to an exclusively European history of banishment and forced emigration.

While further research is needed into the worldwide itineraries of nineteenth-century exiles, the memory of exiles around the world suggests some stimulating lines of inquiry. Thus in 2018, the Beninese visual artist Estache Kuassi Agoumkpé, born in 1983, embarked on an artistic tour around France, Martinique, Algeria, and Benin, presenting nine paintings of "the African pantheon of resistance", retracing the course of King Béhanzin, sovereign of Dahomey (1845–1906). After being defeated in 1892 by the French general, Alfred Amédée Dodds, Béhanzin spent the rest of his life in exile. It was under his reign that Dahomey was colonized by the French in 1892. On being deposed and then arrested in 1894, Béhanzin sought to negotiate his removal to a distant land. He was sent to Martinique, where he was initially an object of curiosity, before he and his court quickly fitted into local life, taking part in religious ceremonies and receiving notables. Each year Béhanzin wrote to the French government to obtain his return to his native land. In 1906, the French authorities granted him the right to leave Martinique, but only for Algeria, where he died. His remains were transferred to Djimè, in Benin, in 1928. The case of King Béhanzin belongs to the world history of colonial conflict, while also being a component in the history of fallen governors and sovereigns. His example provides a way of linking Africa and the Caribbean into our analysis, together with two contexts we have scarcely mentioned, namely European imperialism and colonization.

Many other sovereigns and protagonists resisting European domination were banished and exiled. After taking in Polish, Italian, and Spanish exiles in the nineteenth century, Algeria became a place of banishment for many sovereigns. The young Emperor Hàm Nghi (1871–1944), accused of being at the head of Vietnamese resistance in Tonkin to French occupation after the ambush of Hue on July 5, 1885, also went into exile in Algiers, at the age of eighteen. Viewed by the French authorities as an influential politician, he was never allowed to return to China. He nevertheless maintained relations with Vietnamese pupils at the Algiers high school and with French officers and missionaries traveling between Indochina, Algeria, and mainland France. Thanks to these intermediaries he was able to maintain a link with Indochina. Despite being under surveillance throughout his life, Hàm Nghi in fact played no political role, and became a painter and sculptor: he was the pupil of the Orientalist painter Marius Reynaud and of the sculptor Auguste Rodin. Another exiled sovereign in Algeria, Ranavalona III, queen of Madagasca, finished her days in Algiers in 1917.

The British also deported sovereigns to strip them of any political role in resistance to colonization. After the First Anglo-Sikh War, Maharani Jind Kaur (1817–1863), the regent of the Sikh empire (1843–1846), was imprisoned in India then deported by the British. She finished her life in Victorian London, and on her death, her body was transported to Bombay where it was incinerated. At the end of the century, several African kings who refused colonization were deported to the Seychelles. Prempeh I, king of the Ashanti (part of present-day Ghana) was exiled for thirty years after the Anglo-Ashanti war of 1894–1896. Chwa II Kabalega, king of Bunyoro in Uganda, was deported from 1899 to 1923; Mwanga II kabaka (king) of Buganda, was deported in 1899; Sayyid Khalid, briefly sultan of Zanzibar, was deported to the Seychelles in 1916, and then to Saint Helena. These cases remind us that authorities used their empires to relegate not solely homegrown protesters and rebels, but also those from colonial lands.

The most frequently used term to refer to the fate of such outcasts was that they had been "deported" or "imprisoned". Looking beyond the confines of European colonial powers, this work wishes to pave the way to comparisons and contrasts with exiles in Africa and Asia, which, it is to be hoped, will lead on to another book. Exile was not only European; it was not simply imitated and appropriated outside Europe. Works by Edward Blumenthal on the South American world,[4] and by Romy Sánchez on Cuba and the Caribbean,[5] have already demonstrated the scale and significance of exile and its associated movements within the political life of these spaces, and it may be posited that exile was in abundant use elsewhere. In the wake of research by Joanna Waley-Cohen, Frédéric Constant has recently shown that exile was part of the sentencing scale in China.[6] It was used as an act of clemency, in which members of the elites were condemned to exile, hence stripped of the honors normally associated with proximity to the royal domain. In China, too, there was a distinction between military exile and civilian exile. For those condemned to military exile, there were several possible destinations to avoid their being grouped all in one place, with distance indexed to the severity of punishment.

Thus a global history of exiles, whether looking at the exiles of kings and queens, of members of political elites, or the forced emigration of working-class people, requires comparison between the provisions for departure and reception, and examination of itineraries transcending individual continents. The history of "what exile is", to use Victor Hugo's famous expression, is necessarily a collective one, attentive to all that made the refugee community – yet alert to the irreducible singularity of the political spaces and configurations under study.

---

[4] Edward Blumenthal, *Exile and Nation-State Formation in 19th-Century South America* (New York: Palgrave-Macmillan, Transnational History Series, 2019).
[5] Sánchez, *Quitter Cuba.*
[6] Joanna Waley-Cohen, *Exile in Mid-Qing China: Banishment to Xinjiang, 1758–1820* (New Haven, Yale University Press, 1991); Frédéric Constant, "Punir par l'espace: la peine d'exil dans la Chine impériale," *Extrême-Orient Extrême-Occident* [online], 40 (2016, placed online November 21, 2018, accessed April 17, 2021, https://journals.openedition.org/extremeorient/599.

Printed sources

Arago, Étienne. *Une voix de l'exil*. Genève: Blanchard, 1860.
Armengol y Cornet, Pedro. *A las Islas Marianas ó al golfo de Guinea? memoria... sobre si convendria establecer en las islas del golfo de Guinea, ó en las Marianas, unas colonias penitenciarias... por D. Pedro Armengol y Cornet*. Madrid: E. Martinez, 1878.
Bernard, Guillaume. *Quatre ans en exil*. Lille: Maison de la bonne presse du Nord, 1894.
Brocher, Victorine. *Souvenirs d'une morte vivante. Une femme dans la Commune de 1871*, préface de Lucien Descaves. Lausanne: A. Lapie, 1909.
Cattaneo, Carlo. *Ugo Foscolo e l'Italia*. Milan: Politecnico, 1861.
Correspondance de Victor Schoelcher présentée par Nelly Schmidt. Paris: Maisonneuve et Larose, 1995.
Crispi, Francesco. *Lettere dall'esilio 1850–1860, raccolte e annotate da T. Palamenghi-Crispi*. Rome : Casa editrice Tiber, 1918.
Déjacque, Joseph. *Les Lazaréennes*. New Orleans: J. Lamarre, 1857.
Descaves, Lucien. *Philémon, vieux de la vieille*. Paris: P. Ollendorf, 1913.
Dramard, Louis. *Voyages aux pays des proscrits : scènes de la vie d'exil*. Paris: C. Marpon et E. Flammarion, 1879
Farini, Luigi Carlo. *Lo Stato romano dal 1815 al 1850*. Turin: Ferrero and Franco, 1853.
Garnier-Pagès, Louis-Antoine. *Histoire de la Révolution de 1848*. Paris: Pagnerre, 1866.
Giurati, Domenico. *Memorie d'emigrazione*. Milan: Treves, 1897.
de Gontaut-Biron, Marie Joséphine Louise. *Mémoires de la duchesse de Gontaut, gouvernante des enfants de France pendant la Restauration, 1773–1836*. Paris: Plon, 1891.
Hugo, Victor. *William Shakespeare*. Brussells: A. Lacroix, Verboeckhoven et Cie, éditeurs, 1864.
Hugo, Victor. *Actes et paroles. Pendant l'exil*. Paris: J. Hetzel et Cie, A. Quantin, 1882–1889.
Hugo, Victor. *Histoire d'un crime*, IV, 12, " Les expatriés ", édition électronique de Jean-Marc Hovasse et Guy Rosa.
Hugo, Victor. *Les Misérables*. Paris: E. Hugues, 1879–1882, cinquième partie, Jean Valjean, Livre premier, " La guerre entre quatre murs ".
de Lamartine, Alphonse. *Histoire de la révolution de 1848*. t. 1. Paris: Garnier frères, 1859.
Lefrançais, Gustave. *Souvenirs d'un révolutionnaire de juin 1848 à la Commune*. Paris: La Fabrique éditions, 2013.
de Lubersac Abbé. *Journal historique et religieux de l'émigration et déportation du clergé de France en Angleterre*. London: Cox, 1802.
Malato, Charles. *Les Joyeusetés de l'exil*. Paris: Stock, 1897.
Malato, Charles. "Some Anarchist Portraits". *Fortnightly Review* 333 (september 1894): 327–328.
de Miñano, Sebastián. "Emigraciones, emigrados ". *Revista Enciclopédica*, VI (1843).
Plauchut Edmond. *Le Tour du monde en cent vingt jours ; Un naufrage aux îles du Cap Vert ; Une excursion à la tombe de Magellan*. Paris: Librairie internationale, 1865.
Marx, Karl, and Engels Friedrich, *Inventer l'inconnu. Textes et correspondances autour de la Commune*. Paris: La Fabrique, 2011.

Marx, Karl and Engels Friedrich, *Les Grands hommes de l'exil*. Marseille: Éditions Agone, 2015, édition établie et préfacée par Sylvie Aprile, traduit de l'allemand par Lucie Roignant.
de Ménerville, Madame, *La Fille d'une victime de la Révolution française. Souvenirs d'émigration, 1791–1797*. Paris: 1934.
Michel, Louise. " *Je vous écris de ma nuit* ". *Correspondance générale, 1850–1904*, édition établie et présentée par Xavière Gauthier. Paris: Max Chaleil, 2000, 1re éd.
Nadaud, Martin. *Léonard, maçon de la Creuse*. Paris: François Maspero / La mémoire du peuple, 1976.
Puccinelli, Mina. *L'Homme obscur qui ment : roman historique de la France*. Brussells: E. Cheval, s. d.
Quinet, Hermione. *Edgar Quinet depuis l'exil*. Paris: Calmann Lévy, 1889.
de Rémusat, Charles. *La Vie de village en Angleterre. Souvenirs d'un exilé*, Paris : Libraire académique, 1863, 2e éd.
Renard, Georges. *Un Exilé*. Paris: P. Ollendorff, 1893.
Ruffini, Giovanni. *Lorenzo Benoni. Mémoires d'un réfugié italien*. Paris: Magnin, Blanchard et Cie, 1859.
Saint-Ferréol, Amédée. *Appendices de mes mémoires*. Brioude: Imprimerie D. Chouvet, 1893.
Saint-Ferréol, Amédée. *Les Proscrits français en Belgique ou la Belgique contemporaine vue à travers l'exil*. Brussels: Librairie européenne C. Muquardt, 1870, 2 vol.
Schurz, Carl. *The Reminiscences of Carl Schurz*. New York: McClure Company, 1907, vol. 1.
Straszewicz, Joseph. " Claudine Potocka ", *Les Polonais et les Polonaises de la révolution du 29 novembre 1830*. Paris: Beaulé et Jubin, 1839.
Saint-René Taillandier. " La Sibérie au XIXe siècle ", *Revue des Deux Mondes*, t. 11 (1855).
Sand-Barbès. Lettres d'hier et lettres d'aujourd'hui. Correspondance d'une amitié républicaine 1848–1870, Préface de Michelle Perrot. Paris: Le Capucin, 1999
Tardivel, Jules-Paul. *Vie du pape Pie IX : ses œuvres et ses douleurs*. Paris: J. N. Duquet, 1878.
del Vecchio, Bartolomeo. *Un voyage de Rome à Genève ou mémoire d'un exilé*. Genève: Chez les principaux libraires, 1850.
Voltaire, *Correspondance, deuxième partie*. Paris: Leroi, 1835.
Tanski, Joseph. *Cinquante années d'exil*. Paris: Lalouette, 1880.
Vallès, Jules. *La Rue à Londres*. Paris: Éditions de la Pléiade.
Woolf, Virginia. *Une Chambre à soi*. Paris: Denoël, 1992.

Bibliography

About, Ilsen, and Denis Vincent. *Histoire de l'identification des personnes*. Paris: La Découverte (coll. Repères), 2010.

Adda, Leila. "Les apports culturels des réfugiés politiques en Tunisie au XIXe siècle." In *Da maestrale a scirocco. Le migrazioni attraverso il Mediterrano* edited by Federico Cresti et Daniela Melfa, 65–81. Milano: Giuffré, 2006.

Acciai, Enrico. *Garibaldi's Radical Legacy. Traditions of War Volunteering in Southern Europe (1861–1945)*. London: Routledge, 2020.

Anceau, Éric, *et al.* (dir.), *Histoire des internationales. Europe, XIXe-XXe siècles*. Paris: Nouveau Monde Éditions, 2017.

Antoine, François, *et al.* (dir.), *Déportations et exils des Conventionnels*. Paris: Société des études robespierristes, Collection études révolutionnaires, 19, 2018.

Aprile, Sylvie. "Exil et exilés français sous le Second Empire." *Hommes & Migrations*, 1253 (2005): 88–97.

Aprile, Sylvie. "L'expérience de l'étranger: vivre et enseigner en exil après le 2 décembre." *Documents pour l'histoire du français langue étrangère*, [online], 32 | 2004, accessed April 29, 2021. http://journals.openedition.org/dhfles/1244.

Aprile, Sylvie. "Exil et éloignement, la famille comme recours." In *Éloignement géographique et cohésion familiale (XVe-XXe siècle)* edited by Jean-François Chauvard and Christine Lebeau, 31–49. Strasbourg: Presses universitaires de Strasbourg.

Aprile, Sylvie. "De l'exilé à l'exilée: une histoire sexuée de la proscription politique outre-Manche et outre-Atlantique sous le Second Empire." *Le Mouvement Social* 225/4 (2008): 27–38.

Aprile, Sylvie. *Le Siècle des exilés. Bannis et proscrits de 1789 à la Commune*. Paris: CNRS Éditions, 2010.

Aprile, Sylvie. "Le proscrit pèlerin: le voyage de l'exilé sur les traces de ses prédécesseurs." In *Le Voyage et la mémoire au XIXe siècle*, edited by Sarga Moussa et Sylvain Venayre, 189–207. Paris: Éditions Créaphis 2011.

Aprile, Sylvie. "Déposer un brevet sans déposer les armes? Exilés et inventeurs français durant le Second Empire." *Revue d'histoire du XIXe siècle* 53/2 (2016): 79–96.

Aprile, Sylvie. "Expériences et représentations de la frontière. Proscrits et exilés au milieu du XIXe siècle." *Hommes & migrations* 1321 (2018): 75–82.

Aprile, Sylvie, *et al.* (ed.). *Comment meurt une République. Autour du 2 Décembre 1851*. Paris: Créaphis, 2004.

Armand-Dreyfus, Geneviève. *L'Exil des républicains espagnols en France. De la Guerre civile à la mort de Franco*. Paris: Albin Michel, 1999.

Bacchin, Elena, *Italofilia. Opinione pubblica britannica e Risorgimento italiano 1847–1864*. Torino: Carocci, 2014.

Bantman, Constance. *The French Anarchists in London, 1880–1914. Exile and Transnationalism in the First Globalisation*. Studies in Labour History n°1, Liverpool: Liverpool University Press, 2013.

Bantman, Constance. ""Anarchistes de la bombe, anarchistes de l'idée" : les anarchistes français à Londres, 1880–1895." *Le Mouvement Social* 246 (2014/1): 47–61.

Bantman, Constance, and Ana Claudia Suriani da Silva (ed.). *The Foreign Political Press in Nineteenth Century London. Politics from a distance.* London: Bloomsbury Academic, 2017.

Bantman, Constance. "Louise Michel's London years: A political reassessment (1890–1905)", *Women's History Review*, 26/6 (2017): 994–1012.

Barbançon, Louis-José. *L'Archipel des forçats: Histoire du bagne de Nouvelle-Calédonie, 1863–1931.* Lille: Presses Universitaires du Septentrion, 2003.

Barbançon, Louis-José. "Les transportés de 1848 (statistiques, analyse, commentaires)." *Criminocorpus* [online], January 2008, accessed May 24, 2019, http://journals.openedition.org/criminocorpus/153.

Barbier, Louis-José. *Les républiques de François-Vincent Raspail: entre mythes et réalité*" (PhD diss, Université d'Avignon, 2016).

Bastid-Bruguière, Marianne. "L'origine polonaise de l'enseignement universitaire du chinois moderne en Europe: Michel Alexandre Kleczkowski (1818–1886)." In *Ex Oriente Lux. Księga Pamiątkowa dla Romana Sławińskiego.* Krakow: Krakowska Szkoła Wyższa, 2005, 29–59.

Bayley, Joanne. "Think Wot a Mother Must Feel": Parenting in English Pauper Letters." *Family & Community History*, vol. 13,1 (2010):5–19.

Beaupré Nicolas and Rance Karine (ed.). *Arrachés et déplacés. Réfugiés politiques, prisonniers de guerre et déportés (1789–1918).* Clermont-Ferrand: Presses de l'Université Blaise Pascal, 2016.

Bensimon, Fabrice *et al.* (ed). *"Arise Ye Wretched of the Earth". The First International in a Global Perspective.* Leiden/Boston: Brill, 2018.

Bensimon, Fabrice. ""À bas les Anglais !" Mobilisations collectives contre les Britanniques dans le nord de la France en 1848." *Diasporas. Circulations, Migrations, histoire* 33(2019/1): 75–90.

Becquet, Hélène. *Marie-Thérèse de France. L'orpheline du Temple.* Paris: Perrin, 2012.

Belardelli, Giovanni. *Mazzini.* Bologna: Il Mulino, 2010.

Ben Amos, Avner. *Le vif saisit le mort. Funérailles, politique et mémoire en France (1789–1996).* Paris: EHESS, 2013.

Bertrand, Gilles, *et al.* (ed.), "Fraternité, pour l'histoire du concept". Grenoble: *Cahiers du CRHIPA*, (2012).

Binder Johnson, Hildegard. "Adjustment to the United States." In *The Forty-Eighters. Political Refugees of the German Revolution of 1848*, edited by A. E. Zucker, 43–78. New York: Columbia University Press, 1950.

Bistarelli, Agostino. *Gli esuli del Risorgimento.* Bologna: Il Mulino, 2011.

Blanc-Chaléard, Marie-Claude, *et al.* (ed), *Police et migrants. France, 1667–1939.* Rennes: Presses Universitaires de Rennes, 2001.

Bled, Jean-Paul. *Les Lys en exil ou la seconde mort de l'Ancien Régime.* Paris: Fayard, 1992.

Blumenthal, Edward. "Les mots de l'exil dans le droit international du xixe siècle, entre Amérique Latine et Europe." *Hommes & Migrations* 1321 (Spring 2018): 43–51.

Boniface, Léonce. "Un proscrit varois de décembre 1851 dans le comté de Nice, le docteur César Provençal (1814–1868)", *Provence historique*, tome 3, fasc. 14 (1953): 126–130.

Bourgin, Georges. "Mazzini et le comité central démocratique en 1851". *Il Risorgimento italiano. Rivista storica*, VI, (1913): 366–375.

Bourguinat, Nicolas. "Traces et sens de l'Histoire chez les voyageuses françaises et britanniques dans l'Italie pré-unitaire (1815–1861)." *Genre & Histoire*, 9 (Autumn 2011).

Bourguinat, Nicolas, et al. (ed.), *La Guerre de 1870, conflit européen, conflit global*. Montrouge: Les Éditions du Bourg, 2020.

Brégeard, Olivier. "Une communauté fragile, les Français de New York au milieu du XIXe siècle." *Annales de démographie historique* (2001): 43–53.

Brice, Catherine et Aprile Sylvie (ed.). *Exil et fraternité en Europe au XIXe siècle*. Pompignac: Éditions Bière, 2013.

Brice, Catherine. "Politique et propriété: confiscation et séquestre des biens des exilés politiques au XIXe siècle. Les bases d'un projet." *Mélanges de l'École française de Rome – Italie et Méditerranée modernes et contemporaines*, n° 129–2 (2017).

Brice, Catherine. "Confiscations et séquestres des biens des exilés politiques dans les États italiens au XIXe siècle. Questions sur une pratique et projets de recherches". *Diasporas. Circulations, migrations, histoire*, n° 23-24 (2014): 147–163.

Brice, Catherine, ed. *Frères de sang, frères d'armes, frères ennemis: la fraternité en Italie (1820–1924). Actes du colloque, École française de Rome, Rome, 10–12 mai 2012*. Roma: École française de Rome, 2017.

Brice, Catherine. "La Commission des barricades de la République romaine (1848–1849): une "technologie politique" ? Réflexion sur les contextes mouvants de l'innovation." *Diasporas. Circulations, migrations, histoire* 29(2017): 131–153, https://doi.org/10.4000/diasporas.791.

Brice, Catherine. "Les monuments de papier. Exil, archives et politique après le Quarantotto." In *La passione per la Repubblica. Studi dedicati a Marina Tesoro* edited by Arianna Arisi Rota, and Bruno Ziglioli: 66–79. Pisa: Pacini editore, 2019.

Brice, Catherine (ed). *Exile and the Circulation of Political Practices in the 19th Century*. Cambridge: Cambridge Scholars, 2020.

Bron, Grégoire. "L'exil libéral portugais du début du XIXe siècle (1808–1834)." *Mélanges de la Casa de Velázquez*, 48–1 (2018): 315–321.

Bron, Grégoire. "The exiles of the Risorgimento: Italian volunteers in the Portuguese Civil War (1832–34)." *Journal of Modern Italian Studies* 14/4 (2009): 427–444.

Bron, Grégoire. "La diplomatie du libéralisme portugais et la solidarité aristocratique internationale (1828–1832)." *Ler Historia* 68 (2015): 9–31.

Brundage, David. *Irish Nationalists in America. The Politics of Exile, 1798–1998*. Oxford: Oxford University Press, 2016.

Bruyère-Ostells, Walter. *La Grande Armée de la Liberté*. Paris: Tallandier, 2009.

Burgess, Greg. *Refuge in the Land of Liberty. France and its Refugees, from the Revolution to the end of Asylum, 1787–1939*. New York: Palgrave, 2008.

Cabot, Bastien. *"À bas les Belges!". L'expulsion des mineurs borains (Lens, août-septembre 1892)*. Rennes: Presses universitaires de Rennes, 2017.

Caddeo, Rinaldo. *La Tipografia elvetica di Capolago*. Milan: Alpes, 1931.

Caestecker, Frank. *Alien Policy in Belgium (1840–1940). The Creation of Refugees, Guestworkers and Illegal Aliens*. Oxford: Berghahn books, 2000.

Canal, Jordi (ed.), *Exilios. Los éxodos políticos en España, siglos XV-XX*. Madrid: Sílex, 2007.

Canal, Jordi, et al. (ed.). *París, ciudad de acogida*. Madrid: Marcial Pons, 2010.

Canal, Jordi. "Guerres civiles en Europe au XIXe siècle, guerre civile européenne et Internationale blanche." In *Pratiques du transnational. Terrains, preuves, limites* edited by Jean-Paul Zúñiga, 57–77. Paris: Centre de Recherches Historiques, 2011.

Caron, Jean-Claude, et al. (ed.). *Entre violence et conciliation: La résolution des conflits sociopolitiques en Europe au XIXe siècle*. Rennes: Presses universitaires de Rennes, 2008.

Carpenter, Kirsty, et al. (ed). *The French Émigrés in Europe and the Struggle against Revolution, 1789–1814*. Basingstoke: Macmillan, 1999.

Castells Olivan, Irene. *La utopía insurreccional del liberalismo. Torrijos y las conspiraciones liberales de la década ominosa*. Barcelone: Crítica, 1989.

Celaya, Diego Gaspar. *La guerra continúa. Voluntarios españoles al servicio de la Francia libre. 1940–1945*. Madrid: Marcial Pons, 2015.

Chase, Malcolm. *Le Chartisme (1838–1858). Aux origines du mouvement ouvrier britannique*. Paris: Publications de la Sorbonne, 2013.

Chevalier, Christophe. "Acteurs non étatiques et relations internationales au XIXe siècle: le cas du comité d'Ostende (1866–1870)", *Relations internationales* 174 (2018/2): 7–22.

Chopelin, Paul, and Bruno Dumons (ed.). *Transmettre une fidélité. La Contre-Révolution et les usages du passé (France, Espagne, Italie, XIXe-XXe siècles)*. Brussels: Peter Lang, 2019.

Çiçek, Nazan. *The Young Ottomans: Turkish Critics of the Eastern Question in the Late Nineteenth Century*. London and New-York: I. B. Tauris, 2010.

Clemente, Alida, "Il business del viaggio nella Napoli dell'emigrazione (1887–1925)", in *Il viaggio degli emigranti in America Latina tra Ottocento e Novecento*, edited by Giuseppe Moricola, 21–46. Naples: Alfredo Guida, 2008.

Coates, Timothy, *Convict Labor in the Portuguese Empire, 1740–1932*. Leiden/Boston: Brill, 2014.

Combes, André. "Les francs-maçons réfugiés en Angleterre (1850–1880)", *Chroniques d'histoire maçonnique* 33–34 (1985).

Comín Comín, Francisco, et al.. *Las cajas de ahorro de las provincias de ultramar, 1840–1898: Cuba y Puerto Rico*. Madrid: Fundación de las Cajas de Ahorro, 2010.

Cordillot, Michel. *La Sociale en Amérique. Dictionnaire biographique du mouvement social francophone aux Etats-Unis*. Paris: Éditions de l'Atelier, 2002.

Cordillot, Michel. *Utopistes et exilés du Nouveau Monde. Des Français aux États-Unis de 1848 à la Commune*, Paris: Vendémiaire, 2013.

Corti, Paola. "Women Were Labour Migrants Too: Tracing Late-Nineteenth-Century Female Migration from Northern Italy to France", in *Women, Gender, and Transnational Lives. Italian Workers of the World*, edited by Donna R. Gabaccia et Franca Iacovetta. Toronto: University of Toronto Press, (2002): 133–159.

Coupain, Nicolas. "L'expulsion des étrangers en Belgique (1830–1914)", *Revue belge d'histoire contemporaine*, XXXIII 1–2 (2003): 5–48.

Coutant de Saisseval, Guy. *Les Légitimistes vendéens au Portugal, la chouannerie portugaise, 1832–1834*. Fontenay-le-Comte: impr. de P. et O. Lussaud frères, 1954.

Cruickshanks, Eveline, and Edward Corp (dir.), *The Stuart Court in exile and the Jacobites*. London-Rio Grande: the Hambledon Press, 1995.

Dansette, Adrien. *Le Second Empire. Du 2 décembre au 4 septembre*. Paris: Hachette, 1972.

Delaunay, Jean-Marc. "Des réfugiés en Espagne: les religieux français et les décrets du 29 mars 1880". *Mélanges de la Casa de Velázquez* 17(1981): 291–319.

Delfau, Gérard. *Jules Vallès, l'exil à Londres. 1871–1880*. Paris: Bordas, 1971.
Deluermoz, Quentin. *Commune(s) 1870–1871*. Paris: Éditions du Seuil, 2020.
Derrien, Marie, *et al.* (dir.), "Genre et engagement en temps de guerre (XVIe-XXIe siècles)", *Genre & histoire*, 19, (2017).
Desurvire, Emmanuel. *Charles-Edmond Chojecki, L'oeuvre et la vie, une biographie*. Sl: Éditeur Emmanuel Desurvire, 2014.
Deschamps, Bénédicte. "Echi d'Italia. La stampa dell'emigrazione", in *Storia dell'emigrazione italiana*, edited by Piero Bevilacqua, Andreina De Clementi, Emilio Franzina. Roma: Donzelli Editore (2002): 313–334.
Deschamps, Bénédicte. "Dal Fiele Al Miele: La Stampa Esule Italiana Di New York e Il Regno Di Sardegna (1849–1861)", *Annali Della Fondazione Luigi Einaudi* 42(2008): 81–98.
Devos, Denise. "La loi de réparation nationale du 30 juillet 1881: source de l'histoire de la répression de l'insurrection de décembre 1851", *Revue d'histoire du XIXe siècle* [online], 1 | (1985).
Diaz, Delphine. *Un asile pour tous les peuples. Exilés et réfugiés étrangers en France au cours du premier XIXe siècle*. Paris: Armand Colin, 2014.
Diaz, Delphine, *et al.* (dir.), *Exils entre les deux mondes. Migrations et espaces politiques atlantiques au XIXe siècle*. Bécherel: Éditions les Perséides, 2015.
Diaz, Delphine. "Indésirables en métropole, utiles en Algérie? Les réfugiés politiques étrangers et la colonisation (1830–1852)", *Revue d'histoire du XIXe siècle* 51 (2015/2): 187–204.
Diaz, Delphine. "Les expulsions de réfugiés étrangers: pratiques administratives et mobilisations de l'opinion publique en France, 1832–1852", *Diasporas. Circulations, migrations, histoire* 33 (2019/1): 19–34.
Diaz, Delphine. "La figure de l'étranger en France de la monarchie de Juillet à la IIe République: de la tête de Turc au bouc émissaire." In *Boucs émissaires, têtes de Turcs et souffre-douleur*, edited by Frédéric Chauvaud, Jean-Claude Gardes, Christian Moncelet et Solange Vernois, 133–144. Rennes: Presses Universitaires de Rennes, 2012.
Delphine Diaz, "Paris, capitale de l'exil intellectuel européen au cours du premier XIXe siècle." In *La Vie intellectuelle en France, XIXe-XXIe siècles* edited by Christophe Charle et Laurent Jeanpierre, 308–314. Paris: Éditions du Seuil, 2016.
Diaz, Delphine. "Les réfugiés en France au prisme des circulaires du ministère de l'Intérieur (1830–1870): pour une étude conjointe des discours et pratiques de l'administration." *Hommes & Migrations*, 1321 (Spring 2018): 33–40.
Diaz, Delphine. "The Risorgimento Italians' Journeys and Exile Narratives: Flight, Expedition or Peregrination?." In *Italianness and Migration from the Risorgimento to the 1960s*, edited by Céline Regnard *et al.* (eds). New York: Palgrave Macmillan, 2022, forthcoming.
Diaz, Delphine. "Exil et circulations politiques autour de 1830: les réfugiés étrangers en France." In *La Liberté guidant les peuples: les révolutions de 1830 en Europe*, edited by Sylvie Aprile, Jean-Claude Caron and Emmanuel Fureix. Seyssel: Champ Vallon, 2013: 226–240.
Diaz, Delphine. "Pour une histoire européenne de l'exil et de l'asile politiques au XIXe siècle: le programme de recherche AsileuropeXIX." *Diasporas. Circulations, migrations, histoire* 28(2016):163–173.

Diaz, Delphine. "Femmes, genre et exil en Europe à l'époque contemporaine." *Encyclopédie pour une histoire nouvelle de l'Europe* [online], 2016. Accessed April 29, 2021. Permalien: https://ehne.fr/node/987.

Diaz, Delphine, *et al.* (ed.), "Dans l'intimité de l'exil", *Revue d'histoire du XIXe siècle*, 61(2020/2).

Díez, García, and Thaidigsmann Barón; Francisco Javier (dir.), *El siglo XIX en el Prado*. Madrid: Museo Nacional del Prado, 2007.

Doran, Christine. "Women in the Philippine Revolution", Philippine Studies, vol. 46, 3 (1998): 361–375.

Dornel, Laurent. *La France hostile. Socio-histoire de la xénophobie (1870–1914)*. Paris: Hachette, 2004.

Dornel, Laurent. "Alexis-Alejo Peyret le passeur: émigration d'élites et transferts culturels", in *Des Pyrénées à la Pampa. Une histoire de l'émigration d'élites (XIXe-XXe siècles)*, edited by Laurent Dornel, 33–50. Pau: Presses de l'Université de Pau et des Pays de l'Adour, 2013

Dornel, Laurent (ed.), *Le Retour*. Pau: Presses universitaire de Pau et des pays de l'Adour, coll. "Espaces, frontières, métissages", 2017.

Dufoix, Stéphane. *Politiques d'exil. Hongrois, Polonais et Tchécoslovaques en France après 1945*. Paris: Presses universitaires de France, coll. "Sociologie d'aujourd'hui", 2002.

Dumons, Bruno (ed.), *Rois et princes en exil : une histoire transnationale du politique dans l'Europe du XIXe siècle*. Paris: Riveneuve, 2015.

Dundink, Stefan, Karen Hagemann et John Tosh (ed), *Masculinity in Politics and War. Gendering Modern History*. Manchester: Manchester University Press, 2004.

Dundink, Stefan, and Karen Hagemann, "Masculinty in Politics and War in the age of democratic Revolutions", dans Ida Blom, Karen Hagemann et Catherine Hall (dir.), *Gendered nations. Nationalisms and Gender Order in the Long Nineteenth Century*, Oxford-New York: Berg Publishers, 2000, 3–21.

Dupasquier, Marcel. *Edgar Quinet en Suisse (1858–1870)*. Neuchâtel: À la Baconnière, 1959.

Dupont, Alexandre. "*Ayudemos a Francia*: les volontaires espagnols dans la guerre franco-allemande de 1870–1871", *Mélanges de la Casa de Velázquez*, 45–1(2015): 199–219.

Dupont, Alexandre. *Une Internationale blanche. Les légitimistes français au secours des carlistes (1868–1883)*. Paris: Publications de la Sorbonne, 2020.

Dupont, Alexandre. "Soignantes et consolatrices? Femmes contre-révolutionnaires dans la Seconde guerre carliste (Espagne, 1872–1876)", *Genre & Histoire* [online], 19 | Spring 2017.

Dupont, Alexandre. "Le genre de la contre-révolution au XIXe siècle", *Encyclopédie pour une histoire nouvelle de l'Europe* [online], 2016, accessed November 21, 2018: https://ehne.fr/node/1201.

Dupont, Alexandre. "L'impossible déchéance de nationalité. L'État français face au volontariat militaire pro-carliste (1872–1876)", *Le Mouvement Social* (2017/2): 99–110.

Dupont, Alexandre. "Les États européens au défi de la contrebande maritime. La contrebande d'armes depuis Anvers, Newport et Marseille dans les années 1870", in *Fraudes, frontières et territoires* edited by Béatrice Touchelay. Paris: IGPDE, 2020.

Durand, Antonin. "Éloigner les Barabbas: sur une campagne d'expulsion d'étrangers en Piémont en 1853", *Diasporas. Circulations, migrations, histoire*, 33 (2019/1): 119–136.

Elliott, Marianne, and Robert Emmet. *The Making of a Legend*. London: Profile, 2003.
Fettah, Samuel. "Les consuls de France et la contrebande dans le port franc de Livourne à l'époque du *Risorgimento*", *Revue d'histoire moderne & contemporaine*, 48/2 (2001): 148–161.
Feys, Torsten. "Riding the Rails of Removal: the Impact of Railroads on Border Controls and Expulsion Practices", *Journal of Transport History*, vol. 40, n° 2, (2019): 189–210.
Feys, Torsten. "International railroads and human mobility controls at the Franco-Belgian border (1840s-1860s)", *Diasporas. Circulations, migrations*, histoire, 33(2019/1): 35–54.
Finn, Margot. *After Chartism. Class and nation in English radical politics, 1848–1874*.Cambridge: Cambridge University Press, 1993.
Firmino, Sophie. *Les Réfugiés carlistes en France de 1833 à 1843* (PhD diss, Université François Rabelais de Tours, 2000).
Freitag, Sabine (ed). *Exiles from European Revolutions. Refugees in Midvictorian England*, New York/Oxford: Berghan Book, 2003.
Fornaro, Pasquale, and Jean-Yves Frétigné, *Garibaldi : modèle, contre-modèle*, Mont-Saint-Aignan: Publications des Universités de Rouen et du Havre, 2011.
De Fort, Ester. "Esuli, migranti, vagagonfi nello Stato sardo dopi il Quarnatotto", in *Rileggere l'Ottocento. Risorgimento e Nazione* edited by Maria Luisa Betri, 227–250. Turin: Comitato di Torino Dell'Istituto per la storia del Risorgimento italiano, 2010.
De Fort, Ester. "La Mecca d'Italia", *1860–1861. Torino Italia Europa*. Turin: Archivio Storico della Città di Torino, 2010.
Di Fiore, Laura. "Documentare il dissenso. Sistema identificativo e controllo politico (1815–1860)", *Meridiana*, 78(2013): 53–75.
Di Fiore, Laura and Chiara Lucrezio Monticelli, "Sorvegliare oltre i confini. Il controllo delle polizie napoletana e pontificia dopo il 1848", *Passato e Presente*, 101(2017): 47–70.
Fourn, François. *Étienne Cabet ou le temps de l'utopie*. Paris: Vendémiaire, 2014.
Fournier, Éric. *La Critique des armes. Une histoire d'objets révolutionnaires*. Paris: Libertalia, 2019.
Fureix, Emmanuel. *La France des larmes. Deuils politiques à l'âge romantique (1814–1840)*. Ceyzérieu: Champ Vallon, 2009.
Fugazza, Mariachiara et Karoline Rörig (ed.), *La Prima donna d'Italia. Cristina Trivulzio di Belgiojoso tra politica e giornalismo*. Milan: FrancoAngeli, 2010.
Furiozzi, Gian Biagio. *L'emigrazione politica in Piemonte nel decennio preunitario*. Florence: L.S. Olschki, 1979.
Gabaccia, Donna R.. *From the Other Side. Women, Gender and Immigrant Life in the US, 1820–1990*. Bloomington: Indiana University Press, 1996.
Gabaccia, Donna R. *Italy's many diasporas*. Seattle: University of Washington Press, 2000.
Gacon, Stéphane. *L'Amnistie. De la Commune à la guerre d'Algérie*. Paris: Éditions du Seuil, 2002.
Garmendia, Vincent. "Note sur la présence carliste en Aquitaine à l'époque de la seconde guerre carliste", *Bulletin Hispanique*, t. 96/2 (1994): 435–451.
Garrigou, Alain. *Mourir pour des idées. La vie posthume d'Alphonse Baudin*. Paris: Les Belles Lettres, 2010.
Garrigou, Alain. *Histoire sociale du suffrage universel en France, 1848–2000*, Paris: Éditions du Seuil, 2002.

Gauthier, Xavière. *La Vierge rouge. Biographie de Louise Michel*. Paris: Les Éditions de Paris, 2013.
Gerbet, Pierre. "La vie des réfugiés politiques à Clermont-Ferrand de 1815 à 1870", *Extrait du Bulletin historique et scientifique de l'Auvergne*, LXIII(1943): 17–21.
Green, Nancy L. *Repenser les migrations*. Paris: Presses universitaires de France, 2002.
Green, Nancy L. "Trans-frontières: pour une analyse des lieux de passage", *Socio-anthropologie*(1999): 48.
Gobat, Michel. *Empire by Invitation William Walker and Manifest Destiny in Central America*. Cambridge: Mass., Harvard University Press, 2018.
Gobat, Michel. "The Invention of Latin America: A Transnational History of Anti-Imperialism, Democracy, and Race", *The American Historical Review*, vol. 118, 5(2013): 1345–1375.
Goddeeris, Idesbald. *La Grande Émigration polonaise en Belgique (1831–1870). Élites et masses à l'époque romantique*. Bern: Peter Lang, 2013.
Goddeeris, Idesbald. "Des révolutionnaires polonais à Bruxelles (1830–1870)", in *Le Bruxelles des révolutionnaires, De 1830 à nos jours* edited by Anne Morelli. Brussels: CFC-Éditions, collection "Regards sur la ville", 2016.
Godineau, Laure, *Retour d'exil. Les anciens communards au début de la Troisième République* (PhD diss Université Paris 1 Panthéon-Sorbonne, 2000).
Godineau, Laure. "Le retour d'exil, un nouvel exil ? Le cas des communards", *Matériaux pour l'histoire de notre temps*, 67 (Pour une histoire de l'exil français et belge) (2002): 11–16.
Godineau, Laure. "Paris attendu, Paris retrouvé. Les exilés communards et le peuple de Paris, de la nostalgie aux retrouvailles", in *Être Parisien* edited by Claude Gauvard and Jean-Louis Robert, 379–390. Paris: Publications de la Sorbonne, 2004.
Gouževitch, Irina and Dimitri Gouzevitch. "La voie russe d'accès des femmes aux professions intellectuelles scientifiques et techniques (1850–1920)", *Travail, genre et sociétés* 4 (2000/2): 55–75.
Grandjonc, Jacques. "Les émigrés allemands sous la monarchie de Juillet: documents de surveillance policière 1833-février 1848", *Cahiers d'études germaniques* 1(1972): 115–249.
Guarneri, Carl J. *The Utopian Alternative. Fourierism in Nineteenth-Century America*. Ithaca and London: Cornell University Press, 1991.
Gubin, Eliane, and Valérie Piette. "Sur la singularité de l'exil politique féminin dans une perspective historique, Femmes exilées politiques. Exhumer leur histoire", *Sextant*, 26(2009): 157–168.
Guidi, Laura. "Donne e uomini del Sud sulla via dell'esilio", *Storia d'Italia. Annali 22. Il Risorgimento* edited by Alberto Mario Banti et Paul Ginsborg,227–230. Turin: Einaudi, 2007.
Guillaume, Valentin. *L'autre exil. Trajectoires migratoires et stratégies d'insertion de la Grande Émigration polonaise de 1831 dans l'Ouest de la France*, (Phd diss., EHESS, 2016).
Harrison, John C. Fletcher, *Robert Owen and the Owenites in Britain and America. The Quest for the New Moral World*. London: Routledge and Kegan Paul, 1969.
Hérisson, Arthur. "Une mobilisation internationale de masse à l'époque du Risorgimento: l'aide financière des catholiques français à la papauté (1860–1870)", *Revue d'histoire du XIXe siècle*, 52/1(2016): 175–192.

Hervé, Jérôme. "Des réfugiés politiques italiens en Maine-et-Loire: accueil et intégration (1845–1900)", *Annales de Bretagne et des Pays de l'Ouest* [online], 109–4| 2002.

Hidetaka Hirota, *Expelling the Poor. Atlantic Seaboard States and Nineteenth-Century Origins of American Immigration Policy.* New York: Oxford University Press, 2017.

Hoffmann, Léon-François. "Victor Hugo, les Noirs et l'esclavage", *Françofonia*, 16, 30 (1996): 47–90.

Humair, Cédric. *1848. Naissance de la Suisse moderne.* Lausanne: Éditions Antipodes, 2009.

Hunt, Lynn. *The Family Romance of the French Revolution.* London: Routledge, 1992.

Hutchins, Stanley. "The Communard Exiles in London", *Marxism Today* 15(1971): 180–186.

Ihl, Olivier. "Louis Marie Bosredon et l'entrée dans le "suffrage universel". Sociogenèse d'une lithographie en 1848", *Revue d'histoire du xixe siècle*, 50(2015): 139–163.

Isabella, Maurizio. *Risorgimento in Exile. Italian Émigrés and the Liberal International in the Post-Napoleonic Era*, Oxford: Oxford University Press, 2009.

Isabella, Maurizio and Konstantina Zanou (ed.), *Mediterranean Diasporas, Politics and Ideas in the long 19th Century.* New York: Bloomsbury, 2016.

Jasanoff, Maya. *Liberty's Exiles: American Loyalists in the Revolutionary World.* New York: Alfred A. Knopf, 2011.

Jeannesson, Stanislas. "Le concert européen", *Encyclopédie pour une histoire nouvelle de l'Europe* [online], 2016, mis accessed October 2018, 31, https://ehne.fr/node/97.

Jensen, Richard Bach. *The Battle against Anarchist Terrorism: an International History, 1878–1934.* Cambridge: Cambridge University Press, 2014.

Jones, Thomas C.. "Définir l'asile politique en Grande-Bretagne (1815–1870)", *Hommes & Migrations*, 321 (2018): 13–21.

Jones, Thomas C. "Rallier la République en exil. L'Homme de Ribeyrolles", in *Quand les socialistes inventaient l'avenir: presse, théories et expériences, 1825–1860*, edited by Thomas Bouchet, Vincent Bourdeau, Edward Castleton *et alii*, 348–360. Paris: La Découverte, 2015.

Jordi, Jean-Jacques. *Espagnols en Oranie. Histoire d'une migration (1830–1914).* Nice: Éditions Jacques Gandini, 1996.

Kale, Steven D. *French salons. High Society and Political Sociability from the Old Regime to the Revolution of 1848*, Baltimore: John Austin University Press, 2004.

Karpat, Kemal H. "Kossuth in Turkey: the Impact of Hungarian Refugees in the Ottoman Empire 1849–1851", in *Studies on Ottoman and Political History. Selected Articles and Essays*, edited by Kemal H Karpat,169–184. Leiden-Boston-Köln: Brill, 2002.

Kasterska, Marya. "Les tombeaux polonais dans les cimetières parisiens", *La Pologne, politique, économique, littéraire et artistique*, 15 novembre (1926): 721–725.

Kelly, Debra, and Martyn Cornick (ed), *A History of the French in London: Liberty, Equality, Opportunity.* London: Institute of Historical Research, 2013.

Kerby A., Miller, "Emigrants and Exiles: Irish Cultures and Irish Emigration to North America, 1790–1922", *Irish Historical Studies*, Vol. 22, n° 86 (Sep. 1980): 97–125.

Kinard, Jeff. *Lafayette of the South: Prince Camille de Polignac and the American Civil War.* College Station: Texas A & M University Press, 2001.

Lamberts, Emiel (ed), *The Black International. L'internationale noire (1870–1878).* Brussels: Presses universitaires de Louvain, 2002.

Lasoen, Kenneth, "185 years of Belgian Security Service", *Journal of Intelligence History*,(2016): 96–118.

De Lorenzo, Renata. *Borbonia Felix, il regno delle Due Sicilie alla vigilia del crollo*. Roma: Salerno editrice, 2013.

Le Gall, Jean-Marie. *Un idéal masculin. Barbes et moustaches, XVe-XVIIIe siècles*. Paris: Payot, 2011.

Le Gall, Laurent, et al. (ed.), *La Politique sans en avoir l'air. Aspects de la politique informelle, XIXe-XXIe siècles*. Rennes: Presses Universitaires de Rennes, 2012.

Leblay, Anne. *Proscrits ibériques à Paris au temps des monarchies constitutionnelles (1814–1848)* (Phd diss, EHESS, 2013).

Léger, Céline, and Jean-Marie Roulin (ed.), "Retours d'exil", *Autour de Vallès*, 50, 2020.

Lehning, Arthur. "Une lettre de Joseph Déjacque à Pierre Vésinier du 20 février 1861. *Bulletin of the International Institute of Social History d'Amsterdam*, Leiden, E. J. Brill 1(1951): 16–19.

Leleux, Marc. "Fraternisation et concurrence: liens et limites d'un rapport au travail. L'exemple des ouvriers belges dans le département du Nord du milieu du XIXe siècle à l'entre-deux-guerres", *Revue du Nord*, 372(2007): 837–855.

Lemesle, Hélène. *Vautours, singes et cloportes, Ledru-Rollin, ses locataires et ses concierges au XIXe siècle*. Paris: Association pour le développement de l'histoire économique 2003.

de Leone, Enrico. "L'apport des patriotes italiens dans la formation de la Turquie moderne", *Turcica*, Paris, t. 3 (1971): 181–192.

Le Rider, Jacques, "Malwida von Meysenbug et Alexandre Herzen", *Revue des études slaves*, tome 78, fascicule 2–3(2007).

Lilti, Antoine. *Le Monde des salons. Sociabilité et mondanité à Paris au XVIIIe siècle*. Paris: Fayard, 2005.

Llorens, Vicente. *Liberales y románticos. Una emigración española en Inglaterra 1823–1834*. Madrid: Editorial Castalia, 1968.

Lopez, René and Emile Temime, *Migrance. Histoire des migrations à Marseille, t. 2, L'expansion marseillaise et "l'invasion italienne" (1830–1918)*. Aix-en-Provence: Edisud, 1990.

López Tabar, Juan. *Los famosos traidores : los afrancesados durante la crisis del Antiguo Régimen (1808–1833)*. Madrid: Biblioteca nueva, 2001.

Loriaux, Florence. "Femmes et exil durant la Première Internationale", *Carhop* [online], 8/2008, accessed November 20, 2018. URL: https://www.carhop.be/images/femmes_exil_premiere_internationale_f.loriaux_2008.pdf.

Loyer, Élie-Benjamin. "Expulser les indésirables: un aspect de la gestion des populations immigrés sous la Troisième République (1880–1939)", *Diasporas. Circulations, migrations, histoire*, 33(2019/1): 44–73.

Lucena Giraldo, Manuel, *Historia de un cosmopolita. José María de Lanz y la fundación de la Ingeniería de Caminos en España y América*. Madrid: Colegio de Ingenieros de Caminos, Canales y Puertos, 2005.

Lucrezio Monticelli, Chiara. *La polizia del papa. Istituzioni di contollo sociale a Roma nella prima metà dell'Ottocento*. Rubbettino: Soveria Mannelli, 2012.

Luis, Jean-Philippe. *L'Ivresse de la fortune. A. M. Aguado, un génie des affaires*. Paris: Payot, 2009.

MacClancy, Jeremy. *The Decline of Carlism*. Reno: University of Nevada Press, 2002.

McKeown, Adam. "Les migrations internationales à l'ère de la mondialisation industrielle, 1840–1940", *Le Mouvement Social* 241/4, (décembre 2012): 31–46.

McPhee, Peter. *Les Semailles de la République dans les Pyrénées-Orientales, 1846–1852: classes sociales, culture et politique*. Perpignan: Les Publications de l'Olivier, 1995.
Malandain, Gilles. *L'introuvable complot. Attentat, enquête et rumeur dans la France de la Restauration*. Paris: EHESS, 2011.
Mardin, Şerif. *The Genesis of Young Ottoman Thought: A Study in the Modernization of Turkish Political Ideas*. Princeton: N. J., Princeton University Press, 1962.
Marley, Laurence. *Michael Davitt: Freelance Radical and Frondeur*. Dublin: Four Courts Press, 2007.
Martellini, Amoreno. "Il commercio dell'emigrazione: intermediari e agenti in Europa, in Africa e nel Levante",in *Storia dell'emigrazione italiana, vol. 1, Partenze*, edted by Piero Bevilacqua, Andrea De Clementi, Emilio Franzina,293–308. Rome, Donzelli (2001).
Martin, Jean-Clément, *Violence et Révolution. Essai sur la naissance d'un mythe national*. Paris: Éditions du Seuil, 2009.
Martinez, Paul K. *Paris Communard Refugees in Great Britain, 1871–1880*, PhD dissertation, University of Sussex, 1981.
Martinez, Paul K. "Amis éprouvés et sûrs: les réfugiés blanquistes en Angleterre, 1871–1880", in *Blanqui et les blanquistes* edited by Philippe Vigier, 153–172. Paris: Société d'histoire de la Révolution de 1848-SEDES, 1986.
Martykánova, Darina. "La movilidad en la circulación de conocimientos en el espacio atlántico: La excepcionalidad significativa de José María Lanz (1764–1839)", in *Trayectorias trasatlánticas (Siglo XIX), Personajes y redes entre España y América* edited by Manuel Pérez Ledesma, 15–44. Madrid: Ediciones Polifemo, 2013.
Marzagalli, Silvia (ed.), *Les Consuls en Méditerranée, agents d'information, XVIe-XXe siècle*. Paris: Classiques Garnier, 2015.
Marzagalli, Silvia. "Études consulaires, études méditerranéennes. Éclairages croisés pour la compréhension du monde méditerranéen et de l'institution consulaire à l'époque moderne", *Cahiers de la Méditerranée*, 93, (2016)11–23, http://journals.openedition.org/cdlm/8469.
Mathorez, Jules. "Les réfugiés politiques espagnols dans l'Orne au XIXe siècle", *Bulletin Hispanique*, 4, (1915): 260–279.
Mayaud, Jean-Luc (ed), *1848. Actes du colloque international du cent cinquantenaire tenu à l'Assemblée nationale à Paris, 23–25 février 1998*, Paris: Créaphis, 2002.
Marco, Meriggi. "Come procurarsi un passaporto: il caso di Napoli a metà Settecento", dans Claudia Moatti et Wolfgang Kaiser (dir.), *Gens de passage en Méditerranée de l'Antiquité à l'époque moderne, Procédures de contrôle et d'identification*, 399–412. Paris: Maisonneuve & Larose, 2007.
Mervaud, Michel. "Lettres d'Ogarev à Natalie Herzen", *Cahiers du monde russe et soviétique*, vol. 10, 3–4 (juillet-déc. 1969). 478–523.
Merzario, Raul. *Il paese stretto. Strategie matrimoniali nella diocesi di Como secoli XVI-XVIII*, enaudi, 1981.
Michel, Ersilio. *Esuli e cospiratori italiani in Corsica (1850–1861)*. Milano: Tyrrhenia, 1929.
Michel, Ersilio. *Esuli italiani in Albania (1821–1859)*, Milano: Istituto per gli studi di politica internazionale, 1940.
Michel, Ersilio. *Esuli italiani in Tunisia 1815–1861*. Milano: Istituto per gli studi di politica internazionale, 1941.
Moisand, Jeanne. *A Spanish Commune and its Worlds*. London: Routledge, 2021, forthcoming.

Moisand, Jeanne. "Les réfugiés du *Numancia*. Le traitement des cantonalistes espagnols en Algérie française (1874)", *Diasporas. Circulations, migrations, histoire*, 33 (2019/1): 159–172.

Morán Orti, Manuel. "La cuestión de los refugiados extranjeros: política española en el trienio liberal", *Hispania. Revista española de historia*, 49, 173 (1989): 985–1016.

Morelli, Anne. "Introduction. Exhumer l'histoire des femmes exilées politiques", "Femmes exilées politiques. Exhumer leur histoire", *Sextant*, 26 (2009) 7–15.

Moreno Fraginals, Manuel. *Cuba-España, España-Cuba. Historia común*. Barcelona: Grijalbo Mondadori, 1995.

Montenach, Anne, *Femmes, pouvoirs et contrebande dans les Alpes au XVIIIe siècle*. Grenoble: Presses Universitaires de Grenoble, 2017.

Mourlane, Stéphane. "Les anarchistes italiens dans les Alpes-Maritimes et le Var à la fin du XIXe siècle: le choix de la marginalité", *Cahiers de la Méditerranée* 69 (2004) 189–198.

Moya, José C. *Cousins and Strangers: Spanish Immigrants in Buenos Aires, 1850–1930*. Los Angeles: University of California Press, 1998.

Moya, José C.. "Remigration: Patterns of Leaving and Returning from Prehistory to the Advent of Globalization" in *Return Migration in Romance Cultures,* edited by Andreas Gelz, Marco Thomas Bosshard, 21–44. Freiburg: Rombach, 2014.

Noiriel, Gérard. *Immigration, antisémitisme et racisme en France (XIXe-XXe siècle). Discours publics, humiliations privées*. Paris: Fayard, 2007.

Noiriel, Gérard. *Réfugiés et sans-papiers. La République face au droit d'asile, XIXe-XXe siècle*. Paris: Hachette, 2006.

Noiriel, Gérard. *La Tyrannie du national. Le droit d'asile en Europe 1793–1993*, Paris: Calmann-Lévy, 1991.

Nordman, Daniel. "Sauf-conduits et passeports", in *Dictionnaire de l'Ancien Régime. Royaume de France XVIe-XVIIIe siècle* edited by Lucien Bély 1122–1124. Paris: Presses universitaires de France, 1996.

Offord, Derek. "The correspondance of Alexander Herzen with James de Rothschild", *Journal in Slavic Studies*, University of Toronto, Academic Electronic, TSQ, n° 66, 2003.

Pan-Montojo, Juan, and Juan Luis Simal, "Exil, finances internationales et construction de l'État: les libéraux et "joséphins" espagnols (1813–1851)", *Revue d'histoire du XIXe siècle*, 53/2 (2016): 59–77.

Pageot, Pierre. *Le Périgord terre d'asile. Réfugiés, évacués rapatriés en Dordogne au cours des XIXe et XXe siècles*. Paris: L'Harmattan, 2005.

Papiez, Katarzyna. "Adampol/Polonezköy, refuge et colonie agricole. Un laboratoire de la polonité en exil dans l'Empire ottoman au XIXe siècle", *Hommes & Migrations*, 1321(2018): 65–73.

Parini, Lorena. "La Suisse terre d'asile: un mythe ébranlé par l'histoire", *Revue européenne des migrations internationales*, 13–1, 1997 (51–69).

Pécout, Gilles. "The international armed volunteers: pilgrims of a Transnational Risorgimento", *Journal of Modern Italian Studies*, 14/4, (2009): 413–426.

Pécout, Gilles. "Pour une lecture méditerranéenne et transnationale du Risorgimento", *Revue d'histoire du XIXe siècle*, 44(2012): 29–47.

Perales Díaz, José Antonio. *Fronteras y contrabando en el Pirineo occidental*. Pamplona: Gobierno de Navarra, 2004.

Pérennès, Roger. *Déportés et forçats. De la Commune de Belleville à Nouméa.* Nantes: Ouest-Éditions et Université Inter-Âges de Nantes, 1991.

Peyrou, Florencia. "The role of Spain and the Spanish in the creation of Europe's transnational democratic political culture, 1840–70", *Social History* 40/4 (2015): 497–517.

Polasky, Janet L. *Revolutions without Borders: the Call to Liberty in the Atlantic World.* New Haven – London: Yale University Press, 2016.

Polfliet, Marieke. *Émigration et politisation : les Français de New York et La Nouvelle-Orléans dans la première moitié du XIXe siècle (1803–1860)*, (Phd diss, Université de Nice Sophia Antipolis, 2013).

Ponty, Janine. "Réfugiés, exilés, des catégories problématiques", *Matériaux pour l'histoire de notre temps*, 44 (1996): 9–13.

Porter, Bernard. *The Refugee Question in mid-Victorian Politics.* Cambridge: Cambridge University Press, 1979.

Premisler, Sylvie. "L'émigration politique espagnole en France (1872–1876, 1894–1912)", *Cahiers du monde hispanique et luso-brésilien* 21(1973): 117–135.

Prudhommeaux, Jules. "Un commis voyageur en communisme icarien. Chameroy, disciple de Cabet", *Révolution de 1848*, 120–121–122 (1927–1928).

Ranvier, Adrien. "Une féministe de 1848: Jeanne Deroin", *Revue d'histoire du XIXe siècle* 26(1908): 317–355.

Rediker, Marcus. *The Fearless Benjamin Lay. The Quaker Dwarf Who Became the First Revolutionary Abolitionist.* Boston: Beacon Press, 2017.

Regnard, Céline. "Le maintien de l'ordre au défi de l'augmentation du transit migratoire. Marseille, New-York, 1855–1914", in *Policer les mobilités. Europe-États-Unis, XVIIIe-XXIe siècle,* edited by Anne Conchon, Laurence Montel, Céline Regnard 87–102. Paris: Éditions de la Sorbonne, 2018.

Reinecke, Christiane. "Governing Aliens in Times of Upheaval: Immigration Control and Modern State Practice in Early Twentieth-Century Britain, Compared with Prussia", *International Review of Social History*, 54 (2009): 39–65.

Riall, Lucy. "Eroi maschili, virilità e forme della guerra", in *Storia d'Italia. Annali 22. Il Risorgimento*, edited by Alberto Mario Banti et Paul Ginsborg, 253–288. Turin: Einaudi, 2007.

Riall, Lucy. "Travel, Migration, Exile: Garibaldi's global Fame", *Modern Italy*, 19/1 (2014): 41–52.

Riall, Lucy. *Garibaldi. Invention of a hero.* New Haven – London: Yale University Press, 2007.

Richard, Élodie. "La déportation comme alternative à la prison, un concours de l'Académie royale espagnole des sciences morales et politiques (1875)", *Hypothèses*, vol. 6, 1(2003): 99–109.

Richard-Jalabert, Éliane. "Marseille, ville refuge pour les libéraux espagnols, 1825–1848", vol. 72, fasc. 3, 51 *Annales du midi*(1960): 309–323.

Rist, Simone. "L'affaire Herwegh", *Revue des études slaves*, t. LXXVIII, fasc. 2–3(2007): 229–242.

Rizopoulos, Andréas. "Activités maçonniques avec arrière-plan politique – et réciproquement – en Grèce au XIXe siècle".*Cahiers de la Méditerranée* 72 (2006): 203–224.

Rolland, Denis, and Luc Capdevila, "France et Belgique, terres d'exil?", *Matériaux pour l'histoire de notre temps*, 67(2002): 1–10.

Romeo Mateo, María Cruz. "Nuestra antigua legislación constitucional ¿modelo para los liberales de 1808–1814?" in *Guerra de ideas. Política y cultura en la España de la Guerra de la Independencia* edited by Jordi Canal et Pedro Rújula. Madrid, Marcial Pons (2011): 75–103.

Rosental, Paul-André. "Migrations, souveraineté, droits sociaux. Protéger et expulser les étrangers en Europe du xixe siècle à nos jours", *Annales. Histoire, Sciences Sociales* (2011/2): 335–373.

Rude, Fernand. *La Suisse et les étrangers. Immigration et formation nationale (1848–1933)*. Lausanne: Antipodes, 2004.

Rudé, George. *Protest and Punishment: Story of the Social and Political Protesters Transported to Australia, 1788–1868*. Oxford: Oxford University Press, 1978.

Rüger, Jan. *Heligoland: Britain, Germany, and the Struggle for the North Sea*. Oxford: Oxford University press, 2017.

Ruiz de Gordejuela Urquijo, Jesús. *La expulsión de los españoles de México y su destino incierto, 1821–1836*. Sevilla: CSIC, Escuela de Estudios Hispano-Americanos, 2006.

Ruttmann, Ulrike. *Wunschbild – Schreckbild – Trugbild. Rezeption und Instrumentalisierung Frankreichs in der deutschen Revolution von 1848/49*. Stuttgart: Franz Steiner Verlag, 2001.

Rygiel, Philippe. *Une impossible tâche? L'Institut de Droit International et la régulation des migrations internationales (1870–1920)*, mémoire d'habilitation à diriger des recherches, Université Paris 1 Panthéon-Sorbonne, 2011.

Salomé, Karine. *L'Ouragan homicide. L'attentat politique en France au xixe siècle*. Paris: Champ Vallon, 2011.

Salyer, Lucy E. *Under the Starry Flag. How a Band of Irish Americans Joined the Fenian Revolt and Sparked a Crisis over Citizenship*. Cambridge (Ma): Harvard University Press, 2018.

Sanchez, Romy, and Juan Luis Simal, "Lexiques et pratiques du *destierro*. L'exil politique espagnol en péninsule et à l'Outre-mer, de 1814 aux années 1880", *Hommes & Migrations* 1321/2 (2018): 23–31.

Sánchez, Romy. "Ceuta : quand la barrière de l'Europe était un bagne colonial", *Mélanges de la Casa de Velázquez* (2018): 331–339.

Sánchez, Romy. *Quitter Cuba. Exilés et bannis au temps du séparatisme, 1834–1879*. Rennes: Presses Universitaires de Rennes, collection "Les Amériques", 2021, forthcoming.

Sarlin, Simon. *Le Légitimisme en armes: histoire d'une mobilisation internationale contre l'unité italienne*. Roma: Presses de l'École Française de Rome, 2013.

Sartorius, Francis. "Des communards exilés (1871–1879)", in *Le Bruxelles des révolutionnaires, De 1830 à nos jours* edited by Anne Morelli 72–81. Brussels: CFC-Éditions, coll. "Regards sur la ville", 2016.

Sartorius, Francis. "Des débuts de la monarchie de Juillet à la fin du Second Empire: intellectuels et hommes politiques français en exil en Belgique", *Revue d'histoire du xixe siècle*, 11(1995/1): 35–49.

Schaffer, Simon (dir.), *The Brokered World: Go-Betweens and Global Intelligence, 1770–1820*, Sagamore Beach: Science History Publications, 2009.

Segala, Lygia. "Prescriptive Observation and Illustration of Brazil: Victor Frond's Photographic Project (1857–61)", *Portuguese studies*, vol. 23, 1 (2007): 55–70.

Senn, Alfred Erich and Nancy Hartmann, "Les révolutionnaires russes et l'asile politique en Suisse avant 1917", *Cahiers du monde russe et soviétique* 3–4, (1968): 324–336.
Shaw, Caroline E. *Britannia's Embrace. Modern Humanitarianism and the Imperial Origins of Refugee Relief.* Oxford: Oxford University Press, 2015.
Simal, Juan Luis. *Emigrados. España y el exilio internacional, 1814–1834.* Madrid: Centro de Estudios Políticos y Constitucionales, 2012.
Simal, Juan Luis. "El exilio en la génesis de la nación y del liberalismo (1776–1848): el enfoque transnacional", *Ayer*, 94 (2014): 23–48.
Simal, Juan Luis. "Exils et circulations des idées politiques entre Amérique hispanique et Espagne après les indépendances (1820–1836)", *Revue d'histoire du XIXe siècle* 51(2015): 35–51.
Sohn, Anne-Marie. *"Sois un Homme!". La construction de la masculinité au XIXe siècle.* Paris: Éditions du Seuil, 2009.
Sodigné Loustau, Jeanine. "Une micro-étude: les Carlistes en région Centre (1833–1876)", *Exils et migrations ibériques au XXe siècle* 5 (1998): 303–344.
Soulet, Jean-François. *Les Pyrénées au XIXe siècle.* Toulouse: Eché, 1987.
Spencer, Warren F. *The Confederate Navy in Europe.* Tuscaloosa and London: University of Alabama Press, 1997.
Sperber, Jonathan. *Karl Marx, homme du XIXe siècle*, traduit de l'anglais par David Tuaillon. Paris: Piranha, 2017.
Spieler, Miranda Frances. *Liberté, liberté trahie…: faire et défaire des citoyens français, Guyane 1780–1880.* Paris: Alma, 2016.
Spire, Alexis. *Accueillir ou reconduire. Enquête sur les guichets de l'immigration.* Paris: Raisons d'agir, 2008.
Stasik, Florian. *Polish Political Emigrés in the United States of America, 1831–1864.* Boulde: East European Monographs, 2002.
Stengers, Jean. "Du nouveau sur Marx à Bruxelles", *Bulletin d'information de l'association belge d'histoire contemporaine* 21/2 (1999): 21–22.
Takaki, Ronald. *A Pro-slavery Crusade: the Agitation to Reopen the African Slave Trade.* s. e.: 1971.
Taraud, Christelle. "Les bagnes de l'Empire au féminin. Ou comment déporter les opposants politiques de la métropole dans les colonies françaises au xixe siècle" in "Femmes exilées politiques. Exhumer leur histoire" edited by Anne Morelli. *Sextant* 26(2009): 17–25.
Tardy, Jean-Noël. *L'Âge des ombres: Complots, conspirations et sociétés secrètes au XIXe siècle.* Paris: Les Belles Lettres, 2015.
Tarrius, Alain, and Olivier Bernet, *Mondialisation criminelle. La Frontière franco-espagnole de La Junquera à Perpignan.* Saint-Denis: Édilivre, 2014.
Taylor, Miles. "The 1848 Revolutions and the British Empire", *Past & Present*, 166/1 (2000): 146–180.
Thibaud, Clément. *Libérer le nouveau monde. La fondation des premières républiques hispaniques. Colombie et Venezuela (1780–1820).* Mordelles: Les Perséides, 2017.
Thoral, Marie-Cécile. "Administrer la frontière: les fonctionnaires de l'Isère et la frontière franco-italienne de la Restauration à la monarchie de Juillet", *Histoire, économie & société*, 26/1(2007): 85–105.

Tombaccini-Villefranque, Simonetta, "La frontière bafouée: migrants clandestins et passeurs dans la vallée de la Roya (1920–1940)", *Cahiers de la Méditerranée* 58(1999): 79–95.

Traugott, Mark. *The Insurgent Barricade*. Berkeley: University of California Press, 2010.

Tikhonov, Natalia. "Les étudiantes de l'Empire des tsars en Europe occidentale: des exilées "politiques"?" Anne Morelli (dir.), "Femmes exilées politiques. Exhumer leur histoire", *Sextant* 26 (2009): 27–37.

Toledano González, Lluís Ferran. "Refugio militar y santuario político: el exilio carlista en los Pirineos Orientales", in *Exilios en la Europa mediterránea*, edited by Julio Hernández Borge et González Lopo Hernández Borge, Domingo 131–161.Santiago de Compostela: Universidad de Santiago de Compostela, 2010.

Torpey, John. *The Invention of the Passport. Surveillance, Citizenship and the State*. Cambridge: Cambridge University Press, 2000.

Tosh, John. *Manliness and Masculinities in Nineteenth-Century Britain*. London: Taylor and Francis, 2004.

Tóth, Heléna. *An Exiled Generation*. German and Hungarian Refugees of Revolution, 1848–1871. New York: Cambridge University Press, 2014.

Tronco, Emmanuel. *Les Carlistes espagnols dans l'Ouest de la France, 1833–1883*. Rennes: Presses universitaires de Rennes, 2010.

Turcato, Davide. "Italian Anarchism as a Transnational Movement, 1885–1915", *International Review of Social History* 52 (dec-2007): 407–444.

Türk, Emine. "Il contributo degli esuli italiani alla modernizzazione dello stato ottomano", in *Gli Italiani di Istanbul : figure, comunità e istituzioni dalle riforme alla repubblica, 1839–1923* edited by Attilio De Gasperis et Roberta Ferrazza 287–294. Turin: Fondazione Giovanni Agnelli,(2007).

Van de Sande, Anton, et Hans De Valk, "Italian refugees in the Netherlands during the Restoration 1815–1830. Report on a Current Investigation"*L'Émigration politique en Europe aux XIXe et XXe siècles. Actes du colloque de Rome (3–5 mars 1988)* edited by Ecole française de Rome 191–204. Rome: École Française de Rome, 1999.

Van Vyve, Maïté. "Les perceptions de l'étranger, du réfugié et de l'expulsé dans les débats parlementaires en Belgique (1835–1875)", *Hommes & Migrations*, 321 (Spring 2018): 53–62.

Verlet, Bruno. *Des Pionniers au Texas. 1850–1880*, Paris: Vendémiaire, 2012.

Vermeren, Hugo. "Pouvoirs et pratiques de l'expulsion des étrangers en Algérie au XIXe siècle: un outil colonial de gestion des flux migratoires", *Le Mouvement social*, 258 (2017):13–28.

Vermeren, Patrice. *Le Rêve démocratique de la philosophie: d'une rive à l'autre de l'Atlantique*; suivi de textes choisis d'Amédée Jacques, *Lettre inédite à Victor Cousin* (1837) ; *De l'enseignement public de la philosophie* (1848). Paris: L'Harmattan, 2001.

Veysset, Nicolas. "La fin des dépôts de mendicité au début de la IIIe République", dans André Gueslin, Dominique Kalifa (dir.), *Les Exclus en Europe, 1830–1939*, Paris: Les Éditions de l'Atelier, 1999: 112–123.

Vidal, Laurent, and Alain Musset, "L'attente comme état de la mobilité", dans Laurent Vidal et Alain Musset, *Les Territoires de l'attente: Migrations et mobilités dans les Amériques, XIXe-XXIe siècles*, Rennes: Presses universitaires de Rennes, 2015: 19–28.

Vidalenc, Jean. *Les Passeports: une source d'histoire économique et sociale, problèmes d'utilisation, limites et lacunes*. Paris: Bibliothèque nationale, 1971.

Vilar Ramirez, Juan B., and Marie José Vilar, *La emigración española al Norte de Africa (1830–1999)*. Madrid: Arco Libros, 1999.
Vilches, Jorge. *Progreso y Libertad. El Partido Progresista en la Revolución Liberal Española*. Madrid: Alianza Editorial, 2001.
Vronsky, Peter. *The Fenians and Canada*. Toronto: MacMillan, 1978.
Vuilleumier, Marc. *Histoire et combats. Mouvement ouvrier et socialisme en Suisse, 1864–1960*. Lausanne: Éditions d'en bas & Collège du travail, 2012.
Wagniart, Jean-François. *Le Vagabond à la fin du xixe siècle*. Paris: Belin, 1999.
Walle, Marianne. ""Le pain amer de l'exil". L'émigration des Allemands révolutionnaires (1848–1850) vers les États-Unis", in *Deutschland – Frankreich – Nordamerika: Transfers, Imaginationen, Beziehungen* edited by Chantal Metzger, Hartmut Kaelble, 140–151. Stuttgart: Franz Steiner Verlag, 2006.
Watson Andaya, Barbara. "Gender, Warfare, and Patriotism in Southeast Asia and in the Philippine Revolution", in *The Philippine Revolution of 1896: Ordinary Lives in Extraordinary Times*, 1–30. Quezon City: Ateneo de Manila University Press, 2001.
Wirth, Louis. *Le Ghetto*, traduit de l'américain par Pierre-Jacques Rojtman. Grenoble: Presses universitaires de Grenoble, 1980.
Yaycioglu, Ali. "Janissaires, ingénieurs et prédicateurs. Comment l'ingénierie militaire et l'activisme islamique changèrent l'ordre ottoman", *Revue d'histoire du xixe siècle*, 53 (2016/2): 19–37.
Zeuske, Michael. "Con López a Cuba!", *Ibero-Americana Pragensia*, Año XXVII (1994): 65–88.
Zucker, Adolf Eduard (ed). *The Forty-Eighters. Political Refugees of the German Revolution of 1848*. New York: Columbia University Press, 1950.

List of figures and tables

Fig. 1: Map of revolutions in 1830s-Europe
Fig. 2: José Rodríguez Gil, *Emigración Carlista*, 1876. Private collection, Biarritz
Fig. 3: Map of exile districts in London in the nineteenth century
Fig. 4: Map of Karl Marx's places of residence and sociability in Brussels (1845–1848)
Fig. 5: "Refugees of the 1871 Commune at the Café du Levant in Geneva", *Le Monde illustré*, April 27, 1872, Paris
Fig. 6: "Bal à l'hôtel Lambert", *L'Illustration*, February 8, 1845
Fig. 7: Antonio Gisbert, *Fusilamiento de Torrijos y sus compañeros en las playas de Málaga*, 1888. Museo del Prado, Madrid
Fig. 8: Refugee certificate from the Second Republic. Source: Archives départementales des Bouches-du-Rhône, 4 M 956.
Fig. 9: Francesco Hayez, *Portrait of Cristina di Belgiojoso*, 1832
Fig. 10: Herzen et ses filles, Olga et Tatiana, photograph, January 11th 1855. ITAR-TASS News Agency/Alamye.
Fig. 11: The routes of Hungarian exile, 1849–1852. Map by Heléna Tóth with the assistance of Cambridge University Press (with the authorization of the author and the publisher)
Fig. 12: Itinerary of Terence Bellew McManus. Map by Hugo Vermeren
Fig. 13: The return from exile of Juan Esquerré. Map by Alexandre Dupont
Fig. 14: Itinerary taken by the Alcoya brothers. Map by Alexandre Dupont
Fig. 15: Exile itinerary of Angelo Frignani. Map by Hugo Vermeren
Fig. 16: Faustin, Victor Hugo, 1870. Special collections of the University of Sussex (Brighton). Item SxMs 162/3/9
Fig. 17: Photo of the Polish avenue at Montmartre cemetery in Paris. Photo published under license CC-BY-NC-SA 2.0 Creative Commons
Fig. 18: G. Julien, *The bedchamber of the Comte de Chambord and the garden at Frohsdorf Castle*, 1883. Source: Bibliothèque interuniversitaire de Santé, Paris
Table 1: Some figures concerning the main groups of exiles leaving Europe (1815–1880)

List of contributors

Sylvie Aprile is a Professor in contemporary history at the Université Paris Nanterre. She is a specialist in 19th-century French exile and has published numerous books and articles on exiles in Europe, particularly on the question of gender and political commitment. She has published *Le Siècle des exilés* (CNRS Éditions, 2010) and prefaced and annotated the unpublished work by Karl Marx and Friedrich Engels *Les Grands hommes de l'exil* (Agone, 2015). She has participated in several collective research programs, including *Exil et fraternité*, co-edited by Catherine Brice.

Constance Bantman is a Senior Lecturer at the University of Surrey, UK. She has published extensively on the history of the French anarchist movement from a transnational perspective, including the monographs *The French Anarchists in London, 1880–1914. Exile and Transnationalism in the First Globalisation* (Liverpool University Press, 2013) and *Jean Grave and the Networks of French Anarchism, 1854–1939* (Palgrave Macmillan, 2021). She also co-edited the volume *The Foreign Political Press in Nineteenth-Century London: Politics from a Distance* (Bloomsbury, 2017).

Fabrice Bensimon is a Professor in British history at Sorbonne Université. He co-edited (with Quentin Deluermoz and Jeanne Moisand) *"Arise Ye Wretched of the Earth". The First International in a global perspective* (Brill, 2018). He is currently writing a book on British migrant workers of the industrial revolution.

Catherine Brice is a Professor in contemporary history at Université Paris-Est Créteil and a member of the Centre d'histoire européenne comparée. She works on 19th-century Italy, particularly the cultural history of politics (*La monarchie et la construction de l'identité nationale italienne (1861–1900*, EHESS, 2018). She has also worked on how mobility relates to innovation. In 2016, with Delphine Diaz, she co-edited *Mobilities, Know-how and Innovation in the 19th Century* in *Revue d'histoire du XIXe siècle*. She has edited a volume on *Exile and the Circulation of Political Practices in the 19th Century* (Cambridge Scholars, 2020), and co-edited (with Gilles Bertrand and Mario Infelise) *Exil, asile. Du droit aux pratiques. XVIe-XIXe siècles* (École française de Rome, 2021).

Delphine Diaz is an Associate Professor in contemporary history at the Université de Reims, and a member of the Institut universitaire de France. In 2014 she published *Un asile pour tous les peuples? Exilés et réfugiés étrangers dans la France du premier XIXe siècle*. Her research focuses on political exiles and asylum policies in France and Europe in the 19th century. Between 2016 and 2020, she coordinated the AsileuropeXIX research program, "Towards a European history of exile and asylum during the 19th century", funded by the Agence Nationale de la Recherche. She is the author of a book on the history of refugees in Europe, *En exil. Les réfugiés en Europe de la fin du XVIIIe siècle à nos jours* (Gallimard, 2021).

Laurent Dornel is an Associate Professor in contemporary history at the Université de Pau et des Pays de l'Adour. His research focuses on the history of xenophobia and migrations. He has published *La France hostile. Socio-histoire de la xénophobie* (Paris, Hachette, 2004), and more recently, with Céline Regnard, *Les Chinois dans la Grande Guerre. Des bras au service de la France* (Les Indes Savantes, 2019). He is currently working on colonial labour in France during the First World War.

Alexandre Dupont is an Associate Professor at the Université de Strasbourg. His research focuses on transnational counter-revolutionary circulations, popular resistance to liberalism in rural settings, and study of borders during the 19th century as a specific scale for politics. He is the author of *Une internationale blanche. Histoire d'une mobilisation royaliste entre France et Espagne dans les années 1870* (Paris, Éditions de la Sorbonne, 2020), drawn from his doctoral thesis, as well as numerous articles and chapters on exiles and political circulations across borders.

Antonin Durand holds a PhD in history. After teaching at the École Normale Supérieure's Department of History, he is currently scientific coordinator at the French Collaborative Institute on Migrations. After a first book on the place of mathematicians in 19th-century political life in Italy, *La Quadrature du cercle. Les mathématiciens dans la vie parlementaire (1848–1913)*, (Presses de la rue d'Ulm, 2018), his work now focuses on transnational mobility of European élites and refugees.

Laure Godineau is an Associate Professor in contemporary history at the Université Sorbonne Paris Nord (Paris 13) and a former student at the École Normale Supérieure. Her research focuses on political exiles after the Commune and she has published many articles on the exile of communards after 1871 and their return to republican France in the 1880s. She specialises in 19th-century history and the Paris Commune, and has published *La Commune de Paris par ceux qui l'ont vécue* (Parigramme, 2010), *La Commune de 1871 expliquée en images* (Seuil, 2021) and co-edited (with Marc César) *La Commune de 1871: une relecture* (Créaphis, 2019, 2020).

Romy Sánchez is a historian and Chargée de Recherche at CNRS, and a member of the Institut de Recherches Historiques du Septentrion (Lille). She is a former student at the École Normale Supérieure in Lyon and of the École des Hautes Etudes Ibériques et Hispaniques (EHEHI) – Casa de Velázquez, in Madrid. Her research focuses on political circulations between Cuba, Spain, the U.S., and the wider Caribbean during the long 19th century, with a special interest in exiles. She has co-edited (with Delphine Diaz, Jeanne Moisand, and Juan-Luis Simal) *Exils entre les deux mondes: migrations et espaces politiques atlantiques* (Les Perséides, 2015) and *Dans l'intimité de l'exil* (Revue d'histoire du XIXe siècle, 2020).

Hugo Vermeren is a researcher at the École Française de Rome (EFR), and a specialist of the history of colonial North Africa, Mediterranean mobility, and maritime societies. He is also a fellow of the Institut Convergences Migrations (CNRS / Collège de France) and coordinator of the "Governing Islands: Territories, Resources and Knowledge of Island Societies (16th-21st century)" EFR international program (2022–2026). A former teaching fellow at the Université Paris Nanterre and the Université de Reims, he has published a book entitled *Les Italiens à Bône (1865–1940). Migrations méditerranéennes et colonisation de peuplement en Algérie* (2017) and co-edited a special issue of *Diasporas*, "Expulser et éloigner les étrangers au XIXe siècle".

Index

Ackermann, Rudolf   17
Aconin, Charles   35
Acs, Gédéon   263
Agoncillo, Felipe   190
Aguado, Alejandro María   164
Aguinaldo, Emilio   190
Alavoine, André   113
Alcoya, Victoriano and Nicolás   248, 303
Algarra, Carlos   249
Andrássy, Gyula   245
Angers, David d'   269
Angoulême, Duchess of   64, 274
Anneke, Fritz   185
Anneke, Mathilde   185, 191, 193
Arago, Étienne   128 f., 135
Arconati-Visconti, Costanza   52
Arconati-Visconti, Giuseppe   52
Arnould, Arthur   255, 259
Artois, Louise d'   118, 134
Attellis, Orazio de   143
Azeglio, Massimo d'   46

Badin   101
Bakunin, Mikhail   122, 158
Ballaguy, Jean-Marie   133
Bandiera, brothers   171
Barbès, Armand   102, 199, 253
Barbet, Virginie   131
Barcelona, Jean   179
Barère, Bertrand   129 f., 269
Barrère, Pierre   114, 199, 269
Barrot, Odilon   64
Barthélemy, Emmanuel   136, 195
Baudot, Marc-Antoine   269
Beaugrand, Henri   139
Bebel, August   264
Béhanzin   280 f.
Beira, Princess of   75, 83
Belgiojoso, Cristina di   25, 52, 186–189, 192, 303
Bem, Józef   80
Benítez, Caballero Carlos   143, 250
Benoit, Pierre   100

Berchet, Giovanni   53
Bergeron, André   112 f.
Bergeron, Charles   112
Bergougnioux   202
Berjeau, Jean-Philibert   102, 132 f.
Bernard, Guillaume   99
Bernstein, Eduard   69
Berra, Jean   92
Berry, Duchess of   134, 192
Bey, Ziya   147
Biernacki, Alojzy   272
Blacas, Duke of   19
Blanc, Alphonse   84
Blanc, Louis   68, 102, 125, 132 f., 146
Blanc, Simon   84
Blanqui, Auguste   122, 200
Blind, Karl   264
Boissière, Ernest Valeton de   225
Bonaparte, Joseph   16, 209
Borges, Josep   65, 156
Bornstedt, Adalbert von   55
Bourbon, Carlos of   36, 54 f., 70, 75, 95, 100, 152, 186, 210
Bourbon, Juan of   36
Bourbon-Massimo, Princess Béatrice of   275
Bourbon-Parma, Margherita of   186, 188 f.
Bourra, Louis-Aimé   132 f.
Braganza, Maria das Neves of   192
Branicki, Count Xavier   106
Brătianu, Démètre   29
Brentano, Lorenz   252
Brisbane, Albert   226
Brocher, Victorine   92, 131
Bruguera, Mateu   249 f.
Bucher, Lothar   263 f.
Buonarroti, Filippo   53
Burns, Mary   126
Buruma, Ian   279 f.

Cabet, Étienne   30, 86, 212, 226, 233
Cambacérès, Jean-Jacques   130
Cantacuzino, Princess   96

Cantagrel, Félix   130
Canudes   108
Capy, Charles   227
Carpeaux, Jean-Baptiste   34
Casanova, Emilia   203
Castillo, Carlos del   219
Cattaneo, Carlo   6, 145, 277
Caussidière, Marc   231
Cavaignac, Jean-Baptiste   269
Ceruti, Ramón   221
Chambord, Count of   155, 274f., 303
Charles X   19f., 118, 134, 222, 275
Charras, Jean-Baptiste   113, 198, 244, 270
Chateaubriand, François-René de   265
Chazeaud, Paul   135
Chodźko, Léonard   39
Chojecki, Charles-Edmond   114, 195
Ciseri, Antonio   200
Claflin, Tennessee   224, 235
Clément, Charles-Louis, 45
Clément, Jean-Baptiste   102, 196
Clovis, Hugues   71
Cœurderoy, Ernest   95, 104
Cobbett, William   237
Cohen-Blind, Ferdinand   264
Confalonieri, Federico   53
Considerant, Victor   69, 130, 226f.
Courbet, Gustave   34
Cramer, Jan Wilhelm   189
Crispi, Francesco   144–146, 277
Cuffay, William   231
Custine, Robert de   75
Czartoryska, Anna   120f.
Czartoryski, Adam Jerzy   23, 39, 59, 108, 153
Czosnowska, Countess Laura   195

Dąbrowski, Abbé Jean-Paul   272
Dalou, Jules   34, 259
David, Jacques-Louis   37, 68, 136f., 215, 235, 269
Déjacque, Joseph   116, 138f., 225, 262
Delavigne, Casimir   22
Delescluze, Henri   207
Delorme, Désempare   129
Demontry, James   270
Deroin, Jeanne   121f., 175, 188, 193, 203

Descaves, Lucien   92, 242
Desroches, Antoine Ulysse   203
Dethou, Alexandre   266
Devoy, John   222
Dietrich, Joseph   245
Doboreski, Marcinoï   135
Dramard, Louis   98f.
Drouet, Juliette   106, 129, 195
Drury, Victor   234
Duché, Marius   115, 125
Duché, Tristan   115,125

Eichler, Conrad   232
Emmet, Robert   172
Engels, Friedrich   26, 56, 87, 125f., 138, 185, 195, 205, 271
Esquerré, Juan   247f., 303
Esquiros, Adèle   196
Esquiros, Alphonse   104, 196
Etzler, John Adolphus   225

Fameau, Sylvain   86
Fazıl, Pasha Mustafa   147
Ferdinand VII   16f., 47, 151, 155, 163f., 169f.
Ferrari, Giuseppe   25
Fleury, Laure   196, 197
Fleury, Victor   197
Foscolo, Ugo   6, 18
Fouet, Eugène   114f.
Francis V, Duke of Modena   85
Frediani, Gaetano   147, 259
Freiligrath, Ferdinand   126
Frichot, Christophe-Désiré   227
Frignani, Angelo   97, 255, 303
Frond, Victor   87f., 107, 115, 280

Galli, Florencio   221
Gamond, Zoé de   58
Gardrat, Aristide   116
Garibaldi, Giuseppe   14, 27, 60, 122, 148, 165, 168f., 191, 200, 208, 211, 228, 230
Garrau, Pierre-Anselme   129
Garrett, Almeida   18
Gattai, Simeone   145
Gendebien, Alexandre   52
Gener, Tomás   17

Gerster, Bela   259
Gicquel, Louis   271
Gioberti, Vincenzo   25, 53
Gisbert, Antonio   169f., 303
Goicuria, Domingo   172
Goldman, Emma   194
Goldsmid, Marie-Cécile   92
Gontaut-Biron, Duchess of   47, 118, 133f.
Gratia, Charles Louis   132
Grégoire, Abbé   6, 51, 94, 149, 168, 210, 269
Gregory, J.W.   234
Grousset, Paschal   218
Guesde, Jules   34

Hàm, Nghi   281
Harney, Julian   56, 62
Henry, Émile   35, 54, 269
Heredia y Heredia, José María de   221
Héricourt, Jenny d'   190, 223
Herwegh, Georg   8, 195f., 271
Herzen, Alexander   7, 8, 30, 106, 144, 195–199,
Herzen, Natalia   8, 195
Herzen, Natalia (daughter)   199
Herzen, Olga   197
Herzen, Tatiana   197
Hess, Moses   21, 126
Hetherington, Henry   56
Hugo, Adèle   195
Hugo, Adèle (daughter)   196
Hugo, François-Victor   117
Hugo, Victor   19, 20,, 22, 29, 69, 87, 93, , 105, 106, 115, 117, 129, 136, 138, 141, 148, 149, 196, 201, 202,, 244–247, 256–259, 263, 266, 267, 270, 271, 274, 282,
Huleck, Marie   190
Humboldt, Alexander von   91, 223

Isabella II, Queen of Spain   36, 95, 151, 186

Jacques, Amédée   91, 223
Jarecki, Théophile   109
Jind, Kaur Maharani   281
Joigneaux, Pierre   268, 270

Jones, Michael D.   223
Jourde, François   218
Juchereau, Antoine   109
Juif, Jules   225
Juin, Auguste   56
Julien, Louise   138

Kabalega, Chwa II   281
Kalapsza, János   229
Kemal, Namık   147
Kendeffy, Katinka   245
Kestner, Mathilde   197
Kinkel, Gottfried   86, 183,193,251
Kinkel, Johanna   183, 185, 193
Kleczkowski, Michel Alexandre   221
Kniaziewicz, Karol   272
Konachowski, Michel   254
Konarski, Szyman   126
Kossuth, Lajos   30, 31, 57, 60, 93, 144, 148,167, 208, 228, 229, 232, 244, 251, 263, 274
Kropotkin, Peter   69, 166
Kugelmann, Ludwig   184f.

La Cecilia, Napoléon   122
La Farina, Giuseppe   155f.
Lafargue, Paul   35, 261
Lafayette, Gilbert du Mortier de   22, 46, 51–53, 59, 211, 222
Lamartine, Alphonse de   11f., 77
Lanclou, Auguste   54
Lanz y Valdívar, José María de   17, 147
Lassalle, Ferdinand   263f.
Lay, Benjamin   149
Ledru-Rollin, Alexandre   61, 102, 106, 113f., 212
Leduc, Albert   196
Lefrançais, Gustave   87f., 98, 101, 192, 262
Lelewel, Joachim   23, 39, 52, 59, 62, 69, 126
Lemmi, Adriano   31, 164
Lemonnyer, François   193
Leroux, Pierre   202
Leroy, Charles   87
Liebknecht, Wilhelm   138, 264
Linati, Claudio   211, 221, 280
Lirio, María de   184

List, Friedrich 24, 303
Lopez, Narciso 100
Louis XVIII 11, 19 f., 45, 265
Lovett, William 56
Lubliner, Ludwik Ozeasz 126

Macaye, Ganich de 75
MacNamara, Marquise 120
Madier de Montjau, Céleste 198
Madier de Montjau, Noël 198, 201, 266
Madier de Montjau, Raoul 198
Madou, Jean-Baptiste 79, 94
Maestri, Pietro 146
Malardier, Pierre 101, 133
Malatesta, Errico 122
Malato, Charles 135, 145
Malot, Hector 241, 255
Mamiani della Rovere, Terenzio 25
Manin, Daniele 165 f., 273 f.
Maria II (Queen of Portugal) 149
Mariño de Agoncillo, Marcela 190
Martínez de la Rosa, Francisco 52
Marx, Edgar 138
Marx, Franziska 138
Marx, Heinrich Guido 138
Marx, Jenny 81, 138, 183,
Marx, Jenny (daughter) 185, 188
Marx, Karl 7, 24, 26 f., 27, 35, 56, 81, 87, 125–127, 131, 137, 138, 158, 184 f., 188, 195, 205, 229, 264, 271,
Massé, Jean-Baptiste 266
Mazzini, Giuseppe 7, 25, 27, 31, 56 f., 59, 69, 79, 89, 122, 144, 158, 162, 165 f., 171, 189, 200–202, 208, 260
McManus, Terence Bellew 237, 303
Meagher, Thomas Francis 222
Medinaceli, Duchess of 188
Mejía, Félix 236
Ménerville, Madame de 118 f.
Meszlennyi, Zsuzsanna 251
Meszlenyi, Rudolf 251
Meysenbug, Malwida von 198 f., 267
Michel, Louise 35, 122, 166, 181, 190–192
Michelet, Jules 29
Mickiewicz, Adam 22, 272
Miguel I (King of Portugal) 18, 149, 168
Miñano, Sebastián de 77

Mink, Paule 131
Minuszyc, Antoine 255
Miraflores, Marquise of 188
Mitchel, John 218, 222
Moll, Jan Ignacy 126
Moll, Joseph 56
Monet, Claude 34, 116
Montesquiou, Comtesse Anatole de 54
Mourouzi, Georges 138
Musset, Alfred de 22, 26, 96
Mwanga II 281

Nadaud, Martin 101, 250 f., 266, 268
Napoléon I 11–12, 16, 19, 58, 76, 191, 265
Napoléon III (Louis Napoléon Bonaparte) 28–29, 34, 69, 77, 84, 134, 161 f., 175, 191, 202, 229, 233, 257, 270
Napoléon (Prince) 114
Navière Charles 222

O'Connor, Feargus 57
Odelski, Stanislas 109
Olszewski, Marcel 254
Onis, Samuel 132
Ordynski, Franciszek 30
Orsini, Felice 69, 161, 233
Ovid 135
Owen, Robert 225

Paine, Thomas 237
Pallavicino, Giorgio 165
Parfait, Noël 259
Pasha, Fazıl 146 f.
Pecchio, Giuseppe 18, 53
Pedro II 115, 280
Pelletier, Claude 133, 233 f.
Pepe, Guglielmo 53, 162
Peyret, Alexis 238 f., 252
Peyrusson, Léonard 87
Pin, Elzéar 266
Pisacane, Carlo 171
Pissarro, Camille 116
Pius IX 27 f., 95, 145, 156
Plauchut, Edmond 91
Pociej, Théodore 272
Polignac, Camille de 222
Potocka, Klaudyna 176

Potter, Louis de 52, 137
Pottier, Eugène 261
Powell, Thomas 225
Prempeh I 281
Préveraud, Honoré 84
Proudhon, Pierre-Joseph 195
Provençal, César 244f.
Puccinelli, Mina 190f.
Pulszky, Ferenc 263
Pyat, Félix 69, 231

Quinet, Edgar 22, 96, 102, 113, 138, 199, 244, 267, 269, 270
Quinet, Hermione 181, 196, 267,

Radetsky, Joseph 28
Raffo, Giuseppe 147
Raspail, Benjamin 199
Raspail, François-Vincent 199
Reclus, Élisée 104, 246
Reményi, Eduard 116
Rémusat, Charles de 134
Renard, Georges 242, 260f.
Ribeyrolles, Charles 107, 115, 144, 271
Richard, Victor 94, 98, 102, 219, 253
Rico y Amat, Juan 242
Rieger, František Ladislav 32
Riego, Rafael del 210
Rochefort, Henri 218, 244, 257
Rodríguez, Gil, José 81, 82
Rohr, Jean 254
Romana, Marquis de la 54, 221
Rossi, Pellegrino 28, 92
Rouppe, Nicolas 50
Rousseau, François 86
Rożycki, Karol 272
Ruffini, Giovanni 89f., 97, 100, 267
Ruge, Arnold 125, 263, 271
Rybiński, Maciej 272

Saco, José Antonio 141
Sagasta, Práxedes Mateo 169
Saint-Ferréol, Amédée 29, 97, 130, 138, 267, 268, 269, 270
Samoggy, Paula de 152
Sand, George 52f., 91, 197, 199, 253
Santa Iria, Marquis de 51

Santarosa, Santorre di 18
Santos, Suárez Leonardo 17
Sapieha, Zofia Anna 153
Sayyid, Khalid 281
Schapper, Karl 56
Schlesinger, Louis 232f.
Schœlcher, Victor 81, 84, 101, 105, 266
Schurz, Carl 86f., 251f.
Sclavini, Giovita 53
Sébastiani, Horace 22
Sieradzki, Jules 272
Sorge, Friedrich 31, 205, 233f.
Sorrieu, Frédéric 92
Spaur, Countess 96
Staël, Germaine de 193
Stempowski, Léon 272
Straszewicz, Józef 39, 176
Struve, Gustav 125
Suavi, Âli 147
Sue, Eugène 195
Szakadaty, Pal 245
Sznajde, Franz 272

Tanski, Józef 176
Thiers, Adolphe 64
Thoré-Burger, Théophile 260
Tinayre, Victoire 131
Tissot, James 116
Tommaseo, Niccolò 25
Tone, Matilda 223, 235, 236
Tone, Theobald Wolfe 223, 235, 236
Torrijos, José María de 151, 169f., 303
Türr, István 27, 259
Two Sicilies, Maria-Christina of the 17, 27f., 53, 75, 95, 97, 108, 165f., 169, 171, 192
Tyszkiewi, Wincenty 126

Ursyn-Niemcewicz, Julian 272

Vallès, Jules 99, 131f., 241, 253, 255, 259, 270f., 277
Van Soen, Gustave 130
Vanucci, Atto 277
Varela, Félix 17
Vecchio, Bartolomeo del 90, 97, 99,
Vésinier, Pierre 116, 262

Villaverde, Cirilo 203
Voltaire, François-Marie Arouet 83, 271

Wagner, Richard 28
Walker, William 150, 232 f.
Weitling, Wilhelm 56
Willich, August 56
Willocq, Florence 193

Woodhull, Victoria 224, 235
Woolf, Virginia 183
Worcell, Stanislas 56

Zambeccari, Livio 211, 230
Zola, Émile 255
Zorrilla, Manuel Ruiz 70, 152, 155

www.ingramcontent.com/pod-product-compliance
Lightning Source LLC
Chambersburg PA
CBHW050515170426
43201CB00013B/1960